D0065792

SEX, CULTURE, AND MYTH

Bronislaw Malinowski

RUPERT HART-DAVIS
Soho Square, London
1963

© 1962 by A. Valetta Malinowska

Made and printed by offset in Great Britain by
William Clowes and Sons, Limited, London and Beccles

CONTENTS

I

SEX, FAMILY, AND COMMUNITY   1

II

CULTURE AND MYTH   165

Part One

SEX, FAMILY, AND COMMUNITY

1

MARRIAGE

Human beings, like all higher animals, multiply by the union of the two sexes. But neither conjugation, nor even the production of offspring, is as a rule sufficient for the maintenance of the species. The further advanced the animal in the order of evolution, the longer the immaturity and the helplessness of the young and the greater the need for prolonged parental care and training. It is thus the combination of mating with parenthood which constitutes marriage in higher animals, including man. Even in its biological aspect [as Edward A. Westermarck says], "marriage is rooted in the family rather than the family in marriage."

The biological foundations of human mating

In human societies, however, there are added to the sexual and parental sides of marriage other elements: marriage is given the hall-mark of social approval; it becomes a legal contract; it defines the relations between husband and wife and between parents and children, as well as the status of the latter; it imposes duties of economic co-operation; it has to be concluded in a public and solemn manner, receiving, as a sacrament, the blessings of religion and, as a rite, the good auspices of magic.

Human marriage also appears in a variety of forms: monogamy, polygyny and polyandry; matriarchal and patriarchal unions; households with patrilocal and matrilocal residence. Other forms, such as "group-marriage," "promiscuity," "anomalous" or "gerontocratic" marriages have been assumed by some writers as an inference from certain symptoms and survivals. At present these forms are not to be found, while their hypothetical existence in prehistoric times is doubtful; and it is important above all in such speculations never to confuse theory with fact.

Marriage again is in no human culture a matter of an entirely free choice. People related by descent or members of certain classes are often

This article appeared in the 14th Edition of the Encyclopædia Britannica, *1929, Vol XIV, pp. 940–50; reprinted by permission of Encyclopædia Britannica, Inc.*

debarred from marrying each other, or else they are expected to marry. The rules of incest, of exogamy, of hypergamy and of preferential mating form the sociological conditions of marriage. To these are added in certain societies such preparatory arrangements and conditions as initiation, special training for marriage, moral and economic tests, which have to be satisfied before marriage can be entered upon. The aspects, the forms and the conditions of marriage have to be discussed in turn, though it is not possible to draw a sharp line of division between these subjects.

Love and marriage

Love and marriage are closely associated in day-dreams and in fiction, in folk-lore and poetry, in the manners, morals and institutions of every human community—but marriage is more than the happy ending of a successful courtship. Marriage as an ideal is the end of a romance; it is also the beginning of a sterner task, and this truth finds an emphatic expression in the laws and regulations of marriage throughout humanity.

Love leads to sexual intimacy and this again to the procreation of children. Marriage on the whole is rather a contract for the production and maintenance of children than an authorization of sexual intercourse. The main reason why marriage has not been regarded as establishing an exclusive sexual relationship lies in the fact that in many human societies sexual relations have been allowed under certain conditions before marriage, while marriage did not necessarily exclude the continuance of similar relations.

Marriage, however, remains the most important form of lawful intercourse, and it dominates and determines all extra-connubial liberties. In their relation to marriage the forms of licence can be classified into prenuptial liberty, relaxations of the marriage bond, ceremonial acts of sex, prostitution and concubinage.

Prenuptial intercourse

In the majority of savage tribes unmarried boys and girls are free to mate in temporary unions, subject to the barriers of incest and exogamy and of such social regulations as prevail in their community. But there are other tribes where chastity of the unmarried is regarded as a virtue, especially in girls, and any lapse from it severely censured or even punished. Many of the lowest savages, such as the Veddas, Fuegians, Kubu of Sumatra, Senoi and other Malayan negritos, do not tolerate sexual intercourse before marriage. Among the Bushmen and the Andamanese instances of prenuptial unchastity do occur, but they are not condoned, still less provided for by custom and moral approval. The Australians, however, allow prenuptial freedom, except perhaps a few of the Southeastern tribes.

On a higher level we find considerable variety in this respect. All over the world, in Oceania, in Asia, in Africa and in both Americas, examples could be quoted of peoples who demand continence more or less stringently, and of their neighbours who allow full freedom. In a few cases only can we find the demand of chastity expressed in very definite usages, which physically prevent incontinence, such as infibulation, practiced among the N.E. African, Hamitic and Semitic peoples and reported also from Siam, Burma and Java. The testing of the bride by a publicly exhibited token of defloration, which forms part of certain marriage ceremonies and which expresses the value of virginity, is carried out more or less thoroughly and naturally lends itself to deception and circumvention. It is found sporadically throughout the world, in the noble families of Oceania (Tonga, Samoa, Fiji), in Asia (Yakuts, Koryaks, Chuwash, Brahui of Baluchistan, Southern Celebes), in America (Chichimec of Mexico), in Africa (Mandingo, Kulngo, Ruanda, Yoruba, Swahili, Morocco, Algeria and Egypt) and likewise among many Semitic and Hamitic peoples. In other parts of the world we are merely informed that chastity is praised and prenuptial intercourse censured (Bantu, Kavirondo, Wa Giyama, Galla, Karanga, Bechuana of Africa; Dobu, Solomon Islanders, of Melanesia; Omaha, Mandan, Nez-Percé, Apache, Takelma of N. America; Canelas and Kanaya of S. America, Bódo and Dhimál of Indo-China, Hill Dyaks of Borneo).

Freedom to mate at will may be fully allowed and even enjoined and provided for by such institutions as the mixed houses for bachelors and girls (Trobriand Islanders, Nandi, Masai, Bontoc Igorot). In some communities prenuptial intercourse is not meant to lead to marriage, and there are even cases (as among the Masai, Bhuiya and Kumbi of India, Guaycuru and Guana of Brazil), where two prenuptial lovers are not supposed to marry. Elsewhere prenuptial mating is a method of courtship by trial and error, and it leads gradually into stable unions, and is finally transformed into marriage. Thus among the Trobriand Islanders "sexual freedom" is considerable. It begins very early, children already taking a great deal of interest in certain pursuits and amusements which come as near sexuality as their unripe age allows. This is by no means regarded as improper or immoral, is known and tolerated by the elders and abetted by games and customary arrangements. Later on, after boys and girls have reached sexual maturity, their freedom remains the same, with the result that there is a great deal of indiscriminate mating. In fact, at this age both sexes show a great deal of experimental interest, a tendency to vary and to try, and here again a number of arrangements and customs play into the hands of these juvenile lovers. As time goes on, however, and the boys and girls grow older, their intrigues naturally and without any outer pressure extend in length and depth, the ties between lovers become stronger and more permanent. One decided preference as a rule develops and stands out against the lesser love affairs. It is important to note that such preferences are clearly based on genuine attachment resulting from real affinity of character. The protracted intrigue becomes a matter of public notice as well as a test of mutual compatibility, the girl's family signify their consent and marriage is finally concluded between the two lovers. Similar forms of prenuptial selection are found in other tribes (Igorot of Luzon, Akamba of E. Africa, Munshi of N. Nigeria).

In no instance, however, is prenuptial liberty regarded by the natives as a negation or substitute for marriage. In fact it always is in such communities in the nature of a preliminary or preparation to marriage; it allows the young people to sow their wild oats, it eliminates the cruder forms of sex impulse from matrimonial selection and it often leads youths and girls to exercise a mature choice based on attraction of personality rather than on sexual appeal.

The principle of legitimacy

Perhaps the most important fact in the consideration of prenuptial unchastity is the rule that freedom of sexual intercourse does not generally extend to freedom of procreation. One of the symptoms of this is that in all communities where chastity is demanded and enforced, the lapse from it entails more censure on girls than on boys, while prenuptial pregnancy is penalised much more severely than mere wantonness. But even where prenuptial unchastity becomes an institution not merely condoned but enjoined by tribal law, pregnancy is often regarded as a disgrace.

Among the aristocratic fraternities of Polynesia, the *areoi* of Tahiti and the *ulitao* of the Marquesas, licence between the men and the women was universal, but children of such unions were killed, unless adopted by a married couple. Among the Melanesian communities of New Guinea and the adjacent archipelago which allow of full sex liberty before marriage the occurrence of pregnancy under such circumstances is a grave disgrace to the mother and entails disabilities on the child. The Masai punish a girl for prenuptial pregnancy, although with them the free unions of unmarried boys and girls are an institution. A similar combination of prenuptial full licence with severe punishment of illegitimate childbirth is recorded from several African tribes (Wapore, Bakoki, Banyankole, Basoga, Akikuyu, Nandi, Beni Amer), from America (Indians of Brit. Guiana, Guaycuru and Guana of Brazil, Creeks and Cherokees), from Asia (Lisu of Burma, Nias Islanders of Malay Archipelago), from Melanesia (Mekeo and N. Solomon Islanders) and from Siberia (Aleut). In all such cases pregnancy is no doubt prevented by contraceptive practices, which however have been reported from very few savage tribes by trustworthy informants; or by abortion, which is far more frequent; or expiated by a punishment of the mother, and sometimes also of the father.

The main sociological principle embodied in these rules and arrangements is that children should not be produced outside a socially approved contract of marriage. In several tribes, the remedy for the disgrace of a prenuptial child consists therefore in an obligation of the presumptive father to marry the girl (S.E. Bantu, Madi, Bavuma, Kagoro of Africa; Tepehuane and Hupa of America; Kacharis, Rabhas, Hajongs and Billavas of India and Assam; Kanyans and Punans of Borneo). In some cases again a child of a free union is desired and expected to come, indeed it is a condition to marriage, which is concluded upon its arrival (Sea Dyak, Hill Dyak, Iruleas, Moi, Bontoc Igorot of Asia; natives of Bismarck Archipelago; Lengua, Guarayos and Pueblo Indians of America; Wolofs and Bambata of Africa). Such cases, although they are in a way the opposite of those in which a prenuptial child is a disgrace, involve the same principle: the provision of a father for the child, that is the elimination of illegitimate offspring. As a matter of fact, in all instances where a prenuptial pregnancy is welcomed, the reason for it is that children are regarded in that community as an advantage. The father consequently need not be forced to marry the mother, he does so of his own accord because fruitful marriage is desirable. Thus in all human societies a father is regarded as indispensable for each child, i.e., a husband for each mother. An illegitimate child—a child born out of wedlock—is an anomaly, whether it be an outcast or an unclaimed asset. A group consisting of a woman and her children is a legally incomplete unit. Marriage thus appears to be an indispensable element in the institution of the family.[1]

Relaxations of the marriage bond

Among tribes where chastity is demanded from unmarried girls and youths, marital fidelity is also usually enjoined. As a rule adultery is regarded as a grave offence and more severely penalised than prenuptial incontinence, though exceptions to this rule do exist. In many communities where freedom is granted before marriage, once the matrimonial knot is tied both partners or the wife at least are bound to remain faithful, under more or less serious penalties (Trobrianders, Mailu, Nukuhiva, Maori of Oceania; Land and Sea Dyaks, Kukis, Hajongs, Saorias, Ceramese of Indonesia; Botocudos and Guarayos of S. America; Illinois, Comanche, Iroquois, Pawnee, Californian Indians of N. America; Timne, Ashanti, Konde, Zulu, Kafirs and Thonga of Africa). The penalty inflicted upon an adulterous wife is invariably much graver than upon an unfaithful husband, and considerable differences obtain according to the circumstances of the offence, the status of the third party, the husband's anger and his attachment to his wife.

There are, however, a number of communities in which the marriage bond is broken as regards the exclusiveness of sex with the consent of both partners and with the sanction of tribal law, custom and morality.

[1] See B. Malinowski, *Sex and Repression in Savage Society*, 1927, pp. 212–17.

In some societies the only occasion on which the wife is allowed connection with other men, nay, has to submit to their embraces, is at the very beginning of marriage. This custom has apparently been known in mediaeval Europe under the name of *jus primae noctis*. It certainly exists in many savage cultures (Brazilian Indians, Arawaks, Caribs, Nicaraguans, Tarahumare of S. and C. America; Ballante, Bagele, Berbers of Africa; Bánaro and S. Massim of Melanesia; Aranda, Dieri and other Australian tribes). Such customs are to be regarded not so much as the abrogation of matrimonial exclusiveness, but rather as expressing the superstitious awe with which sexual intercourse, and above all defloration, is regarded by primitive peoples. As such they should be considered side by side with the numerous instances in which girls are artificially deprived of their virginity, without the intercourse of any man; with prenuptial defloration by strangers; with temporary prostitution of a religious character, and with sexual intercourse as a puberty rite.

A greater encroachment upon sexual exclusiveness in marriage is found in the custom of wife-lending as a form of hospitality. This is very widely distributed over the world.[2] It must be realised that this practice is not an infringement of the husband's rights, but rather his assertion of authority in disposing of his wife's person. Very often indeed a man will offer his sister, daughter, slave or servant instead, a fact which indicates that this custom is not so much the right of another man to infringe upon the matrimonial bond as the right of the head of the household to dispose of its female inmates.

Very often sexual hospitality is exercised in anticipation of future reciprocal benefits, and must be considered side by side with the custom of wife-exchange (Gilyak, Tungus, Aleuts of N.E. Asia; Bangala, Herero, Banyoro, Akamba, Wayao of Africa; various Himalayan and Indian tribes; S. Massim of Melanesia; Marquesas, Hawaii, Maori of Polynesia; and various Australian tribes). At times there is an exchange of wives at feasts, when general orgiastic licence prevails (Araucanos, Bororo, Keres of S. America; Arapahos, Gros Ventres and Lower Mississippi tribes of N. America; Dayaks and Jakun of Indonesia; Bhuiyas, Hos, Kotas of India; Ashanti, Ekoi and various Bantu tribes of Africa; Kiwai Papuans). On such festive and extraordinary occasions not only are the sexual restrictions removed, and the sexual appetite stimulated, but the ordinary discipline is relaxed, the normal occupations abandoned and social barriers over-ridden, while at the same time people indulge in gluttony, in desire for amusement and social intercourse. Sexual licence, as well as the other relaxations, liberties and ebullitions at such feasts fulfils the important function of providing a safety-vent which relieves the normal repressions,

[2] See the comprehensive references in Westermarck, *The History of Human Marriage,* 1921, 3 vols., Vol. I, pp. 225–26.

furnishes people with a different set of experiences, and thus again tends to safeguard ordinary institutions.

These cases where wives are exchanged for sexual intercourse only must be distinguished from the less frequent instances of prolonged exchange, with common habitation, more or less legalised. Among the Eskimo of Repulse Bay, "If a man who is going on a journey has a wife encumbered with a child that would make travelling unpleasant, he exchanges wives with some friend who remains in camp and has no such inconvenience. Sometimes a man will want a younger wife to travel with, and in that case effects an exchange, and sometimes such exchanges are made for no special reason, and among friends it is a usual thing to exchange wives for a week or two about every two months" ([William Henry] Gilder, *Schwatka's Search*). Analogous forms of prolonged exchange are found among certain tribes of S. India; while among the Siberian Chukchi a man will often enter on a bond of brotherhood with those of his relatives who dwell in other villages, and when he visits such a village his relative will give him access to his wife, presently returning the visit in order to make the obligation mutual; sometimes cousins will exchange wives for a prolonged period.

Again, among the Dieri, Arabana and cognate tribes of C. Australia, a married woman may be placed in the so-called *pirrauru* relationship to a man other than her husband. Such a man may, with the husband's permission, have access to her on rare occasions. Or if the husband be absent and give his consent the woman may join her paramour for some time at his camp, but this is apparently rare. In order to lend his wife in this way a man must wait until she is allotted by the tribal elders as the *pirrauru* to another man. Then he may consent to waive his marital rights for a short time, though we are expressly told he is under no constraint to do so. Circumstances, jealousy, even the disinclination of the woman are obstacles all of which must make the carrying-out of *pirrauru* rights extremely rare. This custom has been adduced as a present-day occurrence of group marriage, but this is obviously incorrect. It is always a temporary and partial surrender of marital rights consisting of a long and permanent connubium with occasional rare episodes of extra-marital liaison.

It is important to remember that we have come to regard marriage as defined primarily by parenthood. Now social parenthood in native ideas, behaviour, custom and law is not affected by these various forms of relaxation just described. The children are reckoned as belonging to the legal husband, and in this as in many other ways—economic, legal and religious—these temporary relaxations do not seriously disturb the marriage relationship. It must be realised with regard to fatherhood that even where the main principles of physiological procreation are known, savages do not attribute an undue importance to actual physiological paternity. It is almost always the husband of the woman who is considered the legal father of her children, whether he be their physiological father or not.

Concubinage

This can be defined as a legalised form of cohabitation, which differs from marriage in that it implies a considerably lower status of the female partner and her offspring than that enjoyed by the legal wife. It is a terminological confusion to speak of concubinage when there is temporary access to a woman, or exclusively sexual rights in her. On primitive levels of culture real concubinage does not exist. Some similarity to it can be found in the institution of subsidiary wives. In certain polygynous communities there is one principal wife, and the subsidiary ones have a much lower status, as is the case among the Guarani, Central Eskimo, Araucanians, Apache, Chippewa (America); Chukchi, Koryak, Yakut (N.E. Asia); Marquesas Islanders, Tongans, Tahitians, Maori, Marshall Islanders (Polynesia); Awemba, Wafipa, S.E. Bantu, Herero, Nandi, Yoruba, Ewhe (Africa); Ossetes, Kadaras, Khambis (India); Battas, Bagobo, Kulaman (Indonesia).

It is not correct to regard the institutions of temporary and limited partnership described above, such as the *pirrauru* of C. Australia or the protracted exchange of partners among the Eskimo, as concubinage.

Prostitution

The institution of commercial eroticism or prostitution has a very limited range among primitive peoples. It has been reported from Melanesia (Santa Cruz, Rossel Island), Polynesia (Line Islands, Caroline Islands, Easter Island, Hawaii), Greenland, N. America (Omaha), S. America (Karaya, Uitoto, Boro), W. Africa, E. Africa (Banyoro). In its relation to marriage it begins to play a very important part only in higher cultures. On the one hand it provides an easy satisfaction for the sexual appetite to unmarried men or those who for some reason cannot cohabit with their wives. It thus constitutes an institution complementary to marriage. On the other hand, in certain communities of which Ancient Greece is a notable example, i.e., "hetairism," prostitution in a higher and more refined form, allowed some women to devote themselves to cultural pursuits and to associate with men more freely than was possible to those legally married.

On the whole it is rather a subsidiary institution than either a relaxation or a form of sexual preparation. Unlike the other forms of sexual licence, prostitution is neither directly correlated with marriage nor does it affect its integrity so seriously as do the forms of matrimonial relaxation which involve both husband and wife.

The economics of the household and family

We are thus led at all stages of our argument to the conclusion that the institution of marriage is primarily determined by the needs of the off-spring, by the dependence of the children upon their parents. More specially, the mother since she is handicapped at pregnancy and for some time after birth, needs the assistance of a male partner. The rôle of male associate and helpmate is almost universally played by the husband exclusively, though in some extremely matrilineal societies the wife's brother shares with the husband in some of the responsibilities and burdens of the household. The economic as well as the biological norm of a family is thus mother, child and husband—or exceptionally both the husband and the wife's brother.

In the vast majority of human societies the individual family, based on monogamous marriage and consisting of mother, father and children, forms a self-contained group, not necessarily however cut off from society. Within the household there is a typical scheme of division in functions, again almost universal. By virtue of natural endowment the wife has not only to give birth to and nourish the children, but she is also destined to give them most of the early tender cares: to keep them warm and clean, to lull them to sleep and soothe their infantile troubles. Even in this the husband often helps to a considerable degree, prompted by natural inclination as well as by custom. This latter often imposes upon him duties and ritual manifestations such as taboos during the pregnancy of his wife and at childbirth, and performances at the time of confinement, of which the *couvade* is the most striking example. All such obligations emphasize the father's responsibility and his devotion to the child. Later on in the education of offspring both parents have to take part, performing their respective duties, which vary with the society and with the sex of the children.

Apart from the special task of producing and rearing the children, the wife normally looks after the preparation of the food; she almost invariably provides the fuel and the water; is the actual attendant at the hearth or fireplace; manufactures, tends and owns the cooking-vessels; and she is also the main carrier of burdens. In the very simplest cultures the woman also erects the hut or shelter and looks after camp arrangements (Australians, Bushmen, Andaman Islanders). The husband is the protector and defender of the family, and he also performs all the work which requires greater strength, courage and decision, such as hunting game, fishing, heavy building of houses and craft, and clearing the timber.

The division of labour between husband and wife outside the household follows the line of men's and women's occupations which differ with the community, but on the whole make fighting, hunting, sailing, metal work purely male occupations; collecting, agriculture, pottery, weaving predominantly female; while fishing, cattle-tending, making of clothing and utensils are done by one sex or the other according to culture.

The division of labour outside the household does not mean merely that husband and wife collect food and manufacture goods for their family each in a different manner. It means also as a rule that each has to collaborate with other members of the community of the same sex in some wider collective enterprise, from which the family benefits only partially and indirectly. In spite of repeated theoretical assertions as to the existence of the "closed household economy" or even of individual search for food among primitive peoples, we find in every community, however simple, a wider economic collaboration embracing all members and welding the various families into larger co-operative units.[3]

The fuller our knowledge of relevant facts, the better we see on the one hand the dependence of the family upon the rest of the community, and on the other hand the duty of each individual to contribute not only to his own household but to those of others as well. Thus in Australia a great part of a man's yield in hunting has to be divided according to fixed rules among his relatives, own and classificatory. Throughout Oceania a network of obligations unites the members of the community and overrules the economic autonomy of the household. In the Trobriand Islands a man has to offer about half of his garden produce to his sister and another part to various relatives, only the remainder being kept for his own household, which in turn is supported substantially by the wife's brother and other relatives. Economic obligations of such a nature cutting across the closed unity of the household could be quoted from every single tribe of which we have adequate information.

The most important examples however come from the communities organised on extreme mother-right, where husband and wife are in most matters members of different households, and their mutual economic contributions show the character of gifts rather than of mutual maintenance.

The split household under matrilocal mother-right

Most of what has been said so far refers to the marriage based on a united household and associated as a rule both under father-right and mother-right with *patrilocal* residence. This means that the bride moves to the husband's community, when she either joins his family house or camp, or else inhabits a house built for the new couple and owned in the husband's name. Patrilocal marriages are by far the most prevalent all over the world.

Matrilocal marriage consists in the husband's joining the wife's com-

[3] Cf. B. Malinowski, "Primitive Economics of the Trobriand Islanders," *Economic Journal*, 1921; "Labour and Primitive Economics," *Nature*, December 1925.

munity, taking up residence in her parents' house and often having to do some services for them. Matrilocal residence may be permanent; or it may be temporary, the husband having to remain for a year or two with his parents-in-law, and having also possibly to work for them. (Eskimo, Kwakiutl, Guaycuru, Fuegians of America; Bushmen, Hottentots, Bapedi, Bakumbi, Nuer of Africa; negrites of Philippines; Ainu of Japan.) [4]

In a few cases which might be regarded as the extreme development of mother-right combined with matrilocal conditions, the wife remains at her mother's residence and the husband does not even take up a permanent abode there, but simply joins her as a frequent and regular but still temporary visitor (Menangkabau Malays of Sumatra, Pueblo and Seri Indians of N. America, Nairs of Malabar). Such extreme cases of mother-right are an exception. They are the product of special conditions found as a rule at a high level of culture and should never be taken as the prototype of "primitive marriage" (as has been done by Bachofen, Hartland and Briffault).

The most important fact about such extreme matriarchal conditions is that even there the principle of social legitimacy holds good; that though the father is domestically and economically almost superfluous, he is legally indispensable and the main bond of union between such matrilineal and matrilocal consorts is parenthood. We see also that the economic side can have a symbolic, ritual significance—the gift-exchange functions as token of affection—it marks thus a sociological interdependence, while it has hardly any utilitarian importance.

Marriage as an economic contract

This last point, together with the foregoing analysis of the household and family economics, allows us to frame the conclusion that while marriage embraces a certain amount of economic co-operation as well as of sexual connubium, it is not primarily an economic partnership any more than a merely sexual appropriation. It is as necessary to guard against the exclusively economic definition of marriage as against the over-emphasis of sex. This materialistic view of marriage, to be found already in older writers such as [Julius] Lippert, E. Grosse, [Lothar] Dargun, appears again in some recent important works. Criticising the exaggeration of sex, Briffault says about marriage: "The institution, its origin and development, have been almost exclusively viewed and discussed by social historians in terms of the operation of the sexual instincts and of the sentiments connected with those instincts, such as the exercise of personal choice, the effects of jealousy, the manifestations of romantic love. The origin, like the biological foundation, of *individual marriage being essentially economic*, those psychological factors are the products of the association

[4] See also E. A. Westermarck, *The History of Human Marriage*, Vol. II, pp. 360–64; Robert Briffault, *The Mothers*, 1927, 3 vols., Vol. I, pp. 268–302.

rather than the causes or conditions which have given rise to it." And again: "Individual marriage has its *foundation* in *economic* relations. In the vast majority of uncultured societies marriage is regarded almost *exclusively* in the light of *economic* considerations, and throughout by far the greater part of the history of the institution the various changes which it has undergone have been *conditioned by economic causes.*" [5]

This is a distortion of a legitimate view. Marriage is not entered upon for economic considerations, exclusively or even mainly; nor is the primary bond between the two parties established by the mutual economic benefits derived from each other. This is best shown by the importance of matrimonial bonds even where there is neither community of goods nor co-operation nor even full domesticity. Economics are, like sex, a means to an end, which is the rearing, education and dual parental influence over the offspring. Economic co-operation is one of the obligations of marriage and like sexual cohabitation, mutual assistance in legal and moral matters it is prescribed to the married by law and enjoined by religion in most cultures. But it certainly is not either the principal end or the unique cause of marriage.

"Marriage by purchase"

As erroneous as the over-emphasis on economics and its hypostasis as the *vera causa* and essence of marriage is also the tearing out of some one economic trait and giving it a special name and thus an artificial entity. This has been done notably with regard to the initial gifts at marriage, especially when given by the husband. More or less considerable gifts from the husband to his wife's family at marriage occur very widely.[6] The term "marriage by purchase" applied to such gifts usually serves to isolate them from their legal and economic context, to introduce the concept of a commercial transaction, which is nowhere to be found in primitive culture as a part of marriage, and to serve as one more starting point for fallacious speculations about the origin of marriage.

The presents given at marriage should always be considered as a link— sometimes very important, sometimes insignificant—in the series of services and gifts which invariably run throughout marriage. The exchange of obligations embraces not only the husband and the wife, but also the children, who under mother-right are counted as one with the mother while under father-right they take over the father's obligations. The family and clan of the wife, and more rarely of the husband, also become part of the scheme of reciprocities. The presents offered at marriage by the husband are often made up of contributions given him towards this end by his relatives and clansmen (Banaka, Bapuka, Thonga, Zulu, Xosa,

---

[5] Robert Briffault, *op. cit.,* Vol. II, p. 1; the italics are those of the present writer.

[6] See the comprehensive list of references in E. A. Westermarck, *op. cit.,* Vol. II, Chap. xxiii.

Bechuana, Madi of Africa; Toradjas, Bogos of Indonesia; Buin, Mekeo, Roro, Trobrianders of Melanesia), and are not all retained by the girl's parents but shared among her relatives and even clansmen (Achomawi, Delaware, Osage, Araucanians of America; S.E. Bantu, Swahili, Pokomo, Turkana, Bavili, Ewhe, Baganda, Masai, Lotuko of Africa; Ossetes, Samoyeds, Aleut, Yakut, Yukaghir of Siberia; Koita, Mekeo, S. Massim, Buin of Melanesia). The giving of presents is thus a transaction binding two groups rather than two individuals, a fact which is reflected in such institutions as the inheritance of wives, sororate, levirate, etc. A correct understanding of the initial marriage gift can be obtained only against the background of the wider economic mutuality of husband and wife, parents and children, maternal and paternal families and clans.

Another type of marriage gift is the *lobola* found among the patrilineal and patrilocal communities of the S.E. Bantu, who live by combined agriculture and cattle-raising. The wife and children are here regarded as a definite economic and sociological asset. The wife is the main agricultural and domestic worker, while the children are valuable because the boys continue the line and the girls bring in wealth at marriage. Marriage is concluded by the payment of cattle, the amount varying greatly according to tribe, rank and other considerations from a couple of head to a few score. These cattle are known as *lobola*, or "bride-price," as is the current but incorrect anthropological expression. The *lobola* in fact is not the motive for the transaction, nor is there any bidding on any market, nor can the cattle be disposed of at will by the receiver, i.e., the girl's father. Some of them have to be distributed by him according to fixed tribal custom among particular relatives of the girl; the rest he has to use for the provision of a wife for his son, i.e., the girl's brother, or else, if he has no male heir, he contracts another wife for himself, in order to obtain the desired male descendants. In case of divorce the marriage gift has to be returned as the identical cattle given and not merely in an equivalent form. The *lobola* is thus rather a symbolic equivalent representing the wife's economic efficiency, and it has to be treated as a deposit to be spent on another marriage.

In Melanesia the husband's initial gift at marriage is a ritual act, and is always reciprocated by the wife's family. This is the case also among certain American tribes (Tshimshian, Coast Salish, Bellacoola, Delaware, Ojibway, Navaho, Miwok); in Siberia (Mordwin, Ainu, Buryat, Samoyed, Koryak), and in Polynesia (Samoa). This return gift may take the form of a dowry given to the bride by her father or parents or other relatives but also directly or indirectly benefiting her husband (Greenlanders, Brazilian aborigines, Yahgans of America; Ibo, Ovambo, S.E. Bantu, Banyoro, Masai of Africa; Buryat, Yukaghir, Samoyed of Siberia; Toda of India; Banks Islanders, Buin, Maori of Oceania). In some communities the balance of gifts is so much in favour of the husband that instead of wife purchase we could speak of buying a husband for the girl (N. Massim; coast tribes of Br. Columbia; Tehuelches of Patagonia; Yakut). Both concepts, however, that of "wife purchase" and "husband purchase" are obviously inadmissible.

Property and inheritance within marriage

As a rule, whatever the manner of economic inauguration of marriage, and whatever the mutual services exchanged between the partners, the latter have not only their own sphere of activity but their own possessions. The wife usually claims the title and right of disposing of her articles of apparel, of the domestic utensils and often of the special implements and fruits of her pursuit. The importance of woman's work in agriculture, her social influence due to this and her specific claims to the agricultural produce—not the ownership of the land, which is generally vested in man—have given rise to the economic theory of mother-right.

Very often the possessions of the husband and wife are inherited by their respective kindred, and not by the surviving partner. The inheritance of the wife by the husband's brother (the custom of levirate), which is known from the Old Testament, but has a fairly wide range of distribution,[7] is not to be regarded as an economic transaction. Like the inheritance of a widow under mother-right and like the custom of killing the widows and the *suttee* of India, it is the expression of the matrimonial bonds outlasting death, and defining the widow's behaviour afterwards.

Marriage as a legal contract

Marriage is never a mere cohabitation, and in no society are two people of different sex allowed to share life in common and produce children without having the approval of the community. This is obtained by going through the legal and ritual formalities which constitute the act of marriage, by accepting in this the obligations which are entailed in marriage and the privileges which it gives, and by having later on to submit to the consequences of the union as regards children.

The legal side of marriage is therefore not made up of special activities, such as constitute its sexual, economic, domestic or parental aspect. It is rather that special side in each of these aspects, which makes them defined by tradition, formally entered upon, and made binding by special sanctions.

First of all, the whole system of obligations and rights which constitute marriage is in each society laid down by tradition. The way in which people have to cohabit and work together is stipulated by tribal law: whether the man joins his wife or vice versa; whether and how they

[7] See the extensive lists given by E. A. Westermarck, *op. cit.*, Vol. III, pp. 208–10; Robert Briffault, *op. cit.*, Vol. I, pp. 767–72.

live together, completely or partially; whether the sexual appropriation is complete, making adultery in either partner an offence, or whether, subject to certain restrictions, there may be waiving of the sexual rights; whether there is economic co-operation and what are its limits. The details and the typical rules and variations of all this have already been discussed, as well as, incidentally, the ways in which the rules are enforced. But it must be added that in no other subject of anthropology is our knowledge so limited as in the dynamic problems of why rules are kept, how they are enforced, and how they are evaded or partially broken.[8]

Only on one or two points are we habitually informed by ethnographic observers, as to what penalties attach to a breach of law and custom and what premiums are set on their careful and generous observance. Thus, we are often informed how adultery is dealt with, though we usually get exaggerated accounts of the severity of the law on this point. Again, to anticipate, incest and exogamy are usually surrounded with definite sanctions, some social and some supernatural. The manners and morals of daily contact within the household are usually laid down and enforced by that complicated and imponderable set of forces which governs all human behaviour in its everyday aspects and makes people distinguish between "good" and "bad form" in every human society. The validity of the economic duties of husband and wife are as a rule based on the fact that the services of the one are conditional on the services of the other, and that a very lazy or unscrupulous partner would eventually be divorced by the other.

Divorce

This brings us to the subject of the dissolution of marriage. Marriage is as a rule concluded for life—at times beyond death, as mentioned above. It is questionable whether the short period "marriages" reported from isolated districts (Eskimo of Ungava district, some tribes of the Indian Archipelago, Arabia, Persia, Tibet) deserve the name of marriage, i.e., whether they should not be put into a different sociological category; but our accounts of them are too slight to allow of deciding this question. In some tribes we are told that marriage is indissoluble (Veddas, Andamanese, certain tribes of the Indian Archipelago and Malay Peninsula). The general rule, however, is that divorce is possible, but not easy, and entails damages and disabilities to both partners. Even where divorce is said to be easy for husband and for wife, we find on further enquiry that a considerable price has to be paid for the "liberty to divorce," that it is easy only to exceptionally powerful or successful men and women, and that it involves in most cases loss of prestige and a moral stigma. Often

---

[8] Cf. B. Malinowski, *Crime and Custom in Savage Society*, 1926.

also divorce is easy only before children have been born, and it becomes difficult and undesirable after their arrival. In fact the main ground for divorce, besides adultery, economic insufficiency or bad temper, is sterility in the wife or impotence in the husband. This emphasises the aspect of marriage as an institution for the preservation of children.

The threat of divorce and of the disabilities which it entails is one of the main forces which keep husband and wife to their prescribed conduct. At times the husband is kept in check by the payment he gave at marriage and which he can reclaim only when the union is dissolved through no fault of his. At times the considerable economic value of the wife is the motive of his good and dutiful conduct.

The status of husband and wife

The duties of the wife towards the husband are apparently in some communities enforced to a considerable extent by his personal strength and brutality, and by the authority given him by custom. In others, however, husband and wife have an almost equal status. Here again, unfortunately, we find too often in ethnographical accounts generalities and stock phrases such as that "the wife is regarded as the personal property of the husband," as "his slave or chattel," or else again we read that "the status of the wife is high." The only correct definition of status can be given by a full enumeration of all mutual duties, of the limits to personal liberty established by marriage, and of the safeguards against the husband's brutality or remissness, or, on the other hand, against the wife's shrewishness and lack of sense of duty. It is often held that mother-right and the economic importance of woman's work, especially in agricultural communities, go with a high social status of the wife, while in collecting, nomadic and pastoral tribes her status is on the whole lower.[9]

Marriage not only defines the relations of the consorts to each other, but also their status in society. In most tribes, marriage and the establishment of an independent household are a condition for the attainment of the legal status of full tribesman in the male and of the rank and title of matron in the woman. Under the system of age-grades the passage through certain initiation rites is a condition of marriage and this is as a rule concluded soon after it is permitted.[10] In all tribes, however, all normal and healthy tribesmen and women are married, and even widows and widowers remarry if they are not too old, under the penalty of losing some of their influence. The attainment of a full tribal status is always a powerful motive for marriage.

[9] E. Grosse, in *Die Formen der Familie und die Formen der Wirtschaft;* Wilhelm Schmidt and Koppers, in *Völker und Kulturen.*

[10] Cf. Hutton Webster, *Primitive Secret Societies* [2nd ed., rev., 1932]; Heinrich Schurtz, *Altersklassen und Männerbünde,* 1902.

The laws of legitimate descent

Marriage affects not only the status of the consorts and their relations, but imposes also a series of duties on the parents with regard to children, and defines the status of children by reference to the parents.

As we know already in virtue of the universal principle of legitimacy, the full tribal or civil status of a child is obtained only through a legal marriage of the parents. Legitimacy is at times sanctioned by penalties which devolve on the parents, at times by the disabilities under which illegitimate children suffer, at times again by inducements for the adoption of children or for their legitimisation by the presumptive father or some other man.

In connection with this latter point it is necessary to realise that the children have invariably to return in later life some of the benefits received earlier. The aged parents are always dependent on their children, usually on the married boys. Girls at marriage often bring in some sort of emolument to their parents and then continue to help them and look after them. The duties of legal solidarity also devolve on the children, uniting them to father or mother according to whether we deal with a matrilineal or a patrilineal society.

One of the most important legal implications of marriage is that it defines the relation of the children to certain wider groups, the local community, the clan, the exogamous division and the tribe. The children as a rule follow one of the parents, though more complex systems are also in existence, and the unilateral principle of descent is never absolute. This however belongs to the subject of Kinship.

Modes of concluding marriage

In studying the legal aspect of marriage, it is extremely important to realise that the matrimonial contract never derives its binding force from one single act or from one sanction. The mistake has often been made in discussing the "origin of marriage," of attributing to this or that mode of concluding it a special genetic importance or legal value. Marriage has in turn been derived from mere subjugation by brutal force (the old patriarchal theory); from appropriation by capture in foreign tribes ([John Ferguson] McLennan's hypothesis); from feminine revolt against hetairism ([Johann Jakob] Bachofen); from economic appropriation or purchase (the materialist interpretation of early marriages); from pithecanthropic patriarchy (Atkinson, Freud); and from *matria potestas* (Briffault). All these views overstate the importance of one aspect of marriage or even of one element in the modes of its conclusion; some even invent an imaginary state or condition.

In reality marriage is the most important legal contract in every human society, the one which refers to the continuity of the race; it implies a most delicate and difficult adjustment of a passionate and emotional relationship with domestic and economic co-operation; it involves the cohabitation of male and female, perennially attracted and yet in many ways for ever incompatible; it focuses in a difficult personal relationship of two people the interest of wider groups: of their progeny, of their parents, of their kindred, and in fact of the whole community.

The validity of the marriage bond derives its sanctions from all these sources. This expresses one of the most important truths concerning marriage. The complexity of motives for which it is entered, the utility of the partners to each other, their common interest in the children's welfare, last, not least, the interest which the kindred and the community have in the proper upbringing of the offspring—these are the real foundations of marriage and the source of its legally binding character.

All this finds an expression in the modes of contracting marriage. These always contain the element of public approval; the collaboration of the families and the kindred of each partner; some material pledges and securities; some ritual and religious sanctions; last, not least, the consent of the parties concerned.

In the old manuals and statements concerning marriage an important place is usually taken by the classical list of the various "modes of concluding" it: marriage by capture, by purchase and by service, by infant betrothal, elopement, exchange, mutual consent, and so on.[11]

This classification is unsatisfactory. It exaggerates as a rule one aspect out of all proportion, and attributes to this one aspect an overwhelming influence upon the whole institution which it never possesses. "Marriage by purchase" we have already dismissed as a crude misnomer, while "service" is but a detail in the economics of certain marriages. "Marriage by capture," which has played such a prominent part in speculation and controversy from McLennan onward, never could have been a real institution: though a man may occasionally wed a woman captured by force in a war, such an occurrence is always an exception; it never was a rule, still less a "stage in human evolution." Tribal endogamy is the universal rule of mankind. Ceremonial fights and ritual capture occur at wedding ceremonies over a wide area.[12] They are capable of interpretation in terms of actual psychology and of existing social conditions. To regard them as survivals of "marriage by capture" is erroneous, and on this point there is now an almost universal agreement. Capture and violence, as well as purchase from other tribes, or on the slave-market, lead to concubinage, and at times supply prostitutes, but only very rarely legal wives.

[11] Cf. even such an excellent and recent account as the article on "Marriage," by W. H. R. Rivers, in *Hastings' Encyclopaedia of Religion and Ethics*.

[12] See E. A. Westermarck, *op. cit.*, Vol. II, pp. 254–77; A. E. Crawley, [*The Mystic Rose,*] Vol. II, pp. 76–100; Robert Briffault, *op. cit.*, Vol. II, pp. 230–50.

Like the contract itself, so also the modes of concluding it contain a great variety of binding and of determining factors. But a real and relevant distinction can still be made between those marriages which are contracted primarily by rules of tradition; those which are arranged for by the families or the kindred of the consorts; and those which arise from free and spontaneous choice of the mates. In no type of marriage is any of these three elements—tradition, arrangement by families or their consent, and free choice—completely absent. But one or other may be conspicuously predominant.

The most usual type of traditionally prescribed union is cross-cousin marriage, with a wide distribution, practised very extensively all over Oceania, Australia and S. India, and sporadically in Africa, N. America and Asia. The marriage of parallel cousins is less frequent, and found notably among Semitic peoples.[13] Even less common are marriages prescribed between other classes of relatives, e.g., between a man and his brother's daughter (N. Australia, some parts of Melanesia), or his sister's daughter (S. India), or his father's sister (certain parts of Melanesia, Dene of N. America). Another type of prescribed marriage is by inheritance, of which the levirate and sororate are the most notable.

Besides such traditionally defined unions, there are also marriages recognised as convenient and desirable by the respective families and arranged for by them. Infant betrothal (prevalent in Australia and Melanesia), where a definite claim is established; or infant marriage (reported especially from India), where the bond is effectively concluded, are two of the most usual forms of these. The main motive for infant unions is the determination of the families to secure a convenient union. In Australia, where an infant is often allotted to a mature male, the power of old men and their keenness to secure young wives, are at the root of this institution. Whether similar conditions existed, or even still survive in Africa, is an interesting problem.[14]

In many communities, including some advanced nations of Europe, marriage is mainly determined by social or financial considerations, and in this the parents of bride and bridegroom have as much to say as the two people directly concerned. In some primitive tribes two brothers exchange sisters (Australia), or a man's matrilineal uncle or patrilineal aunt has some say (Melanesia). Where the initial payments are very heavy and where they are used to secure a wife for the bride's brother, marriage is usually also a matter of an arrangement rather than free choice.

With all this free choice still remains the most important element. Very

[13] Cf. Sir James George Frazer, *Folk-Lore in the Old Testament*, [3 vols., 1919,] Vol. II, pp. 145 *sqq.*; B. Z. Seligman, "Studies in Semitic Kinship," *Bull. School Oriental Studies*, 1923–24.

[14] See B. Z. Seligman, "Marital Gerontocracy in Africa," *Journal of the Royal Anthropological Institute*, 1924.

often an infant betrothal or some other form of arranged union is broken by one of the people directly affected, and marriage by elopement, with the subsequent consent of family and kindred, overrules all other considerations. Invariably in all communities the majority of unions come from the initiative of the partners. Marriage by free personal choice is the normal marriage, and the choice is mainly determined by personal attraction, which does not mean merely a sexual or erotic attraction. In general the physical appeal combines with compatibility of character, and such social considerations as suitability of rank and of occupation and of economic benefits also influence the choice. Here again the nature of marriage entails a complexity of motives, and its stability has always to be secured by a suitable compromise between conflicting interests.

The religious and ceremonial side of marriage

The sanctity of the marriage bond is not found merely in the Christian religion, nor is it a prerogative of the higher cultures. The supernatural sanction, derived from a solemn, publicly celebrated, spiritually as well as ethically hallowed ceremony, adds to the binding forces of mere law. Marriage is valid as a legal contract in so far as its breach is visited by worldly retributions and its generous fulfilment carries worldly benefits. As a sacrament, marriage in primitive and civilised societies alike is protected by spiritual powers, rewarding those who observe matrimonial duties meticulously and piously, and punishing those who neglect them.

The religious aspect of marriage is therefore closely akin to the legal, in that it adds to the validity and sanctity of other functions, rather than establishes new ones. It finds expression in the acts of establishment and those of dissolution: religious rites are to be found at betrothal and wedding, while divorce is often religiously defined and qualified, and at death the breach of the bond finds its spiritual expression in the duties, observances and ceremonies incumbent on the surviving partner. Besides these ceremonial manifestations in which the bonds of marriage are religiously tied or dissolved, religious ethics establish those rules of matrimonial conduct which are sanctioned supernaturally or felt binding through their appeal to moral sense rather than to self-interest.

Ceremonies of betrothal and wedding

Betrothal can be defined as an act preliminary to marriage, establishing mutually presumptive claims. The period between betrothal and marriage varies, and where it is short, it is often difficult or even impossible to decide whether we deal with an act of betrothal or an inaugural wedding rite. It is also unprofitable to draw a very sharp line of distinction between infant betrothal and infant marriage. Where betrothal imposes real obligations and a valid tie, the rites then observed usually fulfil in their religious bearing the same function as those of marriage, and consist of the same or similar actions, both as regards ritual technique and symbolic meaning. It will be best therefore to discuss the binding rites of marriage and betrothal together.

These rites and ceremonies cover a very wide range, from the simplest act, such as a meal openly taken in common, to complex and elaborate tribal festivities, extended over a considerable period of time. But in every human society marriage is concluded by a ritual enactment. It might be disputed whether such rites in their simplest form present a genuine religious character; but most sociologists would agree that they always possess some religious elements in that they are solemn and public; in their more developed form and in higher cultures they become definitely religious. It will be best in discussing the nature of wedding rites not to draw too pedantic a distinction between their legal and religious aspects, since the two often merge or shade into each other imperceptibly.

"The most general social object" of a wedding rite is [as Westermarck says] "to give publicity to the union." By this the legal as well as the religious sanction of the union is established. The contract is made binding in that all the members of the community bear witness to it; it is hallowed in that the two mates solemnly and openly declare before man, God or other spiritual powers that they belong to each other.

The symbolism of marriage ritual

A marriage rite is as a rule also a ritual act with a symbolic significance, and as such it is often conceived to possess a magical efficacy; it contains a moral precept or expresses a legal principle.

Thus the fundamental purpose of marriage, the continuity of the race, is indicated in wedding ceremonies by ritual, intended to make the union fruitful, to obviate the dangers associated with sexual intercourse, especially with defloration, and to facilitate the various stages of the process of generation from the first act to delivery. Among the fertility rites a prominent place is taken by the use of fruit or grain or other cereals, which are sprinkled over the newly wedded couple or on or round the nuptial bed, or handed to them or brought into contact with them in some other way. Rites, such as the accompaniment of the bride by a little child, the use of various symbols of generation, and the direct offering of prayers and sacrifices, are all intended to make the union fruitful. The breaking of some object at the wedding serves to avert the dangers of defloration and to facilitate the consummation of the union. The undoing of knots and laces, found in many wedding rites, makes for easy delivery at childbirth. In all these acts we see the ritual expression of the biological nature of marriage.

As an official and public recognition of a biological fact, as the most important contract ever entered by two individuals, and as the act which creates a new social entity, the family, marriage is a crisis. Now a crisis in human life is always surrounded by powerful emotions: forebodings and hopes, fears and joyful anticipations. Innumerable wedding rites are in existence which are obviously intended to remove the dangers associated with the crisis of marriage.

Dangers apprehended in subjective forebodings are usually conceived in the form of evil agencies: demons or ghosts or malevolent spirits, forces of black magic, mysterious concatenations of ill-luck. These have to be kept at bay or counteracted, and we find innumerable rites intended to avert ill fortune and bring happiness and good chance to the new household. Among these are the avoidance of certain days and places as unlucky, or on the other hand the selection of certain days as being of good omen; the shutting out of evil influences from the place where the wedding is being celebrated; the making of noises, the firing or brandishing of some weapon; the bathing or washing of bride and bridegroom or sprinkling them with water; the lighting of fires and waving of torches; the circumambulation of the bridegroom's tent or of the church; the beating of the bridegroom's tent, and the observance by the bride and bridegroom of various kinds of abstinences with regard to action and eating. Other forms in which bad luck can be side-tracked are: the disguising of the real actors, who may dress in the clothes of the opposite sex, cover themselves, or paint their faces; the substitution for them of effigies; marriage by proxy; and the contracting of mock marriages with trees or animals or inanimate objects. Finally an important antidote against all supernatural dangers is the state of spiritual invulnerability which is achieved by moral purity and the observance of those mixed ethical and ritual rules which in primitive culture often surround important acts of human life. The most important tabu of this kind, in connection with marriage is obviously the tabu of sex-continence. The principle that the bride and the bridegroom have to abstain from intercourse for some time after the wedding is known all over the world from primitive savagery to the most refined ethics of the Christian church, from Australia to the New World,[15] while on the wedding night there are occasionally other minor abstinences.

It is characteristic that while the bride and the bridegroom are often considered in a state dangerous not only to themselves but also to others, they are at the same time a source of blessing and of beneficent influences. Thus certain rites are supposed to influence favourably the welfare of other persons even independently of their relations to the principals; joining in at a wedding is sometimes believed to produce benefit; a wedding is looked upon as a potential cause of other weddings; while good luck is often expected from contact with the bride or bridegroom or something worn by them.

Marriage is a crisis not merely in the spiritual sense. It is also an actual sociological transition from one state to another, both partners forsaking

[15] Cf. E. A. Westermarck, *op. cit.*, Vol. II, pp. 547–64.

their old families to form a new one. The rupture with the parental family, clan, local community or tribe is expressed in a number of interesting wedding rites. Sham fighting between the bridegroom or his party and the bride's family, or some other kind of resistance made by the latter; the barring of the wedding procession; weeping and other ritual expressions of grief and unwillingness on the part of the bride and her relatives; and the mimic enactment of capture or abduction of the bride—these are mostly the dramatic expression of the fact that the bride has to be torn from her old home, that this is a violent and critical act, a final one.

But the most important type of wedding rite is that which lays down that marriage is a sacramental bond. Here again the symbolism is wide and varied, from the most direct expression of union by the joining of hands or of fingers, the tying of garments, the exchange of rings and chains, to complicated dramatic enactments of the separation and union. An important symbolism of the new ties to be established consists in the performance of some act which in future will constitute one of the normal duties or privileges of married life. Such acts in a way define the nature and exclusiveness of marriage by anticipation in ritual performances. Among them, naturally the most important are the ceremonial performance of the sexual act and the ceremonial participation in a common meal. In certain ceremonies the symbolism lays down the relative domains of marital influence. Thus in some cases the assertion of the husband's power is prominent: he is presented with a whip, or he boxes the bride's ears, or mimically beats her, and so on. In others again the wife may attempt by similar acts to mark her independence and her power over her husband. The economic aspect of marriage is often also expressed in some magical act, intended to ensure prosperity to the future household, e.g., by the smearing of butter and honey by the bride over the pole of the tent to ensure abundance of staple food. Again, the division of economic functions is expressed in other rites, as where the wife tends the fire, prepares and cooks food for her husband, etc.

These examples cover the most important though by no means all the ideas expressed in wedding rites. It is easy to see that the symbolism is extremely rich and varied, and that it embraces almost all the aspects of marriage. There are rites which bear directly upon sex and upon gestation; there are rites with a clear domestic and those with an economic significance; there are rites referring to emotional attitudes at marriage and to moral ideas as to its ends. In technique they are all legal, magical or religious. In short, the ceremonial of marriage covers and expresses all the relevant sides of the institution of marriage, and as such it has been a most fruitful and revelatory subject of anthropological study. It also has been the main source of errors and pitfalls.

In order to avoid them it is important to realise that all ritual symbolism is necessarily vague. Speaking of the marriage ceremonies, Professor

Westermarck rightly lays down that "Anthropologists are often apt to look for too much reasoning at the bottom of primitive customs. Many of them are based on vague feelings rather than on definite ideas." [16] The ritual symbolism at marriage also expresses as a rule mixed and compound meanings in most of the acts. Thus the spilling of corn over the couple may mean fecundity, prosperity, good husbandry as well as union, and probably it vaguely expresses all these elements. Sham fights and captures, tree marriages or marriages by proxy have obviously a plurality of meanings.

Nor is the function of symbolism exhausted by its direct and literal meaning. A ritual act, fixed by tradition, defining the relevant manner of concluding a contract, impresses by pomp and circumstance its social importance and its binding force in the moral sense. The ethical rules and tabus which usually go hand in hand with ritual add to this spiritualising function of wedding ceremonies. The public and official nature of the marriage act, often marked by the presence of an officiating priest, ruler or magician; heralded by banns and public announcements; sealed by witnesses and documents; enhanced by the sacredness of place and of time constitutes the widest and most general function of the rite, and that is to make marriage public, binding, sacred and morally impressive.

The dissolution of marriage in ritual

The binding forces of the marriage contract, and its ritual and moral character, are expressed as clearly at the dissolution by divorce or death as at its inception. Unfortunately our information is so defective on this point that a brief survey only can be given.

Divorce in higher cultures is a religious matter, to be carried out under the supervision of the church, and with the observance of certain formalities which express and safeguard the sanctity of the sacrament. From lower cultures we find only a few examples of divorce rites, where such symbolic acts as the breaking of a rod, the tearing of a leaf, or the casting away of some object are publicly performed (Kacharis, Hajongs, Khasis of N.W. India; Bagobo of Mindanao; Tumbuka of C. Africa; certain Canadian Indians; Maori of New Zealand).

Far more material is at our disposal referring to the persistence of the matrimonial bonds at death. They are never dissolved automatically by the decease of either partner, and their tenacity is greater for the widow than for the widower. But in either case the death of one consort imposes a number of ritual and moral observances on the other, the fulfilment of which is an essential part of the marriage contract.

The widow, or widower, usually plays the most prominent part among all mourners. Thus among certain peoples the widow has to perform

[16] *The History of Human Marriage*, Vol. II, p. 563.

various duties, extending over a more or less considerable period, at the grave of her husband. She has to sleep beside or over it; to supply it with provisions; to keep a fire burning there perpetually (Takulli, Kutchin, Mosquito, Pima Indians of America; Minas, Nsakara, Baganda of Africa; Pentecost Islanders and certain Papuans of Oceania; Kukis of India). Even more telling are the long series of tabus and duties to be observed by the widow before she is allowed to remarry: she must remain chaste, refrain from bathing or renewing her garments, avoid certain foods, etc. (Omaha, Stlathlumh, Creek, Chickasaw, Algonkin, Iroquois, Dakota, Eskimo of N. America; Angoni, Bakoba, Baya, Bawele, Baganda, Akamba, Herero, BaThonga, Zulu of Africa; Amoor tribes and Kukis of India; Bontoc Igorot of the Philippines; Maori of New Zealand; Ainu, Yakuts, Kamchadal of N.E. Asia).

Similar regulations prevent the widower from entering into a new alliance immediately after he has been set free by his wife's death. Thus among many peoples (Greenlanders, Eskimo, Aleut; Dakota, Omaha, Shawnee of N. America; Herero, Bushmen, BaThonga, Zulu of Africa; certain Papuan tribes; the Bontoc Igorots and the Ainu) the surviving husband has to live single for a time during which he is subjected to various restrictions and observances, such as refraining from sexual intercourse.

The most definite affirmation of the persistence of marital bonds is found among those people who completely forbid remarriage to widows (Tikopians, Rotumans, Marquesans, Line Islanders in Polynesia; Chinese; Ainu of Japan; Formosans; Brahmans of India) or to widowers (Ainu, Formosans, Biduanda Kallang of Malay Peninsula).

Even this is overshadowed by the institution of *suttee,* the sentence of death passed by religious tradition over the widow at her husband's death so that her spirit might follow his into the next world. This institution is found not only in India, from where we have borrowed its name, but also among the Comanche, Cree and certain Californian tribes of N. America; in Dahomey and among the BaFiote of Africa; in the New Hebrides, Fiji, Solomon Islands, Pentecost Island and New Zealand of Oceania.

The social conditions of marriage

With this we have finished the analysis of the various aspects of marriage, biological, domestic, economic, legal and religious. It will be necessary still briefly to consider marriage in relation to other modes of grouping, and to discuss certain barriers to and qualifications for matrimony, connected with membership in wider groups.

Marriage is never free in the sense that any man would be at liberty to marry any woman. Natural and physical impediments obviously do not come here under consideration, since we are only concerned with social rules. Thus it is clear that in order to marry, two people must come into contact with each other, and under primitive conditions this is possible only when they belong to the same tribe, or to tribes who meet in peaceful commerce or in warfare. Tribal or natural endogamy is thus the first condition of marriage, but it is of secondary interest to the sociologist, and must be distinguished from strict endogamy.

Endogamy proper is the rule which allows marriage only between members of a section of a tribe and forbids unions between members of two sections. Strict endogamy is rare. It occurs mainly in India where members of the same caste only are allowed to marry. In other parts of India we find a system called *hypergamy* in which a man is allowed to marry a woman of a lower section in his caste. He may also marry a woman of the same section if other conditions allow this. But a woman may not marry a man of a lower section on penalty of loss of status of her whole family. In some communities there is competition to secure husbands of high sections.

In primitive communities endogamy is not very widespread. It occurs in tribes where there is a degraded class of artisans or else stratification by rank (Polynesia; Korea, Japan; Trobriand Islands of Melanesia; Algonkin, Salish of N. America; Masai, Banyankole, Karanga and other tribes of E. and S. Africa). In such cases we often find endogamy in what might be called an approximate form. Indeed such approximate endogamy, as a tendency to marry within the profession, class or rank, is, as an unwritten law, well-nigh universal in primitive and civilised communities.

Another type of endogamy which is very widespread is that associated with religion. In very few religions is marriage outside the group of the faithful permitted. Islam, Judaism, Christianity and Hinduism are cases in point. Primitive religion as a rule need not be intolerant as regards mixed marriages, because there the tribal barriers and lack of communication act with sufficient stringency.

The prohibition of incest

The most widely spread and most rigidly enforced qualification to marriage is the set of rules which prohibit unions between the members of the same family. These are known as the rules of incest, and play a great part in the constitution of the family and in the regulation of primitive kinship. Incest has become also of great importance in modern psychology through the speculations of Freud and the psychoanalytic school.

Although incestuous unions between near relatives are universally abhorred and prohibited, the rules differ greatly from one society to another as regards the prohibited degrees as well as the stringency and character of the sanctions. Marriages between mother and son and between father and daughter are universally prohibited by law, custom and moral sentiment. Statements can be quoted, it is true, of tribes among whom more or less irregular unions between parents and children do occur. Thus marriages between mother and son have been reported from the Caribs, Eskimo, Pioje, Tinne of America; Minahassa of Celebes and Kalang of Java; New Caledonians; and the Banyoro of Africa. Again unions between father and daughter are said to occur among the Minahassa of Celebes, Karens of Burma, and in the Solomon, Marshall and Pelew Islands of Oceania. Even better attested are the marriages between brother and sister (Marshall Islands and Hawaii; ancient Irish, Egyptian and Inca royal families).

When we go beyond the family group, the prohibitions of marriage between uncles and nieces, aunts and nephews, first and second cousins, and so on, vary greatly. In some communities certain of these unions are explicitly encouraged and regarded as desirable; in others forbidden. About preferential marriages between relatives we have already spoken. Extensive prohibitions of marriage between distant kindred exist, besides the Western Christian civilisations also among a number of other tribes and cultures (Salish, Eskimo, Pipites of Salvador, Aztecs, Araucanians, Abipones, Ona, Yahgan of America; Koryak, Yukaghir, Kalmuck of N.E. Asia; Torres Straits Islanders, Mekeo, Polynesians of Oceania; S.E. Bantu of Africa).

Exogamy

This is the system which far larger groups of people are regarded as related to each other and their members forbidden to intermarry. It is found mainly in association with the classificatory nomenclature of kinship terms and the clan organisation. Whether exogamy is genetically connected with incest, i.e., whether it is an extension of the tabu on intercourse and marriage within the family, or an independent institution, is a debated question.[17]

Exogamy embraces the widest number of people, where it is based on the dual organisation and debars from intercourse or marriage one half of the tribesmen and tribeswomen. Normally exogamy is an attribute of clan, i.e., of the group of people who trace their descent to a common ancestor, have in most cases the same totem, and fulfill a number of functions together. The clans are sometimes a subdivision of the tribe, based numerically on the dual principle, as where we have two, four or eight clans. At times there is an odd and more or less considerable number of clans, and exogamy is enforced only within each of these divisions. The prohibitions as a rule apply unilaterally (Iroquois, Huron, Lenape, Mohegan, Miami, Shawnee, Creek, Sauk, Fox, Kickapoo, Blackfoot, Dakota, Seminole of N. America; Arawak and Goajiro of S. America; Tungus, Yakut, Samoyed, Ostyak, Tartars of N.E. Asia; various aboriginal peoples of India; Torres Straits Islanders, Papuans, Melanesians, Polynesians

[17] See E. A. Westermarck, *op. cit.*, Vol. II, pp. 192–218; Sir James George Frazer, *Totemism and Exogamy,* 1910, Vol. IV, *passim;* B. Malinowski, *Sex and Repression in Savage Society,* 1927, Part IV.

and Micronesians of Oceania; Hottentot, S.E. Bantu, Anyanja, Wayao, Awemba, Makololo, Akonde, Masai, Akamba, Baganda and other E. African tribes; Ashanti and other W. African tribes). Only in a few cases has exogamy to be observed with regard to the clans of both parents (Omaha, Osage of N. America; certain Naga tribes of Assam; S. Massim of Melanesia, Herero, Lango of Africa).

A specially complex set of conditions prevails in the tribes of C. Australia, where there is a twofold division into (a) totemic clans, which are not strictly exogamous; and (b) matrimonial classes, which strictly correspond to kinship divisions, and which are not only exogamous, but regulate marriage to the extent that a member of one of them has to marry into one and one only of the remaining three or seven classes, as the case may be.

The forms of marriage

From the foregoing description it will be clear that there is a considerable range within which the constitution of marriage can vary. For as we have seen there can be many different arrangements in the domestic, legal, economic and ceremonial sides of marriage, and each of their manifold combinations constitutes a distinct form of marriage.

The term "form of marriage" has been as a rule applied to what might be called the *numeric variation* in marriage, i.e., the variation according to the number of consorts united to each other; and the main "forms of marriage" usually listed are monogamy, polygyny, polyandry and group-marriage. To deal with this classification adequately it is necessary to distinguish hypothetical assumptions from actually existing social arrangements. From this point of view we can at once eliminate "group-marriage," since our previous analysis has shown that the *pirrauru* relationship of Australia and similar institutions among the Eskimo and in Siberia can not in their parental, economic, legal or religious functions be regarded as a form of marriage.

Polyandry

This is the name given to a union in which several men are legally bound in marriage to one woman. Polyandry is the rarest of the numeric varieties of marriage, and unfortunately the one on which, in spite of its great theoretical importance, we possess but very meagre and inadequate information. Polyandry is not found among any of the more primitive peoples, and its distribution is almost completely confined to the highlands of S. India and C. Asia, with isolated exceptions, such as one African tribe (Bahima) and some Eskimo, among whom it occurs, but infrequently.

In Tibet and the adjacent countries there exists polyandry of the fraternal type, i.e., several brothers share the wife in common. All the husbands live together with their common wife as members of the same household, and cohabit successively with her. Children born of these marriages are sometimes regarded as the legal descendants of the eldest brotherhusband only; in other cases it appears that when a child is born it is attributed to him by whom the mother asserts that she has conceived it.

Among the Nayars of S.W. India there is a so-called form of polyandry which has played an important though rather deceptive part in the theories of marriage. A girl goes through a form of marriage with a man, but then really consorts with a number of men who need not be related to one another. She lives apart from her partners, who cohabit with her successively by agreement among themselves. Owing to the matrilineal institutions of this people, the children of such marriages inherit from their mother's brother, but the social importance of fatherhood is seen in the fact that the woman, when pregnant, always nominates one or other of the men as the father of the child, and he is obliged to provide for it and to educate it.

Another account is that by Dr. Rivers, of the Toda polyandry, which can be taken as the representative of the simpler type of this institution in S. India. Among the Toda, several men, usually two or three brothers, share the wife, but it is the rule that they cohabit with her in succession. Again, the children are not owned in common by the husbands, but each child is allotted individually to one, not with reference to any presumption of physical paternity, but in virtue of a ritual act performed by the man over the child, an act which establishes social paternity and confers legitimate descent on the child.

Polyandry is thus a compound marriage, in which cohabitation is usually successive, and not joint, while children and property are not shared by the husbands.

Polygyny

This is a form of marriage in which several wives are united to one man, each having the status of legal consort, while her offspring are regarded as the legal descendants of the husband. As an institution polygyny exists in all parts of the world. There are very few primitive tribes about whom we are informed that a man is not allowed, if he can, to enter into more than one union. Many peoples have been said to be monogamous, but it is difficult to infer from the data at our disposal whether monogamy is the prevalent practice, the moral ideal, or an institution safeguarded by sanctions. It must be remembered at once that polygyny is never practised throughout the community: there cannot exist a community in which every man would have several wives, since this would entail an enormous surplus of females over males.[18] The second important point with regard to polygyny, which is seldom brought out clearly, is that in reality it is

[18] Cf. however the important contribution to this subject by G. Pitt-Rivers, *The Clash of Culture and the Contact of Races*, 1927.

not so much a form of marriage fundamentally distinct from monogamy as rather a multiple monogamy. It is always in fact the repetition of a marriage contract, entered individually with each wife, establishing an individual relationship between the man and each of his consorts. As a rule each relationship is little affected legally or economically by the others.

Where each wife has her separate household and the husband visits them in turn, polygynous marriage resembles very closely a temporarily interrupted monogamy. In such cases there is a series of individual marriages in which domestic arrangements, economics, parenthood as well as legal and religious elements do not as a rule seriously encroach on each other. The polygyny with separate households is more universally prevalent. Among the great majority of the Bantu and Hamitic peoples of Africa, where the number of wives, especially in the case of chiefs, is often considerable, each wife commonly occupies a separate hut with her children, and manages an independent household with well-defined legal and economic rights. Where, on the other hand, as among many N. American tribes, two or more wives share the same household, polygyny affects the institution of matrimonial life much more deeply.

In most cases the motive for polygyny is economic and political. Thus in the Trobriand Islands (Melanesia) the chief's income is due to his wives' annual endowment. In many African communities the chief derives his wealth from the plurality of his wives, who by means of the produce of their agricultural labour enable him to exercise the lavish hospitality upon which so much of his power rests. A multitude of wives, however, may increase not only a man's wealth but also his social importance, reputation and authority, apart from the influence of the number of his children. Hence we find in many Bantu communities of Africa that the desire to have many wives is one of the leading motives in the life of every man; while the fact that in many Melanesian and Polynesian communities polygyny is a prerogative of the chief testifies to the social prestige attaching to it.

Monogamy

Monogamy is not only the most important form of marriage, not only that which predominates in most communities, and which occurs, statistically speaking, in an overwhelming majority of instances, but it is also the pattern and prototype of marriage.

Both polyandry and polygyny are compound marriages consisting of several unions combined into a larger system, but each of them constituted upon the pattern of a monogamous marriage. As a rule polygamous cohabitation is a successive monogamy and not joint domesticity; children and property are divided, and in every other respect the contracts are entered individually between two partners at a time.

Monogamy as the unique and exclusive form of marriage, in the sense that bigamy is regarded as a grave criminal offence and a sin as well as a sacrilege, is very rare indeed. Such an exclusive ideal and such a rigid legal view of marriage is perhaps not to be found outside the modern, relatively recent development of Western Culture. It is not implied in Christian doctrine even. Apart from such isolated phenomena as the recent Church of Latter Day Saints (Mormons) and the heretical sect of Anabaptists (16th century), polygyny was legally practised and accepted by the Church in the middle ages, and it occurs sporadically as a legal institution accepted by Church and State as recently as the middle of the 17th century.[19]

Monogamy as pattern and prototype of human marriage, on the other hand, is universal. The whole institution, in its sexual, parental, economic, legal and religious aspects, is founded on the fact that the real function of marriage—sexual union, production and care of children, and the co-operation which it implies—requires essentially two people, and two people only, and that in the overwhelming majority of cases two people only are united in order to fulfil these facts.

Conjugation necessarily takes place only between two organisms; children are produced by two parents only, and always socially regarded as the offspring of one couple; the economics of the household are never conducted group-wise; the legal contract is never entered upon jointly; the religious sanction is given only to the union of two. A form of marriage based on communism in sex, joint parenthood, domesticity, group-contract and a promiscuous sacrament has never been described. Monogamy is, has been and will remain the only true type of marriage. To place polygyny and polyandry as "forms of marriage" co-ordinate with monogamy is erroneous. To speak about "group-marriage" as another variety shows a complete lack of understanding as to the nature of marriage.

Theories of marriage

The last conclusions reveal once more the important truth of scientific method that a full knowledge of facts cuts the ground from under most hypothetical speculations. The theories of human marriage have mainly been concerned with its "origins" and "history," and attempts were made at ranging the various "forms of marriage" into an evolutionary series. Once we come to recognise that marriage is fundamentally one, and that its varieties correspond not to stages of evolution, but are determined by the type of community, its economic and political organisation, and the character of its material culture, the problem becomes one of observation and sociological analysis, and ceases to move on the slippery plane of hypothesis.

The view that marriage originated in "promiscuity," "hetairism" or

[19] Westermarck, *op. cit.*, Vol. III, pp. 50–1.

"matrimonial communism," and that monogamy is a product of gradual development through a multitude of stages, has been advanced by Bachofen, Morgan and McLennan; has found wholehearted or partial support by a number of eminent writers (Lord Avebury, [Mrs. Margaret] Fison, Howitt, [E. B.] Tylor, Spencer and Gillen, [Albert Hermann] Post, [Wolfgang] Köhler, [Maxime] Kovalevsky, Lippert, Schurtz, Frazer and others); and has been criticised and combated by [Charles R.] Darwin, Westermarck, [Andrew] Lang, Grosse and Crawley.

The writings of [Lewis H.] Morgan's school suffer from an overemphasis of the sexual aspect, often coupled with prudish reticences; from a misinterpretation of linguistic evidence; from a neglect of the parental and economic aspect of marriage. They are full of fantastic and meaningless concepts such as "promiscuity," "group-marriage," "primitive communism," which as a rule are not even laid down with sufficient concrete details to give hold to our imagination and remain mere words on paper. The German writers of this school, who have contributed a voluminous output, especially in the *Zeitschrift für vergleichende Rechtswissenschaft,* have certainly not neglected the legal side of marriage, but in applying to primitive societies the dry legal formalism of modern jurisprudence, and in ruthlessly forcing all facts into the cut and dried scheme of "marriage stages," they have contributed but little which will have lasting value.

The recent advocates of Morgan's and Bachofen's view, notably [W. G.] Sumner, Rivers, [A. G.] Keller, Briffault, have given a much better and more concrete outline of the hypothetical early stages of marriage. But even this last stand of the "group-marriage" theory is based on an inadequate analysis of the institution and an unwarranted assumption of early sexual and economic communism as well as of group-motherhood.

Modern theories of marriage follow closely the lead of Darwin on the biological side, of Westermarck in his sociological analysis, and of Crawley in some of his psychological suggestions. Such writers as [R. H.] Lowie, [Alfred L.] Kroeber and Howard in America; [Richard] Thurnwald, W. Schmidt and Koppers in Germany; A. R. Brown, Malinowski, and Pitt-Rivers in Great Britain, both in their theories and in their field work show a far greater interest in the sociological analysis of marriage, in its relation to the family, in the correlation of its aspects, in the sociological working of sexual customs, whether these be tabus, relaxations or excesses, in their reference to marriage.

Some new light on marriage has been thrown by those psychoanalysts, notably J. C. Flügel, who are prepared to give serious consideration to facts in their bearing upon the Freudian doctrine. Finally important contributions to the theory of marriage have been made by those students who approach the problem in its practical applications: the eugenists: students of population; and scientific aspects of social hygiene.

Marriage like most problems of anthropology is ceasing to be a subject of speculation and becoming one of empirical research.

BIBLIOGRAPHY

Leathley, S. A., *The History of Marriage and Divorce*, 1916.

Goeller, E., *Das Eherecht im neuen kirchlichen Gesetzbuch*, 1918.

Shukri, Ahmad, *Muhammadan Law of Marriage and Divorce*, 1917.

Vandyopadhyaya, Sir Gurudasa, *The Hindu Law of Marriage and Stridhana*, 1915.

Granet, M., *La polygynie sororate et le sororat dans la Chine féodale*, 1920.

Vergette, E. D., *Certain Marriage Customs of some of the Tribes in the Protectorate of Sierra Leone*, 1917.

Howitt, A. W., *The Native Tribes of South-East Australia*, 1904.

Spencer, B., and Gillen, F. J., *The Arunta*, 1927.

Spencer, B., *The Native Tribes of the Northern Territory of Australia*, 1914.

Frazer, J. G., *Totemism and Exogamy*, 1910.

Thomas, N. W., *Kinship Organization and Group Marriage in Australia*, 1906.

Westermarck, E. A., *The History of Human Marriage*, 3 vols., 1921.

Schoeffer, S., *Das Eheproblem*, 1922.

Iwasaki, K., *Das japanische Eherecht*, 1904.

Westermarck, E. A., *Les cérémonies du mariage au Maroc*, 1921.

2*

2

THE FAMILY: PAST AND PRESENT *

The family, that is the group consisting of mother, father and children, has been and to a large extent still remains the main educational agency of mankind. This is the verdict of sound modern anthropology, this is the knowledge derived from history and dictated by common sense.

Ancestor worship, the command to "honour thy father and thy mother," the cult of a God the Father and of a Mother Goddess, have been the corner stones of most human religions. The modern scientific student of genetics is inclined to judge the quality of the offspring by that of the parents. The contemporary sociologist counts cultural inheritance and home influences as the dominant factors in the shaping of human character. Psycho-analysis with its stress on the "domestic complex," that is the memories derived from the early contact between the child and its parents, and Behaviourism, with its assertion that "conditioning" matters more than endowment, also imply that the influences of the domestic setting must be dominant in education.

At present, however, the family is being seriously threatened and its future searchingly questioned. "The family is going to disappear within the next fifty years"; "sex is now used for recreation and not for procreation"; "family life is obviously a study in lunacy"—such statements could be multiplied from modern sociological and pseudo-psychological literature. The type of reproduction and education outlined by Aldous Huxley, as a

---

* A fuller documentation of the anthropological views here summarised will be found in the articles s.v. "Marriage" [see Chapt. 1 of Sex, Culture, and Myth], "Kinship" [see Chapt. 6], and "Social Anthropology" in the 14th Edition of the Encyclopædia Britannica; the article s.v. "Culture" in the Encyclopaedia of Social Sciences (New York); also in the article "Parenthood— The Basis of Social Structure" [see Chapt. 3].

This article appeared in November 1934 (Vol. XV), pp. 203–06 of The New Era in Home and School, the monthly magazine of The New Education Fellowship, 9, The Butts, Bratton, Westbury, Wilts., England, and is reprinted by permission.

satire, in his *Brave New World*, has been seriously propounded by some writers whose authority is not altogether negligible.

There is no doubt that some of the dominant intellectual trends of our day have exercised a corroding influence on the stability of marriage and the family, notably, Psycho-Analysis, Behaviourism, some advocacies of "sex communism" and of the extreme hedonistic point of view. Some overt legislative attacks against marriage and the family, mainly in Soviet Russia, seem also seriously to threaten the future of the domestic institutions. The most important, however, are those influences which go beyond academic attack or clumsy legislative encroachment, which are insidious, inevitable, and pervading at the same time. I mean such facts as the technique of contraception, the growing financial, hence also legal and moral, independence of woman, and the fact that the household is rapidly ceasing to be a profitable economic enterprise, or even a convenient place for the joint existence of the family.

The modern woman does not need the cloak of marriage in order to satisfy her sexual life; modern man does not need to resort to prostitution nor clandestine intrigue. Each can earn his or her own living, can play a rôle in public and political life, can move about independently and need not marry when he wants occasionally to mate. Should there be even a child, it is possible with the modern ease in transport and anonymous reappearance somewhere else, to slip away and eventually to hand the child over to be brought up in some sort of communal nursery, kindergarten and then school. With most incentives gone, with the advantages of marriage fading away and the hardships of home life increasing, one often wonders not that marriage is affected, but that people still marry and bring forth families, that after divorce they remarry—in short that humanity still reproduces mainly in the old-fashioned manner.

It is at this point that the modern anthropologist who studies the past of human history in order to obtain an insight into the future can offer an explanation as well as some indications of development.

The anthropologist himself, in fact, has been confused in his theoretical work by a number of factors such as primitive mother-right, the sexual freedom of savages, the importance of the clan, tribe or horde and its encroachment on the family—factors which closely resemble the modern snags of domestic life. There was a time when anthropology despaired of the existence of the family in the past, even as sociologists nowadays despair of the family in the future. We had the famous theories of primitive promiscuity, of group marriage, of early matriarchy, and of the gradual and painful evolution towards monogamy and family.

These views which still have a wide currency in popular and pseudo-scientific literature have been now definitely discarded by professional anthropologists. The change has come through a better knowledge of facts. Reports about the existence of so-called group marriage in Central Australia, in Siberia, or New Guinea, have been recently found to be incorrect. With the fuller knowledge of facts and the changing outlook we have arrived also at more precise concepts and different methods of approach. We no longer glibly speak about "sexual communism," "group marriage," "primitive matriarchy" and the "clan as a reproductive unit." The modern anthropologist is no longer busy dissecting the various aspects of the family and marriage into "promiscuity," "marriage by purchase," "patriarchy" and so on, and then projecting such self-contained entities on an evolutionary line. The competent observer has discovered that "father-right" and "mother-right" exist side by side, that marriage is compatible with pre-nuptial laxity, that the clan and family instead of excluding, complement each other. In fact, through all variations the most stable units which are found everywhere are the family and individual marriage.

An entirely different problem therefore has emerged for a modern anthropologist. It is no longer the question of deciding whether the family or individual marriage has superseded or followed the clan, whether early representatives of the human species were entirely promiscuous or highly virtuous, whether mother-right precedes patriarchy or vice versa. The problem for the modern anthropologists is rather to show the relation of these different social groups, agencies and institutions.

Let us take as an example the question of sexual morality. The distinction embodied in the modern slogan "sex for recreation and not for procreation" has been drawn by most savages—drawn, enforced and institutionalized. If we were to divide the lowest savages into Primitive Puritans and Early Hedonists, the former—the Veddas of Ceylon, the Orang Kubu of Sumatra, the Yahgan of Tierra del Fuego—look at matters in a way on which from the "moral" point of view even Queen Victoria herself could not improve. Every one of them regards with horror any lapse of an unmarried girl, with disfavour any libertinage on the part of an unmarried boy, and they are very much shocked by the very mention of adultery.

On the other hand, the central Australian as well as the typical Bantu and Polynesian, the Papuan or the Sudanese, takes a different view. Free love making is allowed, at times there are restrictions and definitions on the type of erotic satisfaction which can be found in the company of the other sex. But one rule is always precise and often extremely stringent: there must be no pregnancy without marriage. The punishment for transgression is sometimes severe to the extent of public and cruel execution of both culprits. Among the Djagga—who belong to the Bantu tribes practising female circumcision—I was told blood-curdling tales of how such executions were actually carried out in the olden days.

In most tribes, however, some speedy and easy remedy is found: immediate marriage is enforced after pregnancy has taken place; or a compensation is demanded from the man, which makes the girl more desirable; or in some cases where children are the main asset of marriage, the man himself marries the girl of his own free will as a reward rather than as a penalty.

This example shows that it is futile to discuss pre-nuptial licence without reference to the institution of marriage. A more detailed analysis—for which some material will be found in the articles quoted—shows that marriage in all human societies is the licencing of parenthood rather than of sexual intercourse. Marriage affects the course of sexual life very profoundly. In fact, pre-nuptial intercourse almost everywhere is not an end in itself but rather a form of trial union, a method of courtship, a means of experimenting in the possibilities of marriage.

If this view be correct, we can say that even a considerable relaxation in sexual conduct does not need to affect profoundly the institution of marriage and the family. It also proves that the key to the problem does not lie in the study of the sexual impulse detached from its wider context of personal relations and of parenthood. We can say that the desire on the part of the woman to have children with the right man, and the realization by the male that only as a father can he reach full tribal status and influence, lead to marriage and the establishment of a household.

Thus, even as it is futile to study the sexual impulse without understanding its psychological context of personal relations between man and woman, so also it will always remain irrelevant to study marriage as a personal relationship without investigating its rôle in tribal life. Without personifying society we can say that everywhere tribal tradition puts a premium on effective and successful parenthood. In societies like those of Africa where the core of religion is ancestor-worship, a man who dies without male issue passes into oblivion, while during his life he remains without real influence in the tribe. Female issue is equally desirable in societies where the bride price is one of the fundamental legal institutions. The whole legal and economic constitution of a typical Bantu tribe, of a Polynesian or Malayan society, is associated with the principle that it is economically advantageous, morally desirable and socially honourable for a man to be the father of many children and for the woman to be a mother of both sons and daughters. The strength of some more highly developed communities, notably the Chinese, the Semites, and the Indians, is associated with the same social and moral forces.

Turning now to another aspect, there is no doubt that at present many economic forces work against the family, and that the State, even in such of its forms as profess to favour marriage and the family, works against it. This is very different from what obtains under more primitive conditions. Take a typical Bantu: he marries because he wants children, but also largely because without a wife he cannot set up a household and cannot cultivate his fields. For this is a joint man's and woman's work. His wife will provide for him his domestic comforts. She will cultivate his gardens and prepare his food. The children also, even while they are being educated in tribal matters, work with him and work for him. In his old age he entirely depends on his children who by tribal law and morality have to support him.

If instead of taking an African Bantu, we were to pass to any other native community or dwell on the old order of things in China, we would find exactly the same conditions. And let me add at once, the study of primitive religion, customary law, and early morality would show that all the forces combine to make wealth in children, that is a strong family and a large family, the greatest asset to man and woman.

Here modern conditions are certainly more alarming than those discussed in connection with the sexual aspect. In the large towns and among industrial workers to-day, the self-contained household is no more an inevitable necessity. It is even less so among the middle class. In the modern life of big cities, what with the difficulty of domestic service, the ease of obtaining food and help in service flats, the life of a household seems to be disintegrating. The family is rapidly ceasing to be a group based on joint production, or even on joint consumption of goods. The economic advantages for a man or woman to marry are negligible compared with the inducements of a Bantu or Oceanic or a Chinese peasant.

The crushing death duties now imposed by most States, above all in Great Britain, have already disintegrated the economic continuity of lineage. Modern taxation, with the insignificant advantages given to large families, works essentially against and not for the family. In addressing educationalists one can point out a characteristic detail: the fact that married women in many countries are deprived of any chance of obtaining teaching posts in State schools. Marriage here as in many professions becomes a liability, and motherhood a stumbling block to a woman's career. A full analysis would show that not only do modern economic and technical conditions work against the family, but that the State instead of assisting the family very often militates against it.

But here again an anthropological analysis would prove that some such disintegrating forces of an economic nature have at an earlier stage worked at the expense of the family, yet without destroying it. The family has survived the economic onslaught and extortion of greedy chiefs, as well as the excessive forms of taxation in the highly organized little states of Africa or Oceania. It has survived the disintegrating influences of forced labour and slavery. It is compatible with individual exploitation of the soil and with communal land tenure.

Again the clan, as I have shown in the article on "Kinship" above mentioned, is not something which overrides the family but it is a group which can be shown to grow out of the family—to be a by-product of family life.

Thus, whichever of the modern disintegrating forces be considered, it is possible to show that the family has in the past withstood and overcome their onslaught. Individual marriage and the family have somehow readjusted and survived the attacks of antagonistic political, economic, legal and hedonistic influences. The group consisting of mother, father and children emerges always as a social unit in which the biological process of procreation is carried out under legal safeguards with a substantial economic foundation, surrounded by moral and religious values. Anthropology proves that the physiological forces of maternal love, the attachment between husband and wife and the interest of the father in his wife's offspring cannot be readily thrown away and superseded by the impersonal concern of the State, by the lukewarm enthusiasm of charity or by the cold interest of scientific planning.

This "message of comfort" does not mean that we should be satisfied with a supine acquiescence in the operation of modern disintegrating forces. A policy of vigilance, indeed of active and constructive reform, is necessary. The exclusive concentration on the sexual side of marriage which we find prevalent in modern sociological literature is, I think, one-sided to say the least. The most important need is to realize that in the future we must create economic, legal and social conditions with real advantages to those who enter marriage and produce large families.

The study of the family teaches us that a civilization which would destroy the family would also destroy the continuity of tradition, the interest in building up economic enterprise, and with this also the integrity of human character.

3

PARENTHOOD—THE BASIS OF SOCIAL STRUCTURE

"Daddy, what an ass you are!" This was the final sentence in an argument which I had with my youngest daughter, aged five. I had not been able to convince her or to sway her opinion. . . . I ceased arguing and reflected. I tried to imagine what would have happened had I thus addressed my father some forty years ago. I shuddered and sighed. Fate was unkind in making me appear forty years too soon.

Four hundred years earlier for such a reply a child would have been beaten, put into a dark room, tortured or disciplined into death or moral annihilation. Four thousand years ago, perhaps, in the Bronze Age, a bloodthirsty patriarch would have killed it outright. But forty thousand years back or thereabouts (I am not very strong on dates or hypotheses) the weak, matrilineal father might have smiled on his offspring even more indulgently than I was able to do, and without that wry twist on his face which comes, I suppose, from undigested patriarchal traditions. In any case, among my present-day Stone Age savages of the South Seas, I have heard children address a father as frankly and unceremoniously, with the perfect equivalent in native of the English "you dam' fool!" while he argued back without any show of patriarchal dignity.

The wheel of change turns round and brings back again things that once lived and only yesterday seemed dead and lost beyond retrieving. To the anthropologist there is nothing new under the sun. He teaches us to look with weary indulgence at the most disconcerting extravagances of our time, he adopts a wise foresight and philosophic caution towards the most intoxicating promises of reform. In this lies his value to the all-too-sanguine sociological radical.

The anthropologist remains unmoved even when faced with the most

This article appeared in The New Generation: The Intimate Problems of Modern Parents and Children, *edited by V. F. Calverton and Samuel D. Schmalhausen, with Introduction by Bertrand Russell, Allen & Unwin, London, and The Macaulay Co., New York, 1930, pp. 113–68, and is reprinted by permission.*

shocking, dangerous and ominous signs of youthful moral decay, with revolts of children against parents, with such symptoms as "petting parties" and increasing divorce. He teaches us that such things have been before and that they have passed without having killed or poisoned the soul of mankind. And in this lies the comfort of anthropology to the wise conservative. The die-hard who despairs or loses his head and temper in planning all sorts of repressive and reactionary measures of retrogression is beyond consolation, or the reach of any serious argument either.

There is no problem in which comfort and caution, as well as vision and intelligence, are more needed than the one discussed in this volume. It is indeed the most actual and burning question of to-day—the revolt of modern youth against the conventions represented by the parental generation; the fight of the young for freedom, and the resistance offered by the old.

The relations between parents and children, as well as our views on them, are undoubtedly undergoing a profound change. As our knowledge increases the very facts themselves shift and modify under our eyes. Psychoanalysis has no sooner delved its complexes out of the Unconscious, than we see them enacted in real tragedies, individual and collective. The so-called freeing of children in the Soviet Republic has assumed catastrophic dimensions. The same new liberty takes less acute, but not less puzzling, forms, in the United States, in England and in Germany. The facts revealed by Judge Ben Lindsey, and in the works of W. I. Thomas, G. V. Hamilton and other students of juvenile delinquency, seem to disclose an entirely new world of precocious vice. The champions of the old order try, above all, to silence the denouncers, to put a taboo on any discussion. When that seems an insufficient remedy they suggest crude, repressive measures. The Fascist State and its imitative fellow-dictatorships of Southern Europe are Prussianizing education, and they thus hope to stem the evil and to produce, under stern state control, the ideal citizen and moral being at high speed and under high pressure.

The relations between the two generations are in the melting pot. New forces are at work, the old [and new]* principles are in solution, and we really cannot foretell what the results will be. The sober scientific outlook, the weight of facts on which it must be based, the breadth of vision which it can give, seem more urgently needed than ever. We must therefore turn to science.

It is the function of science to control the future on the basis of a correct analysis of the past and present: Knowledge gives foresight in the light of experience. In discussing the future of parenthood and the family the sociologist will do well to reflect on what these institutions

---

* As in manuscript; not carried over to publication.

are, how they develop and how they are related to human nature. Above all, how they work and how they have worked in the various societies of the past and present.

The anthropologist, as we said at the outset, comes in here as a useful helpmate of the student of modern conditions. He studies human cultures and the organization of societies within the widest compass of human experience. He can provide the background of comparative knowledge against which all modern problems must be discussed. He should be able to lay down the laws which define the constitution and nature of the family and parenthood. He should be able to demonstrate how certain elements vary, disappearing in some societies, hypertrophied in others, while yet the fundamentals of relationship between parents and children remain stable and universal. These fundamentals are the true constituent elements of marriage, parenthood and the family. Their discovery, definition and establishment is the real task of scientific anthropology.

It might be objected that the student of society would look in vain for simple, concordant and acceptable answers from present-day anthropology. Looking up Westermarck or Crawley he would find that marriage was monogamous from the outset. If he referred to the writings of Rivers and Sidney Hartland, or the popular works of Briffault, Ivan Bloch, Ploss-Bartels or [Ferdinand Emil] Reitzenstein, he would find that promiscuity, group-marriage, and an overwhelming proto-feminism existed in primitive mankind, and that family and marriage are late products. He would learn a great deal about the gorilla and the missing link, he would be told lewd and lurid stories about pithecanthropoid raping and about communistic and classificatory savages; he would enjoy short stories about long words, such as exogamy, incest-fixation, endopatrophagy, marriage-by-capture-cum-polyandry. He would emerge learned but not necessarily wise, not any wiser certainly, as to what has been in the matter of family and marriage, of parents and children. He would even find himself thoroughly muddled as to what present-day savages do think or feel in these matters. For these poor savages are being constantly used as pawns in controversy and props in hypotheses, rather than as living beings and the subjects of a living science. The institutions of the native races of to-day instead of being used as material for sociological study, as a basis for scientific induction, are regarded as "survivals" of past stages and indices of vanished historical periods.

There is one movement in anthropology, however, which is built on a strictly comparative foundation and studies facts primarily with an empirical and sociological interest. The functional school of anthropology has made considerable contributions towards this problem and the results will be briefly presented here.[1]

[1] For a brief account of the general character of the Functional method see article s.v. "Social Anthropology" in the 14th Edition of the *Encyclopædia Britannica* written

The theoretical issues, as we have said, have been so muddled by controversy and misguided methods that it will be necessary to have a direct look at conditions as they exist in primitive societies still open to observation. Let us for a moment forget all anthropological quarrels and theories: let us lift the veil of prejudice and controversy, look at facts directly, and to this end arrange an experiment in thought if not in reality.

Let us imagine an intelligent observer stranded among an entirely savage tribe—a sort of ethnographic Robinson Crusoe. He could reveal to us many interesting points in method of field-work, as well as collect valuable observations. For, with an uncorrupted sample of primitive humanity before him, himself unbiased by the missionary's zeal and one-sided view of native culture, unhampered by the planter's greed, and the administrator's spurious sense of power, he would have unlimited opportunities for a sympathetic study of the people around him. At the same time, unlike the learned modern field-worker, he would have no theoretical preconceptions, he would not be partially blinded by his previous vision of primitive humanity as dictated by theories and hypotheses. Such an ideal observer, interested and yet unprejudiced, intelligent yet with his common sense still intact, would register the facts of primitive life as they appeared to him, so to speak, in layers, illuminated by deepening psychological and sociological insight.

At first he would probably be struck by a number of customs, shocking in their crudity, cruelty and strangeness; and at the same time he would be equally impressed by a body of beliefs, usages and institutions so entirely similar to our own as to be almost indistinguishable to an untrained eye. Among these latter our ethnographer would probably pick out the institutions of the family and the bonds of kinship as an outstanding example of the "uniformity of human nature."

Indeed, at first sight, the typical savage family, as it is found among the vast majority of native tribes—of the few apparent exceptions I shall speak presently—seems hardly to differ at all from its civilized counterpart. Mother, father and children share the camp, the home, the food and the life. The intimacy of the family existence, the daily round of meals, the domestic occupations and outdoor work, the rest at night and the awakening to a new day, seem to run on strictly parallel lines

---

by the present writer, who is also responsible for the label "Functional" now generally attached to the movement of which he is a follower. "Kinship" and "Marriage" have also been treated from the Functional point of view in two articles in the *Encyclopædia* [Chapt. 6 and Chapt. 1 of *Sex, Culture, and Myth*]. The method is also exemplified in *Sex and Repression in Savage Society* (1927) and *The Sexual Life of Savages* (1929) which deal with the problem of sex and parenthood. Professors A. Radcliffe-Brown and R. Thurnwald, Dr. R. W. Firth and Captain Pitt-Rivers are also associated with the Functional movement while the following writers are spiritually akin to it: Havelock Ellis, R. H. Lowie and E. Westermarck, G. A. Dorsey and E. Sapir, A. A. Goldenweiser and Margaret Mead.

in civilized and in savage societies, allowance being made for the difference in the level of culture. The members of the family are evidently as closely bound together in a native tribe as they are in an European society. Attached to each other, sharing life and most of its interests, exchanging counsel and help, company and cheer, and reciprocating in economic coöperation, the same bonds unite them as those of our family; similar distances and barriers separate them from other families. In Australia and among most North American Indians, in Melanesia and in Siberia, among the majority of African tribes and in South America, the individual undivided family stands out conspicuous, a definite social unit marked off from the rest of society by a clear line of division.[2] An observer would have to close his eyes or read himself blind in the works of Morgan, Köhler, [Heinrich] Cunow or Rivers not to see this.

Had our ethnographic Robinson Crusoe an abundance of time for the study of native customs and sufficient intelligence and method to reflect upon them, he could substantiate his first impression by weighty arguments. Thus he would find that what could be called the instinctive foundation of maternal love is clearly traceable in his native society. The expectant mother is interested in her future offspring, she is absorbed in it from the moment of its birth, and in the carrying out of her social duties of suckling, nursing and tending it, she is supported by strong biological inclinations. In a tribe where there are such practices as infanticide or frequent adoption, the natural innate tendencies of maternal love may become rebelliously subservient to custom and tribal law, but they are never completely stifled or obliterated. In any case, once a child is spared, kept and nursed by the mother, maternal love grows into a passion. And this passion develops as the mother has to guide, watch over and educate her child, and lasts through life. To this the child responds with an exclusive personal attachment to the mother, and the mutual bond remains one of the strongest sentiments in any human society.

What might strike an observer with even greater force would be the position of the father. Expecting, perhaps, from a savage man a certain degree of ferocity towards wife and children, he might be astonished to find instead a kind and considerate husband and a tender father. At his worst—I mean in tribes where, through custom and tradition, he plays the not always amiable rôle of a stern patriarch—he is still the provider of the family, the helpmate at home, and the guardian of the children up to a certain age. At his best and mildest, in a typical matrilineal community, he is a drudge within the household, the assistant nurse of his

[2] The generalizations of this essay will be fully substantiated in a forthcoming volume on *Primitive Kinship*. Compare also the article s.v. "Kinship" in the 14th Edition, *Encyclopaedia Britannica* [see Chapt. 6 of *Sex, Culture, and Myth*]; and the writer's *The Family among the Australian Aborigines* (1913).

children, the weaker and fonder of the two parents, and later on the most faithful and often the most intimate friend of his sons and daughters.

If our observer wanted to lay yet deeper foundations for his initial view of the permanence and importance of the individual family, he might point out a number of traditional usages, customary and legal norms referring to common habitation, household occupations and mutual economic duties—all of them making the undivided individual family a definite legal unit. The relation of mother to child, clearly dictated by natural inclinations, is yet not entirely left to them. The mother, besides feeling inclined to do all she does for her child, is none the less obliged to do it. An unnatural mother would be not only blamed but punished, and the bad or careless father would equally have to suffer under the lash of public opinion or be punished by some definite legal measure.

Thus, as likely as not, the final conclusion of our authority would be that in matters of kinship, family life and children, matters among primitive people are much as they are with us. That is to say, the personal bonds of kinship are the same in primitive tribes and in civilized societies; and the affection within the family, the habits, uses and laws of the savage household are entirely reminiscent of a peasant's or poor man's home in Europe. The mother, tied by physiological bonds to her children, fulfils the same part as every mother has to fulfil; the father in a savage community seems to be there for exactly the same purpose as the patriarchal head of the family in modern European society; to watch over the safety of his children, to provide for them and to guide them through life.

The picture here attributed to a supposed ethnographic Robinson Crusoe is not imaginary. It is just this sort of information about parental love, the kindly treatment of children, their obedience and affection in return, the enduring of family bonds throughout life, which some of our earliest and best authorities present in their ethnographic accounts. Nor is this picture at all unreal, though it is certainly one-sided. Our early ethnographic information, which shows us the individual family as a universal unit in mankind, which emphasizes motherhood, dwells on the impressive facts of family intimacy and common habitation, and tells us what the native feels and how he behaves; this information gives us not only a true picture, but it brings into relief some of the most essential and valuable features of kinship.

Yet, obviously, it is a one-sided picture. For if we were satisfied with it, there would really be no problem of primitive kinship at all. The earlier authorities, the patient missionaries who worked among uncontaminated natives, the intelligent traders who perhaps had the best opportunities of getting in touch with the savage, yet lacked the most important requisites for scientific observation: the interest for the theoretical problem, the faculty of discerning a social institution through its concrete manifestations and the methods of collecting objective evidence. It is significant that most of the progress into the deeper regions of the problem of kinship, most of the discoveries of its less obvious aspects, were made by workers in the study, or at least stimulated by speculative interest. Unfortunately speculation carried away the scholars, and took them out of touch with facts.

Let us return therefore to reality and show what it might have revealed to our imaginary observer in the hidden aspects of kinship, those, that is, which so far have escaped his attention, and in which the real difficulty of primitive kinship resides.

Longer residence among the savages, better acquaintance with their language and culture, and above all patient and mature reflection upon what he saw, would have suggested to our observer certain questions and revealed certain anomalies in the typical family life. Thus, for instance, had he been stranded in a matrilineal society he would, in due course, have been impressed by the constant appearance of the mother's brother, by the assumption of authority on his part over his sister's household, and by the number of obligations which he had to fulfil towards it; and this, despite the fact that the husband was still on the spot, endowed with a great deal of marital and paternal influence.

Following up this line of inquiry our observer would have been bound to strike the rich vein of native theories of procreation and descent. Perhaps he would have found that in the tribe where he lived the natives had no idea of physiological paternity, that instead they alleged that certain spiritual agencies were responsible for the birth of the child. If, fired by this discovery, our observer had traveled to other countries to follow up his research, he would have been extremely puzzled to find a surprising variety in theories of procreation, in the conclusions drawn from them, and in the institutions which embody these theories.

In certain tribes the mother is regarded as the only parent related by the bond of body and blood to the child. Maternal kinship is exclusive, the mother's brother is head of the family, the father is not united by any kinship tie to the child, there are no legal rights, no inheritance, no solidarity in the agnatic line. Yet, and this might have puzzled our observer considerably, the father, even in such tribes, is in many respects very much like the ordinary patriarchal father, and his position is defined by certain rival customs and laws, apparently in disharmony with the general matrilineal constitution.

Again, in another community, the observer would have found that, in spite of the ignorance of fatherhood, kinship is traced in the paternal line; the mother has very little influence over the legal affairs of the household and no influence in the determining of descent. In some cultures, on the contrary, the father would be considered as the only real procreative agent, while the mother is there regarded but as the soil that receives the seed.

In yet another community descent—that is, the system of determining the child's social status—is reckoned neither through father nor through mother, but is determined by the circumstances of the child's birth, or by some social act performed during the woman's pregnancy or after her confinement, as is the case among the Todas, in Central Australia, and in certain parts of Oceania.

Thus in the study of the problems of descent the inquirer would be led into a complicated network of social rules, beliefs and ideas, astonishingly complex, abstruse and involved, if compared with his initial conclusion that "in the matter of kinship things are much the same with the savages as they are with us."

What makes this subject difficult not only to grasp but even to discover is the fact that the natives have no explicit "theory of kinship" or of descent. They live in a particular set of social conditions, have certain concrete rules which they obey, some of which they also formulate, and have a number of beliefs controlling their kinship attitudes. But to bring all these diffused and dispersed data into one pattern is far beyond the mental grasp of the most exceptionally intelligent native, even in a relatively high culture. The unity of systems of kinship and descent is achieved by the facts of social life and through the integrating power of social organization. It is the ethnographer's task to discover and describe this unity, and that he can do only by observing the social organization at work, a task of no mean difficulty.

The study of the problems of descent would lead the observer to the discovery of a type of kinship organization little known in our modern European communities, though still existing among certain Celtic and Slavonic peoples of Europe. The majority of native tribes are divided, not only into families, but into larger groups which yet possess to a certain extent a kinship character.

Thus, in certain areas, the tribe falls into two halves or moieties. Each of these has its name, its collective sense of unity and usually a special myth defining its character and its relation to the other moiety. The division of certain Australian tribes into the moieties of Eaglehawk and Crow, and the bipartition of the Western North American Indians are classical examples of this division. Usually this halving of a tribe is associated with strict prohibition of marriage within the moiety, so that a man of the first must marry a woman of the second and vice versa. Thus the two moieties are knit together into one whole, and every individual family must consist of both elements.

. . .

In other tribes there are four clans or classes, in others again eight, the further bisection regulating marriage, playing a conspicuous part in ceremonial life, and usually having some economic importance. Among still other peoples there is an odd number of clans which cannot be brought under the dual or any numerical principle.

What makes these modes of grouping really puzzling is their kinship character. The members of a clan regard themselves as kindred, trace their descent from a common ancestor, conceive of their exogamous prohibitions as of a variety or extension of incest, and, in certain circumstances, behave as if they were of the same body and blood.

Arrived at this point, the observer would find himself surrounded by a host of queries, problems and difficulties which he had never suspected in the early days when his attention was exclusively concentrated on the institution of the family, and when kinship presented to him no problem whatever.

We have imagined our commonsense ethnographer starting with the family and arriving gradually at the recognition of the clan. Had he been thrown by chance into a society where the larger group is more prominent, it is likely that only towards the end of his inquiries might he have been able to arrive at the conclusion that the individual family still exists and plays an important part.

This would happen, for example, in a matrilineal community where the whole group live in a big communal house, where the father is conspicuously absent from the family, and visits his wife in a clandestine manner at night, spending most of his time in the men's clubhouse. But in such a society we find in reality the same state of affairs as previously described, turned, so to speak, inside out. For though usually absent the father is none the less an indispensable member of the household. He has to marry the woman if his children are to enjoy full legal status in the tribe. He remains the guardian of the family in certain matters, he still has to fulfil economic duties, and is very often bound to act as the representative of his wife and children on ceremonial, religious and magical occasions. Family life, written large on the surface of their existence among most primitive peoples, is here the recondite aspect of social organization, but is nevertheless real and important.

In all early societies there are to be found the two main facets of kinship: the relation between individuals and the relation between groups— though not necessarily developed clans. And it is the tracing of the connection between these two aspects which forms the main problem of the sociology of kinship, and from which arise all the difficulties.

Perhaps the most baffling and disquieting of all the questions connected with kinship is the queer linguistic usage known as "the classificatory system of relationship." As he mastered the language our observer would find that the child who applies the words "mother" and "father" to his own parents is taught to bestow these titles upon some other people. The mother's sister is called by the same name as the mother, the father's brother is addressed as "father," and he also extends the terms *mother, father, brother, sister,* etc., to certain classes of more distant relatives and clansmen, while for certain other relatives he is taught to use entirely new terms of kinship—but these he also applies not to one person but to several people. This so-called "classificatory" use of kinship terms is prevalent among the vast majority of savage communities, although it is not universal.

This discovery made, our observer is faced by a really difficult problem. Language and linguistic usage seem apparently to break the bonds of family, to obliterate fatherhood by substituting a "group of fathers" for the individual one, a "group of mothers" for their own mother, and so on. Since our observer is well acquainted with the language and social organization of the natives, he will not adopt the easy explanation of this linguistic usage as a mere form of politeness, nor imagine that the appellations of kinship are extended merely as "terms of address." He knows that the terms are applied according to strict rules to a number of people whose relationship is traceable by pedigree or defined by membership in the clan. He knows also that behind the linguistic usage there is a set of mutual obligations between the man and all those whom he calls "father," "mother" and so on. The "fathers" act as group on certain occasions, at ceremonies, in legal matters, in economic coöperation, and they are therefore a well-defined social class and not merely a name.

Having come to realize this, our observer might make another mistake, perhaps even more dangerous than that of regarding the family as the exclusive kinship unit and of overemphasizing its resemblance to our European family. Tired by all the difficulties and contradictions which face him at every fresh discovery in kinship, he might happen upon a new and apparently simple solution: "Surely the crux lies in the fact that these people have an entirely different view of kinship and an entirely different system of reckoning and regarding relatives. The cardinal point of their conception is the idea of group-relationship. In this we have to take the cue from the language and realize that as the people have no special words in their vocabulary to distinguish their *real* parents, *real* children, *real* spouses, and so on, even so these individual relatives matter little or nothing to them. We must discard our own ideas, adopt the primitive, the classificatory view of kinship, and correlate it perhaps with certain original institutions of mankind, which we can easily infer from the character of the systems of nomenclature."

And here we see our observer drifting gradually into speculations about primitive conditions, survivals and past stages of human development, and, with the best intentions, turning his back on facts, and following the road into which most of his anthropological predecessors have been lured.

. . .

I have tried to summarize with the aid of our imaginary observer some of the outstanding difficulties and puzzles of primitive kinship as they have actually presented themselves in the course of anthropological research. In the history of the problem there was indeed a time when tradition and science were, so to speak, under the first impression of the facts, when the early unsophisticated view was universally held, that primitive kinship based on the family is essentially similar to our own, that mankind lived from the beginning in the typical patriarchal family.

This was the view we inherited from classical antiquity and took over with the Bible from Semitic mythology. It was prevalent during the Middle Ages and right up to the second half of the last century. It dominated Christian theology—was in fact part of it. It was retained by the Encyclopaedists who found in it a natural institution, suitable to natural man. The early observations of missionaries and travelers did not in any way seriously upset it. Thus it could take definite scientific form at the hands of students of Indo-European linguistics and archaeology, and even later of such writers as Fustel de Coulanges and Sir Henry Maine, who both had good knowledge of anthropological evidence. Maine can in fact be regarded as the chief scientific upholder of the patriarchal theory.

Then came the discoveries of Bachofen, Morgan and McLennan which overthrew the position once and forever. They disclosed remarkable and unsuspected aspects of primitive kinship; mother-right, avunculate, the clan system and exogamy, the importance of the levirate, polyandry and cross-cousin marriage, and above all the classificatory nomenclature. These discoveries, remarkably enough, were made primarily from the armchair, by the reconstruction and reinterpretation of ancient customs and certain previously known ethnographical facts. Morgan's discovery of classificatory nomenclature was the only one made in the field, and he immediately carried it into the province of speculation.

Yet these armchair discoveries are perhaps among the most signal proofs of the power of scientific thought in anthropology. For soon a wealth of facts began to pour in from various parts of the world, confirming the inspired vision of Bachofen, the shrewd reconstructions of McLennan, and the imaginative schemes of Morgan. However distorted most of the hypotheses were in their final version, there is no doubt that their main tenet, the affirmation of the depth and importance and above all the variety of primitive kinship, was based on a strong sense of reality.

The sudden and dramatic turn which opinions on the family and marriage took was not, however, without its evil consequences: it created the rift in anthropological opinion to which allusion has already been made. So that at present, anthropology is divided into two camps on almost every point associated with the theory of primitive marriage, sexuality and parenthood. The one side, roughly speaking, regards monogamy as the original form of marriage, patriarchy as the dominant principle of early kinship, and the family as the cell of society. The other side believes in a state of primitive promiscuity or communistic marriage, in the clan as playing the rôle of an early domestic institution, and classificatory kinship as being the principle of original parenthood.

Both sides are certainly in error insofar as each overlooks one essential aspect of human kinship and over-emphasizes the other. To overcome this deadlock which results in sterile controversy and dialectical exercise we must attempt to understand the reasons which caused either camp to assume a hostile position, from which they cannot move or come to terms.

It is not difficult to see why the old patriarchal theory became untenable and how the revolution in ideas came about. With the discovery of primitive mother-right and classificatory nomenclature, as well as with the recognition of early forms of marriage incompatible with the monogamous ideal, most of the old tenets had to be discarded. Biblical patriarchy could not be reconciled with the dominant position of the mother's brother, nor the tracing of kinship through the mother with the old Latin preponderance of paternal kinship. And mother-right had to be accounted for.

Why is it that, under primitive conditions, maternity seems to have so much greater importance and to become associated even with power? The solution which floated before the visionary mind of Bachofen is well known. His intuition told him that originally mankind had lived in sexual promiscuity in which there was no marriage and no fatherhood. The rôle of woman was so degraded in fact that even maternity did not lead to social influence, and women, debased by male lust, were of no real political importance. Against this condition they revolted. They asserted woman's claim to her children, they created the right to love and to exercise choice though not yet exclusiveness in mating. Woman had a natural male protector in her brother and avunculate became an institution associated with mother-right. Thus order was born with mother-right, and order as well as law and morals became founded on woman's right to choose her lovers and to own her children. A beautiful theory, or rather myth—inspiring, revolutionizing, all our ideas, irradiated with the charm of the Eternal Feminine, making primitive woman a primeval Beatrice who leads men out of the Hell of Promiscuity into the Heaven of Love and civilization!

The patriarchal theory was submitted almost simultaneously to yet another attack. It was less inspired but even more penetrating and formidable, since it came armed with a wealth of fact and of almost incontrovertible linguistic argument. Morgan's hypothesis of promiscuity and group-marriage came from that inexhaustible source of scientific conjectures—the etymological study of words. The words—in this case classificatory kinship terminologies—appeared, however, to be so clear in their purpose, so telling in their historical reminiscences, that the early stages of marriage were brought back to us, as it were, preserved in fragments of native vocabularies.

Morgan's attack was directed, remarkably enough, against the very strongholds of the patriarchal theory, the biological foundation of fatherhood. But Morgan himself was under the influence of patriarchalism, in that he regarded the father as the dominant parent and the most important person in the counting of kinship. He felt that if the classificatory uses of kinship terminologies could be explained as regards the father, all other classificatory uses would become plain. To him, then, the real problem was the classificatory plurality of fathers, as expressed by native linguistic usage.

Now the best explanation of the plurality of fathers is the proverbial uncertainty of fatherhood alluded to by Homer and expressed in Latin legal maxims. But this uncertainty of fatherhood, in order to give rise to a classificatory use of the term, had to be conceived as definitely institutionalized. And here the ever-fascinating hypothesis of primitive promiscuity once more presented itself as a plausible and natural explanation which made everything clear and consistent. If all members of a primitive horde mated promiscuously, then all the men of the older generation would stand in the relation of potential fathers to the child. If he wanted to be correct he would have to use the term "father" to all of them jointly. And, consistently with that usage, he would call the women of the older generation "mothers," those of his own generation "wives"; while the men of his own generation would be "brothers," and those much younger than himself potential "sons" and "daughters."

Thus the classificatory use of kinship terms was completely explained as the linguistic expression of promiscuity, and of its later development, group-marriage. The hypothesis, moreover, is, to Morgan and his followers, the only explanation possible of classificatory kinship terminologies. The fact that classificatory nomenclatures still exist in primitive communities from which promiscuity has completely disappeared, and where group-marriage exists only in "traces," is due (according to our authorities) to the persistency with which words and verbal usages "survive" after their sociological foundation has vanished. Thus the two most puzzling phenomena of primitive social organization—mother-right and the classificatory terminology of kinship—led by different roads to the same assumption, that promiscuity of group-mating was the primitive form of marriage; that the communal horde, or the clan, represented the primitive family; and that group-kinship was the form of early parentage.

A flood of arguments and corroborative evidence began to pour in as supporting this famous hypothesis. Such survivals as ceremonial capture in marriage rites, customs like the *couvade*, the levirate and cross-cousin marriage—above all the interminable variety of standardized sexual liberties and excesses, were adduced in support of a primeval communism in wives. It seemed for a time as if the older view were completely to be swept off the scientific map, as if the family, monogamous marriage, sexual exclusiveness and jealousy were to be regarded as late and artificial acquisitions, completely irrelevant in the shaping of human morals, institutions and laws.

Then came a reaction, cogent, destructive and, as reactions often are, somewhat one-sided. The biological warning of Darwin, amplified and sociologically supplemented by Westermarck, put a serious query against the assumption of promiscuity and group-marriage as incompatible with selective mating, that is as a condition which would inevitably lead to racial degeneration and social disorder. McLennan, though in agreement with Morgan's main hypothesis, pointed out certain obvious linguistic fallacies involved in taking the classificatory terms at their face value; and his arguments were taken up later by Andrew Lang, Crawley and Westermarck. Finally Westermarck, the main leader of this reaction and the champion of monogamy, pointed out that both marriage in single pairs and the family play a conspicuous part in the most primitive societies known to us, and that the father is by no means a mere communal cipher, but is always the head of the undivided family and household, even where kinship is traced through women.

And here the argument still stands. One side, represented by Westermarck, Andrew Lang, Crawley and Pater Schmidt, insists on the importance of the family, individual kinship, and the paramount relevance of biological factors; while the other, led by Durkheim and Rivers, Sidney Hartland, Frazer and Briffault, granting all this more or less grudgingly, discounts the sociological value of biological factors, insists on the communistic inclinations of primitive man, presents classificatory terms and classificatory legal usages, mother-right and the avunculate, as puzzles which cannot be solved except by the hypothesis of communal marriage and group-kinship.

There is no doubt that each side neglects one fundamental aspect of the subject. Looking at facts through the eyes of our imaginary observer, we saw that neither the family nor the clan can be ignored. Both exist and they do not exclude each other but rather are complementary. We must not neglect the family or parenthood in primitive society because it is a familiar and drab subject. We must not overemphasize group-kinship because it is so strange and exotic; because it lends itself to speculations about the communistic savage; because it seems to explain so well sensational and "queer" features, such as classificatory terms, mother-right and exogamy and various sexual excesses. The temptation is great to overlook the obvious—the *tout comme chez nous*—but it must be resisted. On the other hand, we must not be biased by an overdose of "common sense," which is too often but another word for mental laziness. We must not decree away classificatory terms as "polite modes of address" or "slovenly speech habits," as has been done. Nor must we discount sex orgies, relaxations or strange taboos as "minor aberrations of savage superstition."

The functional anthropologist regards facts as being of equal value whenever they really loom large in native life and social organization, irrespectively of whether they are drab or amusing—whether they appear strange or familiar from the European point of view. And when these facts consistently appear together, when they obviously form part of an organic whole, the functional anthropologist is not prepared to tear this organic whole to pieces and then to place the torn fragments on an evolutionary scale. The questions usually asked are: is promiscuity the original institution from which marriage and the family but gradually developed; or, on the contrary, are the family and monogamous marriage the starting point, and communal kinship and sexual laxity only temporary aberrations? These questions are for us irrelevant and fictitious.

The real question is: what is the relation between the family and the clan—between individual and classificatory kinship? These are not stages which succeed each other, and can be found here and there, accidentally mixed or overlapping. It is absurd to regard one of them merely as a "survival," the other as an innovation. They are two aspects of kinship which always appear in conjunction, though the clan or classificatory side is sometimes almost in abeyance. But since they work side by side they must fulfil functions which are on the one hand related, on the other certainly not identical. These distinct functions must be discovered and defined. The first and capital problem of primitive kinship is therefore to establish the relation between the family and the clan, between individual and classificatory kinship. By solving this problem we shall be able to arrive at a clear conception of kinship—to define it functionally in a way which covers the two phases and assigns to each its respective place in culture.

With this problem, that of classificatory terminologies is obviously intimately connected. If we cannot explain them as a monstrous linguistic fossil, as an encumbrance always dragging one stage behind in evolution; if we have to regard them as live parts of language; we shall have to ask again: what is the function of the classificatory principle of terminology? What is there in the actually existing social conditions of primitive mankind which these terminologies express and with which they are correlated?

Mother-right and father-right again cannot possibly be stages or shadows of stages. Each of them is always associated with its opposite or correlate. They are the two sides of the big system which defines filiation in each community. The real problem is: why does such a system always involve an overemphasis of one side, that of the mother or of the father;

what does this overemphasis really mean, and what serviceable part does it play in social organization? And here it is easy to see that, since motherhood is biologically the far more important fact, it is the paternal side of kinship which presents the problematic facet of the case. Interesting customs such as the *couvade*, psychological problems such as relate to the ignorance of fatherhood and its social consequences, are among the problems which must also be functionally solved. And, once we embark upon questions of filiation and the counting of kinship, we are faced directly by the whole complex of problems concerning derived kinship, that is, the contribution of clans and moieties to the cohesion of society; the function of collective solidarity; the function of exogamy and of group-reciprocity.

These are the pieces of our puzzle and on the whole most of them seem so disconnected, so ill-fitting, that the natural reaction of the explaining mind was to cut them up into proper shapes and regard them either as stages or as fragments of compound cultures, trait-complexes or *Kultur Kreise*.[3] To the functionalist, however, the relatedness of the various aspects and institutions is the most important characteristic of culture, and here the universal coexistence, the dovetailing, the obvious many-sidedness of kinship, make us see in all the facts of sexuality, marriage, family and clanship one integral institution: the Procreative Institution of mankind.

What is the main function of this big institution? The obvious answer is—the propagation of the species, but it is easy to see that the continuity of culture is as deeply involved in kinship as is the continuity of the race. Let us start with the biological fact, since that is the more tangible and definite. What is the procreative unit in human society? The answer is so obvious, the fact that one male must be married to one female in order to produce offspring is so patent, that the answer that it is the

[3] The anthropological reader of this essay will have noticed that the contributions of the so-called Historical or Diffusionist school have received but small attention in my argument. As a matter of fact they have been almost insignificant, both in quantity and in quality. The treatment of the family and kinship by the American school is sound, but it is not historical, it is comparative, I should almost say functional. Here belong the contributions of Lowie, Goldenweiser, [Edward Winslow] Gifford, Kroeber, [Clark] Wissler and Dorsey and the few but sound remarks scattered through the writings of E. Sapir. [Fritz] Graebner's and Schmidt's method of regarding father-right and mother-right, clanship and the individual family as independent cultural traits belongs, on the other hand, to the type of cultural surgery which is incompatible with the functional treatment of human institutions. Fortunately Schmidt and Koppers are inconsistent, and in their last big work (*Der Mensch aller Zeiten*), following E. Grosse, they treat the elements of kinship as organically connected parts of a bigger unit, and even try to correlate them with economic, environmental and political factors.

human family, consisting of mother, father and child which is the procreative unit, appears at first sight an unnecessary truism.

It may come as a shock therefore to the man in the street when he is
told that it is really round this question that most learned anthropological
discussions center and that, even now, there is a profound disagreement
in the views held. Thus in the latest voluminous discussion on the question we are told that "the clan like the family is a reproductive group
and not a political organization," and again, "We must dismiss entirely
from our minds the notion that, while the patriarchal family is a sexual
group depending upon certain intimate relations, reproductive and economic, the clan is a group resting upon some other principle; that while
the one is a reproductive group, the other is a social or political organization." [4] Obviously these statements are paradoxically worded, for the
author patently does not intend us to assume, what in fact he actually
says, that under the clan system group babies are conceived in collective
copulation and brought forth out of a communal womb in an act of
joint parturition. Whatever might be the similarity between the clan and
the family, the sexual relations as well as the reproductive conditions
within the clan are carried out by single pairs.

The only way in which we can plausibly interpret the above contention is that the author does not really dispute the fact that biological
procreation happens in pairs, but merely discounts the validity of this
biological fact as regards ties of kinship and social relationship. He regards,
in other words, zoölogy as not relevant for social organization. It would
be possible to imagine that since human instincts are almost indefinitely
plastic, the communally constructed clan can completely replace the
biologically constructed family. Though the child is produced by one
man and woman only, if this child were brought immediately under the
control of a group of fathers and mothers, the early influences which
shape its kinship ideas and kinship theories would be collective and not
individual.

If we thus reformulate Mr. Briffault's extravagant statement it opens
before us the real problem of kinship. [5] The statement becomes reasonable.
But of course this does not mean that it is true.

[4] R. Briffault, *The Mothers,* Vol. 1, pp. xvi, 591.

[5] This indeed is the way in which it has been framed by Rivers: "A child born into
a community with moieties or clans becomes a member of a domestic group other than
the family in the strict sense." (*Social Organization,* p. 55.) This point of view has also
been expressed by the same author in his hypothesis of group-motherhood (*op. cit.,*
p. 192 *sqq.*) and in his whole conception that in the early stages of development of
society the clan filled that place in social organization which the family occupied afterwards. (See, e.g., *History of Melanesian Society,* pp. 6-15; *Kinship and Social Organization,* p. 75; article s.v. "Kinship" in *Hastings' Encyclopaedia of Religion and Ethics.*)

We have thus to open the question of what the *initial situation* of kinship really is. Is the child actually born into the clan or into the family; is it brought directly under the influence of groups or of individuals? Are there such things as "group-motherhood" or "group-fatherhood" or have we always only individual mothers and fathers, and that not only in the biological, but also in the cultural and social sense of the words?

In laying down the study of the *Initial Situation of Kinship* as the capital problem of kinship, in demanding the exact analysis of the sociological configuration of the earliest experiences, we are doing, somewhat tardily, for social anthropology what psychology has been doing for the study of the mental development of the individual in general; nor is it only psychoanalysis which forces us back to the cradle in order to study the formation of complexes and the charging of the Unconscious with most of its subsequent drives! Behaviorism, in showing that it is the conditioning of reflexes or, as I should prefer to say, the moulding of innate dispositions, which matters most, is also leading us back to the study of the period when this moulding takes place on the largest scale. Above all, the most important contribution to modern psychology and social science, the Theory of Sentiments propounded by Shand and McDougall, demands that all human values, attitudes and personal bonds should be studied along the line of development, with special consideration of the earliest periods.

The concept of the Initial Situation of Kinship, which I first introduced in my article on "Kinship" in the 14th Edition of the *Encyclopaedia Britannica,* places the emphasis on the study of the first stages of kinship sentiments. And, indeed, if the study of any and all human sentiments must be done along the life history of the individual, in a biographical treatment so to speak, this must be done in the case of kinship above all things. Because in kinship the most typical and the fundamental process is that in which biological facts are transformed into social forces, and unless this be understood well, the whole question is placed on a false foundation and we get the chaos of controversy with which we are faced at present.

It is hardly necessary, perhaps, to add that in laying down the problem of the Initial Situation we are doing more than merely introducing a concept and a terminological entity. In doing this we are really opening a number of definitely empirical questions referring to the cultural transformation of the biological elements, sex, maternity and fatherhood; we are focussing our argument on the linking-up of courtship, marriage and kinship; last, but not least, we are demanding a clear answer to the question as to the relation between procreation, domesticity, and the legal or political aspects of kinship.

Let us then proceed to the analysis of the Initial Situation of Kinship

and try, through a comparative survey along the widest range of variations, to see whether some general principles can be established with
reference to it.

Maternity is the most dramatic and spectacular as well as the most
obvious fact in the propagation of species. A woman, whether in Mayfair
or on a coral island of the Pacific, has to undergo a period of hardship
and discomfort; she has to pass through a crisis of pain and danger, she
has, in fact, to risk her own life in order to give life to another human
being. Her connection with the child, who remains for a long time part
of her own body, is intimate and integral. It is associated with physiological effects and strong emotions, it culminates in the crisis of birth,
and it extends naturally into lactation.

Now what is it that the advocates of "group-motherhood" want us to
believe? Neither more nor less than that, with birth, the individual link
is severed and becomes merged in an imaginary bond of "collective
motherhood." They affirm that such powerful sociological forces are at
work, such strong cultural influences, that they can override and destroy
the individual attitude of mother-to-child. Is this true? Do we really find
any sociological mechanisms which succeed in severing the mother-child
relationship, dumping each into the group of collective mothers and collective children? As a matter of fact all these hypotheses are pure figments and, looking at facts as we did through the eyes of our imaginary
observer, we were led to the conclusion that maternity is as individual
culturally as it is biologically. The point is of such capital importance,
however, that we must look more in detail at the arguments by which
individual maternity has been challenged by such writers as Rivers and
Briffault.

They have alleged that communal suckling, the frequent and indiscriminate adoption or exchange of infants, joint cares and joint responsibilities, and a sort of joint ownership of children create an identical bond
between the one child and several mothers, which would obviously mean
that every mother would have also a group of joint children. In these
views there is also implied the assumption that conception, pregnancy
and childbirth, which obviously are individual and not communal, are
completely ignored by society as irrelevant factors, and that they play no
part in the development of maternal sentiments.

Let us examine the implication of the group-motherhood hypothesis
first, and then decide whether a communal game of share and exchange
in children and infants is, or ever could have been, played.

Now, in the first place, it is a universal fact that conception, pregnancy, childbirth and suckling are sociologically determined; that they
are subjects of ritual, or religious and moral conceptions, of legal obligations and privileges. There is not one single instance on record of a

primitive culture in which the process of gestation is left to nature alone. Conception, as a rule, is believed to be due as much to spiritual as to physiological causes. Conception, moreover, is not a process which is allowed to take its natural course as a result of prenuptial intercourse. Between the freedom of sexual life and the freedom of becoming a mother a sharp distinction is drawn in all human societies including our own, and this is one of the most important sociological factors of the problem and to it we shall presently return.

Most important of all, a legitimate, socially approved of, conception must always be based on an individual legal contract—the contract of marriage.[6]

Once conception has taken place the prospective mother has always to keep taboos and observe ceremonial rules. She has to abstain from certain foods and carry out lustrations; she has to undergo more or less complicated pregnancy ceremonies; she has to wear special decorations and clothes; she is regarded sometimes as holy, sometimes as unclean; last, not least, she is very often sexually tabooed even to her own husband. All these ceremonial, moral and legal rules are, by the very nature of the facts, individual. Their motive is invariably the welfare of the future offspring. Most of them establish individual ties between the prospective mother and her future offspring. Maternity is thus determined in anticipation by a whole cultural apparatus of rules and prescriptions, it is established by society as a moral fact, and, in all this, the tie of kinship between mother and child is defined by tradition long before birth, and defined as an individual bond.

At the crisis itself, that is at birth, the ceremonies of purification, the idea of special dangers which unite mother and child and separate them from the rest of the community, customs and usages connected with midwifery and early lactation—this whole cultural apparatus continues to reaffirm and to reshape the bond of maternity, and to individualize it with force and clearness. These anticipatory moral influences always put the responsibility upon one woman and mark her out as the sociological or cultural mother over and above her physiological claims to that title.

All this might appear to refer only to the mother. What about the child? We can indeed completely discount Freud's assumption that there is an innate bond of sexual attraction between mother and child; we must reject further his whole hypothesis of "the return to the womb." With all this we have to credit psychoanalysis with having proved that the earliest infantile experiences, provided that they are not completely broken and obliterated in childhood, form a foundation of the greatest im-

---

[6] In order to avoid possible misunderstandings I should like to remind the reader that plural marriages such as polygyny and polyandry are always based on an individual legal contract between one man and one woman, though these contracts may be repeated.

portance for the later individual relationship between the child and its mother.

Now here again, the continuity between prenatal cares, the earliest infantile seclusion of mother and child, and the period of lactation, which in native society is much longer than with us, the continuity of all these experiences and their individual unity is in primitive societies as great as, if not greater than, with us.

And this is the point at which we have to deal with the unprofitable assumption of communal lactation. In the relatively small savage communities where there occur perhaps one or two childbirths in a year within reach of each other the idea of mothers synchronizing conception and pregnancy and clubbing together to carry out lactatory group-motherhood, at the greatest inconvenience to themselves, the babies and the whole community, is so preposterous that even now I cannot think how it could ever have been promulgated by Dr. Rivers and upheld by Mr. Briffault.

As to a "communalizing" adoption, in the first place, even where it is most frequent, as in certain Polynesian and Melanesian communities, it simply substitutes one maternity for another. It proves undoubtedly that cultural parenthood can override the biological basis, but it does not introduce anything even remotely like group-maternity. In fact the severance of one bond before another is established is a further proof of the individuality and exclusiveness of motherhood. In the second place the custom of indiscriminate adoption is prevalent among a few savage societies only.

We can thus say that motherhood is always individual. It is never allowed to remain a mere biological fact. Social and cultural influences always indorse and emphasize the original individuality of the biological fact. These influences are so strong that in the case of adoption they may override the biological tie and substitute a cultural one for it. But statistically speaking, the biological ties are almost invariably merely reinforced, redetermined and remoulded by the cultural ones. This remoulding makes motherhood in each culture a relationship specific to that culture, different from all other motherhoods, and correlated to the whole social structure of the community. This means that the problem of maternity cannot be dismissed as a zoölogical fact, that it should be studied by every field-worker in his own area, and that the theory of cultural motherhood should have been made the foundation of the general theory of kinship.

What about the father? As far as his biological rôle is concerned he might well be treated as a drone. His task is to impregnate the female and then to disappear. And yet in all human societies the father is regarded by tradition as indispensable. The woman has to be married before she is allowed legitimately to conceive. Roughly speaking, an unmarried mother is under a ban, a fatherless child is a bastard. This is by no means only a

European or Christian prejudice; it is the attitude found amongst most barbarous and savage peoples as well. Where the unmarried mother is at a premium and her offspring a desirable possession, the father is forced upon them by positive instead of negative sanctions.

Let us put it in more precise and abstract terms. Among the conditions which define conception as a sociologically legitimate fact there is one of fundamental importance. The most important moral and legal rule concerning the physiological side of kinship is that no child should be brought into the world without a man—and one man at that—assuming the rôle of sociological father, that is, guardian and protector, the male link between the child and the rest of the community.

I think that this generalization amounts to a universal sociological law and as such I have called it in some of my previous writings *the principle of legitimacy*.[7] The form which the principle of legitimacy assumes varies according to the laxity or stringency which obtains regarding prenuptial intercourse; according to the value set upon virginity or the contempt for it; according to the ideas held by the natives as to the mechanism of procreation; above all, according as to whether the child is a burden or an asset to its parents. Which means according as to whether the unmarried mother is more attractive because of her offspring or else degraded and ostracized on that account.

Yet through all these variations there runs the rule that the father is indispensable for the full sociological status of the child as well as of its mother, that the group consisting of a woman and her offspring is sociologically incomplete and illegitimate. The father, in other words, is necessary for the full legal status of the family.

In order to understand the nature and importance of the principle of legitimacy it is necessary to discuss the two aspects of procreation which are linked together biologically and culturally, yet linked by nature and culture so differently that many difficulties and puzzles have arisen for the anthropologist. Sex and parenthood are obviously linked biologically. Sexual intercourse leads at times to conception. Conception always means pregnancy and pregnancy at times means childbirth. We see that in the chain there are at least two possibilities of a hiatus; sexual intercourse by no means always leads to conception, and pregnancy can be interrupted by abortion and thus not lead to childbirth.

The moral, customary and legal rules of most human communities step in, taking advantage of the two weak links in the chain, and in a most remarkable manner dissociate the two sides of procreation, that is sex and parenthood. Broadly speaking, it may be said that freedom of intercourse

---

[7] Compare article s.v. "Kinship" in the *Encyclopædia Britannica*, 14th Edition [Chapt. 6 of *Sex, Culture, and Myth*]; also *Sex and Repression in Savage Society* (1927) and Chapter VI of *The Family among the Australian Aborigines* (1913). In this latter the relevant facts are presented though the term is not used.

though not universally is yet generally prevalent in human societies. Freedom of conception outside marriage is, however, never allowed, or at least in extremely few communities and under very exceptional circumstances.

Briefly to substantiate this statement: it is clear that in those societies, primitive or civilized, where prenuptial intercourse is regarded as immoral and illegitimate, marriage is the *conditio sine qua non* of legitimate children—that is children having full social status in the community.

In the second place, in most communities which regard prenuptial intercourse as perfectly legitimate, marriage is still regarded as essential to equip the child with a full tribal position. This is very often achieved without any punitive sanctions, by the mere fact that as soon as pregnancy sets in a girl and her lover have to marry. Often in fact pregnancy is a prerequisite of marriage or the final legal symptom of its conclusion.

There are tribes, again, where an unmarried mother is definitely penalized and so are her children. What is done under such conditions by lovers who want to live together sexually and yet not to produce children is difficult to say. Having had in my own field-work to deal with the case in point, I was yet unable to arrive at a satisfactory solution. Contraceptives, I am firmly convinced, do not exist in Melanesia, and abortion is not sufficiently frequent to account for the great scarcity of illegitimate children. As a hypothesis, I venture to submit that promiscuous intercourse, while it lasts, reduces the fertility of woman. If this side of the whole question still remains a puzzle it only proves that more research, both physiological and sociological, must be done in order fully to throw light upon the principle of legitimacy.

There is still one type of social mechanism through which the principle of legitimacy operates, and that is under conditions where a child is an asset. There an unmarried mother need not trouble about her sociological status, because the fact of having children only makes her the more desirable, and she speedily acquires a husband. He will not trouble whether the child is the result of his love-making or not. But whether the male is primed to assume his paternity, or whether child and mother are penalized, the principle of legitimacy obtains throughout mankind; the group of mother and child is incomplete and the sociological position of the father is regarded universally as indispensable.

Liberty of parenthood, therefore, is not identical with liberty of sexual intercourse. And the principle of legitimacy leads us to another very important generalization, namely, that the relations of sexuality to parenthood must be studied with reference to the only relevant link: marriage, conceived as a contract legitimizing offspring.

From the foregoing considerations, it is clear that marriage cannot be defined as the licensing of sexual intercourse, but rather as the licensing of parenthood.

Since marriage is the institution through which the inchoate, at times even disruptive, drives of sex are transformed and organized into the principal system of social forces, it is clear that sexuality must be discussed, defined and classified in relation to marriage. From our point of view we have to inquire as to what is its function in relation to marriage.

We have first to inquire, is chartered and limited sexual liberty subversive and destructive of marriage and family; does it ever run counter to these institutions? Or, on the contrary, is regulated and limited intercourse outside matrimony one of those cultural arrangements which allow of a greater stability of marriage and the family, of easier adjustment within it, and of a more suitable choice of partner?

It is obvious that once we erect chastity as a positive ideal, once we accept the Christian principle of monogamous marriage as the only decent way of regarding this institution, we have prejudged all these questions and stultified the whole inquiry. And it is astounding how even those who attack the institutions of Christian morality and marriage and regard themselves as absolutely free of preconceptions, still remain under the influence of the ideal or at least of its pretenses. Thus all sociologists, from Bachofen to Briffault, were inclined to regard communistic orgies, relaxations of the marital tie, forms of prenuptial freedom, as "survivals," as traces of a primeval sexual communism. That, I think, is an entirely wrong view, due to an involuntary tendency to regard sexual intercourse outside marriage as something anomalous, as something which contravenes marriage; a view directly implied in our Christian ideal of monogamy.

Let us look at facts in the correct perspective; see, that is, how sexuality is related to marriage in various primitive communities. Let us first classify the various types of regulation in relation to marriage. Those communities where virginity is a prerequisite of decent and legal marriage, where it is enforced by such surgical operations as infibulation; where wives are jealously guarded and adultery is a rigorously punished offense—those communities present no problem to us. There sex is as absolutely subordinated to marriage as in the Christian monogamous ideal, and far more so than in our Western practice. But such communities are comparatively rare, especially at a primitive level, and generally we find some form of customary license outside marriage.

Here again we must distinguish with direct reference to marriage, which really means to parenthood. Prenuptial license, that is, the liberty of free intercourse given to unmarried youths and girls, is by far the most prevalent form of chartered freedom, as well as the most important. What is its normal course and how is it related to marriage? Does it as a rule develop habits of profligacy; does it lead to a more and more promiscuous attitude?

Even a study of those forms which are nearest to us and should be best known—that is, the prenuptial usages of European peasants—should have furnished the clue to the comparative anthropologist. The German peasant speaks of "trial nights"; he justifies his institution of *Fensterln* (windowing, i.e., entering through the window) by the commonsense axiom that unless he has full sexual experience of his future bride he is unable to make a sound empirical choice. The same view is taken by the savage Melanesian, by the West African, by the Bantu, and by the North American Indian; last, but not least, by some of the new generation—young intellectuals. We have, therefore, in prenuptial license, in the first place, an institutionalized method of arranging marriage by trial and error.

And this is by no means a mere pretense, though often the desire for trial leads to errors. In fact, however, the general course of prenuptial intrigue conforms naturally to the pattern of the principle. The number of intrigues does not increase, the appetite for change and variety does not grow with experience. On the contrary, with age and a ripening insight into the nature of sexual relations, two definite phenomena occur. On the one hand the character of the intrigues changes: they become stronger and deeper. New elements enter into them; the appreciation of personality and the integration of erotic attraction with the spiritual character of the lover. On the other hand, and correlated with the first process, we find that the mere attraction of sexual experiences loses a great deal of its charm.

We see, therefore, that if we look at prenuptial sexuality in a dispassionate sociological spirit, and if we contemplate it in its relation to marriage, we find that it fulfils two functions. It serves as an empirical foundation to a mature, more spiritual choice of a mate, and it serves to drain off the cruder sexual motives from affection and attraction. It is thus, on the one hand, the sowing of wild oats, on the other a trial-and-error method of concluding marriage.

If we look at the relaxations of the matrimonial bond we see that they fulfil a not altogether dissimilar function. There is the temporary exchange of wives. We find it in wife-lending at tribal feasts or during the occurrence of catastrophes; in the institution of *pirrauru* in Central Australia; in the prolonged wife-lending among the Eskimos or in Siberia. Such customs simply mean that from time to time a man and a woman already married are allowed to have sexual experiences with other people.

Sexual, let us keep in mind, is not synonymous with conjugal, though the polite parlance of puritanic hypocrisy has made it so. Temporary cohabitation, above all, never implies community of children. Its function consists, in the first place, in that it once more satisfies in an approved, licensed way the desire for change which is inherent in the sexual impulse. In the second place it sometimes leads to the discovery that the new, temporary partnership is more suitable, and so, through divorce, it leads to a marriage on the whole more satisfactory. Here, again, postmarital extra-connubial sexuality is an arrangement both of trial and error, and also a safety vent. The first function is more prominent in the standardized forms of wife-lending for more prolonged periods; the second, in the occasions of orgiastic license at big tribal festivals, where often many of the usual bonds and restrictions are suspended.

We see, then, that the regulated forms of nonconjugal intercourse, far from being adverse to, and subversive of marriage, are its adjuncts and adjuvants. They allow a greater selectiveness; a selectiveness in which compatibility is established as well as cruder sexuality eliminated. They allow, therefore, of the conclusion of marriages based on an affinity of character combined with sexual compatibility. They eliminate, also, from the institution of marriage the disruptive forces of sex which come from unsatisfied intercourse, monotonous and one-sided satisfaction. They counterbalance, therefore, the repressive forces of the strict matrimonial discipline of sex.

For it is important to realize clearly that in savage societies sexual repression is as rigid and definite as sexual license is clear and prescriptive. The savage is by no means untrammeled sexually. The difference between civilized and savage codes lies, in fact, in a greater definiteness of the latter—though even here I would not like to be dogmatic. At any rate, in a community where, by rules of exogamy, one-half, or at least a considerable number, of all the women are not lawful as wives or lovers; where the taboos of occupation, of status, of family and of special occasions considerably restrict the opportunities of intercourse; in communities where there exists the severest code of conduct in public and private, imposed upon husband and wife, brother and sister, and people standing in definite kinship relations—in such communities it is clear that repression acts with at least as great a force as with us. And this means that the forces of reaction against the trammels and restraints imposed by society are very powerful. Thus sex, throughout humanity, is regulated; there are restrictions as well as liberties and the institutions which allow of the latter can only be understood in their function when we refer them to the fundamental procreative institutions—those of the family and marriage.

We see, therefore, that parenthood and marriage furnish the key to the functional understanding of regulated sexuality. We see that sexual regulations, the liberties and the taboos, constitute the road to marriage and the way of escape from its too rigid bonds and consequent tragic complications. The sexual impulse has to be selective in human as well as in animal communities, but its selectiveness under culture is more complicated in that it has to involve cultural as well as biological values. Trial and error are necessary and with this is definitely connected the interest in variation and impulse towards novelty. To satisfy the fundamental function of sex we have the institution which makes full sex, that is parenthood, exclusive and individual. To satisfy the correlated selective components of sex, we have the dependent institutions of regulated license. To sum up, we have found that parenthood gives us the key to marriage, through the principle of legitimacy, and that marriage is the key to a right understanding of sexual customs. It may be added at once that the dissociation of some sexual experiences from the primitive idea of marriage, coupled with the real interrelation of the two, yields to the sociologist an interesting background for the consideration of modern problems of sexuality, marriage and divorce.

The principle of legitimacy has led us to the consideration of sex in its relation to marriage, and brought us to the functional definition of sexual excesses as component parts of the integral procreative institution. All this hinges, of course, on the fact that sex leads to conception, but that since sex and conception are not absolutely linked together, they can be culturally dissociated in more than one way. The whole question possesses, however, one aspect which is of the greatest sociological importance and upon which we have barely touched so far. This is the native theory of procreation and the sociological consequences of this theory.

In the first place the degree of knowledge about the physiology of procreation varies considerably from one culture to another, as we saw with the help of our imaginary observer. From an almost absolute ignorance of physiological paternity we pass to an extreme overemphasis of the part played by the semen in procreation; from highly complicated animistic theories as to what happens when the new being is prepared in the spiritual world for the present one, to an almost complete unconcern with the whence of human life; from a great sociological influence of those ideas to a complete disconnection.

Theories vary, legal ideas are more or less linked up with the dogmatic views, but, as subject matter, all these facts are to the functional anthropologist of paramount importance. The views about procreation may or may not be a relevant social force. Where they are, they show the extreme importance of mythological and animistic foundations in a legal system. The modern anthropologist has once more to claim the functional study of such beliefs as against their treatment in the light of mere curiosity. In my investigations of the matrilineal system in the Trobriand Islands, I found that the whole doctrine of matrilineal identity in kinship is based on the natives' theory of procreation. I found also that the important sociological part played by the father is based on certain secondary, derivative views as to paternal influence upon the offspring in its embryonic state. (Compare *The Sexual Life of Savages*, Chap. VII.)

The whole theory of paternity, its dependence upon a direct physiological bond between father and child or merely upon the bond indirectly established between father and offspring through marriage—this theory should be studied in functional connection with the various taboos, ritual observances, ceremonial, magical, economic and legal acts performed by the father at conception, during pregnancy and at childbirth. The famous custom of the *couvade* will naturally occur to every reader in this connection; the custom, that is, in which the husband mimics the pangs and vicissitudes of childbirth. But the *couvade*, if we place it in its setting of cognate phenomena, is but one of a whole series of customs which shows that the father has a number of legal and magical obligations to fulfil, and that, in performing them, he works for the welfare of his offspring and his wife. In other words, from the functional point of view, all those customs which we might label as belonging to the *couvade* type are an exact parallel to those which establish cultural maternity.

We see thus that individual paternity, as well as individual maternity, is established by a whole series of customs and rites; that, although maternity is the more important biological fact, both parents are connected with the child through a culturally determined relationship. This cultural relationship, however, is not artificial, in the sense that it should be independent of natural inclination. The traditional usages, the taboos, the magical rites, which in an anticipatory manner secure the welfare of the child, express the natural emotions of both parents. Wherever observations on the subjective side of the question have been made, it has been found that both prospective parents love their offspring in anticipation, that they are interested in it from the moment of its birth, that they bestow on it the tenderest cares and most lavish affection during infancy.

For the child is linked to both its parents by the unity of the household and by the intimacy of daily contacts. In most communities both parents have to look after it, to nurse it and to tend it. The father may, in extreme matriarchal communities, be legally the guest and the stranger in his wife's house; he may be regarded as being of an entirely different bodily substance from his child; yet he loves it and looks after it almost as tenderly as the mother does.

Thus the initial situation of kinship, both culturally and biologically, consists in individual parenthood based on marriage. Parenthood, in human societies, is not merely a biological fact, but it is just in its cultural definition that we find the greatest emphasis on the individual relationship, that is, on individual paternity and maternity. We have answered thus the problem and, in answering it, we have shown that we have not merely introduced a new term—*initial situation*—but that this has led us to the discovery of the principle of legitimacy, to a new treatment of sexuality in reference to marriage, and to the investigation of native theories of procreation as related to social organization and legal systems.

With the conclusion that parenthood, as determined by cultural as well as by biological forces, constitutes the Initial Situation of Kinship, we have laid our foundation but we have not completed our task. The importance of the initial situation consists in its influence, in its controlling power over the later life of the individual and upon the formation of the wider social ties. It is in the relation of parenthood to the other forms of social grouping that the real problem of kinship consists.

Modern psychologists agree that parenthood, as the dominant influence of infancy, forms the character of the individual and at the same time shapes his social attitudes, and thus places its imprint upon the constitution of the whole society. But to show how this actually happens is really a sociological task.

The Social Anthropologist who studies the formation of primitive kinship ties must follow parenthood to its furthest ramifications. He must show the weanings, the extensions, the ebbing and strengthening of the ties. He must establish the final triumph of parenthood as the only stable force working right throughout life, as the pattern of most relations, as the foundation on which even the religious cults and dogmatic conceptions of a community are based.

The human family is not merely a procreative institution. The earliest cares gradually but surely shade into the training of the child's own impulses. From this early training in such elementary matters as cleanliness, safety, the use of its limbs, voice, etc., education proceeds to the teaching of manual craftsmanship, and later again, the imparting of tradition and social rules.

The initial situation, based on physiological facts and innate impulses, thus gradually ripens into cultural education. The mother is an invariable agent in all this: the father usually stands by her as an almost equivalent helpmate, though at times his rôle is much less significant. The most burdensome form of human coöperation, the training of the young by the old, is bound up with the tenderness and affection which comes from maternity and which seems somewhat mysteriously associated with fatherhood.[8]

The training of body and mind, the transmission of standardized behavior and moral ideals in skill, knowledge and values, must go hand in hand with the transmission of material goods. To teach craft you have to provide the tools, to instruct in magic you have to part with your secret formulae and procedures. To impart your family tradition and the privileges of your status you have to transmit rank, position, even social

---

[8] The innate tenderness of the father seems to me to be derived from his social rôle of guardian of the woman during her pregnancy, rather than from some mysterious instinct which would allow a man to identify a child produced by his semen. Compare my *Sex and Repression in Savage Society*, p. 214; *The Sexual Life of Savages*, Chap. VII. Compare also Bertrand Russell's *Marriage and Morals*, where this point of view has been adopted.

identity. In this last case, unless you transmit social status, the passing on of its traditional definition is worthless.

Thus education, sooner or later, leads to the handing over of material possessions, of social privileges, of a great part of one's moral identity. And here the first break occurs in the simple direct growth of the family relationships. In some societies the father has to step back when it comes to the most important moral and sociological education, he has to let his wife's brother instruct his children and hand over to them what might be called "social continuity." The father is, in such cases, never completely replaced by the mother's brother. He is still the head of the household, but an important duality begins in the allegiance and in the social duties and obligations of the child.

In societies where kinship is counted through the father the distortion is less obvious, at least to European eyes. But, on the one hand, in some societies on a primitive level, the father's sister very often assumes an important place as a female counterpart of the father, and on the other hand, in all such societies, the relation to maternal relatives becomes irrelevant and there is a one-sided overemphasis of the father's line. Most important of all, the father, in pronouncedly patriarchal communities, changes his rôle. From the tender and often indulgent parent, which he was to the small child, he becomes the autocrat of the household, the wielder of the *patria potestas*, and often at times a tyrant, while the mother's brother acts as the friend and tender male helpmate of the children.

Thus, while the early cares and physiological dependence on parenthood lead to education and this again to the transmission of social identity, privileges and possessions, a serious shock occurs at this stage of the simple process. And, indeed, it is usually a shock even in the manner in which it is carried out. At times children are forcibly removed from their home and brought to that of their grandparents, as among the Southern Bantu, or placed in special bachelor houses or men's club houses or sent to another village. Or again, while they live at home, they may have to carry on certain more or less easy tasks under a new authority, that of the village headman or totemic chief, and submit to a new routine, if not discipline. The typical form, however, in which the severance of the child from the home and the impression of new kinship ideas takes place, are the initiation ceremonies. There, passing through ordeals, seclusion and privations, the child is weaned from home, from the influence above all of the mother, and instructed in clan mythology and clan morality. At the same time he forms new bonds, finds himself a member of an Age Grade or other male organization, but above all, when there is a clan, he is taught the solidarity and unity of this group, of which he is now a full member. Later in life, it may be added, marriage constitutes a violent wrench in the whole kinship outlook of both sexes, though more so in the case of a girl.

With all this the family bonds are never completely destroyed: they are only profoundly modified and overlaid by other associations. For the series of shocks by which the bilateral family kinship becomes transformed into wider classificatory ties is associated with another series of what might be called reconstructive processes.

When weaning, which takes place late in life in primitive societies, is over, the child, who may have been sent away from home or during the process forcibly kept from contact with the mother, returns to her, and, though weaned, continues to be dependent on her for food. Again at initiation the mother may be directly reviled and discredited to the son. He may even be permanently kept from home after the ceremonies are over. This profoundly modifies his relation to the mother, to the home and to his whole early kinship horizon. And yet, he maintains close, strongly emotional, though perhaps surreptitious, relations with his mother; his old home remains the only family circle to which he belongs and to which he frequently returns; probably he still feeds at home or is sent food from home. Again, when, under mother-right, the maternal uncle replaces the father as regards authority and influence, the paternal relationship is deeply changed. Yet the father becomes often even more of a friend, a private adviser and a real helper; and very often a whole body of usages grows up which compensate to a large extent for the loss of authority. At marriage the man or woman enters, or rather creates a new household, but both the old households still remain homes to husband and wife. As grandparents' homes they are open to their offspring. Even at death the parental tie is not broken, as we already know.

Thus the primary bonds of parenthood grow and mature and retain to the last some of the original pattern. We might almost call this growth of bilateral ties natural because it continues in direct pursuance of physiological facts, because it is based on the emotional readiness of the parents to help their children and on the correlated response of children to parents.

But parenthood asserts itself in yet a different manner. The configuration of the child's own household, as it consists of his father and mother, of his brothers and sisters, is repeated all around him. As soon as or even before he has become an active and effective member of his household, he is received into the households of his grandparents, of the brothers and sisters of his parents. He thus forms new ties in virtue of his relationship to father and mother and very much on the same pattern as his own family ties are formed. The household is thus the workshop, so to speak, where kinship ties are built.

The formation of the new ties, in the sense in which we are speaking now, is essentially individual. Thus, one of the nearest relatives outside the own household is invariably the mother's sister. This woman often assists at childbirth, helps the mother during the first few days when the infant needs most care and attendance, often visits the household, in case of the mother's illness takes charge of the child. She is in short an assistant mother, or substitute mother. In matrilineal communities she would be the person who, legally, would replace the mother in the case of her death or inability to look after the child. In patrilineal societies this part might be played by the wife of the father's brother, very rarely only by the father's sister. But in any case the nearest relatives of both mother and father are, to the child, secondary parents.

It must be remembered that in primitive societies any form of what might be called "social insurance"—that is, organized assistance and replacement in case of death or misadventure, such as we have in the charitable and benevolent institutions of civilized communities—can only be done directly and personally. We see, accordingly, in primitive societies, an extraordinary development of what might be termed the substitution by kinship and a definite system of vicarious duties and responsibilities devolving on the nearest of kin. This principle of substitution is clearly seen in the way in which the children are trained to regard the mother's sister as a substitute mother and to call her by the same term which they apply to the mother.

The father's brother is likewise called father, his wife, mother; the children of the mother's sister and of the father's brother usually are named by the same terms as the own siblings. If we study primitive kinship terminologies, not as ready-made products but in the process of formation along the life history of the individual, we find that the essence of so-called classificatory kinship consists in gradual extensions on the basis of vicarious substitution. The substitute mother or father is, in certain respects, equivalent to the real one. He or she appears in the intimacy of the household, side by side with the real parent; he or she renders to the child services similar to those of the real parent, at times replacing the real parent and acting as the substitute. The salient facts of this process are that the substitute parent resembles in certain respects the original one and that the naming expresses this partial assimilation.

To sum up: as the individual grows up the process of direct extension of kinship ties surrounds him with other households, related to him through his parents and constituting what might be called the neighborhood of kindred. Sometimes this neighborhood of kindred is directly on the territorial basis and coincides with the local grouping of households, at other times the kindred are scattered over a wide area.

We have just followed the development of the parental ties in the later life of the individual. Let us now see how the processes of development which we have studied affect the family. Here an interesting generalization arises directly out of the survey of facts: the development of parenthood into kinship is by no means a simple process or even one process. It shows a manifoldness in which, however, two main aspects are visible. We have on the one hand the consolidation and later the transformation of the family group and on the other the clan. Let us once more turn to these two institutions.

In our account of the imaginary observer's career we showed that the family would appear "so obvious" to him that he might be in serious danger of overlooking it. The clan, on the other hand, is so unexpected and recondite that he might equally well miss seeing it. But once having noticed it, he would see in it that strange, powerful and obtrusive institution, which has fascinated generations of anthropologists into ignoring the family almost completely.

We are in a position now to discard the classical and all too facile solution that the clan is a domestic institution. We know that among present-day natives it never plays the part of the family, and that it is improbable, nay, inconceivable, that the clan or any similar institution should ever have had a domestic, still less a procreative, function.

Is the clan then merely a political or legal institution? This second facile answer must also be discarded. The clan, connected with classificatory kinship terms, pervaded by ideas of kinship and descent from one ancestor, is in the psychology of natives intrinsically based on conceptions of bodily unity. Thus, though the clan is neither a substitute for nor equivalent of the family, it stands in some sort of intimate relationship to that institution. But it is not such a general statement that we want, but a precise answer to the question as to what type of relationship exists between the family and the clan.[9]

Both the family and clanship begin at home. When a child is born it becomes *ipso facto* a member of its mother's or father's clan, and all subsequent clan relations are derived from this fact. But the effective importance of clanship at birth is nil, while that of parenthood really constitutes the whole universe of the infant. We have seen that as he grows up the influence of the clan increases. With the gradual severance from the household, with his entry into economic coöperation, with his initiation into the mythological and esoteric lore of his people, with his assumption of the legal bonds of citizenship, with his growth, that is, into full participation in the ordinary and ceremonial life of the tribe, the native

[9] As will be seen, the main problem of kinship in my opinion is the understanding of extended kinship, that is clanship, in its relation to the family. I should regard a one-sided over-emphasis of the family as almost as erroneous as that of the clan. When my friend Mrs. B. Z. Seligman writes about ". . . the numerous conversations I have had with Professor Malinowski, spread over a number of years, during which he always spoke of the importance of the family and I defended the clan" (*Journal of the Royal Anthro. Inst.*, Vol. LIX, p. 234), I think that she imputes to me too exclusive an attachment to the family. I should like to have earned the title *Familiae Defensor*, but in reality I have for some time past been aware that the real solution lies in the right and full appreciation of both sides of kinship—the classificatory as well as the individual.

becomes more and more clearly aware of the validity of the clan and his place in it.

Again, as we have seen, parenthood gradually changes, but we know that only very superficially does it fade away. The mother, at first the source of all sustenance and protection, diminishes in importance at weaning, at initiation, with the child's entrance into the bachelor's house or girls' community. The father, at first the only male on the horizon, a tender and loving parent, becomes, in a patriarchal community, primarily the wielder of authority, while in a matrilineal, he has to give over a number of his prerogatives and services to the mother's brother.

To all appearances, then, the clan grows, the family decays. The hypothesis might impose itself that the one passes into the other, so that the family is the institution of childhood, the clan that of adult life. Even this, however, as we know, is too simple a solution. Let us then return to the life history of the individual.

And here we must make a short, methodological digression. The approach to the problem of kinship through the study of the development along the life history of the individual should have been obvious. Kinship is the most personal fact in human life and an organic fact at that. It starts with birth, it grows and modifies as the organism matures, it passes through several crises, above all that of marriage. Even with death its bonds are not completely broken, for kinship is the basis of ancestor worship and similar religious cults. Its treatment in this historical or we might say biographical way yields the only really satisfactory solution. And yet this simple approach has so far been neglected. The projection of the evolutionary line of development has completely blinded anthropologists to this straightforward and simple method which alone can yield the clue to all the puzzles and difficulties.

We have just said that on a superficial view the family fades. But this is only partially correct, for the family lasts throughout life. The parents who start as protectors of their children, become, in their old age, the wards and charges of these children. At the death of an old man or woman the children are the chief mourners, and the spirits of previous generations communicate primarily with their own offspring.

In fact, we saw that, at first, the family, as a definite group, grows rather than fades. The infant who at first was but a passive being tended by its parents, as a child, takes a definite place in the household, where, side by side with the mother and father, the group is completed by his brothers and sisters. This growth and consolidation of the family continues until a time when it splits, so to speak, and one side of it, the maternal or paternal, becomes overstressed, the other overruled, only to assert itself in various covert reactions and reaffirmations.

This twofold or split growth of kinship, or rather the coexistence of two processes, is, I believe, the source of most difficulties. I maintain that right through life there is, on the one hand, the process of growth and constant reaffirmation of the simple bilateral family pattern. On the other hand, and side by side with this, there is a breaking-up, connected with a unilateral over-emphasis of the legal side of the maternal or the paternal bond. The influence of these two processes, in a way antagonistic to each other, can be traced in the classificatory terminologies, in legal systems, in sexual attitudes, in what might be called "complexes," that is, reactions of individual feeling and even of custom against the official attitude prescribed by tradition.

Each process has its special mechanism. The direct growth of the family is helped by the local grouping of households, by coöperation within the neighborhood, by the fact that, for many purposes, the relatives of both father and mother are relevant to the child. Last, but not least, by the rules of incest which everywhere exist over and above the rules of exogamy. The splitting and breaking up of the family on the unilateral principle and the correlated building up of clan ties is achieved gradually in some communities by the teaching of the rules of descent and the introduction into tribal tradition and ritual, or dramatically in others at initiation, by esoteric clan ceremonial and mystery performances, and by the rules of clan exogamy and classificatory terminologies and institutions.

Thus kinship, as an integral system of personal bonds, is a complex social phenomenon. This complexity in the growth of kinship has not been the source of anthropological troubles only. It is also the source of many tribal maladjustments; of the constant strife between clan solidarity and personal allegiances, between rules of exogamy and individual preferences, between the dominance of the group and the assertion of the individual.[10]

Marriage is a crisis and one which affects deeply all kinship relations. Through marriage two individuals establish a new household, each of them acquires a new body of relations, those in law, and presently they will become the source of a new set of relationships, those of their children to the rest of the community. But in each new household there is repeated all that has been described before in reference to the initial situation. There is one set of facts, however, to which some more attention must still be given, and that is the conditions of infantile sexuality and the rules of incest.

Whether the Freudian is right or wrong about infantile sexuality, there is no doubt at all that the precautions as to its future development are taken pretty early in primitive societies. The taboos are imposed very soon

[10] This duality of influences and principles of conduct was the main argument of my two books *Crime and Custom in Savage Society* (1926) and *Sex and Repression in Savage Society* (1927).

in life. The prohibition of any sexual or erotic interest between members of the same household is universal. It is independent of mother-right or father-right: the taboo embraces both parents under either system of counting kinship. It is also independent of ideas about procreation, of the state of morality in a culture, of forms of marriage and of residence. The taboo on incest is a universal rule throughout humanity, endures through life, and is usually the strongest, most deeply felt moral prohibition.

But even with all this, great varieties obtain. In some communities, especially in Oceania, there is an absurd over-emphasis of the taboo between brother and sister. In others, the mother and son relationship is much more strongly prohibited, only very seldom is father-daughter incest regarded as an equally heinous offence.

The most important differences, however, are to be found in the extension of incest taboos. The strict prohibition obtains only as regards the family in the narrowest sense. Beyond this a variety sets in, usually associated with the unilateral counting of kinship, but even then with an extraordinary number of divergences. The full unilateral extension of incest gives rise to the well-known phenomenon of exogamy. This rule—almost invariably associated with the existence of clans—lays down that marriage must never take place between members of the same clan.

Exogamy develops out of incest, gradually, within the life history of the individual. The boy or the girl moves within a number of cognate households, those of the father's brother, for instance, and the mother's sister. The extension of kinship by direct growth on the family pattern embraces both these households. The offspring of both would be addressed as brothers and sisters, they would be the favorite playmates, while their parents would be addressed by the same terms as their own parents and felt to be substitute or secondary parents. But fairly early in life a difference would set in and become gradually sharper and more pronounced as the children grew up. One household, under mother-right that of the mother's sister, would become officially and legally kindred. The boys there would be legally treated as equivalent to the own brothers, while as regards the sisters a definite taboo would set in. They could not be treated in an erotic manner; from any play which involved sexual interest, they would have to be excluded, while on the other hand they would gradually assume a special relationship very much like that of their own sisters.

And as life progresses, more and more households, related on the mother's side, would be included in this type of relationship. The family terms of relationship would be extended to all these people, the community of the clan name and the unity of common totemic descent would unite all these men and women as clansmen and clanswomen. They would become legally united, under an obligation to defend each other in all clan feuds; owning, perhaps, some amount of property together; coöperating in enterprises; jointly financing feasts, wars and other undertakings. Above all, between the men and the women there would obtain a special, somewhat constrained, sober, non-erotic relationship—at least on the surface, for lapses from exogamy are not unknown. And, in the carrying out of religious or magical duties the members of the same clan would very often act as one group.

Thus it can be said that in no other aspect can the twofold nature of the kinship process and the twofold character of the products be seen as clearly as in the incidence of the sexual taboos. Exogamy is the result of a one-sided extension of the kinship attitude of avoiding sexually those bodily related. But this one-sided growth of incest in no way invalidates the full strength and bilateral character of the original taboo. Family incest remains prohibited by an independent set of rules. Both the processes and the products are related but autonomous.

We have arrived at the end of our descriptive survey. The individual whose life history we have followed is now married, at the head of his new household. He is still attached to his old family and he stands in a new relationship to the household and his wife. Besides this, however, he has formed a whole series of other bonds. He has contracted the bonds of extended kinship uniting him to several households, directly related to his parents. He has taken over with his wife a similar group of her extended relatives. But he has, above all, through the consistent one-sided extension of ties, acquired a definite status in a strictly circumscribed group—the clan.

As a result of the complex process of formation of kinship bonds we see the individual encompassed by a series of kinship rings, member of several kinship groups. In the genetic sense the most important of them is the family. But all of them have their respective functions to perform, and each assumes now and then a dominant importance. Nor is their multiplicity devoid of complications and conflicts. The legal figment of exclusive kinship in the one line, that is of clanship, is never fully adjusted to and balanced with the claims of the family. The complexity of kinship is the main source of social troubles and maladjustments, next, perhaps, to sexual jealousy, rivalries of ambition and economic greed.

Our results show up the absurdity of the usual dilemma in treating kinship: it is not *either* individual *or* communal, either the family or the clan. Kinship in primitive communties is both individual and collective, and it is also the kinship of the extended kindred group, of the relationship-in-law—it presents, in fact, a multiplicity of facets. We have seen how all this comes about and to what results it leads.

We have also become aware of how the multiplicity of facets is maintained. The tribal life of a primitive people is not absolutely homogeneous.

It falls, above all, into two main phases: private and public, that of everyday concerns and that of ceremonial activities; that, in short, of the Profane and of the Sacred. Whether this distinction is absolute, whether it lends itself to all the theoretical manipulations to which it has been submitted by [Emile] Durkheim and his school, is irrelevant. But there is no doubt that, throughout the world, most of a people's time is spent in economic concerns on a small scale—in the tilling of the soil, in hunting and fishing, in the patient carrying out of craft and industry. This type of existence is dominated by the household: each family work their own plot of ground or do their own collecting of food; they cook and feed together; they spend a great deal of their time and take their amusements within the family circle. It is in this phase of tribal life that the family is paramount. These Profane seasons are not any less "social" than is ceremonial life. Custom and tribal law control and dominate the individual side of kinship as much as they do the collective side.

But in every tribe there are times when the whole community collects, magical ends are pursued and spiritual values reasserted. Economic needs are often satisfied by communal hunting or fishing or by feeding the assembled people from a communal stock of stored vegetables. At such periods sexual life is often stirred to greater activity and since the tribe is assembled on a vast scale, the rules of exogamy come definitely into operation. This ceremonial phase of tribal life is dominated by the institution of the clan. Clansmen and clanswomen have often to act together; families are broken up in the performance of ceremonial duties; and individual relationship is definitely subordinated to the classificatory principle. It is a recrystallization of the sociological system within the tribe, rationally motivated to the adult, impressive to the youth, often bewildering to the child. This dissolution of the family at ceremonial occasions, as I have often witnessed it myself in Melanesia, is a real and powerful factor in the moulding of the twofold operation of individual and collective kinship.

There are, of course, also what might be called intermediate phases. There is economic coöperation on a large scale, though not yet on a tribal one. This is done by the local group and the ties of extended kinship usually govern ownership, mutual help, reciprocity, as well as the sharing of results.

There are the respective legal duties controlled by individual and extended kinship. And, again, there is clan solidarity operative in vendetta and in communal rights to objects of great value or with mythological claims. Here the clan once more becomes paramount. There is, finally, war with all its magic and ritual of declaration and peace-making, and here the clan and the relationship between clans dominates the situation.

Thus the several facets of kinship function alternatively on different occasions, each is correlated, at least in its principal manifestations, to one phase of tribal life. Through all the manifestations, however, the element of parenthood is, in one way or another, ostensible. It is, of course, the permanent foundation of the bilateral family; it directly affects the bonds of extended kinship; in one of its sides it is the starting point and the nucleus of clan unity. And throughout the whole process of growth and splitting of kinship, in all its manifestations, the influence of the initial situation makes itself felt in the classificatory usages of kinship terms, first formed in the family and then gradually and successively extended to all the wider groupings.

Terminology is one of the main mechanisms expressing the growth of kinship and controlling it. We must still say a few words about it. I have left it on purpose till this stage of the argument because the study of kinship words has dominated and warped the study of kinship facts to an extraordinary extent. Words are associated with kinship ties and in a way control them. But it is impossible to understand the meaning of words except by correlating them to social realities, for they are the products of social intercourse and they grow out of life. It is really in the study of their growth as the by-products of the development of personal ties that we can gain insight into their nature.

Let us face the classificatory puzzle at its very core—the terms used for parents by children. Each man addresses several elderly males and females by the same terms, father and mother respectively. Now we have already seen that, sociologically, a man has always one real father and one real mother but that there is a series of people who grow into his life as substitute fathers and mothers. They become more and more diluted, so to speak, more and more shadowy in their parental character. Yet, at times—and as regards the unilateral extensions, which in due time yield the clan—the fathers and mothers, the brothers and sisters, appear in solid blocks of kindred. But this takes place only on certain occasions and from certain points of view. The own parents dominate the home, ordinary life, most of the emotional and personal interests. The classificatory "blocks" appear at ceremonies or on legal occasions.

How is this sociological reality translated into linguistic usage? To a superficial observer it would appear that only one word is used and that consequently there is only a group-relationship. But better linguistic acquaintance would show that the word is used in several senses with each time a different accent, different phraseology, and within a different context. We might speak of a series of homonyms—better even, of a series of words represented by the same sound but, in actual speech, always distinguishable. The correct way would be to say that the native word for *mother* is always "indexed," so to speak, by emotional inflection, by context and by phrasing.

Now, native languages swarm with homonyms. And these are not due to the often alleged "poverty of language" or "slovenliness of speech." Most homonyms are significant metaphors. Primitive magic is full of them. The use of simile and metaphor is in verbal magic what a sympathetic act is in ritual. We ourselves use kinship terms, such as father and mother, in our prayers—again as metaphors. What function do such metaphors fulfil in our prayer and in primitive magic? They impose a binding obligation on our divinity. We address Him as Father so that he might be merciful and answer our approach in childlike confidence with a fatherly response. The native metaphorically addressing his blue skies as a Black Cloud imposes a binding obligation on the impersonal forces that be to turn drought into rain.

Can this principle of binding metaphor in the use of kinship terms account for the development of classificatory terms? The native starts, as a child, with one meaning of kinship terms, moulded on the personal relationship within the family which is his initial situation, linguistically as well as socially. This primary meaning, later on, he is taught to extend to one relative after the other. Roughly speaking, the first extension is that of the term so far used only for the real mother to the mother's sister. This extension is no more a complete assimilation of meaning than is the sociological relationship of the child to the mother's sister identical with that which obtains between it and the mother. I have watched the process of this primary extension among Melanesian savages and have seen how difficult it is merely to induce the child to use the term in an extended meaning. The child has to form a new meaning for the old word. In reality he acquires a new word with the same form but a different subject-matter. He will use the word in a different manner and under different circumstances. When, after some resistance, he comes to apply the term mother to his mother's sister, he does not confuse the two people nor mix up the two ideas; he does not, in other words, carry out a complete linguistic identification. By the time the child learns to use his language with discrimination and to get the feel of it, he knows that he merely emphasizes a similarity and passes over the differences.

What is, to pass now to our sociological terminology, the function of this one-sided linguistic emphasis? Well, the similarity in the relationship between mother and mother's sister is the basis of all the legal obligations of the newly acquired relative. It is in virtue of being a potential equivalent to the mother that the maternal aunt is under an obligation to the child. It is therefore this side of the relationship which is linguistically expressed. We have here, therefore, a metaphorical use of the word, though the metaphor here is not magically but legally binding. The partial equivalence is verbally transformed into a fictitious identity because this identity is relevant to the child.

The same argument applies, obviously, to the direct extension of the term father to father's brother, and of the terms brother and sister to those first cousins with whom, under a unilateral counting of descent, relevant kinship establishes an identity of substance.

It is interesting to note that the twofold process of kinship growth finds its counterpart in the formation of kinship terminologies. Among the people who are directly kin to the parents there are those to whom no direct extension of an already existing kinship attitude is possible. Apart from the grandparents, the father's sister and the mother's brother, as well as their offspring, technically called cross-cousins, are usually named by new terms of kinship. These people, as we know, occupy sociologically a special position; they are the people who give the extra-familial imprint to the process of unilateral over-emphasis. It is impossible here, however, linguistically to follow up this intricate and difficult process in detail. We shall have to be satisfied with having laid down the main principle.

The important thing is to note that there are phases of kinship terminology even as there are phases in the social reality of kinship. The native vocabulary in kinship is never a homogeneous whole. It is always a compound of several layers: one of them, the terms of individual usage, corresponds to the primary meanings derived from the initial situation. We might describe as the second layer of kinship terminology, that which results from the direct extension to the nearest kindred of the parents. There is a body of terms used to more distant relatives, traceable through genealogy and prominent within the local grouping. There is the body of terms obtained in that sudden extension of relationship which comes with marriage. Finally there is the system of classificatory usages applied to the tribe at large and describing this time groups and not individuals. In this last use, and in this only, are the terms really classificatory. They form a very limited part of the whole range of linguistic usages and they correspond to those phases of tribal life when the clan exerts its sway over the individual and when, in ceremonial or legal activities, clan faces clan within tribal life.

Bluntly put, this simply means that it is nothing short of nonsense to speak of any native terminology as classificatory in its integral character. Native terms are used in a classificatory way only on occasions. All the explanations by "survival," by the association with group-marriage, are to us as futile as the explanation by "polite terms of address." Even the laborious and learned correlation of classificatory kinship terminologies with the clan system, worked out by Rivers, is spurious. For, in the first place, the classificatory use of terms never completely corresponds to the clan division; and, in the second place, the limited correspondence controls only the one form of use.

We have established that the so-called classificatory character of native kinship terms is the result of a series of extensions. In these the linguistic pseudo-identification has a definite function. By the binding metaphor of language it gives expression to the substitution of one relative for another if need be, and it thus strengthens, linguistically, the system of social insurance which is the basis of primitive cohesion. Here, again, we find that it is in the relations of the several layers within the same system of terms that the real nature and functional value of the whole can be established. Yet the very existence of the stratified character of primitive terminologies has been completely ignored by previous anthropological workers.

We have now followed the development of kinship along the line of the life history of a typical primitive tribesman. It was necessary, here and there, to indicate the possible varieties which arise under different conditions of mother-right or father-right respectively, of different sexual taboos and forms of license. Yet with all this it was possible to give a coherent and representative picture of human kinship on primitive levels. We have demonstrated that its initial situation is in the family; we have shown the derived character of the extended bonds; we have traced the social mechanisms through which derivation takes place; we have been able to assign the proper place to sex in relation to marriage, and of marriage in relation to the family, and lastly to define clanship and classificatory kinship as the final and most highly derived products of parenthood. Throughout we were able to arrive at a number of sociological generalizations; to lay down a series of laws, which define the relations of the various component parts of the one big system which controls the continuity of the human species and of human culture.

Perhaps the most important of our generalizations is that all these phenomena, sex, mating, parenthood, clanship and classificatory terminology, can only be understood if we consider them in relation to each other, as parts of a big procreative institution. The core of this institution is the human family: that is, parenthood culturally defined and marriage as a social contract. The principal function of the compound institution is the continuity of the human species, but in direct dependence on this procreative function, the family has to act as the principal agency in the education of the child. By education was here understood the full cultural equipment of the individual for tribal life and the placing of him in the framework of the community.

Sex, we were able to prove, is subordinated to marriage, and marriage is fundamentally determined by parenthood in that it is a social charter for the establishment of a legitimate family rather than a license for sexual intercourse. Thus, the main function of parenthood consists in the transformation of the biological endowment into lifelong emotional ties and in the making of these into complex cultural forces. It is, therefore, the essence of human parenthood that, through the building of strong emotional attitudes on biological foundations, it endures, it leads to the establishment of a lifelong social relationship of mutual obligations and services. This, however, since human beings never live in single families but in groups of them, entails the building of new ties in virtue of the parental ones and directly on the pattern of them. Parenthood, thus, is invariably the starting point of wider social relationships.

Yet these extensions, which in many respects grow along the natural lines of the family constitution—that is, in following up the kinship bonds of both father and mother—have to be limited in some ways to one line only. The transmission of material possessions, of status, and of rank, is in all human societies submitted to definite rules. The main principle of all such rules is that one line only of parenthood should be counted as legally relevant. We have seen that unilateral descent, succession and inheritance are intimately bound up with order and simplicity, with cohesion and continuity of tradition. At the same time, once the paternal or the maternal side is legally over-emphasized as relevant and the other overlooked, the extension of kinship leads to the formation of new, wider groupings, technically named clans or sibs.

Thus the extension of family ties takes place along two channels, not always clearly differentiated in the reality of tribal life, but sharply distinguishable in their functional determination and in the effects which they produce. We have followed both processes and shown that their results correspond to their function. We studied, on the one hand, the gradual consolidation of family ties: the formation of new bonds in direct extension and on the pattern of the family; the persistence of the old household and the grouping of other related households around the original nucleus. The product of this process is the consolidated parenthood as it affects the mature individual, the extended family or *Grossfamilie;* and the bilateral, genealogically defined system of kindred and relatives.

On the other hand, we studied the second process which begins fairly early in life with the traditional decree making one side and one side only relevant in legal kinship. We have shown how, through a series of acts, such as initiation and other transition rites, with the gradual imposition of tribal duties, the clan takes hold of the individual, principally in ceremonial and legal matters, but to a large extent also in economic coöperation and political affairs.

In all this we have seen that kinship, though it starts from a common source, that of procreation, develops a number of aspects. Kinship, in its tribal or collective aspect, is by no means identical with kinship in its domestic aspect. As the ties extend in the unilateral process their original family character becomes more and more attenuated and diluted by other ingredients. In the bilateral process of direct growth the family pattern remains more permanent, but even there it must be remembered that the parental relationship is modified when the child becomes an adult. But though the developed family of the adult tribesman has also lost a considerable number of the elements of which it was made up to the infant and child, yet it still consists of the same people. The ties which bind them together are the direct development of those which in childhood united offspring to parents.

The developed kinship system of an adult tribesman, which comprises both classificatory and individual ties as well as several minor ones, bears only a remote, at times mainly figurative resemblance to the family ties as these were in infancy. But in all the processes which lead to the final kinship system, each new set of ties is built under the influence of the initial situation and as an extension of it. We must, however, establish a more precise distinction between the component parts of the compound system.

The primary and fundamental elements of the parent-to-child relationship—the fact of procreation, the physiological services, the innate emotional responses—which make up the family bonds vanish completely from the relationship within the clan. Totemic identity, the unity of clan-names, the mythological fiction of common descent in one line, magical, religious and legal coöperation, are new elements which enter into clan relationships and which constitute the greatly modified kinship of the clan.

But though the clan is essentially non-reproductive, non-sexual and non-parental—though it is never a primary basis and source of kinship—its connection with the family is real and genetic. The clan grows out of the family and kinship round one of the parents by the affirmation of the exclusive relevancy of this one parent, by the injunction of legal solidarity with kindred of one side only, often accompanied by legal fictions and linguistic metaphors in classificatory terminologies.

It is necessary to insist on this fundamental difference between the clan and the family just because the two institutions have been so hopelessly confused. The clan, as we know, has been defined as a domestic institution, as the savage equivalent of the family, as a reproductive group. But as a matter of fact, the clan is never an independent, self-sufficient kinship unit. It differs from the family in that, by definition, any type of sexual relationship is excluded from the clan; thus the husband-wife relationship, which is one of the fundamentals of the family, has no counterpart within the clan. Again, the relations between the older and the younger generations within the clan, or between age grades, are neither counterparts nor copies of the parent-to-child relation. Above all, there is nothing, not even a trace, of what might be regarded as reproductive functions within the clan. Sex, as we know, is rigidly excluded, matrimony even more so. And as we have just seen, there is nothing corresponding to the early infantile relation between parent and child. The initial situation always falls outside the clan.

What then corresponds, on the wide, communal or collective scale to the family? The clan, as we know, is in its very inception based upon the elimination of either the paternal or the maternal side from relevant kinship. In the collective system, therefore, it is the clan of the relevant parent plus the clan of the irrelevant parent plus the clans related to Ego by marriage and other forms of affinity—it is all these clans which together embrace the classificatory body of relatives. Classificatory nomenclature always refers to the tribe or to a large part of it, and never to one clan only. It is not the clan, therefore, but the tribe as a correlated system of clans which corresponds to the family on the classificatory level of kinship.

With this we are able to define the clan functionally as the institution which standardizes one-sidedly the extended aspect of parenthood. The clan, however, unlike the family, is always part of a larger system, never a self-contained unit. The full functional reality of clanship is only achieved by the integration of the clans as correlated units into a larger tribal whole.

We can also, now, define kinship as, in the first place, the personal bonds based on procreation socially interpreted; and, in the second place, as the complex system of wider bonds derived from the primary ones by the twofold process of direct extension and of unilateral reinterpretation.

We have now redeemed all or most of our promises. We have laid down from the functional point of view the relation of the family to the clan and explained their coexistence. We have given a functional definition of kinship, after having ascertained its multiple character. We have shown that the unilateral over-emphasis of kinship fulfils the function of contributing to order and continuity in the transmission of culture. We have assigned a place to sexual excesses as a trial-and-error method of mate selection and as a safety-valve to the natural experimental impulse of sex. We have shown that the function of incest taboos and of exogamy is the elimination of sex from sentiments which are incompatible with its violent destructive force and its further elimination from the sober working partnership on which parenthood and clanship are based. We have shown that the function of classificatory terminologies is verbally to document, by the legal force of binding metaphor, the obligations of secondary parenthood and derived relationships.

In all this there was hardly any question of origins, of distribution or diffusion. The type of explanation here given is not altogether familiar even to the modern anthropologist. Its main characteristic consists in showing that certain forms of social organization, universally found, contribute towards cohesion, continuity of tradition, the interlocking multiplicity of bonds, the better integration of individual sentiments, and the more efficient working of the social machinery. In the particular case of Kinship, we were able to show that cultural processes tend to follow the direction of innate biological drives, that physiological facts are made gradually to ripen into sentiments and these again lead to purely cultural institutions.

The functional method allows us, then, to establish the laws of biographical growth; to place the various elements of the kinship institution in their correct perspective; to establish a relevant relationship between them.

Exactly as the correlation of efficient military organization with political power, and of large political units with conquest are sociological laws; exactly as the persistence of slavery at certain levels of culture can be related to industrial efficiency, commercial power, and again to strong political organization; so the correlation of the multiplicity of kinship bonds with stability, order, strong family life, gives us relevant sociological laws.

The functional method leads us to a full and comprehensive grasp of facts; to their correct description; to the exact definition of the various elements of the problem and to a detailed correlation of the various phases of kinship. This it can do and no more. But without at least a preliminary treatment from the functional point of view, the anthropologist runs a serious risk of distorting facts, of defining them incorrectly and of setting before himself insoluble problems to which he then proceeds to give imaginary solutions. This has been the bane of the Science of Man and the present attempt, if it does no more than place the problem on a correct foundation, will have been amply justified.

With all this I do not want to pretend to an attitude of false modesty. I am convinced that the functional treatment is the only really adequate approach to the subject. The Jack-in-the-box explanations of all the kinship and sexuality puzzles appear to me altogether spurious and unnecessary. And they are based, one and all, on a terrible mutilation of facts through an altogether unjustifiable carving and lopping. But, above all, I feel that in this symposium—in company, that is, with practical sociologists interested in the present and future of parenthood and in its past in so far as it bears on the present and future—I am really at home. For the comparative science of man can be of use to sociology just in so far as it is able to show the essentials of kinship and of the family, of parenthood and of marriage; the true nature of sexual excess and of sexual morality. The anthropologist has scientifically to define the real and effective morals of marriage and parenthood, that is, the sound sociological laws which control these institutions. He must show where the family comes in, whence it draws its forces, how far it is inevitable and where it can be dispensed with. It is just this type of generalization which we have been able to achieve here.

It is clear, therefore, that anthropology must supply the student of modern society not with precedent but with sociological law. Were we to prove that unbridled promiscuity was the main pastime of Mr. Pithecanthropus Erectus and his wife, this, in itself, could not justify "petting parties" and certain similar institutions. Nor need our views on modern communism or upon its compatibility with human nature be profoundly influenced by the discovery that primitive forms of communism have occurred occasionally in early societies. The argument from "natural inclination" is as spurious as that from primeval precedent. But if we can prove that marriage as a legal contract and the family as a culturally defined group of parents and children, can be traced through all the changes and vicissitudes of history, if we can show that even license serves to strengthen the family and marriage, our outlook becomes more plastic and tolerant and our judgment more competent. In the first place, we look with a certain diffidence upon any attempt to subvert or reform these institutions through any radical change. Revolutionary decrees for the abolition of the family and for the substitution of legalized free-love for marriage are bound to be abortive, for they run counter to the sociological laws which we have proved to be universal.

At the same time the mere stubbornness of the moral reactionary who does not want even the form of such institutions changed, who opposes the discussion of divorce, of contraceptives or of the "revolt of modern youth," works against the cause of true conservatism. For in the first place the knowledge of real facts establishes the value of marriage and the family. And in the second place, nothing subverts the substance of a social institution so much as a blind adherence to outworn forms and obsolete habits which survive by mere inertia.

The anthropologically trained sociologist cannot deal in rosy ideals or in Utopian millenniums. There was never a perfect child nor a perfect parent and there never will be. A complexity of motives and interests and the persistence of conflict have met us at every turn of our investigation.

Functional anthropology is thus an essentially conservative science. The institutions of marriage and the family are indispensable, they should be saved at all costs in the present wrecking of so many things old and valuable. But, like all really conservative tendencies, the functional view advocates intelligent and even drastic reform wherever this is necessary. If marriage and the family are in need of a much greater tolerance in matters of sex and of parental authority, these reforms ought to be formulated, studied and tested in the light of the relevant sociological laws and not in a mere haphazard, piecemeal fashion.

4

APING THE APE; *or, an anthropologist looks at the modern world from his primitive cave-dwelling*

"You have killed passion," said the sad Old Man.

"We have discovered pleasure," retorted the Flapper. "We have discovered pleasure which satisfies and does not destroy. Passion was dangerous, it tore you to pieces and cast you high and dry on the rocks of tragedy or the sands of disillusionment. We do not want to relive Tristan and Isolde, nor yet the story of Anna Karenina. We in turn have torn passion into small bits and scattered them over the gay nights of our existence."

"Yes, and in forgetting how to suffer you have forgotten how to love."

"What *you* call love is just a romantic and sentimental pose. It doesn't fit into modern life; it doesn't mean anything to me or to any of us—any more than it meant anything to the full-blooded primeval savage. We are tired of that conspiracy of Continental Romantics and mid-Victorian prudes and its sentimentalities. We have no sympathy with the lovesick maiden or the brokenhearted hero. To us they are pathological specimens—hormones and liver and a couple of complexes. Our kind of love is much wider—more comprehensive. We don't pick and choose by your hazy sentimental ideals, but by our needs of the moment. We have made love a thing of give and take all round—nicely pooled and redistributed."

"In my gay young days," mused the sentimental Old Man, "there was a song in Paris, 'J'aime la femme et la folie.' This was also an abstract love for an impersonal object, syndicalised and communal. It was loving woman as a prostitute. Now [man] love[s] woman as the Mother-Image or as the Communal Wife. The most modern among you have made man and woman into interchangeable parts in the well-oiled mechanism of the routine of organised petting parties."

"Anyhow," said the Flapper, "we know now how to use contraceptives —and how to use our economic independence and easy divorce. You'll never

drive us back into the old patriarchal marriage—we have finished with
the degradation and enslavement of women, with religious taboos and
irrational chastity. J. B. Watson says that in fifty years there will be no
such thing as marriage. Love is an entirely private and personal affair—as
you would see if you read Havelock Ellis. Look at Bertrand Russell, too—
he shows clearly enough that jealousy, which you probably think is a
rather grand emotion, is mostly made up of possessiveness and is nothing
but a burden on a man or woman. Everybody has a *right* to be happy—
Dora Russell has given us the charter for that."

The wise Old Man began to explain that Havelock Ellis and Bertrand
Russell have said many other things as well, many wise things, showing
that marriage and family life are after all not to be jettisoned lightly—
but the Flapper had snapped off the argument and was already beyond the
reach of wisdom and of sentiment or of Old Age.

This is a paraphrase of a conversation which I heard sometime, somewhere; was it in Bloomsbury or in Greenwich Village, or in Charlotten-
burg . . . I cannot remember; or was it only in a bad dream—one of
those Freudian dreams which are not altogether wish-fulfilments?

The headlong rush into . . . ?

Such things make you feel old and sad and wise if you belong to the
pre-war generation. Things have hurried past us, and much has been
destroyed without which life seems very empty and unsettled. The Great
War started the social havoc, then came Einstein and destroyed the
physical world. The motor-car and now the aeroplane are destroying
natural beauty and defiling nature—that is, to us old-fashioned people.
But perhaps the most unsettling and destructive thing is this uncertainty
which we feel. Is contemporary civilisation going through a crisis of unprecedented magnitude or is it comfortably developing on progressive
lines? Are we being driven with a vertiginous speed somewhere, somehow,
to an unknown goal, unknown but essentially destructive—or are we
merely rationalising human existence, as we have rationalised our theories,
our industries, and our street traffic?

That there is some destruction all around us, there is no doubt. We are
tired, we are even frightened—so tired and frightened at times that
repression seems the only comfortable way out. We don't want to listen
to the threats of the decline of the Western World—that everything is
going to the dogs.

But let us sample the problem and concentrate our attention on the
crisis in marriage and the family, as well as in love-making suggested in
the overheard conversation. Here again the essence of what is happening
is difficult to assess. Looked at from one angle, civilisation's time-
honoured arrangement of marriage and the family appears as the only

institution really safe, founded as it is on the bed-rock of human nature, defined by immemorial tradition, unassailable by most of the forces of modernism. A great many conservatives (using this term in the widest sense, i.e. those attached to tradition and permanence), looking at marriage from this angle, would simply discourage any change and leave alone this sheet-anchor of social stability. "The Englishman's home is his castle"—the proverb in its sociological symbolism stands for the belief that the domestic institution will remain the stronghold of Anglo-Saxon culture and of modern culture in general.

But looking at it from this angle only we would be blinding ourselves completely to realities. Sex and the freedom of sex have become important subversive forces. They have been adopted almost as the insignia of revolutionary attitudes by the new generation, who spiritualise promiscuity and regard "old-fashioned" morality as the last entrenchment of repressive taboos and prejudices. They find marriage and the family one of the main obstacles to their achievement of personal happiness. On the other hand, those who believe that a wholesale reconstruction and reorganisation of society is necessary, whether on lines of Communism or Fascism or any other social creed, naturally and reasonably feel that as long as the State does not control the reproduction as well as the education of the young, the domestic circle will remain the stubborn guardian of the old order.

On the whole neither the believers in automatic stability nor those who anticipate the complete extermination of marriage and legitimate parenthood within a generation or two are very helpful to us—they are not true to the reality of fact. Yet the whole discussion is carried on from these extreme positions; it is not so much a discussion as an angry shouting across wide spaces. And what is the rôle of the prophets of cold reason, as we might call the scientific experts in whom the modern man places such implicit trust? And who is going to be the real expert on marriage? As an anthropologist, I should like to claim for my science, not to say for myself, the privilege of being able to speak dispassionately and intelligently on the past, present and future of marriage and family. But anthropology, especially when it talks about marriage, has a bad name, and it deserves it.

For the last three quarters of a century or so, students of primitive cultures have quarrelled about the "origins of marriage," about the morality of primitive man, about his fidelity, his jealousy, and his parenthood. They were to all appearances divided into two irreconcilable camps.

"Up till relatively recent times, about the middle of the last century, matters appeared to the students of the subject in a very simple fashion. The two great authorities of our Christian civilisation, the Bible and Aristotle, contain positive statements about the origins of marriage and the importance of the family. To the mediaeval theologian and to the nineteenth century sociologist, marriage appeared respectively as a divine, and as a natural institution, and the patriarchal family as the cell of society, while any deviations from monogamy were regarded as exceptions, lapses or irrelevancies. Even as late as 1861 Sir Henry Maine could affirm that it was difficult to see 'what society of men had not been originally based on the patriarchal family.' This simple doctrine, the Adam and Eve theory of primitive marriage, as we might call it, was based on authority rather than on observation, on reticences rather than on the frank discussion of facts, on belief and moral prejudice rather than on a dispassionate desire for truth. Anthropology, therefore, was doomed to modify if not to explode this theory, and it did so with a vengeance."

I have quoted this passage verbatim from a previous article of mine written about ten years ago, because I have recently been classed by a group of militant Misbehaviourists and pseudo-anthropologists as a supporter of Sir Henry Maine's views, and the nickname "Adam-and-Eve theories of marriage origins," which I coined myself, has been affixed to me (sic!) without any acknowledgment of course!

Let me return however to the history of the problem. As I said, the explosion of the naïve Adam-and-Eve views was so destructive that it blew everything to pieces. Towards the middle of the last century a number of scholars hit upon what appeared to be an illuminating as well as a sound and genuine scientific discovery. They suddenly received a revelation, partly from facts, partly from that "inner consciousness" which revealed to the German philosopher the nature of the camel (or was it an elephant?). The revelation told them that it was not a paradisiacal monogamy but licentious, horrid promiscuity in which primitive man lived; that far from having a well-regulated family he lived in a horde where everyone mated with everyone else, where the children were communally held by group mothers and group fathers, where there was no order, no morality, no anything.

The first perhaps to hit upon the new ideas was Bachofen, a stodgy and learned Swiss lawyer. Pondering over old texts, Greek and Latin mythologies, and legal documents, he found that in olden days most human societies lived under mother-right, that is, women were the stronger sex, descent was counted from the mother, and the father was an irrelevant item in the household. This was well in accordance with the fact that in many primitive communities motherhood is of greater importance than paternity.

The solution of this state of affairs which came to Bachofen as one of those scientific illuminations which create an epoch—though often an epoch of muddle and side-tracking—is well known. His inner vision showed him original mankind living in sexual promiscuity, with neither marriage nor fatherhood nor morality. Woman was desecrated by male concupiscence, she was enslaved, she was nothing more than a prostitute. But women, by nature morally stronger than the male sex, revolted

against this desecration. They established individual marriage, discriminative maternity, and in doing so they introduced law, order and morality.
A great American ethnologist, Lewis H. Morgan, was led by the study
of the so-called classificatory terminology of kinship to frame similar
hypotheses. According to him, human society originated in complete
sexual promiscuity, passed then through the consanguine family, the
punaluan household, group marriage, polyandry, polygyny, and what-not,
arriving only after a laborious process of fifteen transformations in the
happy haven of monogamous marriage. About the same time, McLennan
and Lord Avebury in Great Britain, [Félix] Giraud-Teulon in France,
Post in Germany were coming to similar conclusions and substantiating
them with elaborate arguments. From savage countries came corroborating
evidence furnished by an army of observers: Howitt from Australia,
[Robert Henry] Codrington and Fison from Melanesia, [Jan Stanislaw]
Kubary from the Micronesian Islands, [George A.] Wilken from the
Malay Archipelago, [Alfred] Grandidier from Madagascar, Kovalevsky
from the Caucasus.

This revolution in scientific views about the origins of marriage for a
time completely held ground, but the sudden and dramatic way in which
opinions on the family and marriage had veered round naturally produced
fatal consequences. No revolution has ever borne unadulterated fruits.
And here also, after a time, there came a reaction, extreme, destructive,
and as reactions often are, one-sided and far too sweeping. Darwin,
Andrew Lang, Crawley, and last not least, Westermarck, put the assumption of primitive promiscuity and group marriage to a searching criticism
and it was found that these new theories of the complete absence of
marriage from primitive cultures, of the communal character of early
mating and family—that these hypotheses can be no more accepted than
the old Adam-and-Eve theory of marriage, at least they cannot be accepted
wholesale.

For almost half a century the deadlock between the two rival schools
lasted. Even a few years ago I was able to write that "Anthropology is
divided into two camps upon almost every question connected with primitive marriage, sexuality and family life. Like many a savage tribe, anthropologists are in this matter organised according to the dual principle,
divided into two moieties or phratries, one claiming descent from a
patriarchal pair, the other from the communistic horde, the one having
as its totemic ancestor the monogamous ape, the other the promiscuous
baboon, the one having Morgan for its patron saint, the other Westermarck." But since then matters have considerably improved, and I certainly would not endorse my by now antiquated statement. At present we
are steering through many difficulties towards a synthesis which embraces
the schools of Morgan and of Westermarck. Adam-and-Eve anthropology
had to be exploded. The naïve and simple solution explaining everything

by promiscuity or mother-right had also to be critically rejected. And now we are moving towards a position which has to recognise the reality of many of the facts which one or other of the schools tried to ignore—the co-existence of family and clan, of sexual license and of strict morality— and we have to evolve a theoretical treatment which is much more complex but also much more instructive.

The play of myth and precedent in anthropology

Why has our science been for such a long time a source of great entertainment to the public, who are amused by it and at times at it? Because though it could have been a real force in modern life, a great practical moral influence, it has so far been mainly playing at problems, constructing fairy tales about primitive man, while its only moral trend has been an invitation to modern man to imitate his primeval ancestor. Incredible as it sounds, aping the ape was to a large extent the motto, the watchword, of research into pre-history and the study of savage cultures.

Let me demonstrate this briefly. For a long time the main anthropological game was the search for origins. "Primitive man," that is, primeval man, the missing link, had to be reconstructed. Modern savages provided us with the stage properties by which this reconstruction was carried out. Primitive man had to be very savage, he had to be amusing, but above all, he had to be painted very much in black and white, he had to present the clearcut character of "unspoilt human nature."

But here came the snag. Once you put the essentially wrong problem: "What is primitive man in his really original nature?" and once you assume that this nature must be very outspoken, you are likely to exaggerate any marked or striking feature into the dominant characteristic. Thus if we look through the theories of "original man" we can collect an amusing and kaleidoscopic variety of primitive silhouettes. We have the bloodthirsty savage who haunted many of the older accounts of primitive life, the missionaries' tales and the Red Indian stories. By contrast, such contemporary writers as Father W. Schmidt, Professor Elliot Smith and Dr. [William James] Perry have discovered the paradisiacal primitive man, puritanically chaste, kindhearted, and essentially peace-loving, a sort of pacifist who would walk straight up to Geneva and vote for universal disarmament. For a long time primeval man was denied all religion, he was a benighted heathen, the savage full of superstitions, and then we had a complete reversal; Andrew Lang discovered primitive monotheism, the good paters, Schmidt and Koppers, endowed him with high morality, strictly monogamous tendencies, and a completely Roman Catholic nature. At times, he was the cunning child of nature, and then again for variety's sake, M. [Lucien] Lévy-Bruhl made him into the prelogical mystic.

Thus we have a myth-making tendency which depicts to us the Golden Age or the natural state or the original nature of man in very firm outline.

Most incredible of all, then comes the cry of return to nature and of following the good example of unspoilt primitive character. No sooner does Dr. Perry tell us that primitive man is a pacifist than one of the leading minds of our age, Mr. G. Lowes Dickinson of Cambridge, whose work on pacifism is really constructive and respectworthy, cannot refrain from adding the naïve argument of "imitating the primitive pacifist" to his relevant cogent plea for disarmament. The late Dr. Rivers, a foremost anthropologist of the past generation and a truly brilliant thinker, advanced Socialism in England because he imagined that Melanesian savages were communists. One or two quite intelligent writers on Feminism have based their reformatory conclusions on the fact of primitive mother-right. Free love has been advocated for the last fifty years all over the world by pious references to primitive promiscuity.

All this is, to use an apt American expression, junk. The myth of a luminous past, however inspiring that may be, cannot be made to lighten our future, to serve as a beacon towards which humanity has to progress. It cannot be said too emphatically: First of all, we shall never be able to reconstruct man's original nature in one single term, or even in two or three terms; man has always been more or less what he is: a very complex creature, mixed of mind and spirit, of good and bad, of earthly lust and divine love, of destructive impulses and desires to build up—in short, the savage, the primitive, the man-ape, was probably very much as you and I are. In the second place, whatever primitive man might have been means nothing, absolutely nothing, to what he is going to become. We might quite as well preach cannibalism or the killing of aged parents, or the burning of widows or the carrying of skulls round the neck, because these customs are very likely to have been practised by the primitive man-ape.

There is now in progress a very decided revulsion among at least one school of anthropology—the Functional—against this retrospective precedent-making. The Functional school wants to place the science of man on a really scientific basis. Exactly as the chemist or physicist by experiment and comparative method constructs the laws of inanimate nature, as the biologist discovers the principles of the process in live matter, so the anthropologist should establish the laws of sociological and cultural process. This of course does not mean that the only task of anthropology is to establish the laws of development on a large scale, that is, either tracing it back to its origins, or else forecasting what may happen two thousand years hence. This ambitious task anthropology has undertaken and it has failed to carry out its undertaking. But even if it confines itself to a much less ambitious task, that of establishing the necessary relations between the various aspects of culture, religion, law, morality, social organisation, economics and so on; even if it is limited to showing the real nature of such institutions as marriage, the family, the state, the religious association, even then anthropology can supply us with the basis for most sociological and cultural problems of today, yesterday and tomorrow.

Functional Anthropology is, then, a determined effort to make the study of man into a science, and this can only be done by establishing the necessary concatenation between cultural facts and by establishing a law of culture. And here the anthropologist, and side by side with him the sociologist and historian, is seriously handicapped. The student of inanimate nature, as well as the man who experiments on guinea pigs, amoebas or plants, has his laboratory, but it is not possible to experiment on human beings—still less on human societies. We cannot stage mother-right in Bulgaria and strict patriarchal institutions in Iowa. We cannot have license and promiscuity in Spain and enforce strict chastity in Portugal: Portugal would rebel. Papal theocracy, lock, stock and Pius XI, cannot be transplanted to New Hampshire and a Soviet regime as a control established in Massachusetts. The only thing which remains for the social student is the comparative method. And here anthropology, the comparative study of cultures over the widest range possible, is a really scientific handmaid of social science. Are you interested in Communism? You want to know really whether this is a horrid invention of those devilish Bolsheviks; whether it originated in the fantasies of Marx, of Engels, or of St. Augustine—or perhaps whether it was invented by Plato. Well, cast a sweeping glance over Stone Age societies, over the kingdoms of Africa, the Pigmies, the Middle Cultures—and what will you find? In every human society there is a fair balance between individual property and the partial surrender for the common treasury, in co-operative work, in contributions, in taxation. "Communism" and "Individualism" are not inventions of philosophers; they are not black and white antitheses—though in this form they lend themselves to political vituperation. They are really correlated economic forces which have always to work conjointly. Functional Anthropology reveals to us that most of the social tendencies, of the political issues, of the economic forces, have been at work from the beginning. They certainly are to be found even in the lowest cultures. They assume different forms, they work through different mechanisms, but they are there. And from the way in which they have been working in the past we may learn something about the way in which they are likely to work in the future.

Instead, therefore, of preaching a return to precedent, Functional Anthropology teaches us by the experience of the past all about the working of human institutions, such as marriage, the family, the state, the co-operative group, the religious community. Functional Anthropology reveals to us the universal features of human society. It shows us what the main business of cultures has been throughout humanity; how this business has been carried on; what mechanisms have been at work. Instead of telling us fairy tales about what had been once upon a time, it simply gives us an insight into the working of human society, of human culture, of the human mind. It is far less amusing—this has to be confessed at once—than the old fairy-tale anthropology. But science is not one of those things which makes life exciting. Science, with its sober determinism, with its less and less pretentious range of questions, with its reduction of everything to a diagrammatic treatment—science has been weeding the adventurous, the romantic, the unexpected, out of life. I shrink and shudder at the idea of what science will make out of life if it ever becomes applied to life. Anthropology has been for a long time the stronghold of the romantic, anti-scientific spirit and that wonderful antiquarianism which gave us beautiful day-dreams about primitive man. I love the old anthropology, and, alas, have to be one of its destroyers.

Let us return to marriage. Functional Anthropology teaches us that marriage is as marriage does. It does not, of course, maintain that marriage has always been exactly as it is now and with us. Marriage has changed widely. But through all the changes and vicissitudes, all history, all development, all geographical setting, the family and marriage still remain the same twin institutions; they still emerge as a stable group showing throughout the same fundamental features—a group consisting of father, of mother and of children, forming a joint household, co-operating economically, united by a contract and surrounded by religious sanctions which make the family into a moral unit.

The position which I and other anthropologists working in the Functional spirit and by the Functional method have arrived at is one of synthesis, though not of compromise. It is so much so that we have all been misunderstood by either side and accused either as reactionary obscurantists or else as aggressive demoralisers. One or two documents might be of interest.

Says Professor Edward Sapir, one of America's foremost anthropologists: "The present sex unrest has been nibbling at more or less reliable information reported by anthropologists from primitive communities. Any primitive community that indulges or is said to indulge in unrestricted sex behaviour is considered an interesting community to hear from." Since I am one of those who collected this "more or less reliable information" and have written the "excited books about pleasure-loving . . . Trobriand Islanders"—to quote the stigmatising expressions of Professor Sapir—I have to bear part at least of the censure which my learned colleague metes out to those who use anthropology as a means of perverting the young. My critic seems to forget that in my "excited books" I have insisted on the fact that "Trobrianders have as many rules of decency and decorum as they have liberties and indulgences," and that far from trying to be "exciting" or unsettling, I have made it clear that the "best way to approach sexual morality in an entirely different culture is to remember that the sexual impulse is never entirely free, neither can it ever be completely enslaved by social imperatives." I have certainly not described my "primitive community" as "indulging in unrestricted sex behaviour," but Professor Sapir would appear to class me with the Impuritans and Anthropological Perverters.

On the other hand, only a few weeks ago a distinguished publicist, speaking about my opinions on marriage past and present, wrote: "If, as Professor Malinowski seems to argue, our modern system is so rooted in the immemorial tradition as to be part of human nature itself—and even of animal nature, too—then it would be rash to tamper with it lightly, lest we undermine the whole foundations of society." And the same publicist labels me as representing the "Fundamentalist attitude" in that I maintain "that marriage always has been and should be as it is." And yet another publicist, this time an extreme prophet of Misbehaviourism, describes the plight of the modern emancipated woman, "who is told by Professor Malinowski, or some other Adam-and-Eve anthropologist, that the family is the foundation of human society." Classing me with Dean Inge, Professor Westermarck and Jix (Mr. Joynson-Hicks, now Lord Brentford, sometime Home Secretary of Great Britain), he laments that "the appalling wreckage of human lives which is the outcome of those fantastic views is beyond computation." And he indicts me among others in the final anathema: "Classic authorities on the history of human marriage have more to answer for than Spanish Grand Inquisitors. Their hands are imbrued with blood and tears." Now there may be some comfort to be had from being hit by both sides, from being alternately labelled as Arch-Immoralist and Grand Inquisitor of Puritanism: truth is unpleasant to all who think in extremes, and he who speaks the truth will not be popular with either side, who believe in having the monopoly. Now it may be amusing to be misinterpreted, misquoted and cudgelled by any extremist (though as a matter of fact I should like to add that Professor Edward Sapir is not an extremist and that his views on marriage, family, and sex are entirely in agreement with mine, and his slight slap at me I regard as uncalled for). But, after all, when you write books you want them to be not only read and misquoted, but understood. Besides the flattery of invective I sometimes wish also for the prosaic but satisfying compliment of sympathetic understanding and assent. So let me indulge in another day-dream: I shall imagine the Functional Anthropologist surrounded by a misguided but intelligent crowd of modern flappers and pseudo-Bolshevists, Impuritans and Feminists, Introverts and Misbehaviourists. They all listen to the Functional Anthropologist, lap up his words, take them to heart, and come out wiser and better people. The Modern Man starts on marriage: "The whole thing hardly seems worth wasting one's breath over. Your orthodox Christian marriage with its claptrap of religious junk, vindictive legal interference and coercion is an intolerable

burden. . . . Are we going to allow this ramshackle affair to strangle
personal happiness, to interfere with social advances? Or shall we finally
put it on a rational basis? There would seem good and fine things to be
jettisoned with it, no doubt. Some of them are probably due to mere
sentimentalising from which it is difficult for us to rid ourselves. Some
are mere Pauline perversions, or survivals from that horrid destructive
Puritanism which had its virtues, but which now has become sheer vice.
Can you give me a single intelligent reason why human affection should
be submitted to law or personal choice to the ceremonial approval of a
bevy of clergymen; or the uniting of personalities be made the object of
an economic bargain?"

"Your arguments," replied the Functional Anthropologist, "have, in
spite of their rhetorical setting, a great deal of truth in them. It is quite
true that the modern law of divorce, let us say, is both immoral and
vindictive. In the majority of cases obviously false evidence has to be
staged in order to dissolve marriages which should be dissolved because
they do not work and cannot work. But the real question is whether we
shall spill the child with the bath, and, because legislation in certain
states of the Union and in certain European countries is silly on one point
or another, whether in order to improve it we shall destroy the family and
marriage."

Absolute monogamy—away with it!

"There is no need to destroy marriage!" the Modern Man replied. "It has
destroyed itself. It is a compound of anachronisms, of survivals. As an
anthropologist, you ought to know it best. Take love and the law. At the
beginning of things love was satisfied to the full measure in primeval
promiscuity, and law did not interfere, since there was no institution of
marriage at all. Under matriarchal conditions, women chose their lovers
but were not submitted to their husbands. This we can and should imitate.
Law became only necessary when under patriarchal tyranny women were
made into chattels and were traded into the possession of the male. What
made everything wrong was the influence of religion—above all, of Christianity. Primitive marriage is never religious, as Franz Boas has told us:
'The religious sanction of marriage exists in hardly any primitive tribe.' "

"On this point I am forced to dissent from the opinion, even though it
has been given by a real and a great anthropologist like Franz Boas. I
have also emphatically to disagree with him when he tells us that 'the
customs of mankind show that permanent marriage is not based primarily
on the permanence of sexual love between two individuals, but that it is
essentially regulated by economic considerations. Formal marriage is connected with transfer of property, for it is obvious that you would at once
make an attempt to apply it to modern conditions.' "

4*

"Certainly," said the Modern Man. "If we want to base modern marriage on love, on which it never has been based before—if we want to make it into something better than a bargain—we have to destroy the whole patriarchal tissue of lies and laws, whether bolstered up by St. Paul's Epistles or the Old Testament, or the writings of Professor Westermarck. May I quote once more the conclusion of our greatest American anthropologist, whose learning, competence and value you yourself recognise fully? 'Instability is found as much in modern civilization as in simpler societies. Man is evidently not an absolutely monogamous being. The efforts to force man into absolute monogamy have never been successful. . . .' "

"This is a most unfortunately worded generalization—especially unfortunate since it comes from Franz Boas. It is based on the usual dialectic trick: you erect a straw enemy and destroy him after a short but somewhat inglorious fight. 'Absolute monogamy' is an ideal, and a good ideal at that, but in my opinion the history of human marriage is not a series of erroneous and futile efforts at 'forcing man into absolute monogamy.' We have rather before us a variety of forms, and the study of these tells us that the fundamental, ever-recurring form of marriage is monogamy in the sense of an individual legal contract between one man and one woman; that this fundamental form is the only one which works satisfactorily; that it is at the base of all the combined forms, including polygyny and polyandry; and that all evolution tends more and more towards the monogamous form of marriage.

The five matrimonial errors of anthropology

"Small wonder that anthropology has become discredited in its application to modern life. The arguments which you have given me, and which are constantly being used, are one and all based on anthropological fallacies. It is untrue that marriage ever has been or could have been an exclusively economic bargain. It is untrue that there are any indications of a primitive state of wholesale promiscuity. It is untrue that marriage in the past has ever been in any community a loveless, cold-blooded contract. It is untrue that there has ever been a pure matriarchal stage. Finally, it is blatantly false that marriage in any community has lacked religious sanctions. I cannot understand how an anthropologist of the measure of Franz Boas could have committed himself to such a statement.

"And not only that," continued the Functional Anthropologist. "Holding this bag of anthropological tricks in one hand, you are not satisfied with using them consistently, but even as you produce them you juggle them and turn them either way to suit your argument. At times you dangle the 'primeval custom' before our eyes as a valuable precedent: let us have promiscuity, because the man-ape was promiscuous; let us desentimentalize marriage, because it was not originally a sentimental arrangement; let us abolish coercion because primitive man was free to mate as he liked. As soon, however, as you take an objection to some institution or other, you brandish it before us as a repellent relic of savage barbarism. The economic side of marriage, the coercion of the woman, does not please you. It is a survival from horrid patriarchal marriage and ought to be abolished. We must get rid of the superstitions of the Australian aborigines and the mid-Victorian gentleman, you argue at once. You don't like the religious side of marriage. It would probably simply be wasting my breath on you if I wanted to prove that Boas is wrong and that in fact marriage throughout humanity is essentially a religious sacrament, because you would simply tell me: 'That is another reason for doing away with religious sanctions. It was good for the superstitious savage, but not for us enlightened people.' "

Marriage—a cocktail or a symphony?

Somewhat cornered, the Modern Man replied: "Your argument so far is mainly negative. But supposing even that you know better than any one of your predecessors and colleagues, what is your view of marriage? What morals can you draw from the past for the present and the future?"

"Well, the most important truth is that marriage has always been a combination, a synthesis of elements. In every form of primitive marriage there are the elements of love and of free choice, but also economic considerations, usually accompanied by elaborate legal contracts and associated with religious sanctions. Marriage was always of necessity a compromise—and a compromise does not give you the full measure of a snake-proof Garden-of-Eden happiness."

"In other words, your whole philosophy boils down to saying that marriage is a cocktail of all things, good and bad, pleasant and otherwise, sweet and bitter. We have to gulp it down—is it as a tonic, or for mixed pleasure, or perhaps as an appetiser?" asked the Ironical Young Lady.

"A harmony or a symphony or even a cocktail if you like—even a cocktail can be good, though I as a good European have never yet condescended to like any one. But it is not the mixed or compound character of marriage that I stress—it is the permanent constitution of the compound. If marriage under a variety of conditions has always had this strange combination of legal coercion as well as of personal choice, there is obviously something inherently necessary in this combination. It cannot be an anomaly of Elizabethan Puritanism or the rulings of the Council of Trent, or of mid-Victorian prudery. We are led to enquire into why marriage should be at the same time a mystic bond of personal affection and a coercive chain of legal ruling. And again, if we find that the biological urge to mate, which is so often given an extremely wide range of satisfaction, still leads people to surrender their personal liberty to the bond of marriage, surely we must conclude once more that marriage satisfies some other needs besides that of sexual union.

The return to suttee

"And then," continued the Functional Anthropologist, "this question of a religious intervention. The anthropologist, however learned, may have his moments of oblivion. To say that marriage has no religious sanctions in any primitive community is probably based on the fallacy of identifying the religious character of marriage with the wedding ceremony. The wedding act itself is very often disconcertingly simple and 'secular.' I have myself seen natives of Melanesia taking what is to them a most momentous step in life by the simple act of sitting together on either side of a large wooden platter and eating a few baked yams with one another. But the same people, as soon as the wife became pregnant, went through a strict discipline of ethical taboos, kept under a religious sanction. They both became enmeshed in a series of magical performances; they entered en rapport with the spiritual world of supernatural beings. When the child was born they had to carry out in virtue of their marriage contract a series of religious ceremonies soon after the birth and periodically during the various crises of their offspring's life. Finally, when separated by death, the survivor had again to document the religious nature of marriage by acting as chief mourner. And this is the pattern of the religious aspect of marriage in most communities. But of an exclusively secular marriage in a primitive community I have never heard—nor can I conceive of it."

"And what is the moral to be drawn from that?" asked one of the audience. "Do you want us to return to a fully religious type of marriage —introduce perhaps suttee—and submit our marriage laws to a new Grand Inquisition?"

"I do not think so. All my lessons are indirect and not by return to precedent. The universal religious character of marriage is to me mainly relevant as a symptom of the high value in which marriage is held by every community. The main function of religion is to hall-mark certain contracts, certain arrangements; to make them important and ethically binding. You modern people may have decided completely to jettison formal religion. Have you also discredited all moral attitudes? Have you lost all sense of value and sanctity? If so, there is no common matter for our discussion, so I shall assume the contrary. But if you have values left, can you not understand that the main lesson—and an entirely rational lesson— to be drawn from anthropology is that the institution of marriage has had this enormous value to all human communities however primitive?"

"Yes, but what is the raison d'être of this high value set on marriage?

Have we not done in our modern world with the motives as well as the forms?"

Flapper v. fetish of sentiment

"Yes," added the Flapper, who had been listening and now joined in the discussion. "We have lost your great fetish of matrimonial sanctity—the sacred, sentimental love. You have sanctified love by making it into a forbidden fruit with sex as its core. Sex is the most forbidden part of the forbidden fruit. With all its sanctity you moralists could never swallow it. It did stick in your throat—Adam's apple, the symbol of patriarchal hypocrisy. We have completely transformed love—we have made it into pleasurable love-making. And there are no precedents to teach us anything. Your anthropology breaks down completely at this point. Birth control, the equality of sexes, economic independence of women, are brand new. We have to create an entirely new world for the new, free, love."

"But that is an old story." The Functional Anthropologist smiled at the Flapper. "The oldest story of all—that of the new generation creating always a new world for the first time. Your experimental love-making based on equality of sex, on contraception or avoidance of physiological results, and on economic independence, has a very long history. The pattern of behaviour which allows a free pre-nuptial unchastity is well known not only to the anthropologist who has studied the world of islands scattered over the Pacific, or the African societies, or any part of the primitive world for that matter, but also to anyone who knows the life of European peasantry with their 'trial nights,' their 'window visits,' their finding out not only whether two people are physiologically well suited, but whether they can produce a child together.

"And the story is always the same," went on the Functional Anthropologist. "In the long run, the young people, free to mate at will, become tired of change, of mere sexual pleasure, and it grows stale on them even as petting parties grow stale and sterile after a time. In our community, since there is a stigma attached to the system, since it very often goes hand in hand with alcoholic poisoning and an abnormal life, many people go under. In a primitive community, where personal sensibilities are lower, where the whole arrangement is traditionally sanctioned, the process runs smoothly. Young people sow their wild oats gradually and naturally. They cast off the surfeit of sex with experimental dabbling in sex, and they gradually find out that erotic approaches only have value when they are accompanied by a real attachment, by the charm which comes from congenial personality and the affection which clings to the right sort of character. And the social system expresses and sanctions this natural trend of psychological affairs. A liaison of long standing is expected to mature into marriage."

The importance of being married

"I still can't understand," said the Flapper, impressed but not convinced, "why these people marry at all."

"There is some surface mystery about it, but if you observe any native tribe or any European peasants, or even your friends in the free communities of the Petting Tribe in our culture, you will find the same phenomena. There is a desire for a full, open, public declaration of the fact that I and my lover are lovers; that nobody else should interfere between us; that we have legal rights to one another."

"But that simply is possessive jealousy," said the Flapper, at once roused into moral indignation and feminine protest as this horrid word, the symbol of patriarchal tyranny, formed in her speech centres.

"Certainly, if you wish to call it by this name. Jealousy is one of the most fundamental sentiments of man and woman alike. I have done my field work in a matriarchal community with as much freedom given to sexual impulses as anywhere else in the world, with as high position given to woman and as much economic independence secured to her in marriage as has ever been recorded—and yet, there, men and women, when really in love, were morbidly, passionately jealous of each other. Their jealousy might bend before custom, but it was always there. And since custom guaranteed exclusive sexual rights only after marriage, two young people, after they became certain that they loved each other, always wanted to marry. They wanted to declare their love publicly. They wanted to be certain of each other's permanent affections. Nothing would satisfy them but marriage. And marriage gave them also the full status in society. And this, by the way, is not the exception, but the universal rule among all primitive communities. A man is not a full member of the tribe before he marries, and a woman who is a spinster is an anomaly—a monster in fact. So much so that she does not exist. One of the most profound differences between primitive and civilised societies is that there are no unmarried people among the so-called savage and barbarous nations of the world."

"Where is all this leading to?" asked the Flapper, half puzzled, half ironical.

"There are several conclusions to be drawn. For the moment I was trying to show to you that the legal contract—that is, the public act declaring mutual appropriation—is not a pathological outgrowth of puritanism, since it exists among the most non-puritanical communities. Love, by its very nature, tends to be mixed up with law. Society—and by this I don't mean a super-personal being, but the integral of the various moral and cultural forces embodied in tradition—society then decrees that in order to be a full member of a tribe a man must marry, and a woman must become a wife. And this traditional force of law, order and morality decrees also that marriage must be distinct, sharply demarcated from an ordinary liaison."

"What do you mean by this?"

"Well, in the first place, marriage gives entirely different privileges to both partners. Even when, as in the various non-puritanical communities, two people are known to live together as lovers and fully allowed to do so, they do not receive any guarantee of permanence and exclusiveness until they are married. In the second place, the act of marriage changes what was a simple, personal relationship into a sociological event. Marriage usually implies a considerable amount of economic contribution from the family of either consort and the establishment of an independent household, of which the man becomes the master and woman the mistress. Marriage thus gives to man and woman a sphere of action, of influence, which they desire to have, but—and this is the most important thing to remember—in this new establishment both partners have to work together. They know it well, and they chose each other on account of their compatibility of character. The blending of sexual attraction with the deeper values of personality lies in the very nature of marriage."

Bigger and better petting parties

"But," said the Flapper pensively, "what you seem to advocate there is Bigger and Better petting parties on the Trobriand pattern. Shall we have our marriage organised by allowing young people to mate promiscuously and gradually to select each other by trial and error? If this is your argument you don't seem to differ profoundly from the Misbehaviourists against whom you seem to have been inveighing."

"If I were to advise you to imitate my Trobrianders or any other savage tribe it would only be if you chose to adopt their whole cultural outlook, their limited range of emotions, the coarseness and one-sidedness of their physiological equipment. In fact, knowing that you are racially not a Trobriander I should say that you would run the risk of moral and emotional bankruptcy if you were to imitate them. You modern people preach the building up of human personality and yet you wish to destroy marriage, the relationship in which personality is best expressed; and parenthood, the relationship in which the building up of new personalities is vested."

The anthropologist, the sensible woman, birth control

Here, at this last sentence, a stray figure entered into the discussion—a lonely figure, the Sensible Woman.

"It seems strange," she said, "that, speaking as an anthropologist, you only now touch upon what to me seems the capital point in marriage—that is, children. Surely you can't discuss the relationship of human mating without thinking of its fruits."

"This," replied the Anthropologist, "is quite true. One of the most mysterious rules of primitive life is that an unmarried woman must not become pregnant, even as we in our society—or let us better say in that of our mothers or grandmothers—would always condone more easily a 'false step' if it did not lead to its natural consequences. Savages usually allow as much sexual liberty as you like, but penalize premarital pregnancy."

"Surely" (here the Birth Control Expert became interested) "this must mean that they know of some means of contraception?"

"Not necessarily. In my own field work I came in contact with communities where unmarried motherhood was very much looked askance at. Remarkably enough, very few girls conceived before marriage, and yet I am absolutely sure that they knew of no contraceptives."

"How do you explain it?"

"I cannot explain it. I know that abortion is sometimes practised which stops short pre-nuptial pregnancy. The natives are not aware of the physiological consequences of intercourse. They explain pregnancy as due to spiritual influences, and against this physiological background they construct a plausible theory of how an ancestral spirit waits until the girl is married. They also have a vague feeling that pre-nuptial conception is a punishment for too much wantonness. But in reality the only explanation that I can offer is that when a young girl from maturity, or even before, practises promiscuous intercourse, she does not conceive. When, with marriage, she is confined to one male, fertility again returns. In some communities, such as those of Polynesia, I am told, rude primitive contraceptives are known, and there certainly abortion is practised on an extensive scale. In other tribes the erotic interests of unmarried people are satisfied without leading to full consummation. In other tribes again, the association between marriage and pregnancy is brought about by the most direct logical, and let us add, charitable rule. As soon as the woman conceives she has to be married by her lover. Since in most of these communities children are an asset and not a liability this rule is enforced by positive inducement and not by penal sanctions.

"But right through a whole range of human societies the principle of legitimacy, the rule that child-bearing requires a male partner, the legal head and guardian of the children, is universal. This rule is really the basis of family life. It declares that the group of mother and child is not complete without the male; that the full procreative group is the family consisting of husband, wife and children."

The masculine matriarch

At this point the formidable figure of the Professing Feminist closed in upon the discussion:

"All this might have been very well among savages, but we modern

women want above all to eliminate the male. If we choose we still shall
have children, but they will be anonymous babies by an anonymous
father."

"Then you want," replied presently the Anthropologist, "a return to the
glorious tradition of the matriarchal past. You want to return to that
feminine society conjured up by the creative imagination of Bachofen and
recently presented in a rehashed and somewhat garbled form by that
publicistic, pseudo-prophet of false feminism, Dr. Briffault."

Here the Sensible Woman interposed: "No, we modern women aspire to
real feminism. The man-aping feminist—the Masculine Matriarch—pays
only lip-service to womanhood. In reality she wants to enslave us to the
masculine ideal. We true feminists don't try to raise the dignity of woman
by eliminating her essential rôles in society. On the contrary, we want to
secure her a position in modern life in that capacity in which she need
not imitate man any more than she can be imitated by him. We want the
woman, as the mother, to dictate some at least of our new laws and new
ideals."

"With this point of view I am fully in sympathy," hastened to add the
Functional Anthropologist. "Some women at least will still desire to become mothers—not all, perhaps, but quite enough to prevent the disappearance of our race. Let us concentrate our attention on them. Will
these women desire also to look after their own children—to be real
mothers—or will they be prepared to hand over the fruit of their love,
of their suffering, the most precious part of their bodily self and of their
sentiments, to some state institution, to a communistic baby farm?

"The teaching of genuine anthropology is that the whole idea of group
marriage and group maternity is preposterous. On the contrary, one of
the most significant quaint and incredible customs of primitive man is
the *couvade,* a custom according to which the husband at childbirth
mimics the physiological disabilities of his wife—goes to bed swooning, his
limbs swaddled, demanding tender cares, potions and a whole show of
anxiety, while his wife briskly gets up from childbed, takes up domestic
duties, and even looks after him. The *couvade* in its outspoken forms is
scattered over the world, but not universal. What is universal is the strict
solidarity of husband and wife during gestation, at childbirth and afterwards. The husband shares in his wife's pregnancy taboos. He plays an
important part at childbirth, warding off the dangers, counteracting the
evil magic. And he takes an active share in the tender care of the infant."

"And what is the lesson of all this?" snorted the Aggressive Feminist.

"The lesson is that the legal 'shackles,' that all the economic burdens
and liabilities, that all the apparatus of a united household—that all this
is not an artificial and unnecessary ingredient of modern marriage. Love
and courtship, as we have seen, lead naturally to permanent cohabitation
based on a legal contract. This contract is necessary because love naturally

leads to the production of children, and children, when produced, must be cared for, cannot be thrown on the rubbish heap or thrown onto the communal care of the Tribe or Society. The mother is the person physiologically designated to do this, to look after it tenderly, to give it all that it needs in nourishment, in emotion, in education, and the man associated with her in love-making has also an innate emotional response which is culturally affirmed in these pregnancy and post-natal observances which we have been discussing. The strong sentiment of paternity makes him respond naturally and take over the rôle of joint partner and protector of his pregnant wife and later of her offspring. Thus we have what you like to call legal coercion, and what more correctly is mutual security due to an open and public contract inevitably associated with the full expression of sexual love. But man cannot live by love alone—still less can woman and her children. An economic basis is necessary for the family. Marriage is inevitably an economic partnership for the common running and provision of the household. Economics is not the prime mover, but an inevitable element of marriage."

"And sure enough—as I had expected you to do—in your argument you have dropped out religion," chipped in the Modern Man, not without irony.

"Religion comes in, as it naturally must, wherever human relations are put to great emotional strain, while, at the same time, based on strong passions and emotional tendencies. Laws and customs with their sanctions and coercive forces can compel people to carry out definite tangible elementary services, but law cannot penetrate the nooks and corners of sentimental life. Definite moral laws based on supernatural sanctions supply the only suitable force on which marriage and parenthood can be based. If we take religion in the widest sense—that is, a system of values based on deep conviction—all personal human relations of this stable and integral nature will have to be submitted to religion."

Behaviourist: "You have been speaking all the time as if Behaviourism had not come to change all our outlook on human nature. You speak of paternal instinct as well as maternal instinct. We know now that all this is nonsense. J. B. Watson has convincingly proved that there are only two real instincts: the shrinking from contact with a frog and the reflex of clutching when a baby is dropped from a height of twenty yards into a cold bath."

"I am not quite convinced yet by the gospel of the Behaviourists," replied the Anthropologist. "But I did not speak of any instincts. Nothing is as destructive of sound psychological thinking as either to believe that all these are 'instincts' or else to believe that human nature is indefinitely plastic. There may be innate tendencies which, under any social and cultural conditions, inevitably integrate into certain patterns. My reading of human history is that the highly complex and certainly not instinctive

attitudes of individual maternity and individual fatherhood are such inevitable patterns or sentiments. I believe that they are deeply correlated
with the structure, not only of our society and Christian culture, but of
every society that ever has existed. I find that it is in the inevitable
concatenation of sexual attraction with deeper personal attraction, desire
to mate with the desire to bring forth children, all the physiological facts
of parenthood with the emotional response to children—I believe that it
is in this concatenation that the strength of marriage and the family lies.
Why, look all around us. With all the facilities of safe and easy satisfaction of lust, with all the preaching about freedom and the need to be
happy, with all the real economic independence of men and women—why,
people should avoid marriage like pestilence. Statistics ought to register
not only a falling birth rate, but the disappearance of registered marriages. Do we find anything of the sort? On the contrary. The mystery
of people still marrying—and divorcing too, certainly, but remarrying
again—people having children, people submitting to all this terrible evil
of married life—this is the real problem, and the answer to the problem I
think I have indicated. You will have to give it yourselves from your
personal experiences and actions."

Modern hetairism

Here a new figure entered the lists, the intelligent and level-headed Man
of the World:

"On the whole, I tend to agree with you. But this is not very helpful
yet—not to me, at least. Your conclusions are conservative and so is all
my personal bias, but after all we have to recognize that things have
changed. You have spoken yourself about the fact that the savages tried
love and mating in a way which does not recommend itself to our tastes.
Where should we move as regards the mere fact of love and sexual relations? You have also indicated that at one point at least there is an unprecedented change in our community. No savages tolerate the bachelor
and the spinster: there are no unmarried people. This I believe, not only
on your authority but from all I have heard, to be exactly true. But we
have now large sections of our community who remain unmarried. What
about them? Are we going to preach to them simply that marriage is
the only goal and the only satisfaction of instinctive drives—that the
family is the best? They have had this preaching for a long time, and
now there are good grounds for assuming that the teaching will gradually
lose influence. We have another tendency in our modern times—a tendency
less established so far, in fact without any rights of citizenship, but a
pronounced tendency nevertheless—I mean the recognition that some
people are not attracted by the other sex at all, but must find happiness
in homosexual friendships. What have you got to say about this problem?"

"I am quite prepared to take up your challenge. In fact I think you have set the problem in absolutely the correct terms. I believe that, with reference to the whole business of procreation, we are rapidly progressing towards what might be called a specific stratification by innate endowment, by the balance between passion and sentiment and by the relation between emotional life and what might be called constructive ambition. I think in the first place—and I have already indicated it—that the gradual absorption of human personality by intellectual work, by political constructive ambitions, by the mere interest in the technique of modern culture, I believe that all this has relegated the physiological interests to a secondary place. At least, these physiological interests are directly in conflict with the active life of a man or a woman immersed in civilization.

"I think that here again, as in every problem which has to do with reproduction, women must be considered first. There are now some women who either have not enough initial interest in maternity or early become absorbed in other pursuits, who do not want to become mothers. Should they be debarred from sex? I personally should answer in the negative. I think that such women have the full right to be happy in their own way. Anyhow, what is the use of arguing about it. Unless we instituted a morality police which would employ half the population of the world to spy on the other half's private doings, unless we instituted key-hole peeping and dirty linen nosing legislation, compared with which the prohibition laws are supremely logical and easily enforceable, unless we prostituted the state in order to protect prostitution and penalize free love, we should be for ever powerless to deal with the free sexual life of the independent woman. We do not expect the modern bachelor to be chaste and innocent, a St. Joseph or St. Stanislas. We have not many illusions—still fewer moral indignations—about the actual virginity of the modern latch-key girl. The class of people who can and do carry on free love already does exist."

"What do you think of Judge Lindsey's 'companionate marriage'?" asked the Flapper.

"Personally I believe that the institutional changes which go under this label are the soundest. I admire Judge Ben B. Lindsey as a staunch fellow-conservative. The advantage of companionate marriage is that it represents the institutionalized, straightforward, honest form of what is already going on in a clandestine and therefore dishonest and uncontrollable manner. Companionate marriage would also allow young people to test the chances of making a success of real marriage. But even the companionate marriage imposes shackles and introduces difficulties which the extreme type of bachelor or spinster psychology would like to eschew.

Stratified morality

"I believe that in due course what will happen is a change in our moral outlook. We shall introduce what might be called stratified morality as well as stratified institutions. The reproductive group—that is, men and women who are prepared to carry on the race, to look after the children and to lead the fullest physiological life—will, I believe, have the premium of natural virtue. That is, they will achieve the fullest measure of human happiness. Yet, with all this, the reproductive group will claim special privileges. Already now there is—to start at the crudest end—discriminative taxation against unmarried people in some countries. In this context I am prepared to give three cheers for Mussolini, small as is our mental and emotional affinity in most other matters. The group of people who need modern conditions can form liaisons and refuse to accept any consequences. They will have to be submitted to greater taxation, to higher exactions of public services and, perhaps, to certain political and social disabilities. I hope they will. Finally, if the claims of the homosexuals are justified, there should be laws which allow them to live happily within a sphere of arrangements in which they are protected from the inevitable odium of the normal sections and at the same time not tempted to infect the others.

"The greatest difficulty for the future which I foresee is some sort of boundaries or isolating layers which would protect the several types stratified by reference to reproduction from each other. For there is no doubt that monogamous morality suffers by contact with the ethics of free love and is driven into retaliating in turn with scorn and moral abuse, with attempts at puritanical police measures, with censorship and the brandishing of taboos. Both sides have legitimate grievances. Is it possible for them to come to terms?"

Facts v. a fool's paradise

"What you say here," rejoined the Man of the World, "is no doubt true enough. But do you imagine three states within the state or three organized groups within each society—the Reproductive Kingdom, the Free Love Republic, and the Homosexual Soviets? This seems to me fantastic."

"No," answered the Anthropologist, "you take me too concretely and literally. I only want to draw your attention to certain facts and ask the question, Are we going to live in a fool's paradise and preach the absolute sanctity of monogamy, brand contraception as 'criminal practices,' talk about the 'new and utterly perverse morality' when the slightest departure from the rigorous canons of Christian marriage is meant, and stupify our moral conscience by this sort of talk while the 'hateful abominations' are going on all around us, and are going on without truly injuring anybody's health, happiness, digestion or spiritual integrity? The terms of invective I have borrowed, as you no doubt recognise, from the last Encyclical Letter of my friend Pius XI. I am afraid I cannot commend him for this latest production of his. This ostrich policy will prevent us from seeing clearly two or three points on which I have insisted. First of all, namely, that the business of reproduction requires a well-established and safely legalized institution of family and marriage. In the second place, that this institution in modern conditions does need additional privileges and an additional bolstering, not only by nice words, but by definite discriminative enactments in its favour. And finally, that there is need for some sort of protective tolerance all round in order to prevent the spread of the infection of moral censure and the infection of moral laxity from one camp to the other."

Fed up with democracy

"But are you not working directly against all the modern trend towards levelling, which is towards complete uniformity—towards one standard for everybody and everything?"

"I think this tendency is already beginning to spend itself. Democracy has not made the world safe for us to live in. It is difficult to imagine even now the same social circle embracing Al Capone and Mahatma Gandhi, D. H. Lawrence and Jix, Henry Ford and Stalin. The driving force of democratic levelling was the abolition, first of all, of hereditary privileged classes, and later of distinctions by wealth and by inherited economic privilege. The levelling has gone too far, beyond the limits of fairness and decency, of justice and real needs. The levelling has degraded man to a spare part in the senseless machinery. The revolt against it must come. We are in fact stratified by taste, by culture, by temperament. I prefer the Viennese Waltz, you prefer the vulgar ragtimes, and a third man may prefer a symphony of Beethoven. Shall we all be compelled to endure the endless drone of international jazz? Can we not have each our own circle and our own institutions in which we can exercise our tastes? The uniformity of fashion, of food and drink (or its absence), the uniformity introduced by the mass production of the cheapest or 'best' brands of everything has attacked and perhaps hopelessly destroyed any differentiation in externals. Are we going to allow this destructive levelling to enter into the most personal of our interests? Are we all going to be made promiscuous by command, or monogamous by law? My belief is that in its very nature marriage is fundamental and permanent, but marriage will never be easy. There is not one simple formula for making it perfect. Whether you follow Bertrand Russell or St. Paul, whether you believe in Judge Lindsey or in St. Joseph, you always have to fight your own personal battle. But as an institution for the regulation of the reproductive process marriage will, I believe, win the day. But with all due deference to traditional morality I see forces in the modern world which will demand an independent and just treatment of unmarried love and perhaps even of homosexual love side by side with the standardized institutions. When they receive this just and fair treatment the now rebellious classes may, I hope, become less aggressive and less destructive to what is to me most valuable in human society: reproduction, marriage, the family and the home."

5

PIONEERS IN THE STUDY OF SEX AND MARRIAGE

SIGMUND FREUD

Psycho-analysis and anthropology

The infection by psycho-analysis of the neighbouring fields of science—notably that of anthropology, folklore, and sociology—has been a very rapid and somewhat inflammatory process. The votaries of Freud, or some among them, have displayed in their missionary zeal an amount of dogmatism and of aggressiveness not calculated to allay the prejudice and suspicion which usually greet every new extension of their theories. Some of their critics, on the other hand, go so far as to dismiss all anthropological contributions of Freud and his school as "utterly preposterous" and "obviously futile," as "an intrigue with Ethnology which threatens disaster to both parties," as "a striking demonstration of *reductio ad absurdum*." [1] This is a harsh judgment and it carries much weight, coming from one by no means hostile to psycho-analysis and thoroughly well acquainted with anthropological problems, especially those discussed by Freud and his school. This seems the right moment to consider impartially, without enthusiasm or prejudice, the scope, importance, and value of Freud's contribution to anthropology.

Through the initiative and under the direction of Prof. [C. G.] Seligman, who at that time was engaged in practical psycho-analysis of war neuroses, I have been able to apply some of Freud's conclusions directly to savage psychology and customs, while actually engaged in field-work among the natives of Eastern New Guinea.

This Letter to the Editor appeared in Nature, *November 3, 1923 (Vol. 112, No. 2818), pp. 650–51, and is reprinted by permission.*
[1] Prof. G. Elliot Smith, in Rivers's *Psychology and Politics*, 1923, pp. 141–45.

Freud's fundamental conception of the Oedipus complex contains a sociological as well as a psychological theory. The psychological theory declares that much, if not all of human mental life has its root in infantile tendencies of a "libidinous" character, repressed later on in childhood by the paternal authority and the atmosphere of the patriarchal family life. Thus there is formed a "complex" in the unconscious mind of a parricidal and "matrogamic" nature. The sociological implications of this theory indicate that throughout the development of humanity there must have existed the institution of individual family and marriage, with the father as a severe, nay, ferocious patriarch, and with the mother representing the principles of affection and kindness. Freud's anthropological views stand and fall with Westermarck's theory of the antiquity and permanence of individual and monogamous marriage. Freud himself assumes the existence, at the outset of human development, of a patriarchal family with a tyrannical and ferocious father who repressed all the claims of the younger men.[2] With the hypothesis of a primitive promiscuity or group marriage, Freud's theories are thoroughly incompatible, and in this they have the support, not only of Westermarck's classical researches, but also of the most recent contributions to our knowledge of primitive sexual life.

When we come to examine in detail the original constitution of the human family—not in any hypothetical primeval form, but as we find it in actual observation among present-day savages—some difficulties emerge. We find, for example, that there is a form of matriarchal family in which the relations between children and progenitors do not exist in the typical form as required by Freud's hypothesis of the Oedipus complex. Taking as an example the family as found in the coral archipelagoes of Eastern New Guinea, where I have studied it, the mother and her brother possess in it all the legal *potestas*. The mother's brother is the "ferocious matriarch," the father is the affectionate friend and helper of his children. He has to win for himself the friendship of his sons and daughters, and is frequently their amicable ally against the principle of authority represented by the maternal uncle. In fact, none of the domestic conditions required for the sociological fulfilment of the Oedipus complex, with its repressions, exist in the Melanesian family of Eastern New Guinea, as I shall show fully in a book shortly to be published on the sexual life and family organisation of these natives.

Again, the sexual repression within the family, the taboo of incest, is mainly directed towards the separation of brother and sister, although it also divides mother and son sexually. Thus we have a pattern of family life in which the two elements decisive for psycho-analysis, the repressive authority and the severing taboo, are "displaced," distributed in a man-

[2] Cf. *Totem and Taboo*, 1918, Chap. IV, 5, and *Massen Psychologie und Ich-Analyse* [*Group Psychology and the Analysis of the Ego*, 1922], Chap. X.

ner different from that found in the patriarchal family. If Freud's general theory is correct, there ought to be also a change in the thwarted desires; the repressed wish formation ought to receive a shape different from the Oedipus complex.

This is as a matter of fact what happens. The examination of dreams, myths, and of the prevalent sexual obsessions reveals indeed a most remarkable confirmation of Freudian theories. The most important type of sexual mythology centres round stories of brother-sister incest. The mythical cycle which explains the origin of love and love magic attributes its existence to an act of incest between brother and sister. There is a notable absence of the parricidal motive in their myth. On the other hand the motive of castration comes in, and it is carried out not on the father but on the maternal uncle. He also appears in other legendary cycles as a villainous, dangerous, and oppressive foe.

In general I have found in the area of my studies an unmistakable correlation between the nature of family and kinship on one hand and the prevalent "complex" on the other, a complex which can be traced in many manifestations of the folklore, customs, and institutions of these natives.

To sum up, the study of savage life and some reflection on Freud's theories and their application to anthropology have led me to the conviction that a great deal of these theories requires modification and in its present form will not stand the test of evidence—notably the theory of *libido,* the exaggeration of infantile sexuality, and the manner in which "sexual symbolisation" is dealt with. The character of the argumentation and the manner and mannerisms of exposition moreover often contain such glaring surface absurdities and show such lack of anthropological insight that one cannot wonder at the impatience of a specialist, such as expressed in the remarks of Prof. Elliot Smith quoted above. But with all this, Freud's contribution to anthropology is of the greatest importance and seems to me to strike a very rich vein which must be followed up. For Freud has given us the first concrete theory about the relation between instinctive life and social institution. His doctrine of repression due to social influence allows us to explain certain typical latent wishes or "complexes," found in folklore, by reference to the organisation of a given society. Inversely it allows us also to trace the pattern of instinctive and emotional tendencies in the texture of the social fabric. By making the theories somewhat more elastic, the anthropologist can not only apply them to the interpretation of certain phenomena, but also in the field he can be inspired by them in the exploration of the difficult borderland between social tradition and social organisation. How fruitful Freud's theories are in this respect I hope to demonstrate clearly in the pending publication previously mentioned.

EDWARD WESTERMARCK

Sexual life and marriage among primitive mankind

Comparative sociology, in many of its branches, started with very simple and homely concepts, and now, after a career of imaginative and somewhat sensational spinning of hypotheses, we find it returning in its latest developments to the position of common sense. The subject of family and marriage, of their origins and evolution, epitomises such a typical course of sociological speculation. In the views about the human family, there was first the uncritical assumption that the family was the nucleus of human society; that monogamous marriage has been the prototype of all varieties of sex union; that law, authority and government are all derived from patriarchal power; that the State, the Tribe, economic co-operation and all other forms of social association have gradually grown out of the small group of blood relatives, issued from one married couple, and governed by the father. This theory satisfied common sense, supplied an easily imaginable course of natural development, and was in agreement with all the unquestioned authorities, from the Bible to Aristotle.

But some sixty years ago, among the many revolutions in scientific thinking and method, the family theory of society seemed to have received its death-blow. The independent researches of Bachofen, Morgan and McLennan seemed to prove beyond doubt, by the study of survivals and ethnographic phenomena, by methods of linguistics, comparative study and antiquarian reconstruction, that the whole conception of primeval monogamous marriage and early human family was nothing but a myth. Primitive humanity, they said, lived in loosely organised hordes, in which an almost complete lack of sexual regulation, a state of promiscuity, was the usage and law. This, the authors of this school concluded, can be seen from many survivals, from the analysis of classificatory systems of relationship, and from the prevalence of matrilineal kinship and matriarchate. Thus, instead of the primitive family we have a horde; instead of marriage, promiscuity; instead of paternal right, the sole influence of the mother and of her relatives over the children. Some of the leaders of this school constructed a number of successive stages of sexual evolution through which humanity was supposed to have passed. Starting from promiscuity, mankind went through group marriage, then the so-called consanguineous family or Punalua, then polygamy, till, in the

This article was a review of The History of Human Marriage *by Edward Westermarck, and appeared in* Nature, Vol. 109, No. 2738 (*April 22, 1922*), *pp. 126–30, and is reprinted by permission.*

highest civilisations, monogamous marriage was reached as the final product of development. Under this scheme of speculations, the history of human marriage reads like a sensational and somewhat scandalous novel, starting from a confused but interesting initial tangle, redeeming its unseemly course by a moral *dénouement*, and leading, as all proper novels should, to marriage, in which "they lived happily ever after."

After the first triumphs of this theory were over, there came, however, a reaction. The earliest and most important criticism of these theories arose out of the very effort to maintain them.

In the middle eighties of last century, a young and then inexperienced Finnish student of anthropology started to add his contribution to the views of Bachofen and Morgan. In the course of his work, however, the arguments for the new and then fashionable theories began to crumple in his hands, and indeed to turn into the very opposite of their initial shape. These studies, in short, led to the first publication by Prof. Westermarck in 1891 of his *History of Human Marriage*, in which the author maintained that monogamous marriage is a primeval human institution, and that it is rooted in the individual family; that matriarchate has not been a universal stage of human development; that group marriage never existed, still less promiscuity, and that the whole problem must be approached from the biological and psychological point of view, and though with an exhaustive, yet with a critical application of ethnological evidence. The book with its theories arrested at once the attention both of all the specialists and of a wider public, and it has survived these thirty years, to be reborn in 1922 in an amplified fifth edition of threefold the original size and manifold its original value. For since then Prof. Westermarck has developed not only his methods of inductive inference by writing another book of wider scope and at least equal importance, *Origin and Development of Moral Ideas*, but he has also acquired a first-hand knowledge of savage races by years of intensive ethnographic field work in Morocco, work which has produced already numerous and most valuable records.

Where does the problem stand now? First of all, the contest is not ended yet, and divergencies of opinion obtain on some fundamental points, while controversy has not lost much of its uncompromising tone. But the issues have narrowed down somewhat. There is no longer a question of accepting the naïve theory which regarded family as a kind of universal germ of all social evolution; nor, on the other hand, does any competent sociologist take very seriously the fifteen successive stages of promiscuity, group marriage, Punalua marriage, etc. Prof. Westermarck and his school do not maintain the rigidly patriarchal theory, and they are fully aware of the importance of matrilineal descent, of the maternal uncle's authority, and of the various kinship anomalies connected with matriliny. The classificatory terms of relationship are, moreover, not considered by Prof.

Westermarck as mere terms of address, but as important indications of status.

The representatives of the opposite school had also to make some concessions, though rather reluctantly and grudgingly. Scarcely any one nowadays would be so irreverent towards our ape-like ancestors and ancestresses as to suspect them of living in a general state of promiscuity. But there is still a formidable list of names, among them some of the most eminent representatives of modern anthropology, quoted by Prof. Westermarck (Vol. 1, p. 103 *n.*), who consider primitive promiscuity as "not improbable," "plausible," "by no means untenable," and use this hypothesis constantly as a skeleton-key to open all questions of sex. Group marriage is still, though somewhat faintheartedly, affirmed to have existed, and even some savages are forced to live up to their evil reputation—in the speculations and bare assertions of some writers. The Punalua family leads an even more shadowy existence, merging into a combined polyandry and polygamy. The most tenacious survival of the Bachofen-Morgan-McLennan theories seems to be the kinship terms, themselves a most fecund breeding-place for all kinds of survival theories.

Thus Prof. Westermarck in this new edition is not altogether relieved of the necessity of dealing with the hypothesis of promiscuity, and in chapters iii-ix he examines the various classes of evidence adduced in its favour. There is a number of statements affirming directly the existence of promiscuous conditions among this or that tribe or people. Some of them come from garrulous and credulous writers of antiquity and have to be discarded as pure fables; others, from modern travellers, equal them in untrustworthiness and futility. On this point no one will certainly controvert the author when he says "that it would be difficult to find a more untrustworthy collection of statements." The investigation then turns to that remarkable group of ethnological facts—*jus primae noctis*, licence of festive and religious character, prenuptial and orgiastic sexual intercourse—in which the powerful instinct of sex, curbed and fettered by social regulations, takes, in its own time, revenge on man by dragging him down to the level of a beast. Prof. Westermarck fully admits the importance and extent of these phenomena; his survey indeed shows the extreme range and the often astounding perversity of these deviations. But he declines resolutely to see in any of these facts a survival of pristine promiscuity, for in all cases the facts reveal most powerful motive forces, and can be attributed to definite psychological and social causes. The theory of survival is moreover irreconcilable with the fact that we find, side by side with licentious tribes, savages who maintain strict chastity; that some of the most primitive ones are virtuous, whilst the most luxuriant growth of licence is found in more advanced communities; that, finally, civilisation instead of abolishing these phenomena only modifies them.

The chapters on customary and regulated sexual licence are full of penetrating suggestions, and the facts, skilfully marshalled, are made to speak for themselves, and will supply a lasting compendium for students of sexual psychology. But what appears most valuable in this, not less than in other parts of the work, are the methods and implications of the argument. Prof. Westermarck has an abhorrence of the now fashionable tendency of explaining the whole by its part, the essential by the irrelevant, the known by the unknown. He refuses to construct out of meagre and insufficient evidence a vast, hypothetical building, through the narrow windows of which we would have to gaze upon reality, and see only as much of it as they allow. The obvious, common-sense and essentially scientific way of proceeding is to get firm hold of the fundamental aspects of human nature—in this case the psychology of sex, the laws of primitive human grouping, the typical beliefs and sentiments of savage people—and, in the light of this, to analyse each fact as we meet it. But to construct the unverifiable hypotheses of primitive promiscuity and interpret facts in terms of figments is, as Prof. Westermarck shows, a method which leads nowhere and lures us from the true scientific path.

Some of the other chapters of Prof. Westermarck's book give us another approach to the psychology of sex and to the theory of human marriage. Sex is a most powerful instinct—one of the modern schools of psychology tries to derive from it almost all mental process and sociological crystallisation. However this may be, there is no doubt that masculine jealousy (chap. ix), sexual modesty (chap. xii), female coyness (chap. xiv), the mechanism of sexual attraction (chap. xv and xvi) and of courtship (chap. xiii)—all these forces and conditions made it necessary that even in the most primitive human aggregates there should exist powerful means of regulating, suppressing and directing this instinct. There is no doubt that all the psychological forces of human sexual passion, as well as the conditions of primitive life, must have tended to produce a primeval habit of individual pairing. We have to imagine a man and a woman forming more or less permanent unions which lasted until well after the birth of the offspring. This, Prof. Westermarck develops in the first chapter of his work. A union between man and wife, based on personal affection springing out of sexual attachment, based on economic conditions, on mutual services, but above all on a common relation to the children, such a union is the origin of the human family. This primeval habit, according to the "tendency of habits to become rules of conduct," develops with time into the institution of family and marriage, and "marriage is rooted in the family, rather than the family in marriage."

Marriage, indeed, right through the book, is conceived in the correct sociological manner, that is, as an institution based on complex social conditions. The greatest mistake of the writers of the opposing school—a mistake which, I think, they have not corrected even in the most recent publications—is their identification of marriage with sexual appropriation. Nor is this pitfall easy to avoid. For us, in our own society, the exclusiveness of sexual rights is the very essence of marriage. Hence we think of marriage in terms of individual sexual appropriation, and project this concept into native societies. When we find, therefore, groups of people living in sexual communism, as undoubtedly happens among a few tribes within a limited compass, we have a tendency at once to jump to conclusions about "group marriage."

To the majority of savages, however, sexual appropriation is by no means the main aspect of marriage. To take one example, there are the Trobriand Islanders, studied by the present writer, who live in the greatest sexual laxity, are matrilineal, and possess an institution which is probably the nearest approach to "group marriage" that exists or could ever have existed. Indeed, it resembles it much more, I think, than does the celebrated *pirrauru* of the Dieri in Central Australia. These natives satisfy their sexual inclinations through all forms of licence, regulated and irregular, and then settle down to marry, decidedly not only or even mainly to possess a partner in sex, but chiefly out of personal attachment, in order to set up a household with its economic advantages, and last, not least, to rear children. The institution of individual marriage and family among them is based on several other foundations besides sex, though sex —naturally—enters into it.

Space does not allow me to follow Prof. Westermarck into his dialectic contests with the most eminent of his contemporaries—with Sir James Frazer and Dr. Rivers about the kinship terms (chap. vi); with Sir James Frazer and Mr. Hartland on matriliny (chap. viii); and with all of them, as well as Spencer and Gillen, on group marriage (chap. xxvi). In all these arguments we find the same extensive use of ethnological material, the same breadth of view and moderation of doctrine, above all, the same sound method of explaining the detail by its *whole*, the superstructure by its foundation. In the treatment of kinship and matriliny, too little concession is perhaps made to the important theories of Sir James Frazer and Mr. Hartland, whose views, unquestionably correct, that ignorance of paternity is universal and primitive among savages, Prof. Westermarck cannot accept. Nor can he see perhaps sufficiently clearly the enormous influence of this savage ignorance on primitive ideas of kinship. As Sir James Frazer says:

"Fatherhood to a Central Australian savage is a very different thing from fatherhood to a civilized European. To the European father it means that he has begotten a child on a woman; to the Central Australian father it means that the child is the offspring of a woman with whom he has a right to cohabit. . . . To the European mind the tie between a father and his child is physical; to the Central Australian it is social." [1] The distinc-

[1] *Totemism and Exogamy*, 1910, Vol. I, p. 236.

tion between a physiological and a social conception of kinship is indeed essential. But, on the whole, Prof. Westermarck's views do not diverge so much from those of Frazer, who, on the other hand, occupies a moderate position among the supporters of the opposite theories. Prof. Westermarck's explanation of exogamy, and of the prohibition of incest—which I think will come to be considered as a model of sociological construction, and which remarkably enough seems to find favour with no one—can only be mentioned here. The excellent chapters on marriage rites (chaps. xxiv-xxvi); the analysis of what could be called the numeric varieties of marriage, monogamy and polygamy (chaps. xxvii-xxviii); polyandry (xxix-xxx); duration of marriage (xxxii-xxxiii), stand somewhat apart from the main argument of the book. Each division is a monograph, a *Corpus Inscriptionum Matrimonialium*, a treatise in itself.

The book is and will remain an inexhaustible fount of information, a lasting contribution towards the clearing up of some of the most obscure aspects of human evolution, and it marks an epoch in the development of sociological method and reasoning.

ROBERT BRIFFAULT AND ERNEST CRAWLEY

Primitive marriage and kinship

Students of primitive mankind still indulge too frequently in bitter and futile controversy; their reputation on this score is deservedly bad, and anthropology, I fear, could well be described as the study of rude man by rude people. Among the various hotly discussed subjects, perhaps the most contentious is primitive sexual life and mating—the much disputed "marriage of the missing link."

The appearance of two remarkable books on this subject, each standing for one side of the vast controversy, is a notable event, and affords a good opportunity for a statement of the problem as it now stands. One of the books, Crawley's *Mystic Rose*, well brought up-to-date by Mr. Besterman, is exactly twenty-five years old, yet it is not only entirely fresh, but also in many respects it is bound to lead modern research for yet another quarter of a century. The other book, Mr. Briffault's *The Mothers*—in size and erudition an imposing achievement—leads us back to the early seventies, to the speculations of Bachofen, Morgan, and

This article was a review of The Mothers: A Study of the Origins of Sentiments and Institutions *by Robert Briffault, and* The Mystic Rose: A Study of Primitive Marriage and of Primitive Thought in its Bearing on Marriage *by Ernest Crawley; it appeared in* Nature, *January 28, 1928 (Vol. 121, No. 3039), pp. 126–30, and is reprinted by permission.*

McLennan. It is, in fact, an attempt to revive their now antiquated point of view that mother-right combined with sexual communism was the original form of organisation. Between them these two books represent a long span of anthropological history; the new contribution its past and the old one its future; while both mirror the present deadlock.

The anthropology of to-day can be divided into two camps on the issue of primitive marriage and kinship: those who believe in original monogamy and those who uphold the hypothesis of promiscuity. Was primitive man sexually promiscuous, or was he monogamous? Was he a thoroughgoing communist in wives and chattels, or a possessive individualist? Was he complaisant or jealous? Was it patriarchy or mother-right which shaped early institutions? Range Andrew Lang, Westermarck, Crawley, Lowie, and Kroeber on one side, and Frazer, Hartland, Rivers, Müller-Lyer on the other, and the latter will vote for communism, group-marriage, mother-right, and complaisance in the "missing link" or primitive man, and the former for his monogamy, jealousy, and private possession.

(1) In my opinion, the problem has been distorted by this black-and-white, yea-or-nay treatment, and I regard it as the main defect in Mr. Briffault's book that he fights on the side of communism, as well as of mother-right, without compromise or reservation. The main thesis of the book is that mother-right was the source of social organisation, that male influence was entirely irrelevant in the dawn of culture, and that kinship, political organisation, the beginnings of law, economic life, magic, and religion were created and completely dominated by woman. To establish this, Mr. Briffault maintains that the maternal instinct is the sole origin of all tender emotions, hence also of all human organisation. Sexual love, on the other hand, leads to cruelty rather than to affection, and has been socially and culturally barren. "The mothers are the basis and the bond of the primitive social group. . . . The male takes no share in the rearing of the young. . . . Fatherhood does not exist."

It is difficult, perhaps, to reconcile this conception of the mother as a source of all affection and all social cohesion with the use which Mr. Briffault makes of her when he tries to explain the origins of exogamy by brutal expulsion of the males. In this context he describes her as: "a fierce enough wild animal . . . uncontrolled and violent . . . an object of horror . . . to the young male, terror-stricken by the anger of a despotic mother." The book is full of such provoking and fantastic exaggerations.

Mr. Briffault leaves no place whatever for the male in early culture. Such extremely important institutions as age grades, secret societies, initiation ceremonies and male political organisations are completely ignored in this work. Again, the rôle of the mother's brother in mother-right is scarcely accounted for; yet a male who intrudes into the very heart of maternal institutions is a formidable difficulty for the champion of an exclusively female culture. Avunculate, one of the most important features of matrilineal societies, is scarcely touched upon by the author—the word is not in the index.

The author then proceeds to prove that group marriage and sex communism exist, and in the course of this discussion commits himself to such extraordinary statements as that "among animals the maternal and derivative, parental, filial, and fraternal instincts operate in accordance with the 'classificatory,' and not with the 'descriptive' system of relationship. It would appear that it is the former that is in a biological sense 'natural,' and the latter which is 'artificial.' " The classificatory system in fact seems so "natural" to Mr. Briffault that he does not discuss it at all, nor does he, in the whole three volumes, give any analysis of primitive kinship, a gap really astounding in a work dealing with mother-right—which is after all but one aspect of primitive kinship.

In the following chapters Mr. Briffault informs us that "girls and women who are not married are under no restrictions as to their sexual relations. . . . To that rule there does not exist any known exception." Since we know that, according to Mr. Briffault, married women also indulge in "group-marriage" and other forms of "licence," continence and individual sexual relations seem to have been completely absent from primitive life. As a matter of fact, the statement quoted is a most misleading generalisation, inaccurate in wording, unsupported by evidence, and based upon a fundamental misconception of human marriage and sexuality. After an account, given from his point of view, of primitive sex communism, group-marriage, sexual selection, and the various manners of concluding marriage, Mr. Briffault proceeds to attribute to woman the discovery of totemism, witchcraft and religion.

It would be easy to indict *The Mothers* for its dogmatic and one-sided affirmations; for the straining of evidence, sometimes to the breaking point; for unsatisfactory definitions—or absence thereof—in such capital concepts as marriage, communism, kinship, avunculate, and mother-right. Much space is wasted in futile controversy; above all in virulent attacks upon Prof. Westermarck, generally by first distorting his views and then destroying them. On the other hand, the contributions of Crawley and Sidney Hartland, and the new and important work of Schmidt and Koppers, are completely ignored. Briffault's three enormous volumes might almost be called an "encyclopaedia of matrimonial errors." The work, however, will be useful to a student, even though he reject most of its conclusions; for it gives a clear, well-written, and certainly unreserved statement of one side of the main problem of anthropology. To the amateur it will prove attractive reading as an introduction; and will be the more useful for its dramatic, strong, and effective narrative, which rivets the attention more forcefully and leaves a sharper imprint upon the memory than a well-balanced, hence less colourful, account might do. As a contribution to science the work has one or two real merits. It is the most exhaustive though one-sided account of the influence of maternity upon the cultural rôle of woman. In the discussion of that subject the author clearly sees and, to the best of his ability, discusses the relation of innate endowment to social institutions in the shaping of human nature; and, in my opinion, anthropology will in the future have to be more concerned with the place of culture within biological development and with the relation of instinct to institution, than with questions of "origin," "evolution," "history," or "diffusion."

(2) The biological foundations of culture, which Mr. Briffault attempts to consider in his new work, have already been fully discussed in *The Mystic Rose,* where the psychology of human relations is explained by what Crawley has termed *physiological thought.* The book sets out to discuss the many strange customs and institutions which centre round sexual life—the *couvade,* sexual taboos, various avoidances, and ceremonies of marriage.

Crawley resolutely rejects all explanations in terms of survival from such original conditions of mankind as "sexual communism," "mother-right," and the total eclipse of the male sex. He regards these as imaginary fantasies constructed against all evidence. He also maintains that the "indiscriminate and careless use of the terms *survival* and *rudiments*" is one of the main sources of anthropological error. On both points anthropology will, in my opinion, have to follow his lead and become inspired by his methods.

The explanation of savage custom and institutions must be given in terms of primitive thought. When Crawley, in his brilliant analysis of savage mentality, declares that "primitive thinking does not distinguish between the natural and the supernatural, between subjective and objective reality," his wording is not quite satisfactory; yet even in this slight misrepresentation of what he terms "primitive logic," Crawley, in forestalling the theories of Lévy-Bruhl, Danzel, [Alfred] Vierkandt, and their followers, must be regarded as the pioneer of modern developments of the problem of primitive psychology. He himself, however, has eschewed the extravagances of some of his successors. He does not commit the fallacy of assuming that the savage has a mind different from that of civilised man. ". . . Human nature remains fundamentally primitive. . . . Primitive ideas . . . spring eternally from permanent functional causes. . . . Ordinary universal human ideas, chiefly connected with functional needs, produce the same results in all ages; and many so-called survivals, which have on the face of them too much vitality to be mere fossil remains, at once receive a scientific explanation which is more than antiquarian." These statements strike the keynote of the soundest developments in modern anthropology. In laying down this point of view, and in carrying it through consistently, Crawley has laid the foundations for the scientific treatment of primitive sexual and social relations.

The main form which "physiological thought" takes in the primitive mind, that is, in the human mind as we find it universally, is a strong apprehension of danger arising from contact with other human beings, especially when there is an element of the abnormal or unusual in the relation. Strangers, people in critical condition—such as sickness, death, or functional crisis—and, above all, people of the other sex, are surrounded with an aura of supernatural fear. In savage culture such dangers are met by two devices: the taboo, and the ritual breaking of it.

Taboo is considered by Crawley as an inevitable by-product of human psychology; and, in a masterly survey of primitive social relations, we are shown how the various imperatives and prohibitions arise naturally out of savage life and savage outlook. Crawley constructs no hypotheses, invokes no *deus ex machina*—he explains quaint features and unrelated details in terms of intelligible and fundamental fact; he introduces order, he links up apparently disconnected phenomena and transforms the strange and unknown welter of "primitive superstition" into a familiar and comprehensible scheme of essentially human behaviour.

The taboo between men and women in its various aspects is treated against the background of mixed attraction and fear, of distrust undermining love—an attitude which is shown to dominate the relations between the two sexes. In this Crawley has anticipated the various theories of primitive society based on the principle of sex antagonism, theories set forth by [Walter] Heape and several other writers long after the first edition of *The Mystic Rose* was published. In Crawley's work we also become acquainted for the first time with that emotional complexity underlying all social relations, especially as between men and women, which has been systematically worked out by A. F. Shand in his theory of sentiment (*The Foundations of Character*). Under the title of "ambivalence" we have had similar phenomena dished up in a somewhat distorted shape in psycho-analytic literature. Crawley, in fact, can be described as the sane and sober forerunner of psycho-analysis, which, when *The Mystic Rose* was written, was unknown beyond a narrow circle of Viennese practitioners. It must also be remembered that psycho-analysis did not turn its attention to problems of primitive culture until a decade after the present book was first published. *The Mystic Rose,* in the due emphasis which it places on sex, in its clear and courageous, but never fantastic or overheated, interest in that impulse, can be placed side by side with Havelock Ellis's *Psychology of Sex* as a pioneer in modern, scientific treatment of human love and mating.

In his theory of ritual and sacrament as mechanisms of breaking the taboo; in his theory of union; in his description of change and exchange;

and in his analysis of the ritual in vital crises, Crawley has been a fore-runner of several now developed branches of anthropology. To him can be attributed the first statement of the theory of *rites de passage*, after-wards so successfully developed by Schurtz, [Arnold] van Gennep, and Hutton Webster. He was the first to regard the sacrilisation of crises of life as the main function of religion—a theory to which he returned in his later work (*The Tree of Life*). His doctrines of change and exchange, of reciprocity and the principle of contact, are akin to the views of the French sociological school, especially of Durkheim, [H.] Hubert, [M.] Mauss, and [Georges] Davy.

Finally, in the last part, a penetrating and original analysis is given of primitive kinship and relationship: that pivot problem and eternal puzzle of the anthropologist. In my opinion it ranks side by side with the first few chapters of Westermarck's *History of Human Marriage* as the best treatment of kinship yet given. Had such writers as the late Dr. Rivers, Mr. Briffault, and other latter-day Morganians read, digested, and as-similated the last three chapters of *The Mystic Rose*, we would have had better field-work and fewer speculations about "anomalous marriages," "group-motherhood," and "savage communism." Even on this last point, Crawley, though not especially interested in economics, had a sound and a realistic view. All anthropological evidence, he maintains, tends "to disprove the common idea that early society had a communistic and socialistic character. The 'rights' of the individual in property, marriage, and everything else were never more clearly defined than by primitive man." Recently we have been told by a great authority that the Mela-nesians are "communistic." That such a view is based on superficial ob-servation, and that Crawley is right here, as almost everywhere else, I have attempted to prove (*Crime and Custom in Savage Society*).

The foundations of Crawley's work are so sound, so firmly established in the bedrock of human nature rightly understood, and of human culture correctly interpreted, that anthropologists will have to build on them for generations to come. To show this, one aspect of his views might be further developed in this place. Crawley has taken the primitive concep-tion of the danger in sexual selection as the fundamental and irreducible datum. He speaks of "that difference of sex and of sexual characters which renders mutual sympathy and understanding more or less difficult"; and he adds: "woman is one of the last things to be understood by man." Again: ". . . woman is different from man, and this difference has had the same religious results as have attended other things which man does not understand." He also speaks of "the instinctive separation of the sexes hardening into tradition and finally made the subject of taboo."

Now I think that here it is possible for modern anthropology to go a step further and to interpret the psychological attitude of primitive man by its cultural function. I maintain that sex is regarded as dangerous by the savage, that it is tabooed and ritualised, surrounded by moral and legal norms—not because of any superstition of primitive man, or emotional view of or instinct about strangeness, but for the simple reason that *sex really is dangerous.*

The sexual impulse has to be experimental if it is to be selective; and it has to be selective if it is to lead to the mating of best with best. This is the eugenic principle which I believe governs human marriage as well as animal mating. Hence sexual jealousy and competition is to be found in human societies, and it harbours serious disruptive forces for any social group living in close contact. In animal societies, rut not only allows the law of battle and sexual selection to operate in especially favourable circumstances, but it also circumscribes the duration of the disruptive impulse and thus eliminates most of its dangers. In man rut is absent, and sex holds him in permanent readiness and tension. Cultural regulations, the various taboos and barriers step in and fetter him, where natural endowment has left him freer than the beast. They safeguard the family by the prohibition of incest, the clan by rules of exogamy, and the bonds of marriage by the ban on adultery and what might be called the principle of legitimacy. This argument cannot be fully developed or substantiated by evidence in this place; nor is it necessary for me to do so, since my views are developed at some length elsewhere (*Sex and Repression in Savage Society*).

In human culture, however, no physical force is sufficient without moral support; no social regulations, however strongly backed by executive power, can be effective without mental assent. The social and cultural rules which separate primitive man and woman in daily existence, at initiation, during the crises of life, in economic occupations, and within certain social groups, cannot stand without the support of some system of thought and belief. Here, indeed, we find all those ideas which express the danger of sex—the ideas of evil and sin—at the very core of love and passion; the conviction that highest happiness in erotic union can only be obtained at the cost of infinite pains and precautions; belief, in short, that sex is religiously sacred, *sacer,* that is, at the same time holy and polluting. The universally human conception of sex must be explained, I think, by its function within culture rather than by mere reference to primitive psychology and the early conditions of life. The sexual taboo, then, and the ideas upon which it rests, appear to us indispensable corollaries of culture and of the influence of this on the increased plasticity of instinct which, since in man it has become more free, more experimental, and therefore more dangerous than in the animal, needs elaborate regulation. The barriers imposed upon sex by culture—that is, the taboos and the correlated primitive conception of sex dangers—appear to us as an inevitable by-product of the change wrought in human endowment by the passage from the state of Nature to that of culture.

I hasten to add that this functional view is implied at many points in Crawley's argument, though it is nowhere clearly formulated by him. It is really implicit in his own concept of the primitive *Weltanschauung*, in which beliefs and ideas do not exist as useless "idle survivals," not as "speculations of rude philosophers," or even as "mistaken associations of ideas." Crawley treats these simple and often quaint "savage superstitions" as what they really are: life forces, indispensable moral values which shape the destinies of mankind with a determinism as binding though not as rigid as that which obtains in the physical world. Thus Crawley has given us in *The Mystic Rose*, what is, perhaps, the first truly scientific work of comparative anthropology, and he must be regarded as one of the founders of what is now known as the functional method of modern anthropology.

HAVELOCK ELLIS

Havelock Ellis has been a personal experience to most thinking men and women of our age—a personal experience which lasts. His scientific work, his artistic vision and the dramatic role which he was made to play as the price of his prophetic influence—and which he played with a consummate dignity and restraint—all these surround him with that mythical halo which but rarely comes to a man during his lifetime. Those of us who have the privilege of personal acquaintance and friendship know well with what charm and nobility he acquits himself of this most dangerous and difficult burden: world-wide fame achieved early in life.

But personal acquaintance is merely a confirmation of the many things which he gives in his published, spoken and acted manifestation; for as all great men, Havelock Ellis lives and reveals himself in his words and deeds. All true and real things in life are simple at heart, yet with an infinite variety of iridescent surface. The thoughts and sentiments of Havelock Ellis are direct in intent, manifold in the grasp of essential facts, and sincere in expression. His philosophic attitude is non-partisan and non-sectarian: he always remains the synthetic metaphysician of life.

The simplest and the most fundamental truths are invariably the most difficult to see and to express. Havelock Ellis tells us that life in its fullest sense is worth living; that sex should be understood, indeed studied scientifically; that on the basis of such knowledge it must be morally vindicated; that a great many of the strict taboos and puritanic values of the past generation will have to change.

Sex is a great and wonderful power for evil and for good, and we must

This article appeared in Birth Control Review (*now* Planned Parenthood News), *March 1931, p. 77, and is reprinted by permission.*

deal with it as we deal with other forces of nature: understand, respect and control it in the light of truth and not in the shadows of prejudice and preconception.

All this Havelock Ellis has given us. He has not proclaimed it as his own great "discovery," but has shown us the facts; illuminated them with his insight; lit them with the fire of his inspiration and enthusiasm. Havelock Ellis has never made sex the only explanation of all mental phenomena, nor has he advocated free indulgence as the remedy of all spiritual and social evils; he never fell into the error of facile pansexualism; nor is his scientific work a system of one-sided doctrines. He was indeed the first scientifically to unveil most of the real mysteries of the sexual instinct. His analysis of the two-fold aspect of this impulse, tumescence and its release; his theory of modesty as a biological asset; his radical distinction between the socially relevant and the essentially personal elements in sex—all this and much more will remain as a classical and a lasting contribution to science.

His pioneering genius consists of a rare combination: common-sense and prophetic intuition. It has made Havelock Ellis anticipate most of the discoveries which are usually ascribed to psychoanalysis, and for which, indeed, he himself gives all credit to Freud, where this credit is really due. The whole path of theoretical development which we can follow in the seven volumes of the *Psychology of Sex* is strewn with innumerable findings bearing on practically all sound modern doctrines in the sciences of the human mind, human society and the human body. Like life itself, and the manifestations of the wide world, Havelock Ellis's work harbors inconsistencies, and it will provoke, now and then, contradictions from even his most enthusiastic followers. One might almost say that to learn from him, by reading his books, is like being in touch with experimental reality, so little *partipris*, parochialism and egocentric vanity is there in his work. So that even on those points where we disagree with Havelock Ellis, we still remain indebted to him for stimulus and inspiration.

There is one aspect of Havelock Ellis's work, however, which he himself has tried to make non-dogmatic and tentative, but which will, I think, remain of permanent value. This is the ethical aspect, and here again it is his supreme tolerance and placidity of mind, combined with his warmth of heart and earnestness of purpose, which makes him go right every time. The dancing "Philosopher of Life" is never frivolous, never cynical and never bitter. He has—in spite of some false appearances and of some aphorisms which have been made about him—nothing of the satyr; nothing of the demon; too little, perhaps, of Dionysos. Some of us, made of a baser metal, may perhaps miss this in Havelock Ellis, the philosopher; even more in Havelock Ellis, the artist; but no serious and honest man will miss it in Havelock Ellis the friend and the counsellor. Take only one issue, but the main issue of sex morality and of all the modern problems connected with it—I mean, of course, birth control. Havelock Ellis from the outset was not only a wise advisor and a consistent supporter of birth control; he was also one of the first to recognize the immense theoretical importance and practical position of birth control in all the vital questions of social ethics. He is unquestionably the most important representative of Neo-Malthusianism in England and in Europe, and serious supporters of birth control in America have chosen him as the Old World Patron Saint of the movement. In his great work on sex, Havelock Ellis has laid the foundation of a new ethical attitude as well as of a new science, and he has given not only an encyclopaedia of facts and a system of ideas, but also a charter of a new freedom.

To me in my earlier youthful enthusiasms Havelock Ellis was first a myth, fraught with artistic and moral significance; later he was an intellectual reality in shaping the plastic phase of my mental development; finally he became a great personal experience when I met him and saw realized in life the anticipation of a great personality. In this, I am glad to say, I feel but one of the legion of his friends and admirers, for all of us like to share that which we regard as good and great. Havelock Ellis provokes just that unselfish admiration and devotion, and in this, perhaps, lies his greatest achievement.

6

KINSHIP

Kinship in human culture

Birth, suckling and the tender cares bestowed by the parents on their offspring establish bonds of union between the members of a family, both in human and in animal societies. The devotion of the suckling mother is not an exclusively human virtue; the watchful and protecting father is to be found among many species of birds and mammals; and the pathetic response of the young to their parents moves the heart of the animal lover as well as of the philanthropist. With many animals, kinship, the protective sentiment of the parents, and the child's response to it, constitute part of the innate endowment indispensable for the survival of the species.

With man, however, we find physiological kinship deeply modified and grown into what is perhaps the most important social institution of mankind. Kinship controls family life, law, social organization and economics, and it deeply influences religion, morality and art. With us the parental relation figures in the ten commandments; maternal love remains the symbol and prototype of many moral virtues; the relations within the Trinity, the obligations between man and his Maker, and those of Christian to Christian are conceived in terms of kinship—Son to Father; child to One addressed as "our Father which art in heaven"; brother to brother. In other societies, the cult of a Mother Goddess, or again ancestor-worship, or kinship with animals or spirits give the dominant tone to religion, morality and art, and directly influence law, social organization and economics. Every human culture is built upon its own system of kinship, that is, upon a special type of personal bonds primarily derived from procreation and family life. Without a deeper understanding of kinship it is

This article appeared in the 14th Edition of the Encyclopædia Britannica, *1929, Vol. XIII, pp. 403–09; reprinted by permission of Encyclopædia Britannica, Inc.*

impossible to grasp the organization, the modes of thought and the general character of human civilization from its humblest origins to its highest development.

The family as the source of kinship

At first sight kinship, the bonds of union between parents and children and between more remote relatives, appears to be simple enough: the typical family, a group consisting of mother, father and their progeny, is found in all communities, savage, barbarous and civilized; everywhere it plays an important rôle and influences the whole extent of social organization and culture.

Indeed it seems hardly to differ at all from its modern, civilized counterpart, as we know it from our own experience. Among native tribes mother, father and children share the camp, the dwelling, the food and the life. The intimacy of family existence, the daily round of meals, the domestic occupations and outdoor work, the rest at night and the awakening to a new day, run in both civilized and savage societies on strictly parallel lines, allowing for the difference in levels of culture. The members of the household are as a rule as closely bound together in a native tribe as they are in a European society, attached to each other, sharing life and most of its interests, exchanging counsel and help, company, cheer and economic co-operation. The same bonds unite them as unite our family, the same distances and barriers separate them from other households. In Australia, as well as among most North American Indians, in Oceania and in Asia, among the African tribes and in South America, the individual undivided family stands out conspicuous, a definite social unit marked off from the rest of society by a clear line of division.

It would be easy to illustrate this picture by a host of actual descriptions. In no ethnographic area is the family absent as a domestic institution. Putting these facts together with our childhood's vision of the first marriage—Adam and Eve in paradise—with the patriarchal traditions of the Bible and of classical antiquity, with the early sociological theories from Aristotle onwards, we might conclude with Sir Henry Maine that it would be impossible to imagine any form of social organization at the beginning of human culture, but that of the patriarchal family. And we might be led to assume that our own type of family is to be found wherever we go, and that kinship is built on the same pattern in every part of the world.

The controversy on kinship

The layman is therefore not unjustifiably taken aback, when on opening a modern scientific book on primitive society, he finds himself confronted by extreme dissension and acrimonious controversy about the very subject on which he expected a simple statement of obvious fact. Broadly speaking, anthropologists are divided on the questions: does the essential unit consist of the family, or of a wider group, such as the clan, the horde, the "undivided commune"; was marriage between single pairs present from the outset or did it evolve from a preceding promiscuity or group marriage; was human kinship originally individual or communistic? One school stands by individual marriage and kinship, and the importance of the family, the other affirms an original communism in sex, economics and kinship—and the two schools are still disputing the issue.

This great anthropological rift, however, is not due merely to the perversity and pugnacity of specialists, nor to any inherent vice of method or insufficiency of material. It often happens in science that the seemingly simplest and most fundamental problems are really the most difficult and remain longest debated and unsettled. As the physicists cannot make up their minds on matter, force or energy, as the chemists change their views on the atom and the elements, as the mathematicians are least certain about space, time and numbers, so the social anthropologists may be forgiven if they still debate, at times hotly, kinship—that conception in which centre all their other problems and ideas.

Modes of counting descent

Kinship, indeed, apparently simple when regarded as ties of union arising within the family out of procreation and the rearing of the young, becomes far more complex when we study it in its further ramifications in tribal life. On one point of great importance a correction has to be made in the traditional view that had undivided sway, before Bachofen, McLennan and Morgan revolutionized social anthropology during the latter half of the 19th century. Kinship is by no means invariably patriarchal; it is not always based on the recognition of the father's primary importance in establishing descent; nor is his right to exercise authority or to hand over his position, wealth and privileges to his son universal. In many societies the mother is the parent through whom kinship is counted, her brother is the male head of the family and inheritance of goods, succession of office and all rights, obligations and privileges are passed from a man to his sister's children.

This legal system is called *mother-right* or more correctly *matriliny*; and the relation between a man and his sister's son, *avunculate*. The circumstance that kinship can be traced through both father and mother has been termed (by Lowie) "the bilateral principle of counting descent"; while the almost universal fact that in any given culture emphasis is laid upon one side only has been defined as the *unilateral* mode of regarding kinship. The bilateral aspect of kinship is never completely obliterated and unilateral counting only means a more or less limited emphasis on one side and never a complete elimination of the other.

The hypertrophy of primitive bonds

Another feature which makes kinship in many a native culture very different from our own is its extraordinary hypertrophy: it transcends the limits of the family, of the local group, at times even of the widest circle of acquaintances.

Perhaps the most baffling and disquieting symptom of these collective aspects of kinship is the queer linguistic usage known as the "classificatory" system of kinship nomenclature. In most savage tongues a man applies such terms as father, mother, brother, sister and so on, not only to the members of his family but, according to rules which vary with the social organization, to classes of people who stand in a definite relation to his parents. In some communities, indeed, for example in Australia, kinship terms go as far as actual social relations and even beyond—that is, even distant strangers never met or seen are regarded as potentially belonging to one class of kindred or another.

Thus language and linguistic usage seem apparently to break the bonds of family, to obliterate parenthood by substituting a "group of fathers" for the individual one, a "group of mothers" for the real mother, and so on. Nor is this usage a mere rule of politeness: the "classificatory" terms are applied according to strict rules, to a number of people, whose relationship is traceable by pedigree or by membership in a clan or class. Behind the linguistic usage there is always a set of mutual obligations between an individual and all those whom he calls "fathers," "mothers," "brothers," etc. The "fathers" or "brothers" act as a group on certain occasions and they are therefore a well-defined social class and not merely a name.

Clan, moieties and classes of relatives

Thus the classificatory use of kinship terms is not alone in grouping people into classes of kindred. The majority of native tribes are actually divided not only into families, but into bigger groups, which yet possess to a certain extent a kinship character. Thus in certain areas, the tribe falls into two halves or moieties. Each of these has its name, its collective sense of unity, usually a special myth defining its character and its relation to the other moiety. The division of certain Australian tribes into the moieties of Eaglehawk and Crow and the bi-partition of the eastern North American Indians are classical examples of this division. Usually this halving of the tribe is associated with strict prohibitions of marriage within the same moiety, so that a man of the first must marry a woman of the second and vice versa. In other tribes there are four clans or classes, in others again eight, these sections regulating marriage and playing a conspicuous part in ceremonial and economic life. Among the majority of peoples, however, there is an odd number of clans which cannot be brought under the dual or any other numeric principle.

What makes it difficult to understand these modes of grouping is precisely their kinship character. The members of a clan regard themselves as kindred, trace their descent from a common ancestor, conceive of their exogamous prohibitions as of a variety or extension of incest, and, under certain conditions behave to each other like kinsmen.

Thus there exist tribes where an individual really seems to acknowledge many "fathers," many "mothers," "sisters," "wives," and so on. And yet in every such case, the man also possesses one real or own relative, a father, a few own brothers and own sisters and certainly an individual mother.

The hypotheses of group marriage and group kinship

As to the fathers, a plausible hypothesis suggests that their plurality might be perhaps due to uncertainty of fatherhood under a system of primitive group marriage. Was not marriage originally promiscuous, communal, between two groups rather than between two individuals? Was not therefore kinship, derived from such group-marriage, originally group-kinship? Is not the classificatory use of kinship terms partly the expression of such group-family relations as they still persist, partly the survival of a more definitely communistic kinship of primeval times? And we see how a plausible reasoning has led many an anthropologist—from Morgan to Rivers, from McLennan to Frazer, from Bachofen to Sidney Hartland—to the theory of a primitive group-marriage and group-family, and to the assumption that primitive kinship was a class kinship, between groups and not between individuals. On the other hand this position has been vehemently disputed by the other school, who cannot reconcile it with the supreme importance of the family, with the apparently primeval nature of marriage between single pairs and with the individuality of Motherhood. By Darwin as well as by Westermarck, by Andrew Lang and by Crawley almost every assumption of the group-kinship school has been disputed, while recently Lowie and Malinowski have tried to show by the analysis of actual facts that the family is after all the foundation of all social order.

Individual and collective kinship

The problem has been undoubtedly vitiated by the uncompromising championship of the clan versus the family, primitive monogamy versus group-marriage, individual relations versus clanship. *The question is not whether kinship is individual or communal—it evidently is both—but what is the relation between its two aspects?* It is an undeniable fact that the family is universal and sociologically more important than the clan which, in the evolution of humanity, it preceded and outlasted. But the clan is in certain communities extremely vital and effective. What is the relation between them? Individual legal prerogatives and self-interest are always predominant, but corporate feeling, co-operation, joint ownership and joint responsibility are important elements in primitive justice and legal organisation. All these bonds and relations, individual as well as communal, are founded on kinship and the sense of kinship. The real task of the enlightened anthropologist is not to join either "school" in denying or belittling one side of kinship or the other, but to establish the relation between the two sides.

The variety of meanings in each classificatory term

The traditional approach to the problem, since Morgan, has been through language. The classificatory character of the terms made a great impression upon anthropologists—but they failed to analyse it linguistically! Now in all human languages we find homonyms, that is, words with a variety of meanings, and in primitive languages such words abound and do not cause any confusion. Thus in technology we frequently find that the same word is used to designate the natural objects from which the material is taken, the material in its raw form, the various stages of manufacture, and finally the finished object. In Melanesia, for instance, the same term *waga* describes a tree as it stands in the forest, its felled and lopped trunk, the dug-out in its various stages, and the finished canoe. Similarly such words as "magical power" (*mana, wakan, orenda,* etc.), "prohibition" (*tabu*), and what not, cover a great variety of meanings.

The first thing to ask then about kinship terms is, whether they really "confuse," "merge" or "lump" the various relatives designated by the same term, or whether on the contrary each time they are used, they receive a distinct meaning, that is, refer to one individual only? As a matter of fact, in actual use kinship terms have always a distinct and concrete meaning and there never is any doubt in the mind of the speaker or hearers as to who is designated in each case. The emotional tone in the first place usually indicates whether a word such as Mother, Father, Son, Daughter, Brother, Sister, is used towards or about "own" relatives, or merely "classificatory" ones. And emotional intonation is an important part of phonetic equipment.

In the second place, there is always an additional apparatus of adjectives, suffixes and other circumlocutions which make it possible to specify whether the actual mother is meant or her sister, or yet another of those whom the classificatory term "mother" embraces. Recently, in Spencer and Gillen's new book (*The Arunta,* 1928) we are given a very rich auxiliary terminology of this kind, which proves that even in that stronghold of classificatory kinship, Central Australia, there exist highly developed linguistic means for differentiating individuals within each class.

Finally we have the context of situation and narrative, the most powerful index of semantic discrimination of meaning in primitive languages. Thus in reality each so-called classificatory term is a class label for a number of distinct words, every one of which has its own specific individual meaning. These individual words are in actual use differentiated from each other phonetically, by the index of emotional tone; lexicographically by the index of circumlocution; contextually by the index of situation. The individual meanings are moreover not built up in a haphazard manner; they are related to each other; they start with a main or primary reference; which then through successive extensions engenders a series of derived meanings.

The initial situation of kinship

What is throughout humanity the initial situation of kinship in which the primary meanings of the terms are formed; and above all is that initial situation individual or collective? Does the child form its kinship meaning on one set of parents, one Mother and one Father, or is it surrounded—at the time when its first sociological categories are being shaped—by a group-family, by classes of Mothers and Fathers? This as we know is the point at issue, and apparently the answer seems to frame itself according as we approach facts from the side of maternity or paternity.

A deeper sociological analysis shows however that the problems of Maternity and that of Paternity are not so different.

Biological and sociological parentage

Biological factors, though important, are not, however, in human societies the omnipotent, exclusively determining element, which they apparently are in animal ones. Legal rules, social institutions, moral and religious doctrines and practices deeply modify the ideas, sentiments and the behaviour of man. Kinship which in its final form is a product of the institutions and doctrines of a society is always shaped by laws and normative ideas. Indeed there is no reason why the transformation should not go so far that the sentimental and legal bond between a child and its mother should not become collective instead of individual. Indeed a brilliant anthropologist (Rivers) has recently propounded the hypothesis of a sociological "group motherhood" as a correlate to "group marriage" and "group fatherhood" and this hypothesis has been made one of the foundation stones in a new matriarchal theory of primitive culture (Briffault).

Thus both maternity and paternity are partly based on biological arrangements of the human organism and innate mental tendencies, and both are deeply modified by social institutions and norms. In both, the facts must be examined carefully; neither a mere zoological induction, nor plausibly brilliant hypotheses about the omnipotence of society can yield a satisfactory answer.

Sex and the uncertainty of fatherhood

It will be best in fact to discuss maternity and paternity together. The two sides of parenthood are linked by sexual life. The laxity of savages has been given a great and undue prominence in discussions on kinship. Wherever sexual relations occur between two groups, as in the Pirrauru custom of Central Australia and sporadically in Siberia and Melanesia; or even merely allowed as between marriage classes and clans, some anthropologists are inclined to speak of "a still existing group-marriage" forgetting that marriage implies far more than the right of sexual intercourse. Again, in various customs of religious and ceremonial nature (temple prostitution, *jus primae noctis*, ritual defloration, bridal night relaxations, sex hospitality and exchange of partners) survivals of a primitive sex communism have been discerned. This, combined with the testimony of classificatory terms, has led to the hypothesis of primitive promiscuity and group family.

In reality, however, *sexual freedom* is an entirely different matter from the *liberty of parenthood*, and between the two there enter some interesting institutions and legal rules.

The principle of legitimacy

In fact the tolerance of free intercourse wherever this exists is not extended to the liberty of conception. The rule in most savage tribes which allow pre-nuptial relations is that unmarried boys and girls may enjoy themselves as much as they like, provided that there be no issue. At times, as among the Areoi, the untrammelled artistic fraternities of Polynesia, heavy penalties are inflicted on the unmarried mother, and illegitimate children are killed or aborted. At times the putative father is penalised unless he marries the girl, or again important economic and social pressure make it advantageous for him to marry her. Almost universally the child born before wedlock has a different status from the legitimate offspring, usually very much to his disadvantage. Very interesting are the cases where, as among the Todas, one of the physiologically possible fathers of a polyandrous household has to perform a special rite in order to assume the legal position of fatherhood. A child deprived of such a legal father is disgraced for life, even though born in wedlock.

And this brings us to the important point. Physiological paternity, the begetting of a child, is not, as a rule, sufficient and may even be irrelevant in determining social fatherhood. In fact native peoples have naturally but an imperfect idea of the mechanism of procreation. Some (Central Australians, certain Melanesians, a few African tribes) attribute the child to the agency of spiritual beings; others again (Ba-Ila, Rossel Islanders, some Australian tribes) over-emphasize the man's share. But in all cases, where the subject has been competently investigated, we find that the mechanism of procreation is conceived in a manner in which some biological knowledge is arbitrarily mixed up with animistic beliefs. This doctrine stands in a definite relation to the kinship ideas and legal principles of a community. Invariably also the bond of kinship, believed to be established by the act of procreation, bodily or spiritual, is of an individual nature and fatherhood has at times to be reaffirmed by a special legal ceremony, also individual.

Natural and sociological maternity

Maternity is obviously as much involved in native doctrines of conception as is fatherhood. Indeed, the ban on pre-nuptial children hits the mother harder than the father, and it penalises always an individual, not a group. An individual woman suffers the disadvantages of an illegitimate child, unless there is a man legally united to her who individually shares her responsibility.

Wherever there is an attempt to cause or prevent conception by religious and magical rites, these refer always to an individual mother and child. The mother becomes usually subject to tabus during gestation which she keeps individually and of which her husband often takes a share. The welfare of the child concerns its own mother and father even before it is born. At birth again various social, magical and moral rules separate the mother from her husband and isolate her with her child. The few female relatives who often assist her are her nearest individual kinswomen. There is no transformation of an individual birth into a group birth—by legal fiction or ritual—but on the contrary there is a social imposition of individual burdens, responsibilities and sentiments upon the real mother. The father, though very much in the shadow, participates through customs of the *couvade* type, vigils and tabus in his wife's confinement, and this he also does individually.

No group parenthood

The ideas and institutions which control conception, pregnancy and birth, show that these cannot be regarded by the anthropologist as mere physiological facts, but as facts deeply modified by culture and social organization. Conception is not left to the chance of free intercourse, even where this is allowed, but its necessary condition is marriage. Parenthood, to be normal, must be made legitimate, that is, based on a socially approved, but individual marriage contract. Society decrees that the initial setting of kinship be the individual family based on individual marriage. And this social decree backs up the natural tenderness and affection which seem to be innate in the human, as well as in the animal, parent. The child again responds with a unique, life-long attachment to the one woman and one man who constitute its first social horizon—that is to its mother and father.

The extensions of kinship

The relation of parents and children is individual, and so is that between brothers and sisters, who are to each other the natural playmates and helpmates of childhood, and remain the legal partners and moral allies in later life.

The household is thus the workshop where kinship ties are forged, and the constitution of the individual family supplies the pattern upon which they are built. We return thus to the simple view so long prevalent in tradition and pre-scientific thought, but now we have established it by a survey and analysis of facts, made it precise—and at the same time qualified it considerably. For the individual household provides only the initial situation of kinship; and the individual parents, brothers and sisters supply only the primary meaning of kinship terms. This fact is of the greatest importance, but to appreciate it fully it is necessary to follow the further development of kinship bonds.

As the child grows beyond the earliest stages of infancy, it is brought into contact with other households—those of the grandparents and those of the brothers and sisters of either parent. Perhaps the most important among these persons is the mother's sister.

The substitute mother

The mother is the physiologically and morally indispensable parent in all societies. Yet there is always the danger of her failing, temporarily or permanently. The substitution of one person for another—in case of death, illness or incapacity—is one of the fundamental elements of primitive organization, and this substitution always takes place on the basis of kinship. In a matrilineal society, the natural substitute for a mother is her sister, usually the one nearest in age. In matrilocal communities, she is on the spot, in patrilocal ones she has to be summoned if it is necessary; even when not needed she will come on long visits. Thus the child, as a rule, becomes familiar early in life with its mother's sister. She again —having perhaps performed important duties during pregnancy and at childbirth—is especially devoted to her potential ward. She often assists the mother, in case of illness replaces her, occasionally may take the child to her own home for a time. She and the mother both know that, under circumstances, she may have to act as a mother to the child. Later on in life the child comes also to realize this and to regard her as *substitute or secondary mother.*

The substitute mother is, in certain respects, equivalent to the real one: the child sees her in the intimacy of the household, side by side with the real mother, receives the same services from her, realizes that at times she replaces the real parent, acting thus as a secondary or substitute mother. The child equally well realizes, however, that this is a very dif-

ferent "Mother" from the real one. A new relationship is thus built up
for which the first one is certainly the pattern, but the process is never
a simple repetition.

Linguistically, the extension of the same term *Mother* to the mother's
sister is obviously no more a complete assimilation than is its sociological
equivalent. The child forms a new meaning for the old word—in fact,
it acquires a new word with the same form, but a different referent and
usually a different phonetic character in its emotional tone. When he calls
his mother's sister "Mother," he neither fuses the two ideas nor confuses
the two people. He merely emphasizes the similarity while he ignores the
differences. This one-sided emphasis corresponds to the fact that similarity
is here the basis of legal obligation. The mother's sister is beholden to
the child in virtue of her equivalence to the mother. It is this which has
to be expressed and the child is taught to call her "Mother" since in doing so it puts her under an obligation. The difference is obvious, irrelevant
—in a way to be obliterated or glossed over. The verbal magic, which is
the first form by which legal obligations are established, has to create a
fictitious identity between Mother's Sister and Mother.

What has been said about the mother's sister applies also to the father's
brother who, under father-right, is often regarded as a substitute father.
His wife would then act as a substitute mother, especially in case of adoption. Under mother-right again, the mother's sister's husband would be the
substitute father.

The special relations of mother-right and father-right

Among the people closely related to the parents there are, however, some
to whom no extension of an already existing kinship attitude is possible.
The grandparents obviously belong here, and also the father's sister and
the mother's brother. Under mother-right and exogamy, the father's sister is never of the mother's kin and cannot be assimilated to the mother
while, though of the father's kin, she is not of his sex and, therefore, cannot be assimilated to him. Under unilateral father-right, she again is the
chief kinswoman of the child. The mother's brother occupies the same
singular position both under mother-right and father-right. New attitudes
have to be built towards these relatives and, as a rule, we find also special
terms for them.

The children of the mother's sister and of the father's brother, or
"parallel cousins" as they are called in Anthropology, are usually regarded
by a savage child as his "secondary" brothers and sisters and addressed
by these terms. To them the primary family attitude is also partially extended, as it is to their parents.

The children of the mother's brother and father's sister—the "cross-
cousins" as they are technically called—usually require the creation of
a new type of bond. The terminologies of the cross-cousins often present

strange verbal assimilations. Thus, in matrilineal societies, the paternal cross-cousin is often called "Father"; and under father-right mother's brother's daughter is labelled "Mother." If we consider, however, that under mother-right, the paternal cross-cousin (father's sister's son) is not Ego's real kinsman—that he is related to Ego only as the father's nearest kinsman—then the verbal identification is less strange. The appellation then really means: "that man who is to me only in so far related as he is my father's nearest in blood." And a similar psychological attitude underlies the strange use of Mother to a cross-cousin and other anomalous terms of this type.

The elimination of sex from workaday life

The unilateral principle which declares that kinship is counted through mother or father only means, in fact, looked at concretely as it enters the life of an individual, that the family bonds are extended on one side only. An important aspect of this one-sided extension is the development of rules of exogamy out of rules of incest. These rules eliminate sex out of the household and the clan respectively. Incomprehensible in their biological function, since biologists agree that occasional inbreeding is innocuous, they can be accounted for by the incompatibility of sexual interest with practical co-operation in everyday life. The emotional tension which accompanies erotic play, the jealousies and dissensions which it arouses as well as its obsessive and distractive influence, make it difficult to mingle sex with serious pursuits. Hence war and hunting, agriculture and trading enterprises, religious and public ceremonial, are often hedged round with sexual tabus.

Domestic life and all those relations which start in the family, that is parent and child, brother and sister, are permanently protected from the upsetting influence of sex by the tabu of incest. Later on, when the savage child, sexually ripe at an early age, enters the wider group of his village community and tribe, an important division is established in all his associations by the unilateral principle. Some people, male and female, become his natural associates in work, legal interests and spiritual concerns. These are his wider kindred, his clansmen and clanswomen, to whom he extends the modified and diluted family attitude, comprising among others, the rules of incest which here become the much wider and weaker tabus of exogamy. The other group consists of women with whom he may amuse himself and pursue his amorous inclinations, and of men with whom he enters into relations of more or less friendly rivalry or reciprocity.

The unilateral principle is thus instrumental in securing for the clan the same condition of sexually undisturbed co-operation as is secured for the family by the prohibition of incest.

Unilateral descent is also intimately bound up with the nature of filiation, that is, with the handing over of status, power, office and possessions, from one generation to the other. Order and simplicity in the rules of filiation are of the greatest importance for social cohesion. Indeed, we find that most political quarrels and tribal dissensions are due, apart from sex, to questions of inheritance and succession—from lowest savagery right up to modern civilization. Rivalries during lifetime, fights and rifts after the death of a man, especially if he be powerful, are of universal occurrence. For, as we know, mother-right and father-right are never absolute and the rules are always elastic and sometimes ambiguous. The generalization may, therefore, be laid down that the simpler and stricter the laws of filiation, the more stringently enforced either mother-right or father-right at the expense of the other, the greater will be the order and cohesion in a community, the smoother will be the transmission of authority, tradition and wealth from one generation to the other.

The further extensions of kinship

So far mainly the principles of extension have been analysed—its driving forces, so to speak: such as the need of substitute parents; the value of eliminating sex from household and clan; the importance of establishing order in filiation. The process itself consists, as in the case of mother substitution, in a series of successive extensions, each of which brings about a partial loosening and modification of the old ties, and the formation of new ones upon the old model.

In the earlier stages, the infant is mainly passive—as when it forms the first bonds by accepting the parental cares; as when it is weaned from the mother; taught to name its parent; to accept a substitute mother and father and to extend to them the parental appellations. Later on when the baby assumes the status of a child, often by donning the first dress, when he begins to follow the parents and takes some part in their pursuits, his interest in new associations and in the formation of new bonds becomes more active too.

Then there comes, in some tribes at least, again a stage of abrupt, passively received training. The rites of tribal initiation, as a rule, entail a dramatic break with the old life and the creation of new bonds. The novice is made to forget his associations with the family, especially with its female members, above all with the mother. In the course of the moral and mythological training which he receives, he is taught in a systematic way what kinship means, he is instructed in the principles of unilateral descent, the rules of exogamy, the duties and responsibilities towards his kindred and relatives. In other tribes, where there are no initiation rites, the same moral and legal education is given gradually, spread over a longer period—but it always has to be received, and it is always given with reference to kinship.

The boy and girl now enter the active life of the tribe. Often the individual has to change his residence, the girl on marrying into another village, the boy on assuming his full unilateral kinship status. In matriarchal and patrilocal communities, for instance, he leaves his father's place and joins his mother's brother. With this a new recrystallization of kinship bonds takes place—always, however, on the same principle: with the old pattern carried over, but adjusted to the individual's new status and to his new conditions of life.

Marriage opens a new phase and constitutes another transition. Here a new set of relatives is acquired, besides the individual mate, and the terminology is enriched by another set of expressions, as a rule some taken over from the old vocabulary of kinship, and some new ones added. Incidentally a new household is founded, with which the whole kinship story starts afresh.

Later on, with old age, with the marriage of children and the arrival of grandchildren, the kinship horizon changes once more, as a rule by the growth and multiplication of the younger generation, lineal and collateral, and by their gradual taking of duties, responsibilities and privileges out of Ego's hands.

The nature of the extensions

Thus each successive transformation of kinship bonds is, as a rule, associated with a biological stage in human life; each corresponds to a different type of social setting; each is conditioned by different functions performed by the group. Kinship invariably begins in the family—mother, father and child, the latter depending for nourishment, comfort and safety upon its parents. From the individual household and the mainly biological functions of the family, the child passes into the social horizon of a few associated households, which by the first extension of kinship, furnish him with his "substitute" parents, brothers and sisters, and by the formation of new relationships, supply his grandparents, his maternal uncle, paternal aunt and his cross-cousins. At, and after, puberty, he learns, in a more explicit and systematic manner, the principles of his tribal kinship and law. This is done through initiation or training within the horizon of the local community. Entering afterwards the stage of active life, as a member of his clan he takes part in most tribal concerns—economic, ceremonial, legal, warlike or religious. Soon, also, he makes a choice of his matrimonial mate, according to the kinship rules regulating marriage in his tribe.

One side of the whole process consists in the gradual assimilation of the new ties to the old ones; the other side, in the creation of new interests, adoption of new functions and formation of new ties. Even when the old ties are purposely destroyed, as in initiation, the new ones are built on their pattern. Throughout the process each extension leads to the formation of new ties and thus to the weakening of the old ones, but never to their complete obliteration, nor to the confusion of the two sets. The new relationships receive some elements of the old ones, which become incorporated in them, but invariably they contain new elements also.

At the end, the individual finds himself not with one confused or amalgamated mass of kindred, but rather, surrounded by a number of gradually widening circles: the family, the collateral relatives, the local kinsmen and relatives, the clansmen, and the relatives within the tribe; and, cutting athwart this concentric system, his own new household and his relatives-in-law.

The persistence of family ties

Why does the family pattern persist throughout these extensions, not only in terminology, but in legal fiction, in totemic tradition and in the character of the various rules? It must never be forgotten, of course, that kinship at the tribal end is by no means identical with kinship at the family end. As the ties widen, their original family character becomes more and more attenuated and diluted by other ingredients. Tribal kinship bears only a remote, at times mainly figurative, resemblance to the family ties, but that it is built under their influence and as an extension of them is beyond doubt.

The main force which brings about this extension is the extreme strength of family ties. The power of the earliest family experiences to influence all subsequent social relations is a universal fact which was not sufficiently appreciated until recently. In spite of their exaggerated claims and fantastic distortions, psychoanalytic writers have helped to show how all-pervading the family sentiments are in society, and how the reminiscences of paternal authority and of maternal tenderness enter into most relations of later life.

In the small communities of savages, where all social relations are direct and personal, where all co-operation is by actual contact, where solidarity and substitution operate within groups of people constantly in touch with each other, the family pattern can be adapted to all wider formations much more concretely and liberally. In all the extensions the new bonds and obligations are formed on account of the old ones; therefore, to an extent, in their image. The unilateral principle deflecting the spread of the family pattern to one side only, makes its sway within the clan only the more concentrated, while it frees from its constraint a whole sphere of relations—those between clans.

The final product of the process of kinship extensions: the clan system, with its twofold relationships within the kinship group and across the groups, is thus the natural product of the influences which drive family kinship into wider spheres of action and of the unilateral principle.

The clan and the family

Nothing is as important and difficult in the study of primitive sociology as the correct understanding of the nature of the clan and its relation to the family. The primary and fundamental elements of parent to child kinship—the bonds of procreation, the physiological services, the innate emotional response—which make up the family bonds, vanish completely from the relationship within the clan. Totemic identity, the mythological fiction of common totemic descent, magical, religious and legal functions, are new elements which have entered into it, and which constitute the greatly modified kinship of the clan.

But though the clan is essentially non-reproductive, non-sexual and non-parental, though it never is the primary basis and source of kinship, its connection with the family is real and genetic. The clan grows out of family kinship round one of the parents by the affirmation of the exclusive procreative relevance of this one parent, by the injunction of legal solidarity with one side of kindred, accompanied often by legal fiction and linguistic metaphor.

The clan differs from the family, however, not only in the nature of its bonds but also in structure. It is the result of the widest possible extension of kinship ties, but on one side only. While the family contains essentially the two principles, male and female, present in procreation, in the physiological division of functions and in sociological protection, the clan is based upon the elimination of either the paternal or the maternal element from relevant kinship. It is rather the clan of the relevant parent, *plus* the clan of the irrelevant parent, *plus* the other clans related to Ego by marriage or other forms of affinity, which together embrace the classificatory body of relatives. In fact the classificatory nomenclature always refers to the tribe or the community or a wider portion of it, and never to one clan only. It is the tribe, therefore, as a correlated system of clans, or such portion of it as is embraced by the classificatory nomenclature, which corresponds to the widest circle of kinship extensions.

It is an easy but dangerous mistake to maintain that "the classificatory system and our own are the outcome of the social institutions of the clan and the family respectively," and to say that as "among ourselves this (the essential) social unit is the family" so "amongst most peoples of rude culture the clan or other exogamous group is the essential unit of social organization." [1] This view carries on Morgan's mistaken opinion that the clan is a domestic institution, made *ad hoc* for purposes of group-marriage, a mistake which has recently been reaffirmed in the phrase that "the clan, like the family, is a reproductive group." [2] All this is a continuous source of error in that it construes the clan into an independent,

---

[1] W. H. R. Rivers, *Kinship and Social Organization*, 1914, pp. 74, 75.

[2] Robert Briffault, *The Mothers*, 1927.

self-sufficient kinship unit, whereas the clan is essentially a group correlated to other groups of a similar nature, and dependent upon their existence. In its simplest form the correlated system is reduced to two clans,
but never to one. It is this compound system which corresponds to the
family, which itself is a self-sufficient independent kinship unit. The clan
in fact never bears the imprint of extended full family kinship, but only
of one side of it.

It is a curious mistake to take savage fiction and linguistic simile at their
face value, and to regard, with Morgan, the clan as a "domestic institution," made *ad hoc* for purposes of group-marriage; or with Rivers, to
imagine that the clan has been the foundation of classificatory nomenclature in the same sense as the family is the basis of our own terminology;
or to affirm that "the clan, like the family, is a reproductive group."

The function of the clan system is neither generative nor domestic;
exogamy is not primarily an injunction to marry a woman of another
clan, but the prohibition of sexual intercourse within the clan. Again
the relations between the older and younger generation within the clan,
or between age-grades, are neither an equivalent nor a copy of the parent
to child relations—above all, not as regards reproductive functions!

The relation of the members of a clan is a modified and extended kinship
solidarity; it implies co-operation in most communal undertakings and
the exclusion of sexual interests. Thus some elements of the later parent
to child and brother to sister relationship are carried over into clanship,
but two elements never enter it: the matrimonial relation and early parent
to child relation. The first of these is extended, in a modified form, into the
relationship between different clans, members of which may pursue amusements and sexual interests in common, as between males and females; and
between individuals of the same sex, render each other reciprocal services
from group to group, and join in enterprises on a tribal scale.

We can now define kinship, in the first place, as the personal bonds
based upon procreation, socially interpreted; and, in the second place, as
the wider bonds derived from the primary ones by the process of gradual
extensions which occur in all communities during the life-history of the
individual. On the level of savagery and lower barbarism, the powerful persistence of family bonds is given freer play, hence the extensions are more
numerous and more definitely systematized; they are backed up by legal
fictions of totemic descent; by ideas of one-sided procreation or mystic
identity; and they lead to the formation of wider groups such as the
clan, moiety or exogamous division.

Kinship is thus a class of social relations, which must be subdivided
into several varieties: primary kinship always founded on marriage and
family; and the derived forms, correlated with the group of cognate
households, the village-community and the clan. The terms of kinship,

which are but linguistic expressions of all these relationships, have obviously also a manifold meaning, which corresponds to the social reality. Thus is explained the existence, side by side of individual and classificatory terms, of the family and the clan, of the individual and communal aspects of kinship. The enigmatic and apparently anomalous character of primitive kinship vanishes with a closer scrutiny of the facts.

To explain kinship there is no need of an appeal to a fanciful history of mankind, beginning with Promiscuity or Hetairism, passing through Group-Marriage, Marital Gerontocracy and Anomalous Marriages, and only ending, after many errors and efforts, in monogamous marriage. Where empirical facts yield a sufficient explanation hypotheses are superfluous—they are a disease of method. Especially erroneous in these speculations is the neglect of domesticity and the influences of everyday life in early childhood, combined, as this neglect often is, with an over-emphasis on sex. Sex, far from being the principal clue to kinship, plays only a subordinate part in its formation, separated as it is from parenthood by the rule of legitimacy. It is the elimination of sex and not indulgence in it which, through the rules of incest and exogamy, really influences kinship and clanship.

The study of kinship, far from demonstrating the small importance of the family, proves the tenacity of its bonds and their persistence through life as a standard for all wider social relations. The age-long experience of mankind, which Anthropology alone can unravel, teaches us that the institutions of marriage and family have never been absent in human history, that they form the indispensable foundation for the structure of human society, and that, however they might become modified in the future, they will never be destroyed nor their influence seriously impaired.

BIBLIOGRAPHY

Classical Works

Bachofen, J. J., *Das Mutterrecht*, 1861.

Maine, H. S., *Ancient Law*, 1861.

Morgan, L. H., *Systems of Consanguinity and Affinity of the Human Family*, 1871.

McLennan, J. F., *Studies in Ancient History*, 1886.

Crawley, A. E., *The Mystic Rose*, 1902; new ed. 1927.

Lang, A., "The Origin of Terms of Human Relationship," *Proc. Brit. Acad.*, 1907 (Vol. 3).

Frazer, J. G., *Totemism and Exogamy*, 1910.

Westermarck, E. A., *The History of Human Marriage*, 5th ed. 1921.

Recent Theoretical Studies

Kroeber, A. L., "Classificatory Systems of Relationship," *Jour. Roy. Anthr. Inst.*, 1909 (Vol. 39).

Rivers, W. H. R., *Kinship and Social Organisation*, 1914; *Social Organisation*, 1924.

Lowie, R. H., *Culture and Ethnology*, 1917; *Primitive Society*, 1920.

Gifford, E. W., *Californian Kinship Terminologies*, 1922.

Malinowski, B., *Sex and Repression in Savage Society*, 1927.

Briffault, R., *The Mothers*, 1927.

Seligman, B. Z., "Marital Gerontocracy in Africa," *Jour. Roy. Anthr. Inst.*, 1924 (Vol. 54).

Descriptive Accounts

Radcliffe-Brown, A. R., "Three Tribes of Western Australia," *Jour. Roy. Anthr. Inst.*, 1913 (Vol. 43); *The Andaman Islanders*, 1925.

Armstrong, W. E., *Rossel Island*, 1928.

Malinowski, B., *The Family among the Australian Aborigines*, 1913; *Crime and Custom in Savage Society*, 1926; *The Sexual Life of Savages in North-Western Melanesia*, 1928.

Rivers, W. H. R., *The Todas*, 1906; *The History of Melanesian Society*, 1914.

Thurnwald, R., *Die Gemeinde der Bánaro*, 1921.

Junod, H. A., *The Life of a South African Tribe*, 1927.

Smith, E. W., and Dale, A. M., *The Ila-Speaking Peoples of Northern Rhodesia*, 1920.

Rattray, R. S., *Ashanti*, 1925.

Spier, L., "The Distribution of Kinship Systems in North America," *Univ. of Washington Pub. in Anthropology*, 1925 (Vol. 1).

Kroeber, A. L., "California Kinship Systems," *Univ. of Calif. Pub. in Anthrop.*, 1917 (Vol. 12).

Czaplicka, M. A., *Aboriginal Siberia*, 1914.

Seligman, B. Z., "Studies in Semitic Kinship," *Bull. School of Oriental Studies*, London, 1923 (Vol. 3).

THE IMPASSE ON KINSHIP

Much ink has flowed on the problem of blood—"blood" symbolizing in most human languages, and that not only European, the ties of kinship, that is the ties derived from procreation. "Blood" almost became discoloured out of all recognition in the process. Yet blood will rebel against any tampering, and flow its own way and keep its own colour. By which florid metaphor I simply mean that the extravagantly conjectural and bitterly controversial theorizing which we have had on primitive kinship has completely obscured the subject, and all but blinded the observers of actual primitive life. Professor Radcliffe-Brown is all too correct when he says "that theories of the form of conjectural history, whether

This article appeared in Man: A Monthly Record of Anthropological Science, *published under the direction of the Royal Anthropological Institute of Great Britain and Ireland, February 1930 (Vol. 30, No. 2), pp. 19–29; reprinted by permission of the Honorary Editor of* Man.

'evolutionary' or 'diffusionist' exert a very pernicious influence on the
work of the field ethnologist," and he gives a very significant example
of the fact-blindness to which this leads.[1]

And these conjectural theories on kinship have simply flooded anthropological literature from the times of Bachofen, Morgan and McLennan,
to the recent revival in kinship enthusiasm, headed by Rivers and his
school, A. R. Radcliffe-Brown, the late A. Bernard Deacon, T. T. Barnard,
Mrs. Reinhold Hoernlé, Mrs. B. Z. Seligman, not to mention myself, or
the Californian kinship-trinity, Kroeber, Lowie and Gifford—one and all
influenced by the work of Rivers. With all this, the problem has remained
enshrined in an esoteric atmosphere. The handful of us, the *enragés* or
initiates of kinship, are prepared to wade through the sort of kinship
algebra and geometry which has gradually developed; memorize long lists
of native words, follow up complicated diagrams and formulae, sweat
through dry documents, endure long deductive arguments, as well as the
piling of hypothesis upon hypothesis.

The average anthropologist, however, somewhat mystified and perhaps
a little hostile, has remained outside the narrow ring of devotees. He has
his doubts whether the effort needed to master the bastard algebra of kinship is really worth while. He feels, that, after all, kinship is a matter
of flesh and blood, the result of sexual passion and maternal affection, of
long intimate daily life, and of a host of personal intimate interests. Can
all this really be reduced to formulae, symbols, perhaps equations? Is it
sound, hopefully to anticipate "that the time will come when we shall
employ symbols for the different relationships . . . and many parts of the
description of the social systems of savage tribes will resemble a work
on mathematics in which the results will be expressed by symbols, in
some cases even in the form of equations"?[2]

A very pertinent question might be asked as to whether we should
really get nearer the family life, the affections and tender cares, or again
the dark and mysterious forces which the psycho-analyst banishes into the
Unconscious but which often break out with dramatic violence—whether
we could come nearer to this, the real core of kinship, by the mere use
of mock-algebra. There is no doubt that whatever value the diagrams
and equations might have must always be derived from the sociological
and psychological study of the intimate facts of kinship, on which the
algebra should be based. The average common-sense anthropologist or observer of savages feels that this personal approach to kinship is sadly lacking. There is a vast gulf between the pseudo-mathematical treatment of
the too-learned anthropologist and the real facts of savage life. Nor is this
merely the feeling of the non-specialist. I must frankly confess that there
is not a single account of kinship in which I do not find myself puzzled

[1] See *Man,* 1929, No. 35.
[2] W. H. R. Rivers, *The History of Melanesian Society,* 1914, 2 vols. Vol. I, p. 10.

by some of this spuriously scientific and stilted mathematization of kinship facts and disappointed by the absence of those intimate data of family life, full-blooded descriptions of tribal and ceremonial activities, thorough enumerations of the economic and legal characteristics of family, kindred and clan, which alone make kinship a real fact to the reader.[3]

And when, after all the floods of ink on kinship, the average anthropologist finds that an authority like Professor Westermarck maintains that most work on classificatory terminologies "has been a source of error rather than knowledge"; when he finds that A. R. Radcliffe-Brown, B. Malinowski and Brenda Z. Seligman cannot agree as to what they mean when they use the terms *kinship, descent, unilateral* and *bilateral;* when he discovers that no sooner has Mrs. Seligman restated the fundamental concept of classificatory terminologies than she is challenged in letters to *Man;* then he really feels justified in mistrusting all this terribly elaborate pseudo-mathematical apparatus and in discounting most of the labour which must have been spent on it.

I believe that kinship is really the most difficult subject of social anthropology; I believe that it has been approached in a fundamentally wrong way; and I believe that at present an impasse has been reached. I am convinced, however, that there is a way out of this impasse, and that some of the recent work, notably that of A. R. Radcliffe-Brown, of Brenda Z. Seligman and of the Californian trinity, has placed the problem on the correct foundation. This has been done by a full recognition of the importance of the family and by the application of what is now usually called the functional method of anthropology—a method which consists above all in the analysis of primitive institutions as they work at present, rather than in the reconstruction of a hypothetical past.[4]

[3] In a book on kinship which I am preparing I shall substantiate this indictment in detail. To mention only the very best field-work: can anyone really unravel Prof. R. Thurnwald's diagrams and synoptics of kinship in his otherwise excellent *Gemeinde der Bánaro?* The "kinship systems" of the Toda, Arunta, Ashanti, Ba Ila, of the Californians and Melanesians, amount to little more than incorrectly translated fragments of a vocabulary. All our data on kinship are insufficient linguistically and inadequate sociologically.

[4] I would like to mention Edward Westermarck and Ernest Grosse as the forerunners in matters of kinship of the modern movement. Perhaps the first monographic description of the family, from an area where its very existence has been most contested, is my *Family among the Australian Aborigines* (1913). In the same year there appeared an excellent article on "Family," in *Hastings' Encyclopaedia of Religion and Ethics,* written by E. N. Fallaize. More recently Kroeber, in his *Zuñi Kin and Clan* [1917], and Lowie in his field-work on the Crow Indians and in his book on *Primitive Society* [1920] have very strongly emphasized the functional point of view in reference to kinship. Quite lately, in her remarkable article on "Incest and Descent," in the *J.R.A.I.,* Mrs. Seligman has definitely announced her conversion to the functional point of view and her recognition of the fundamental importance of the family. (Vol. LIX, p. 234.)

All this recent work is bound to lead us to the correct solution of the many more or less superficial puzzles, as well as of the real and profound problems of kinship. This work is still somewhat diffused and chaotic, however, and there is the need of a comprehensive contribution which will organize and systematically integrate the results of the functional work, and correct a few mistakes still prevalent. In my forthcoming book on kinship I am making an attempt at such a systematic treatment. Here I propose to indicate in a preliminary fashion some of its results.[5]

It is unnecessary, perhaps, in addressing the readers of *Man*, to labour the point of kinship remaining still in an impasse. The several interesting articles in the present periodical, as well as in the *Journal*, show how profoundly even the few most devoted and most spiritually related specialists disagree with one another.[6] As a member of the inner ring, I may say

[5] The subject of kinship, and above all the fact that it invariably originates in the family, was the starting point of my anthropological work. The book on *The Family among the Australian Aborigines* was begun in 1909 and published in 1913. I laid down there a number of principles and concretely worked out some of my general ideas. These I was able more fully to substantiate in my subsequent work in the field and in the study. The development of my views on kinship can be followed from my first field-work on the Mailu, where my treatment is still largely conventional and incorrect up to my article s.v. "Kinship" in the 14th Edition of the *Encyclopaedia Britannica* and my two volumes on sex in savage life. The list of my contributions fully or partially devoted to kinship follows:

1. *The Family among the Australian Aborigines*, London, 1913.
2. "The Natives of Mailu," *Transactions of the R. Soc. of S. Australia*, Adelaide, 1915.
3. "The Psychology of Sex in Primitive Societies," *Psyche*, Oct. 1923.
4. "Psycho-Analysis and Anthropology," *Psyche*, Apr. 1924.
5. "Complex and Myth in Mother-Right," *Psyche*, Jan. 1925.
6. "Forschungen in einer mutterrechtlichen Gemeinschaft," *Zeitschrift für Völkerpsychologie und Soziologie*, Mar. 1925.
7. "Address on Anthropology and Social Hygiene," *Foundations of Social Hygiene*, London, 1926.
8. "Anthropology," article in *Ency. Brit.*, additional volumes, 1926.
9. "The Anthropological Study of Sex," *Verhandlungen des I. Internationalen Kongresses für Sexualforschung*, Berlin, 1926.
10. *Crime and Custom in Savage Society*, London, 1926.
11. *Sex and Repression in Savage Society*, London, 1927 (embodies 4 and 5).
12. *The Sexual Life of Savages*, London, 1929 (embodies 3 and 6).
13. "Kinship," article in *Ency. Brit.*, 14th Edit., 1929 [Chapt. 6 herein].
14. "Marriage," article in *Ency. Brit.*, 14th Edit., 1929 [Chapt. 1 herein].
15. "Social Anthropology," article in *Ency. Brit.*, 14th Edit., 1929 (revised version of 8).

[6] Cf. *J.R.A.I.*, Vol. LVIII, p. 533, and Vol. LIX, p. 231, articles by Mrs. B. Z. Seligman; *Man*, 1929, No. 35, by A. R. Radcliffe-Brown, and No. 148, by E. E. Evans-Pritchard; and letters by Mrs. Seligman (1929, No. 84), by A. R. Radcliffe-Brown (1929, No. 157), and by Lord Raglan (1930, No. 13).

that whenever I meet Mrs. Seligman or Dr. Lowie or discuss matters with Radcliffe-Brown or Kroeber, I become at once aware that my partner does not understand anything in the matter, and I end usually with the feeling that this also applies to myself. This refers also to all our writings on kinship, and is fully reciprocal.

The impasse is really due to the inheritance of false problems from anthropological tradition. We are still enmeshed in the question as to whether kinship in its origins was collective or individual, based on the family or the clan. This problem looms very large in the writings of the late W. H. R. Rivers, of whom most of us in the present generation are pupils by direct teaching or from the reading of his works. Another false problem is that of the origins and significance of classificatory systems of nomenclature. This problem, or any problem starting from the classificatory nature of kinship terminologies, must be spurious, because the plain fact is that classificatory terminologies do not exist and never could have existed.[7] This sounds like a paradox but is a mere truism which I propose to develop later in another article. Connected with the classificatory obsession, there was the rage for the explanation of queer terms by anomalous marriages, which led to one or two half-truths but also to half a dozen capital errors and misconceptions. The conception of mother-right and father-right as successive stages or self-contained entities, recently so well and convincingly stigmatized by Radcliffe-Brown (*Man*, 1929, No. 35), has been embodied in yet another monument of brilliantly speculative erroneousness in Briffault's work on *The Mothers*.

The real trouble in all this is that we have been hunting for origins of kinship before we had properly understood the nature of kinship. We inquired whether mother-right preceded father-right or vice versa, without allowing the facts to convince us, as they must, that mother-right and father-right are always indissolubly bound up with each other. Because we have profoundly misunderstood the linguistic nature of kinship terms, we are able to make the monstrous mistake of regarding them as "survivals," as petrified remains of a previous social state. It is almost ludicrous with what naïveté Morgan assumes throughout his writings that the terminologies of kinship invariably lag one whole "stage of development"—neither more nor less—behind the sociological status in which they are found; and yet that they mirror the past sociological status perfectly. The mere logical circle of the argument is appalling. But even worse is the complete misconception of the nature of kinship terminologies which, in fact, are the most active and the most effective expressions of human relationship, expressions which start in early childhood, which accompany human intercourse throughout life, which em-

[7] For the most recent, brief, clear and most erroneous statements concerning the nature of classificatory terminologies, see the letter in *Man* by Mr. J. D. Unwin (1929, No. 124).

body all the most personal, passionate, and intimate sentiments of a man or woman.

The modern or functional anthropologist proposes, therefore, to understand what kinship really means to the native; he wishes to grasp how terminologies of kinship are used and what they express; he wishes to see clearly the relations between the family, the clan and the tribe. But the more he studies all these elements of the problem and their inter-relation, the more clearly he realizes that we have to do here not with a number of isolated entities but with the parts of an organically connected whole. In the first place, the family and the clan, for instance, which have hitherto been regarded as domestic institutions at various stages of development, appear invariably together. That is, while the family exists in many societies alone, the clan never replaces it, but is found as an additional institution. Again, though certain tribes use kinship terms in a wider sense, they also use them in the narrower sense, denoting the actual members of the family. Or, again, there is no such thing as pure mother-right or father-right, only a legal over-emphasis on one side of kinship, accompanied very often by a strong emotional, at times even customary, reaction against this over-emphasis. And, in all communities, whatever the legal system might be, both lines are *de facto* counted and influence the legal, economic, religious and emotional life of the individual. It is, therefore, nothing short of nonsensical to perform this sort of illegitimate preliminary surgery, to cut the organically connected elements asunder, and "explain" them by placing the fragments on a diagram of imaginary development. The real problem is to find out how they are related to each other, and how they *function*, that is, what part they play respectively within the society, what social needs they satisfy, and what influence they exert.

To put it clearly, though crudely, I should say that the family is always the domestic institution *par excellence*. It dominates the early life of the individual; it controls domestic co-operation; it is the stage of earliest parental cares and education. The clan, on the other hand, is never a domestic institution. Bonds of clanship develop much later in life, and, though they develop out of the primary kinship of the family, this development is submitted to the one-sided distortion of matrilineal or patrilineal legal emphasis, and it functions in an entirely different sphere of interests: legal, economic, above all, ceremonial. Once the functional distinction is made between the two modes of grouping, the family and the clan, most of the spurious problems and fictitious explanations dissolve into the speculative mist out of which they were born.

I shall have, however, to qualify and make much more detailed the above contention. Here I only wish to point out that kinship presents really several facets corresponding to the various phases or stages of its development within the life history of the individual. For kinship is the phenomenon which begins earliest in life and which lasts longest, even as the word *mother* is usually the first word formed and often the last word uttered. Kinship as it appears in the social horizon of a developed adult tribesman is the result of a long process of extensions and transformations. It starts in early life with the physiological events of procreation; yet even these are profoundly modified in human society by cultural influences. The original ties of kinship, which I believe firmly are invariably individual, later on develop, multiply and become largely communal. So that, at the end, the individual finds himself the centre of a complex system of multiple ties; a member of several groups: the family, always; the extended household, in many communities; the local group, almost invariably; the clan, very often; and the tribe, without any exception. I am convinced that if the study of kinship ties had been carried out in the field along the life history of the individual, if terminologies, legal systems, tribal and household arrangements had been studied in process of development and not merely as fixed products—that we would have been completely free of the whole nightmare of spurious problems and fantastic conjectures. It is almost an irony in the history of anthropology that the most ardent evolutionists as well as the most embittered prophets of the historical method have completely missed development and history of kinship in the one case in which this development and history can be studied empirically.[8]

Whenever we become convinced that a phenomenon must be studied in its development, our attention naturally must become focussed on its origins, and let us remember that here we are dealing, not with a fanciful, reconstructed evolution, but with the observable development of kinship in human life and that *origins* here mean simply the whole set of initial conditions which determine the attitudes of the actors in the kinship drama.

These actors are obviously three in number at the beginning—the two parents and their offspring. And, at first sight, it might appear that the drama itself is of no real interest; for is it not merely the physiological process of conception, gestation and child-birth? In reality, however, the process is never a merely physiological one in human societies. However primitive the community, the facts of conception, pregnancy and childbirth are not left to Nature alone, but they are reinterpreted by cultural

[8] My friend Mr. T. J. A. Yates suggests the adjective "biographical" as the simplest description of the method of approach to kinship through its study along the life history of the individual. I shall speak in future of the "biographical method" in order to define what might be called sociological ontogeny. Mr. Yates is now engaged on a comparative study of the functional correlation of mother-right and father-right.

tradition: in every community we have a theory as to the nature and causes of conception; we have a system of customary observances, religious, magical or legal, which define the behaviour of the mother, at times also of the father; we have, specifically, a number of taboos observed during pregnancy by both parents.

Thus, even the biological foundation of kinship becomes invariably a cultural and not merely a natural fact. This unquestionably correct principle has become at the hands of some modern anthropologists the starting point for a new reinterpretation of Morgan's hypothesis of a primitive communal marriage. Rivers, the most conspicuous modern supporter of Morgan's theories, is fully aware that group-marriage implies group-parenthood. Yet group-parenthood, above all group-motherhood, seems to be an almost unthinkable hypothesis. As such it has been in fact ridiculed by Andrew Lang, E. Westermarck and N. W. Thomas. Rivers, however, following in this the brilliant suggestions of Durkheim, Dargun, and Kohler, argues that, since cultural influences can modify maternity in every other respect, it can transform it even from an individual motherhood into a sort of sociological group-motherhood. This writer, and a number of his followers, notably Mr. Briffault, would lead us to believe that what I like to call the *initial situation* of kinship is not individual but communal.

I have adduced these very recent hypotheses about the initial situation of kinship in order to show that its study, far from being an obvious and superfluous statement of a physiological fact, raises a number of sociological questions, even of controversial points. With all this, the study of real empirical facts seems to show that the communal interpretation of the initial situation is definitely erroneous. I can but anticipate here the full presentation of my argument, and say that while I recognize that kinship, even in its origins, is a cultural rather than a biological fact, this culturally defined kinship is, I maintain, invariably individual. All the primitive theories of procreation, though they are a mixture of animistic beliefs and crude empirical observations, invariably define parenthood as an individual bond. The taboos of pregnancy, the rites observed at certain stages of gestation, customs of the *couvade* type, ceremonial seclusion of mother and child, all these individualize the relationship between the actual parents and their offspring.

While most of these facts refer to the individual tie between mother and child, a number of them, such as the couvade, the taboos kept by the pregnant woman's husband, his economic contributions towards pregnancy ceremonies, culturally define paternity, and at the same time individualize this relationship. There is one fact, however, of paramount importance as regards paternity, a generalization so cogent, so universally valid, that it has, to my knowledge, been almost completely overlooked, as it so often happens to the "obvious." This generalization I have called, in some of my previous writings, the *principle of legitimacy*.[9] This principle declares that, in all human societies, a father is regarded by law, custom and morals as an indispensable element of the procreative group. The woman has to be married before she is allowed legitimately to conceive, or else a subsequent marriage or an act of adoption gives the child full tribal or civil status. Otherwise the child of the unmarried mother is definitely stigmatized by an inferior and anomalous position in society. This is as true of the polyandrous Todas (where the child has, in fact, to be sociologically assigned to one father among the several husbands); of the matrilineal Melanesians, of primitive peoples in Australia, in North America, and in Africa, as of monogamous and Christian Europe. The principle of legitimacy works at times in indirect ways, but on the whole the law which demands marriage as the preliminary to family seems to be universal.

I believe that a correct inductive survey of all the evidence at our disposal would lead us to the answer that the initial situation of kinship is a compound of biological and cultural elements, or rather that it consists of the facts of individual procreation culturally reinterpreted; that every human being starts his sociological career within the small family group, and that whatever kinship might become later on in life, it is always individual kinship at first. At the same time this general statement gives us only the broad outlines of the initial situation; this becomes from the outset deeply modified by such elements as maternal or paternal counting of kinship, matrilocal or patrilocal residence, the relative position of husband and wife in a community, length of lactation, types of seclusion and taboos. The study of the initial situation, far from being trite and insignificant, is a rich field of sociological investigation, and a field on which the anthropologist and the modern psychologist meet in common interest.

With the conclusion that individual parenthood, defined by cultural as well as biological forces, forms invariably the initial situation of kinship, the foundations of a correct theory have been laid. But the task is not yet complete. What I have named the initial situation is important in its influence on later life. Parenthood interests the sociologists not only in itself, whether as an exhibition of human tenderness or as an example of the cultural transformation of instinct, but rather in that it is the starting point of most other sociological relationships and the prototype of the characteristic social attitudes of a community. It is, therefore, the processes of the extension of kinship from its extremely simple beginnings in plain parenthood, to its manifold ramifications and complexities

[9] Cf. article on the "Psychology of Sex in Primitive Societies," *Psyche*, Oct. 1923; *Sex and Repression*, 1927, Part V; Chapter VII of the *Sexual Life of Savages;* article on "Kinship" in *Ency. Brit.*, 1929 [Chapt. 6 of *Sex, Culture, and Myth*]. Cf. also *The Family*, Chapters V and VI.

in adult membership of tribe, clan and local group, which, in my opinion, forms the real subject-matter of the study of kinship. It is in the study of these processes that the true relationship between clan and family, between classificatory systems and individual attitudes, between the sociological and the biological elements of kinship, can be discovered.

Most of the mistakes were due to the following false argument: all kinship is biological; the cohesion of a clan is based on kinship; ergo, clanship has a direct biological basis. This conclusion has led to such capital howlers as that "the clan marries the clan and begets the clan"; that "the clan, like the family, is a reproductive group"; and that "a domestic group, other than the family" is the environment of primitive childhood. The perpetrators of these and similar are no lesser anthropologists than Fison, Spencer and Gillen, Briffault, and Rivers.

All this nonsense could never have obsessed some of the clearest minds in anthropology had the study of the initial situation been made the starting point, and the study of subsequent processes of extension the main theme, of social anthropology. For the "origins of the clan system" are not to be found in some nebulous past by imaginary speculations. They happen nowadays under our very eyes. Any reasonably intelligent and unprejudiced anthropologist who works within a tribe with clan organization can see them taking place.

I have, myself, witnessed the "origins of the clan" in Melanesia, and I think that even from this one experience I am able to draw a universally valid conclusion, or at least a generalization which ought to be universally tested. Especially since all the fragmentary evidence from other areas fits perfectly well into the scheme based on Melanesian facts.

The process by which clanship and other forms of communal kinship develop out of the initial situation is in reality not easy to grasp or to define. The main difficulty consists in the fact that it is a lengthy and interrupted process; that its threads are many, and that the pattern can only be discovered after an integration of detailed and intimate observations over a lengthy period of time. And so far, it has been the custom of competent sociologists to pay only flying visits to savage tribes, for which practice the euphemism of "survey-work" has been invented. While the long-residence amateur was unable to see the wood for the trees.

But there is one definite source of difficulty. This is the fact that in the biographical development of kinship we have a two-fold process, or rather two correlated processes, one, roughly, of consolidation and extension of family ties, the other a process in which the family is over-ridden, in which kinship is submitted to a process of one-sided distortion, and in which the group or communal character of human relations is definitely emphasized at the expense of the individual character.

I shall proceed to amplify this statement, but I want to mention here that this duality of kinship growth has given rise to most of the misconceptions, above all to the quarrel as to whether primitive kinship is communal or individual, whether it is essentially bilateral or unilateral.[10]

Kinship in primitive communities has invariably the individual aspect, it has in most cases also the communal one. Each aspect is the result of a different process, it is formed by different educational mechanisms, and it has its own function to fulfil. The real scientific attitude is, not to quarrel as to which of the two actually existing phases of kinship has a moral right or a logical justification for its existence but to study their relation to each other.

Let me first briefly outline the process of consolidation of the family. For it must be remembered that, clan or no clan, the individual's own family remains a stable unit throughout his lifetime. The parents, in most societies, not only educate and materially equip the child, but they also watch over his adolescence, control his marriage, become the tender and solicitous grandparents of his children and in their old age often rely on his help. Thus the early bonds of kinship, which start in the initial situation, persist throughout life. But they undergo a long process which, on the one hand, as we have said, is one of consolidation, and on the other one of partial undermining and dissolution.

The consolidation in its early phases starts with the physiological dependence of the infant upon his parents, which shades into the early training of impulses, and that again passes into education. With education there are associated already certain wider sociological implications of parenthood. The child has to be educated in certain arts and crafts, and this implies that he will inherit the occupations, the tools, the lands or hunting-grounds of his father or his mother's brother. Education, again, embraces the training in tribal traditions, but tribal traditions refer to social organization, to the rôle which the child will play in society, and this the child usually takes over from his father or his mother's brother.

Thus, already, at the phase of education, kinship may either simply and directly confirm the father's rôle in the family, or, in matrilineal societies, it may partly disrupt the family by introducing an outsider as the man in power.

At the same time the dependence of the child upon the household varies to a considerable extent in different societies. He or she may either remain as an inmate in the parents' house, sleeping, eating and spending most of his time there; or else the child moves somewhere else, becomes influenced by other people, and forms new bonds. In communities where there are ceremonies of initiation the sociological function of such customs consists often in divorcing the child from the family, above all from

[10] Cf. for instance the interesting correspondence between Mrs. Seligman and Professor Radcliffe-Brown in *Man,* 1929, Nos. 84 and 157.

maternal influences, and in making him aware of his unilateral bonds of clanship, especially with his male clansmen. This is obviously an influence of a disruptive rather than a consolidating character so far as the family is concerned.

When it comes to adolescence and sexual life, there is an enormous variety of configurations but usually sexuality removes the boy or girl from the family and through the rules of exogamy makes him or her aware of their participation in the clan. At marriage, on the other hand, the own father and mother, at times some other near relative, always individual, come into prominence. The founding of a new household means to a large extent a final detachment from the parental one. But the parents, whether of the husband or the wife, reaffirm the relationship by the already mentioned fact of grandparenthood. Finally, in old age, new duties define the relationship between an adult man and his decrepit father or mother. Thus, throughout all the varieties which we find scattered over the globe, in main outline we find that the individual relation of offspring to parents develops, receives several shocks and diminutions, becomes reaffirmed again, but always remains one of the dominant sentiments in human life, manifesting itself in moral rules, in legal obligations, in religious ritual. For, last not least, at death, parent or offspring alike have to fulfil some of the principal mortuary duties and, in ancestor-cults —which, in a more or less pronounced form are to be found everywhere —the spirits of the departed are always dependent on their lineal descendants. The consolidation of family ties, and of the concept of family and household, manifests itself in the extensions of the early kinship attitudes to members of other households. Thus in most primitive communities, whatever be their way of counting descent, the households of the mother's sister and of the father's brother play a considerable part and in many ways become substitute homes for the child.

I have stressed, so far, the elements of consolidation, let me now muster those of disruption. The actual weaning, the removal from the family, especially from the mother's control, outside influences such as that of the mother's brother, at times of the father's sister or brother, initiation and the formation of a new household—all these influences run counter to the original ties and militate against the persistence of parental bonds and influences. At the same time most of these disruptive influences are not really negations of kinship. They are rather one-sided distortions of the original parental relationship. Thus, the mother's brother, in matrilineal societies, becomes the nucleus of the matrilineal clan. The training in tribal law, especially and dramatically given at initiation, while it removes the boy from the exclusive tutelage of the family, imbues him with ideas of clan identity and solidarity.

Clan identity becomes especially prominent in certain phases of tribal life. During big tribal gatherings, whether for economic enterprise or war, or enjoyment, the bonds of clanship become prominent, the family almost disappears. Especially is this the case in large religious or magical ceremonies such as those reported from Central Australia, Papua, Melanesia and the various districts of North America. On such occasions there takes place a recrystallization of the sociological structure within the community, which brings vividly to the minds of young and old the reality of the clan system.

We can see, therefore, that the clan develops as a derived sociological form of grouping by empirical processes which can be followed along the life history of the individual, which always take place later in life— full clanship taking hold of an individual only at maturity—and which embrace a type of interests very different from those obtaining within the family.

As I have tried to show elsewhere already there is something almost absurd in the tendency of anthropologists to treat the family and the clan as equivalent units which can replace one another in the evolution of mankind.[11] The relation between parents and child—that is, family relations—are based on procreation, on the early physiological cares given by the parents to the child and on the innate emotional attitudes which unite offspring and parents. These elements are never found in clanship. This institution, on the other hand, is based on factors which are quite alien to the family: on the identity of a totemic nature; on mythological fictions of a unilateral common descent from an ancestor or an ancestress; and a number of religious or magical duties and observances. It may be safely laid down that the family, based on marriage, is the only domestic institution of mankind, that is, the only institution the function of which is the procreation, the early cares and the elementary training of the offspring. Kinship thus always rests on the family and begins within the family. The clan is essentially a non-reproductive, non-sexual and non-parental group, and it is never the primary source and basis of kinship. But the clan always grows out of the family, forming round one of the two parents by the exclusive legal emphasis on the one side of kinship, at times backed by a one-sided reproductive theory. The functions of the clan are mostly legal and ceremonial, at times also magical and economic.

Family and clan differ thus profoundly in origins, in the functions which they fulfil, and in the nature of the bonds which unite their members. They differ also in structure. The family always embraces the two principles essential to procreation—motherhood and fatherhood. The clan is based on the partial negation of one of these principles. But the difference goes farther. The family is self-contained as regards its functions. The

[11] See B. Malinowski, article on "Kinship," in *Ency. Brit.*, 14th Edit., 1929 [Chapt. 6 of *Sex, Culture, and Myth*], esp. "The Clan and the Family" [pp. 147–149 of *Sex, Culture, and Myth*].

clan, by the very nature of its formation, is a dependent and correlated unit. The body of actually recognized relatives in the widest, that is classificatory, sense never consists of the clansmen alone. It embraces the own clansmen—that is, kinsmen on the relevant side—the clansmen of the irrelevant parent, the clanspeople of the consort, and members of the other clans who take part in the communal game of exchange of services, so characteristic of the tribes organized on the basis of the clan. It is the tribe, as the body of conjoined and mutually related clans, which at the classificatory level corresponds to the family. The sociological equivalence of family and clan, which has played so much havoc with social anthropology, is a misapprehension due to the omission of functional analysis and of the biographical method in the study of kinship problems.

I have started with a protest against the subordination of the flesh and blood side of kinship to the formal, pseudo-mathematical treatment to which it has been so often subjected. I have justified my criticism in a positive manner by showing that there are fundamental problems of kinship which demand a great deal of first-hand sociological observation and of theoretical analysis: problems which must be solved even before we start kinship algebra. The *initial situation,* the *principle of legitimacy,* the *two correlated processes of extension,* the *multiplicity of kinship groupings*—this is an extensive field for full-blooded sociological research in the field and in the study. Through the biographical approach and the functional analysis which I have advocated, most of these problems become transferred to the realm of empirical research from that of hypothetical reconstruction.

There remain a number of questions, however, on which I was hardly able to touch, above all the notorious puzzle of classificatory terminologies. I have left this latter question on one side on purpose: words grow out of life, and kinship words are nothing else but counters or labels for social relations. Even as, sociologically, kinship is a compound and complex network of ties, so every native nomenclature consists of several layers or systems of kinship designations. One system is used only to the parents and members of the household. Another stratum of kinship appellations is extended to the next nearest circle of relatives, the mother's sister and brother, the father's brother and sister, their offspring and the grandparents. Yet another type of kinship words applies to the wider relatives of the immediate neighbourhood. Finally there are kinship words used in a truly classificatory sense, based partly but never completely on the distinctions of clanship. The sounds used in these different senses are the same, but the uses, that is the meanings, are distinct. Each use, moreover, the individual, the extended, the local and the classificatory, is differentiated by phonetic distinctions, however slight, by fixed circumlocu-

tions, and by contextual indices.[12] It is only through the extraordinary incompetence of the linguistic treatment in kinship terminologies that the
compound character of primitive terminologies has, so far, been completely
overlooked. "Classificatory terminologies" really do not exist, as I have
said already. But I shall have to return to this question once more.

After that, it will be possible for me to criticize directly the logical
game of kinship algebra from Morgan and Kohler to Rivers and Mrs. B.
Z. Seligman; and to show within which limits this game is legitimate
and where it becomes spurious. There remain one or two questions: the
definition of kinship and descent, on which I have been recently criticized
by A. R. Radcliffe-Brown in the present periodical; the nature of kinship
extensions, where I have to deal with the strictures of my friend E. E.
Evans-Pritchard (also in *Man*); the nature of the functional treatment
of kinship, where I have drawn some kindly, but I think irrelevant, criticism from Lord Raglan in the last number of *Man*.

---

[12] Some points here briefly touched upon will be found elaborated in Chapter XVI,
Section 6, of my *Sexual Life of Savages,* and in my Memoir on "The Problem of Meaning
in Primitive Languages" in Ogden and Richards's *Meaning of Meaning*.

Part Two

CULTURE AND MYTH

7

CULTURE AS A DETERMINANT OF BEHAVIOR

That we are passing through a cultural crisis of unprecedented magnitude and of a definitely putrid quality nobody doubts, except, of course, the 999 in 1000 intellectual ostriches who prefer to remain head in sand rather than to face realities. There are also those who react with complete defeatism; who are satisfied with nihilistic prophecies of decay and downfall. Oswald Spengler has made himself the most popular and decorative spokesman of this group.

But there are still a few left who prefer to stand for intellectual integrity, and fight even if victory be uncertain. These can see only one way out of the straits—the establishment of a rational and empirical, that is, scientific, control of human affairs. This is the faith of those united in the present intellectual venture; it is the aim and thesis of this volume.

In this chapter I attempt to show that cultural anthropology can and must provide the foundations of the social sciences. It can do this by defining the nature of human associations, of economic pursuits, legal institutions, magical and religious practices, studied within the widest range accessible to observation and analysis. In order to do this, it is necessary to re-define the aims and scope of cultural anthropology. This science is, in fact, at present detaching itself more and more from the agreeable and fascinating hunt for the exotic, the savage, and the diversified. As a science, it has to concentrate more and more on the universally human and fundamental, even when this lacks the touch of sensationalism

This article was, in its original form, a paper delivered at the Harvard Tercentenary Conference of Arts and Sciences, Sept. 7, 1936. It was published in, and is reprinted by permission of the publishers of, Factors Determining Human Behavior, *by Edgar Douglas Adrian and others, Cambridge, Mass., Harvard University Press, Copyright, 1937, by The President and Fellows of Harvard College. It was republished, after the author's additions, in* Human Affairs, *edited by R. B. Cattell, Macmillan, 1937.*

The first part of this essay (pp. 167–174) appeared in Human Affairs, *but was not included in the Harvard address.*

and remains as dull and drab as the daily life of man and woman, as their quest for food, and their concern with children and cattle.

The science of man is still conceived by laymen as a colorful display of strange oddities and quiddities of the savage; as the antiquarian search for origins, survivals, and evolutionary side-tracks. Why is a cannibal so cannibalistic? Why does he avoid his mother-in-law with so many circumstantial rudenesses? Why does he kill one twin or even two, while we worship quads and quins? Head-hunting, juicy stories about orgiastic ritual, somewhat shocking forms of primitive marriage, obscene mutilations, and mysterious masked dances are undoubtedly more amusing to speak about or even to listen to than economics, law, and social organization. But scientifically these latter are more relevant.

There is no doubt that in the vast museum of human achievement—or failure—in progress there can be found strange hypertrophies, unique distortions, and quaint deviations from the human average. These, however, are but the plums or currants in the pudding of each culture. Take the most primitive or most exotic of human civilizations, and you will find there still the same ordinary universally human standardized institutions: the domestic hearth round which there live, work, love, and hate each other the members of the family; the co-operative group, which goes out to dig roots and search for edible grubs, who till the soil or do the hunting; or, again, the congregation of the faithful who worship a totem or a supreme being, an ancestral spirit or a fetish. For all human beings must be nourished, and they have to reproduce; they must co-operate in technical and economic pursuits; they have to obey rules of conduct, and these have to be enforced in one way or another. They must live, love, and be safe, even before they dance, paint, enact strange ceremonies, and develop sacred or profane fiction. Even in these later pursuits, however, the fears, hopes, and desires of man are not arbitrary, hence not indefinitely or indeterminately diverse.

The search for determinism in the broadest and most fundamental principles of human behavior is, therefore, the first and foremost scientific task of anthropology conceived as basis and starting-point of other social studies. But even in the case of very strange and outlandish customs or institutions, explanation can only mean the reduction of the exotic and singular to elements universally human and familiar. Consider, for instance, head-hunting, or the *potlatch*, running amok, or lying in *couvade*. What can be meant by explaining these in a scientific analysis? Only when we begin to perceive that at the basis of a strange, at first incomprehensible, custom or institution there exist fundamental human tendencies or influences of environment; when we see how that one strange custom depends on and is related to certain pursuits which are universal and, therefore, immediately comprehensible—then, and then only, can we say that we understand the custom.

The *couvade*, for instance, is brought nearer to our comprehension if we consider it as a very strong expression of the physiological claims of paternity, and of the tendency—universal, though usually less marked—for the father to assimilate his role to that of his wife. The *potlatch*, again, is but a highly magnified collective gesture of grandiloquent generosity or conspicuous waste, of which we find symptoms and manifestations in every culture, less obvious, no doubt, and less pointed, but unmistakably akin to the great feasts of the Northwest Indians.

Having lived from childhood in a variety of cultural settings—among the then semi-savage Carpathian mountaineers, and among Baltic barons, having moved from Poland to North Africa and from the Canary Islands to north Germany and France—and later having worked among several exotic cultures, I have more than once experienced the reduction of the exotic to the familiar. When you enter a new cultural setting, the behavior, individual or collective, of the new type of human beings seems strange, unmotivated, irrational, in short incomprehensible. You learn the language, you gradually adopt the strange habits and the new points of view—and imperceptibly what was alien becomes familiar and you feel at home in what recently had been an exotic *milieu*. The universally human running through all the cultures is the common measure of comprehension and adaptation.

With all this, there are no doubt certain queer and extremely exotic habits which will always remain unamenable to explanation, hence quaint and almost repugnant. Even now I cannot understand—indeed I feel a strong repulsion at the very thought of it—how certain human beings can enjoy playing golf, or committing suicide by hara-kiri; how some natives are able to remain for long stretches of time standing in the rain and looking at a few others kick a large round object (this is called among the natives of England "football"); or why some South Sea natives must collect pickled heads, etc. etc. Even in such cases, however, as eating of human flesh, underdone beef, or plum pudding, playing golf, running amok, and the practice of *couvade,* the anthropologist may attempt to survey the psychological raw material of the pursuit, can assume a certain diversity of taste in human beings, and define the pursuit in terms of the universally human.

But it must be clear to anyone with training in natural science or a scientific outlook in cultural matters that the less fundamental a phenomenon, the more complex and concrete the factors which enter into its make-up, the lesser will be the chance of its becoming the subject of a general law, the result of universally valid principles. Science begins and ends with the establishment of general principles valid for all the phenomena which fall within its purview. The science of human behavior, that is, of culture, is not an exception to this rule.

One of the greatest virtues of a scientific worker consists in knowing precisely where to draw the limits of legitimate research; it consists in possessing the courage of a clear and emphatic *ignoramus, ignorabimus.* The humanist has perhaps not yet clearly recognized the beauty of this virtue. He has not drawn strongly enough the line dividing art, intuition, and empathy from scientific research. To a humanist both qualities are necessary; they may be combined; they should never be confounded. Just now when we are faced with the danger of a complete breakdown of the scientific approach and of faith in science, combined with a corroding pessimism as to the value of reason in dealing with human affairs, the power of reason must be affirmed and its functions clearly defined. It is not an accident that Spengler's nihilism and defeatism is founded on an entirely anti-deterministic, hence anti-scientific, conception of culture. To Spengler, "Culture" is an autonomous group-mind or collective genius which expresses its free will in those outward shadowy manifestations which, to the uninitiated and unwary, appear as the substance. The Eye of the Illuminated Seer and Prophet alone perceives that they are but the outer husk, and penetrates beyond to the inner meaning. This grandiose and mystical conception of culture as a Spirit-behind-the-facts has fascinated millions and stultified the work of social science for a generation or two.

The jack-in-the-box conception of culture, as the self-revelation of an immanent Genius or Deity, has been cultivated in German metaphysics; it reaches its peak in Hegel's Historical Idealism. But its full practical application had to wait till the arrival of the latest incarnation of the Absolute—Herr Adolf Hitler.

The conception lends itself not only to a mood of pessimism, but also to an aggressive, strong-fisted, and somewhat egocentric *Wille zur Macht.* It has become the spiritual charter of National Socialism and Fascism, and also (let us be fair) of Communist dictatorships-in-culture. For every dictatorship can make good use of a doctrine which regards all civilization not as the expression of the needs, desires, and fundamental characteristics of the many, but rather as the dictated will of one. No dictatorship can tolerate more than one standard or arbiter of ultimate wisdom and value. It must be truth or Hitler, scientific determinism or Stalin, results of research or Mussolini. Whether you accept doctrinaire Marxism as the ultimate answer to all questions, or the view that one "racial" or "national genius" alone has produced THE civilization (and goes on producing it in the dictates and *pronunciamentos* of a Ministry of Propaganda and Kultur), there is no room for free, uninspired, and untrammelled research into the determinism of historical process, the limits of legitimate legislation, the ethics of oppression, and arbitrary molding of human character and spirit.

On the negative side, therefore, the following survey of fact and argument is directed largely against the gigantic abuses, theoretical and practical, of the Hegelian principle that civilization is but the dictate of an Immanent Genius or the Incarnation of the Absolute. These doctrines, as a matter of fact, are not confined merely to propaganda ministries or to such productions as *Mein Kampf*, the speeches of Mussolini, and the decrees of the Kremlin. From quarters above all suspicion of sympathy with dictatorship there have come quite recently pronouncements strangely in tune with the anti-deterministic view of culture—anthropological theories declaring that there can be no genuine science of culture.

Listen to the venerable leader and veteran of American anthropology, Professor Franz Boas. In an apparently definite statement of his position which is also his *imprimatur* on a strange book by Dr. Ruth Benedict,[1] he tells us that the ultimate task of the anthropologist consists in "a deep penetration into the genius of the culture." He follows this up by telling us that in a survey of diverse cultures we find that "they are permeated each by one dominating idea." But whose idea is it by which a culture is dominated? No doubt the idea of the "genius of the culture." We are dangerously near to the conception of *Volksgeist* or *Volksseele*, the immaculate tribal genius of the German people, with the Jewish grandmother strictly ruled out. For it is the preservation of the purity of race and of its cultural genius on which the modern prophets of the Third Reich are building a "pure culture."

Professor Boas's attitude towards Hitlerism is exactly the same as mine, and his own work in anthropology is classically scientific. Yet in a moment of methodological absent-mindedness he seems to forget that the only salvation for social science is to become a real science, that is, to part company with "tribal geniuses," "pervading spirits of culture," and all such hypostases which are merely a short cut away from the legitimate task—a search for general laws. Indeed he tells us that "the relations between different aspects of culture follow the most diverse patterns and do not lend themselves profitably to generalizations." No generalizations, no universally valid laws, no science of culture. I have also to disagree fundamentally with Professor Boas when he light-heartedly defines other cultures as "abnormal": in stating that the more we know of cultural drives, "the more we shall find that certain controls of emotion, certain ideals of conduct, prevail that account for what seem to us as abnormal attitudes when viewed from the standpoint of our own civilization. The relativity of what is considered social or asocial, normal or abnormal, is seen in a new light." [2]

In my opinion this is not the right way to put anthropology on a scientific basis. The apparently most heterogeneous diversities must be reduced to common factors, for there is a common measure of all culture process and culture configuration. To deny this, as is done by Dr. Ruth

[1] *Patterns of Culture*, 1935.

[2] *Op. cit.*, pp. xii and xiii.

Benedict in her book sponsored by Professor Boas, is to condemn the quest of scientific anthropology from the very beginning. In a comparative examination of several cultures she affirms that they are "heterogeneous assortments of acts and beliefs." She tells us that "they differ from one another not only because one trait is present here and absent there, and because another trait is found in two regions in two different forms. They differ still more because they are orientated as wholes in different directions. They are travelling along different roads in pursuit of different ends, and these ends and these means in one society cannot be judged in terms of those of another society, because essentially they are incommensurable." [3]

The anthropologist, therefore, has to take his staff and walk with one "tribal genius" to its ultimate goal and discuss with this "tribal genius" the ends and aims of its pilgrimage. By some miraculous and prophetic intuition the anthropologist has to apprehend each orientation as a specific, incomparable reality.

The results carried out on this program of genius-hunting and empathy with collective spirits are what might be expected. After long and laborious analyses, we are told by Dr. Ruth Benedict that one culture is Apollonian, the other Dionysiac, that one tribal genius suffers from megalomania, and another from paranoia. There are cultures which are "incorrigibly mild," others "ruthlessly aggressive," yet others "superbly self-satisfied." I could quote from other writers who affirm that culture can only be understood as a form of "collective hysteria," while others speak about "masculine cultures" or cultures "oriented away from the self," about races who are "introvert" or "extrovert," or define a culture as "maternal in its parental aspects and feminine in its sexual aspects."

All such theories reduce anthropology to a purely subjective interpretation of each culture in terms of figurative speech, of pathological simile, of mythological parallel, and other more or less literary or artistic ways of intuition. There is no room left for the scientific analysis.

I had to enter the protest with some emphasis, because the new tendency threatens to dominate the growing generation of anthropologists both in the United States and in this country. Livelier journalism has already hailed Dr. Ruth Benedict and her associates as the prophets of a new vision in humanism. The tendency is so facile and attractive, yet so entirely sterile in my opinion, that no warning could be too strong. Many of the younger generation are drifting into mystical pronouncements, avoiding the difficult and painstaking search for principles; they are cultivating rapid cursory field-work, and developing their impressionistic results into brilliantly dramatized film effects, such as the New Guinea pictures of Dr. Margaret Mead in her Sex and Temperament (1935).

[3] Op. cit., p. 223.

There is diversity in human culture, thank heaven! Empathy into "national characteristics" or "racial genius" is an attractive artistic pursuit.

Oh, East is East, and West is West, and never the twain shall meet,
Till Earth and Sky stand presently at God's great Judgment Seat. . . .

But even when it comes to art, continue to read Kipling's poem and you will find that when it is a question of a relevant pursuit such as horse-stealing or cattle-lifting, robbery or war, then East meets West on an equal footing. The story of *Kim*, and the Anglo-Indian short stories, where East comes to grips with West and the two vie with each other in love and hate, in fights and adventures, all demonstrate one truth—the poet and anthropologist Kipling always divines the common measure of humanity-at-one. The artistic creation of Kim alone shows the road to the correct treatment of empathy and intuition, for Kim is both a Westerner and an Indian, and in all his exploits he moves along the line of common measure.

The private, personal drive of every anthropologist is often to be found in his love of the exotic, in his insatiable hunger for the taste of strange customs and picturesque costumes, for the flavor of new tongues and the new language of ideas and emotions. But from the very fact that a European can sometimes assume the outlook and temporarily even adopt the ways of a stone-age Melanesian or an African nomad, an Indian or a Chinaman, proves that there is a common measure in even the intuitive aspects of culture. And when it comes to scientific analysis, it is necessary to lay the rule hard and fast, absolute and rigid, that to go beyond the search for the common measure is to flounder into the non-scientific. The artist may be there too, in the make-up of a field-worker, or of an anthropological theorist, but he must not confuse his aesthetic task with his scientific problems.

On the positive side, therefore, the arguments which follow are an attempt to establish that there can be a genuine science of culture; that general principles and universally valid concepts are not only necessary, but indispensable; and that the analysis of human cultures can be carried out in the same spirit—both empirical and strictly conforming to logic—which is the only way of dealing with problems of physics, biology, and anthropology as well.

"Culture as a determinant of human behavior"—I read this title as an injunction to prove that there exists a science of human behavior, which is the science of culture. Culture, in fact, is nothing but the organized behavior of man. Man differs from the animals in that he has to rely on an artificially fashioned environment: on implements, weapons, dwellings, and man-made means of transport. To produce and to manage this body of artifacts and commodities, he requires knowledge and technique. He depends on the help of his fellow-beings. This means that he has to live in organized, well-ordered communities. Of all the animals he alone merits the tripartite title of *homo faber, zoom politikon, homo sapiens.*

All this artificial equipment of man, material, spiritual, and social, we call technically culture. It is a large-scale molding matrix; a gigantic conditioning apparatus. In each generation it produces its type of individual. In each generation it is in turn reshaped by its carriers.

Is this big entity itself subject to laws of a scientific character? I for one have no hestitation in answering this question in the affirmative. Culture is a determinant of human behavior, and culture as a dynamic reality is also subject to determinism. There exist scientific laws of culture.

The possibility of a really scientific approach to humanism and anthropology is still contested. It is not superfluous, therefore, to reaffirm the existence of determinism in the study of human culture.

In my opinion the principal ailment of all humanism is the disjunction of empirical approach from theory, of methods of observation from speculative doctrine. It will be best, therefore, first to turn to the testimony of cultural fact itself. It is easiest to grasp the essence of a phenomenon in contemplating its manifestations through a wide range of variation. Let us then make a rapid flight over the globe and obtain bird's-eye views of some highly divergent types of human culture.

The culture of a nomad tribe

Let us descend first on the arid and dusty steppes of central East Africa inhabited by the Masai, the famous fierce warriors of the region. On approaching the native encampment we are met by a group of men, tall, dignified, armed with iron spears and daggers. Their women, svelte and elegant, startle the newcomer with the glitter and rattle of the wrought-iron ornaments encircling their necks, wrists, and ankles. Both sexes still wear the native robes of soft goat- or sheepskin. Not a shred of calico nor European trinket mars the archaic vision of men and women of Africa as they lead us into the ring of low brown huts, made of thatch, plastered with cow-dung, and enclosed with a stout fence of prickly shrub.

Conservative in his material culture, the Masai still clings also to his old tribal ways. He still remains at heart a gentleman robber, herdsman, cattle-lifter, and warrior. When, after years of drought, starvation threatens the Masai among their pestilence-stricken herds, how can they help using force, in which they have been trained through generations, against their fat and flabby neighbors grown weak in their wealth and security? Their whole social organization—age-grades, mutilations and tests of endurance, and military drill—is tuned up to the development of warlike virtues. The Masai warrior—that is, every man between puberty and marriage—lives in a special camp, devoting all his time to the aristocratic arts of doing nothing and preparing for war. He is governed by a democratic regime in which an elected captain administers law and leads the men into battle.

Agriculture they despise, vegetables being food fit only for women. As a Masai warrior put it to me in a convincing argument: "The earth is our Mother. She gives us all the milk we need, and feeds our cattle. It is wrong to cut or scratch her body"—a confirmation of the psycho-analyst's conception of Mother-Earth, by one who had not studied the works of Professor Freud yet!

As to sex morals, they leave entire freedom to immature girls, who consort with the warriors in their camp. At puberty every woman has to undergo a drastic operation, clitoridectomy, which constitutes their marriage rite.

The whole tribe owe allegiance to the *Ol'loibon*, the hereditary rain magician and prophet. He controls them through his gift of divination and his power of producing magical fertility of land and of women.

How can we press this strange, exotic material, as rich and varied and elusive as life itself, into a scientific scheme? The temptation to stop at artistic impressionism is great. We might well feel that it would be best to paint the war-like Masai in exaggerated colors in order to bring out the martial, boisterous, licentious "genius" of this culture.

Indeed, this type of procedure is the latest fashion in anthropology. Since, however, we are in search of a scientific, that is, deterministic approach, let us inquire into what are the main interests of the natives, the pivotal points of their tribal life. We see at once that their interests center around food, sex, defense, and aggression. Divination and prophecy, and their political influence, are related to their military adventures and the vicissitudes of climate. The age-grades are an occupational organization correlated with their military life; they form an educational system in which tribal knowledge is imparted, discipline and endurance inculcated.

Thus culture, as we find it among the Masai, is an apparatus for the satisfaction of the elementary needs of the human organism. But under conditions of culture these needs are satisfied by roundabout methods. The Masai cannot turn to nature directly in order to nourish himself. In the long development of his tribal culture, the institution of pastoral-ism has come into being. The tending, breeding, exchange, and ownership of cattle, incidentally also the need of its defense and protection, impose derived or secondary imperatives on the life of the Masai: the cattle kraal, military camps, seasonal migrations, and fertility magic are the outcome and correlates of pastoralism.

The continuity of the race equally does not work by physiological determination alone. Sexual appetite and personal attraction, the urge to mate, and the desire for children are reformulated culturally. Each phase of the biological process—maturation, puberty, courtship, marriage, and parenthood—is correlated with the mode of life and the arrangements of domesticity and bachelors' camp; and the whole is safeguarded by the military organization. The vast phenomenon of kinship, including the family, marriage, clanship, and the laws of descent, is the cultural counterpart of the physiological process of reproduction.

The needs of man and the aspects of culture

Let us see what the conditions are in a neighboring tribe. Not far from the Masai steppes, on the slopes of the Kilimanjaro, the highest mountain in Africa, live the Chagga, an agricultural, sedentary people. The Chagga, though he also keeps and appreciates cattle, is mainly a tiller of the soil. Yams and pumpkins, peas and millet thrive well on the fertile green fields of the Kilimanjaro. The staple food, however, is the banana. As the Masai culture has been labeled "cattle-complex," so the Chagga culture could certainly be defined as a banana obsession. The Chagga lives on bananas; he lives among bananas—every homestead must be surrounded by its banana grove; and when he is dead he is buried amid bananas.

In contrast to the nomadic Masai, the Chagga have a highly developed body of land laws. Their large-scale system of irrigation is a feat of engineering unparalleled anywhere in native Africa south of the Sahara. Again, unlike the democratic Masai, the Chagga have a well-developed chieftainship. In each district the chief is the supreme judge, the source of law, the military leader, and the high priest of tribal ancestor-worship. The centralized power of the Chagga, however, is not based on aggressive militarism. They have a highly developed system of defense, with extensive, well-guarded earthworks along the frontiers, and enormous subterranean chambers where men, women, and cattle are able to take refuge during a Masai raid.

The Chagga differ from their neighbors, the Masai: they practice agriculture, live in fixed settlements, have a developed system of land tenure; and their religion consists mainly in ancestor-worship. They resemble the Masai in that they practice female circumcision, they have developed age-grades, and they believe in magic by divination. What is the best way of establishing a common measure for the scientific comparison of differences and also of similarities?

Clearly, again, we must compare their institutions—that is, the organized systems of activities, each correlated with a fundamental need. In both tribes we find that to nutrition there corresponds the economic system, dominated among the Chagga by agriculture, among the Masai by cattle-breeding. In both cultures we should have to analyze the economic system by means of such universally valid concepts as the organization of production, the methods of distribution, and the manner in which consumption integrates certain groups of people. Among both we should have to consider the physiological process of reproduction as it is organized into the domestic institutions. The physiological growth of the individual is in both cases institutionalized into the system of age-grades. Political organization comes into being in the satisfaction of the need for safety in the case of the Chagga; in the case of the Masai the military organization and the political system are the outcome of a periodic need for predatory economics. In both tribes there are, again, corresponding organizations for the maintenance of internal law and order. The political system, in its military and legal aspects alike, imposes its own discipline, morale, ideals, and economic requirements.

The transmission of the cultural heritage from one generation to another brings into being the two educational systems of the Chagga and Masai. In both tribes the earlier stages of training are bound up with domestic life, while later on the initiations into age-grades carry on the education in tribal custom and morality.

From the comparison of the two cultures we reach one of our pivotal generalizations. Every culture must be analyzed into the following aspects: economics, politics, the mechanism of law and custom, education, magic and religion, recreation, traditional knowledge, technology, and art. And all human cultures can be compared under the headings of this scheme.

Far from the chaotic, indeterministic defeatism which overwhelms the amateur, and apparently even some professional anthropologists, this approach gives us a solid scientific foundation.

Incidentally, we also arrive at another conclusion. Anthropology, the science of culture, must study the same subjects as those which confront the student of contemporary civilization, or of any other period in human history. It must approach primitive culture from the angle of politics and economics, theory of religion, and jurisprudence. And here anthropology may claim a special position among the other sciences of human society and culture.

Its range is the widest; it relies entirely on direct observation, for its sources are in the student's own field. It is perhaps the only social science which can easily remain detached from political bias, nationalist prejudice, sentiment, or doctrinaire zeal. If this social science fails to develop an entirely dispassionate study of its material, there is not much hope for the other branches of humanism. Hence, in vindicating the scientific character of anthropology we are working at the very foundations of social science. Anthropology has the privilege and the duty of acting as an organizing agency in the comparative study of cultures.

Adaptation to environment and diseases of culture

In order to appreciate the influence of environment upon culture, let us leave tropical Africa and move into the desert of snow, ice, and rock inhabited by the Eskimos. Their winter house, made of stone or of snow, has been described as a marvel of engineering, a perfect adaptation to climate and to the available material. It certainly is an example of thoroughgoing correlation between a material object and the necessities of life. Combining warmth, space, and ventilation, it provides during the long winter night comfortable places in which to lie and listen to the long tales of folklore, or carry on technical activities. The technological excellence of these natives is also shown in the construction of their sledges and their weapons, of their canoes, and of their traps.

In comparison with this, some aspects of their culture seem underdeveloped. The Eskimos have been described as devoid of any political system or of legal institutions. They have been often accused of extreme pacifism in that they do not slaughter each other in organized fighting. Yet this is perhaps not quite correct. For though they have no political chieftainship, they recognize the authority of the Shaman. He also acts in a roundabout way as an important juridical agency. They have their code of law, consisting of many taboos, the breach of which brings down evil not only on the wrongdoer but on the whole community. Tribal calamity can be averted only by public confession. After that the Shaman can magically re-establish tribal prosperity. Thus, as the Masai have anticipated psychoanalysis, so the Eskimos are the forerunners of the Oxford Group movement.

On the other hand, toward sex they have the same attitude as the Masai. They have also a somewhat similar type of political system, always with the exception that the one are extremely warlike, and the others have never heard of fighting.

Our approach to a scientific study of culture, through the various aspects which correspond to the fundamental and derived needs of man, does not break down even here, when we apply it to such a one-sided, in many ways stunted, and in other ways hypertrophied, culture as that of the Eskimos. For the Eskimos eat and reproduce, maintain themselves secure against weather and animals, have developed means of movement in space, and they also regulate the bodily development of the individual. Their culture consists, like all others, of the cardinal aspects: economics, education, law, politics, magic and religion, knowledge, crafts, art, and also recreation.

What about war? Some divisions of the Eskimos have a minimum of military organization. Others are completely ignorant of fighting. Since the polar and central Eskimos have no neighbors, nor yet any cause for internal quarrels and dissensions, they cannot have military institutions. This fact confirms our conception of the instrumental nature of organized activities. Where, as in their westernmost offshoots, the Eskimos are in contact with warlike Indian tribes, they have developed the organization, the virtues, and the apparatus of war.

In the study of war, as of any other aspect of culture, the strict application of scientific determinism is necessary. This is achieved by clear definitions, empirical concepts, and inductive generalization. All the wrangles as to the innate pacifism or aggressiveness of primitive man are based on the use of words without definition. To label all brawling, squabbling, dealing out of black eye or broken jaw, *war*, as is frequently done, leads simply to confusion. One author tells us then that primitive man is a natural pacifist. Another has recently described war as indispensable for the survival of the fittest. Yet another maintains that war is the main creative, beneficent, and constructive factor in the history of mankind. But war can only be defined as the use of organized force between two politically independent units, in the pursuit of a tribal policy. War in this sense enters fairly late into the development of human societies.

Only with the formation of independent political units, where military force is maintained as a means of tribal policy, does war contribute through the historical fact of conquest to the building up of cultures and the establishment of states. In my opinion, we have just left this stage of human history behind, and modern warfare has become nothing but an unmitigated disease of civilization.

I have made this brief digression on warfare because it illustrates one side of the scientific or functional method in cultural analysis. This method is often accused of overemphasizing the perfect integration of all factors within the working whole of culture. This is a misrepresentation. The functional method only insists on the fact that all the elements of culture are related to each other; they are not idle survivals or disconnected traits, but they function—that is, they are at work. It does not pronounce any appreciation or moral comment as to whether this work is good or evil, well or badly adjusted. As in the case of some primitive types of warfare, and certainly of its most recent developments, the instrumental analysis of culture reveals more cogently than dissection into traits the occurrence of catastrophic maladjustments of human society.

As you have noticed just now, and felt, perhaps, throughout the argument of this lecture, there has been a background of critical indictment running right through. I do not want to waste your time with controversy and polemics. At the same time, I do not want you to feel that we are running in open doors in insisting on an objective, sober, empirical, and non-mystical treatment of culture. We are engaged now in laying down the foundations for a sound method in social science. When these are clearly and simply stated, they have a knack of appearing mere truisms. Science in the long run is nothing but common sense and experience built up on a systematic basis, refined and clarified to the utmost limits of conceptual lucidity. So, briefly: I have been insisting that anthropological theory must be objective, which means aboveboard, and presented in a manner amenable to verification. Why? Because some of the leaders of contemporary anthropology still maintain that there is a subjective factor in all humanistic observation. To quote an eminent scholar: "All historical definitions are in their very essence subjective."

I have been driving in the existence of a measure common to all comparative work in anthropology—the existence, that is, of a general scheme of human culture, universally valid. Why? Because it has been stated in so many words that "no common measure of cultural phenomena can be found," and that "the laws of cultural process are vague, insipid and useless."

I have again and again indicated that it is illegitimate to cover our inability to deal with certain facts by such mystic labels as the "genius of culture," or to describe this "genius" as Apollonian, Dionysiac, megalomaniac, or hysterical. Why? Because all these atrocities have been recently committed. Culture has been described as the "collective hysteria" of society. We have had recently a whole rainbow of colorful tags and epithets tied to the neck of each individual culture.

I have insisted that analysis must not be arbitrary; that the dissection of a culture, even as that of a corpse, must obey the laws of its anatomy, and not become mere butchery, a lifting out of "traits" and the lumping of them into haphazard "trait complexes." Why? Because the most powerful school in anthropology still follows the precepts of Graebner, who would have us isolate "traits" and define them by characteristics not founded in the nature of the object or the material. One of the leading American anthropologists tells us that an agglomeration of such traits into a complex "is historically most convincing when the traits are not related to one another." To regard culture as a jumble of disconnected and unrelated details may lead to amusing reconstructions but of doubtful value. In the process, however, it robs our whole concept of culture of all life and significance.

The family as the cornerstone of social structure

But let us leave aside this controversial mood. To make our point clear, let us concentrate on an object—*the* object of objects, in a way—the material embodiment of the premier institution of mankind, the family. We shall choose our example from yet another ethnographic area and contemplate a pile dwelling in Melanesia.

In sharp contrast to the arid steppes of central Africa and the Arctic desert of snow, we are surrounded here by a wilderness of water, coral reef, and swamp. The main symptom of man's adaptation to his surroundings is a remarkable achievement of primitive architecture, the house on piles. It stands firmly on its foundations of stout tree-trunks driven deep into the muddy bottom of the lagoon. Constructed of strong material cunningly fitted and lashed together, it resists the combined attacks of wind, waves, and weather.

To the lagoon dweller such a house is a fortress where he can take refuge and which he can defend. It is a watch-tower from which he can see the approach of suspicious strangers. It is also conveniently near to the coast which he frequently has to visit in order to tend his gardens. The structure of the house is thus determined by the inter-tribal relations of the people, their economic pursuits, by climate and natural environment.

It can thus be studied only within its natural setting. But after man has invented, constructed, and improved his dwelling, and made it into a fortress, an economic asset, and a comfortable home, the house then dominates his whole mode of life. The outer shell of his domesticity influences the social structure of family and kinship.

Indeed, it seems that the higher the cultural development, the more ruthless and brutal becomes the tyranny of machine over man. Are we not at present hopelessly enslaved by our hypertrophied prosperity which we have not yet learned to manage; by our rapid means of communication which allow us to speed, but too often to speed but aimlessly? And last, not least, and worst of all, by our excessive efficiency in the means of collective destruction? Once more a humanist may be allowed to reflect on the fact that the overdevelopment of mechanical science and its applications have completely outgrown the progress of our knowledge of how to adjust our efficiency to really human aims and needs.

Since in my opinion anthropology should begin at home, let me give you an anthropological impression of modern culture and recount a personal experience in which I very poignantly became aware of the power of things over man.

No experience in my exotic wanderings among the Trobrianders and the Chagga, among the Masai and the Pueblo, has ever matched the shock I received in my first contact with American civilization on my first visit to New York, when I arrived there ten years ago on a fine spring evening, and saw the city in its strangeness and exotic beauty. The enormous yet elegant monsters blinking at me through their thousand starry eyes, breathing white steam, giants which crowded in fantastic clusters over the smooth waters of the river, stood before me: the living, dominating realities of this new culture. During my first few days in New York I could not shake off the feeling that the strange "genius" of this most modern civilization had become incarnate in the skyscraper, the subway, and the ferry boat. Large insects in the shape of automobiles crept along the gutter called street or avenue, subordinate but important. Finally, as a fairly insignificant and secondary by-product of the enormous mechanical reality, there appeared the microscopic bacteria called Man, sneaking in and out of subway, skyscraper, or automobile, performing some useful service to their masters, but otherwise rather insignificant. Modern civilization is a gigantic hypertrophy of material objects, and contemporary man will still have to fight his battle in order to reassert his dominance over the Thing.

But what interests us at present is to find the existence of a common measure between the residential part of the skyscraper and snowhouse, pile-dwelling and cow-dung hut.

In the material used, in structure, in architecture, in all, that is, which we can call the form of the object, there is hardly one trait in common. But look at the dwelling as a part of an institution. It appears at once that the principles on which each dwelling is integrated into organized human life and becomes the shell of this life are the same throughout humanity. In the penthouse on top of the skyscraper, in the snow igloo, in the *engadji* of cow dung, in the *niyumba* of thatch, we find the same domestic unit, the family, consisting of father, mother, and children.

Is the resemblance only superficial? No. Functionally it is not merely a resemblance, but an identity. The group is united by the same task, the essential business of reproducing the race. A universal type of legal charter gives juridical validity to the group. The act of marriage bestows legitimacy on the children, grants the consorts mutual privileges and duties, defines the domestic work of husband and wife; above all, it im-poses on them the duty of looking conjointly after the children. Human parents, unlike animals, are not allowed merely to throw up fresh organisms, but they have to introduce fully fledged citizens into the community.

Another fundamental difference between man and the animals is that under civilization parenthood develops into the wider network of relations which we anthropologists call the system of kinship. Here at once a universal generalization can be made. In every human society both parents share in procreation, in tending and training the children, but only one line of descent is legally relevant. Kinship is counted either in the direct mother line or father line. And the anthropologist is also able to state the reason why. Any ambiguity, any confusion in the tracing of filiation inevitably leads to disaster and chaos in laws of inheritance and of succession. Even as it is, with one line of descent, primogeniture, or with the law of borough-English, ultimogeniture, most legal difficulties in primitive and developed communities are due to conflicts in the law of inheritance or succession.

Another universal law of kinship is that, under unilateral descent and the classificatory system of kinship status, parenthood becomes extended into clan relationship. The classificatory use of kinship terms, again, a curious linguistic phenomenon which seems to saddle every individual in primitive culture with a whole bunch of fathers and mothers, of aunts, uncles, sisters, and, alas, even mothers-in-law, is universal. To explain it whole libraries have been written about the existence of primitive promiscuity, group marriage, and the gradual development of monogamy out of complete sexual and parental communism. All this is, in plain American, *bunkum!* Had the classificatory system been discovered by one who spoke the native language well, had it been studied scientifically, a very simple explanation would have been discovered.

The discovery of the actual live function of classificatory terms was made in Melanesia. I was able there to study not the product, that is, the ready-made so-called classificatory system of nomenclature, but the process of extension as it actually occurred in the life of the individual. I found that the piecemeal extension of linguistic usage runs parallel with the piecemeal transference of the child-to-parent attitude. The terms, thus gradually extended, do not in fact lump clansmen and clanswomen into groups of fathers, mothers, wives and husbands, siblings and children. The idea of group parenthood or group marriage appears preposterous to the primitive—he simply would laugh at the volumes of anthropological speculation on primitive promiscuity. It is the unadulterated product of the academic mind. In real native life terminological extensions function as quasi-legal metaphors. They exercise the binding force on the widening circle of kindred, a force which diminishes as the genealogical distance grows. There is an analogy between this phenomenon and the use of words in a spell, both being instances of the creative metaphor of the magical word.

In the same way, had the great variety of the forms of pre-nuptial relations and of relaxations of the matrimonial ties been studied, it would have been recognized that they cannot be remnants of pristine promiscuity because they function as experimental methods of courtship.

Had I more time, I should discuss with you a number of important laws in the theory of kinship: the principle of legitimacy; the determinism in mother-right and father-right; the correlation of clanship and extended kinship with their function in primitive communities; the function which might be roughly described as that of social insurance. We should see that the wider kinship groups disappear because in our more highly differentiated communities the state, charity organizations, friendly societies, and public services take over the functions of kinship. The theory of kinship here placed before you explains the phenomena of primitive life not as survivals or diffusions in terms of this or that recondite hypothesis or fantasy but in terms of observable fact and relations between facts.

[That no scientific theory will be able to explain certain queer customs of kinship and domesticity may be granted. Why do some savages impose strict taboos and avoidances between a man or a woman and the mother-in-law? Apart from the inherent wisdom of such a rule, there is no explanation forthcoming. Why do some communities kill one of a pair of twins; others both; and yet others treat them with special consideration? I doubt whether an answer will ever be given. Why do some people practice clitoridectomy and others infibulation? Why do we find in one culture circumcision, and in another subincision? It is difficult to answer. Speaking of twins, I am certain that many a savage would be most certainly shocked by, and would develop all sorts of hypotheses in order to explain, the interest which has been taken recently by the Western world in quadruplets and quintuplets.]*

The quest for food and primitive economics

We have found throughout our survey that the food quest and other economic activities leave a deep imprint on the whole culture. This truism, however, must be supplemented by a somewhat fuller appreciation of the place of economics in primitive culture. Let us once more concentrate on a concrete case, the system of agriculture of the Trobriand Islanders in Melanesia. Their whole tribal life is dominated by agriculture. During the season of hard work, men and women practically live in the gardens. Then, while the plants sprout and grow, the women still have to do weeding. The men, on the other hand, devote themselves to other things, fishing and trapping, industries, canoe-building, and trading expeditions. One man only, the Garden Magician, still remains hard at work. He has been in fact from the beginning an organizer of work, directing the allotment of land, and, while ostensibly he was carrying on his rites, in reality he acted as tribal entrepreneur. Even when it comes to the harvest he still has to bless the crops and then perform over the stored produce a type of magic which, by reducing the appetite of the people, makes food last longer.

But agriculture as an economic activity does not end with the harvest. The distribution of the products is an important business which penetrates into all the aspects of tribal life. Tribute has to be given to the chief, and on this tribute his political power is largely based. A quota of food has to be put aside for tribal ceremonies, and this finances largely their public and religious activities. Finally, the third stage of the economic process, consumption, presents many interesting aspects in this tribe, as everywhere else. For consumption means not merely eating, but also handling, display, ritual food offerings, and last but not least, sheer waste. For in the Trobriands the passion for accumulated food is so great that people prefer to keep their yams till they rot in the storehouses rather than to see the latter empty.

We see, then, that agriculture must be studied within the context of the whole economic system. For the vegetables are exchanged for fish; they are used in the financing of enterprise and for feeding the craftsmen, for the capitalization of industries. This is especially interesting in the study of the large native jewelry, or, more correctly, tokens of wealth, which

---

* *This paragraph appeared in the Harvard address, but not in* Human Affairs.

play a considerable part in the political system and which are also cere-
monially exchanged in the course of large inter-tribal expeditions, which
are practiced throughout this region. Could we apply the same detailed
study to Masai or to Chagga economics, or those of the Eskimos or Plains
Indians, we would see that they also must be considered under the three
headings of production, distribution, and consumption.

In production we would find everywhere the question of the social
and cultural forces by which labor is organized. We would have to
inquire how productive labor is maintained; in other words, whether
there are beginnings of capital and even of interest. Under the heading
of distribution, we would not merely have to consider the complicated
institutions of African marketing, peddling, and hawking, as well as more
or less extensive forms of inter-tribal trade. We would also have to discuss
the chief's tribute.

I think that throughout the world we would find that the relations
between economics and politics are of the same type. The chief, everywhere, acts as a tribal banker, collecting food, storing it, and protecting
it, and then using it for the benefit of the whole community. His functions are the prototype of the public finance system and the organization
of state treasuries of today. Deprive the chief of his privileges and financial
benefits, and who suffers most but the whole tribe? At the same time,
it would be interesting to see how sometimes, especially in African
monarchies, the chief's political power was abused for selfish and extor-
tionate financial policy; and equally interesting to see what limits there
were to such malpractices. In the few cases where I was able to investigate
into this matter in central East Africa, I found that the subjects could,
and did, rebel, or else used sorcery, of which the monarch was usually very
much afraid.

As regards consumption, we should find that the common eating of
food, its preparation and the joint domestic economy, is one of the
strongest ties of family life. Even more interesting would it be to study
conspicuous waste under primitive conditions. It is possible to show that
such institutions as the Northwest Indian *potlatch* and the large displays
and redistributions of food practiced all over Oceania are not merely a
curiosity. The passion for wealth engenders thrift and stimulates production. The power of wealth as a guarantee of legal contracts or as public
payment for services forms one of the earliest binding forces in which
economic value influences and enhances social organization and solidarity.
The delight which the Trobriander feels in seeing his yams rot corresponds
to an important economic attitude; we have here a standardized sentiment
which crystallized around accumulation and permanence of foodstuffs,
the sentiment which sets economic security above immediate satisfaction.

The anthropologist is often asked by elderly ladies or young girls: "Is
primitive man an individualist or communist? I want to know that,

because I want to know whether human nature is communistic or not." I could refer to one or two instances where a scholar of high repute has played into the hands of the lady questioner, old or young. As a matter of fact, the anthropologist can give an opinion, but only as to the workings of ·the institution of property and not as to that vague entity, human nature. Communism as public control of private property has always existed and must be present in every culture, simple and developed. Communism as absence of individual property does not exist under primitive conditions.

Take the prototype of all wealth, value, and property: soil used for agriculture. Here it is very easy to juggle with words, for on the surface a pastoral, nomadic people are communistic in land. Yet an intelligent analysis shows that in the effective use of land they are not more communistic than the New Yorkers who use their public thoroughfares jointly. The economics of cattle, which is the effective way in which land is used, is always subject to individual ownership. Tillers of the soil who use the land directly invariably appropriate the soil, at least for the period of tilling. A tribe in central Africa, the Bemba, among whom I was able to do some work on this subject, have an unlimited supply of land. The title is vested in the chief. It is controlled by the local headman, and every individual is allowed as much as he likes. But once the boundaries are marked, there is no trespassing, no common use. There is full and exclusive individual appropriation for the period of from three to five years while cultivation goes on. Even then quarrels about land are more frequent than about women.

The Trobrianders have an extremely complicated system of land tenure, the gist of which is that the titular owner very seldom uses his own property, but receives an adequate and conveniently situated portion of land, for which he pays a nominal rent. Among the Chagga, ownership is individual, but if a man owns more than he can actually cultivate, the community disposes of the surplus to someone who is in need of soil.

Complete communism of land actually under cultivation is never found in any primitive society. Production is a process in which man invests labor and intelligent foresight, and at least as much of his wealth as is necessary for planting and for keeping himself alive while he works. No free human being will do it permanently without some legal guarantee, safeguarding for him the results of his efforts. The guarantee given to each free individual that the results of his efforts will be his to use or to give, is tantamount to individual ownership. Where there are slaves, pawns, or serfs, there may be a class of people who work without any claims to the fruits of their labor. But such communism turns men into slaves, serfs, or pawns. May this not be true of all forms of communism?

Another interesting lesson which we can learn from an anthropological survey is in the analysis of profit. We are often told that with the abolition of private profit all evils, such as war, sexual jealousy, poverty, and even drunkenness, will disappear. There is no doubt at all that profit lends itself to abuse through dishonest financial manipulation and the running, in the interest of shareholders, of enterprises which ought to be directed to public service. It must be controlled by public agencies in primitive as well as in civilized communities. But is it necessary to change the whole social order, nationalize all wealth and means of production, in order to reach the desired end? To me the Marxian doctrine of profit entails a complete misconception of the relationship between the economic factor and other motives and drives in human society. The pocket is not the only channel by which wealth can be maldistributed and abuses canalized. Vanity, doctrinaire zeal, incompetence, and personal ambition cause as much havoc as does greed. The men who control production— in Africa or Europe, in Melanesia or America—do not and cannot fill their pockets or bellies with gold. Where they can and do harm is in mishandling and misusing the production and distribution of wealth. In order to prevent that, public control by disinterested agencies is necessary. And here it is obviously better to have a system in which control of wealth, legislation, and the executive use of power are not concentrated in the same hands, but vested in separate agencies. The totalitarian state and the African autocracy are not models of sound economic systems. The real advance lies in the gradual piecemeal reform, involving all the parts of the economic and political organism. An integral revolution destroys, but it does not create. The concentration of all controls in the same hands means the abolition of all control.

Savage exoticisms and scientific anthropology

So far we have concentrated on prosaic, ordinary, non-savage aspects. [Many of you who have come to see a notorious anthropologist perform on the platform have, no doubt, drawn up a hopeful list of anticipations: cannibalism, *couvade*, avoidance of the mother-in-law, and the pious custom of killing and eating aged and decrepit parents, head-hunting and infanticide, sorcery, trial by ordeal, human sacrifice, taboos, totems, and all the other tricks of trade of the entertaining anthropologist.]* It all started with Herodotus, who amused us with talks about lotus-eaters and man-eaters, about queer sexual habits and gastronomic perversions.

[I have been drab and sober on purpose.]* If anthropology is to become the comparative science of cultures, it is high time it stepped out of its herodotage and anecdotage. It must turn to the fundamentals of human culture, in simple and complex, primitive and highly developed forms alike. It must study primitive economics and political systems, the

---

* *The material in brackets appeared in the Harvard address, but not in* Human Affairs.

7

theory of kinship and social organization, early jurisprudence, and systems of education. It must study all of these across the widest comparative range of human experience.

Not that we could not profitably dwell on some of the primitive eccentricities of man. Cannibalism as a system of foreign policy is a sound way of solving international complications: it is a rapid and effective manner of assimilating racial and national minorities. To run away from or to turn your back on your mother-in-law, many of us feel, would be an amiable and highly rational way of securing domestic happiness. The eating up of decrepit parents is a good method of old-age insurance, while expressing fully an appreciation of one's progenitors.

Seriously, however, in most of these queer and sordid customs there is a core of rational and practical principle, and also a quota of belief or superstition which on balance is not always completely foreign to us. Cannibalism is as repulsive to us as the eating of underdone beef or mutton is to the sentimental vegetarian, or the swallowing of live oysters would be to a Jain priest. But after all, meat is meat, and where there is a scarcity of it a strong nervous system cannot be too finicky or allow imagination to run away with it. But cannibalism also involves the fundamental belief that by eating your slain enemy you acquire his personal qualities or his spiritual virtues. And here just stop to think for a moment. Is this belief of a mystical or spiritual union by ingestion so absolutely alien to us? Can you not think of very highly differentiated and spiritual religions where mystic union is achieved by a sacrament in which the spiritual substance is taken by mouth? Between the lowest and crudest customs and the highest spiritual act there may be an unexpected common measure, so that charity may finish abroad when knowledge begins at home. By placing thus each of these strange and queer customs within its proper psychological and cultural setting, we can bring it near to us, we can perceive in it the universally human substratum. In other words, we have to carry out our analysis of primitive belief or superstition by means of universally valid concepts and thus make it amenable to scientific treatment.

There is no doubt that most "queernesses" and exoticisms of savagery reside in what we call "superstition" in others and "belief" in ourselves. Magic is obviously further from our comprehension even than primitive religion. Those acquainted with ethnological literature know how much attention has been devoted to magic. It is usually regarded as a primitive form of mental aberration and as a typical symptom of savagery. Tylor defined magic as a grossly distorted type of animistic philosophy. Frazer's theory presents magic as a perverted form of primitive pseudo science. Professor Freud again sees in magic a typical delusion of paranoia and ascribes it to primitive man's belief in the omnipotence of thought.

The function of magic

In truth magic is nothing of the sort. Here again it might be best to follow a magical act and see what we can learn from it. I was sitting in a lagoon village built on piles when, at an early stage of my Melanesian field work, I had my first experience of a severe monsoon hurricane. After the first few strong blasts a general commotion arose: people could be seen running about and screaming, some were trying to make fast the canoes, others to put away some of their chattels. They were all in panic. The onslaught of the wind was terrific, and I had to muster all my nervous energy to keep up the white man's burden of dignified impassivity.

And then I received my first intimation of the character, the power, and the influence of Melanesian magic. When the wind was at its worst a loud chant suddenly arose from one of the platforms. The hereditary wind magician of the community was about to calm down the storm in order to prevent any destruction which it might wreak. The words of the spell were simple: he ordered the wind to abate, to avaunt, to lie still. He addressed the wind from the mountain, the wind from the lagoon, the wind from the rainy clouds, and ordered them to lie down and lie still. He asserted that no harm could be done to the village.

What was the effect of his imprecations on the wind does not matter to us skeptics, but the effect of his voice on the human beings was truly magical. His voice rose like a mighty wall of safety between the frightened human beings and the unchained forces of nature. It was evident that the villagers now felt safe. They became more and more calm and reassured as the magician proceeded with his long spell. They behaved quite differently after the magic had been chanted. And immediately after he had finished his spell the magician took the practical situation in hand: he gave orders what to do, orders which were immediately obeyed in a disciplined, organized manner.

I realized then and there what the real function of magic is. On the psychological side it leads to a mental integration, to that optimism and confidence in the face of danger which has won to man many a battle with nature or with his human foes. Socially, magic, by giving leadership to one man, establishes organization at a time when organized and effective action is of supreme importance.

We have seen exactly the same function of magic in Trobriand agriculture. There also the magician acts as organizer to the community, while to each individual he gives confidence, spurring him to greater effort. And here I would immediately like to add a rider. If we were to examine either the wind magic or the agricultural magic point by point, we should come to one extremely important conclusion. The activity of the magician never encroaches on the technique or subject matter of practical work. In agriculture the Trobriand magician bestows additional fertility on the soil, forestalls pests and blights, the ravages of bush pigs and wallabies, destruction by drought and other unmanageable causes. He never does magic instead of cutting down the shrub or fertilizing the soil with ashes.

Magic is always carried out on the principle "Magic helps those who help themselves." It deals with the unaccountable, unmanageable elements of luck, chance, and misfortune. It never tackles the ordinary forces of nature, which are always managed by man with his own hands. Exactly the same may be said of the magic of war, of love, of enterprise, and of health. Everywhere magic only steps in where knowledge has declared its inability to deal with the situation. Far from being an assertion of the omnipotence of thought, it is rather a humble declaration that man throws himself on the mercies of higher supernatural forces, revealed through sacred tradition.

We define magic as the ritual act performed to bring about a practical result unachievable by man's unaided force. The ritual act is based on the belief that by the strict observance of traditionally prescribed behavior, bodily and verbal, man can influence the course of nature and the rulings of fate. This belief is always founded on traditional mythology and on the empirical affirmation of the power of magic. Magic has its ethical value in that it affirms the positive issues and thus leads to courage, endurance, and perseverance. It also makes people join in ritual work for the common good.

To define religion quite briefly, it differs from magic in that it does not aim at practical ends in emergencies of ordinary life. Religion, indeed, deals with the permanent and enduring problems of human existence. The acts of religion are not means to a practical end. Each religious ritual is an end in itself; in communion with divinity, in sacrifice the worshipper ministers to the pleasure of his god or gods; in acts of ancestor-worship homage is made and union achieved with the spirits of the dead. Each of such acts brings about its own end and compensation. In one important branch of religious activities, those connected with the death of a human being, we also see that mourning and wailing, ritualized grief, and burial center around a spiritual rather than a practical necessity: that of removing the pollution of death and of insuring the spiritual welfare of the soul of the deceased. But it is easy to see that religion also removes the mental conflict in face of metaphysical danger: religious belief affirms the positive issues in promising man immortality, in bringing him in touch with Providence, in setting him on the right way to reach personal salvation and the good of the community.

The place of knowledge, religion, and magic in culture

How can we link up religion, magic, sorcery, and divination as cultural phenomena with our noble system of interpretation in which we conceive of culture as the vast apparatus for the satisfaction of human needs? We have seen that the fundamental needs of the human organism, those of food, reproduction, safety, freedom of movement, are satisfied under culture by *ad hoc* systems of organized activities. Culture thus establishes the quest for food and the industries, technical constructiveness, courtship and marriage, kinship schemes, and military organizations.

We have seen how this cultural, roundabout way of indirect satisfaction imposes secondary or derived needs. These are not innate drives of the organism but highly derived implications of man's cultural response to innate urges. Thus economic desires, values, standards, legal inhibitions and the consciousness of one's rights and privileges, social ambition and kinship sentiments, political prestige and submissiveness are essentially human characteristics. But they are imposed by the circumstances of human existence in organized communities and not by reflex or instinct or any factor of innate endowment.

But this is not the end. The vast machinery of culture is maintained, regulated, and preserved by the body of traditional lore. This is made possible by language, which allows man to formulate general rules and condense them into concepts. Thus, to systems of action there correspond systems of thought. Action must be based on foresight and on the grip of the context. Man deals with nature and his fellow beings by constructive and imaginative handling of each situation. He has to lay down the results of past experience into systems, fixed, standardized, yet withal plastic. These he hands over from generation to generation.

Systems of human knowledge exist even among the lowest primitives. They must have existed from the very beginning of humanity. The widespread misconception that primitive man has no rudiments of science, that he lives in a hazy, mystical, or infantile world, has to be rejected in the light of our fuller knowledge of primitive cultures.

But though knowledge is easily accounted for, what are the natural foundations of religion and magic? That which establishes man's final superiority over the animals, his power of symbolic and constructive thought, imposes on him also great burdens. It reveals to him the fundamental uncertainty and limitation of his own existence. In order to think clearly man has to look back and remember; he has to look forward and foresee; and that means he is subject to fear as well as to hope. Man, of all the animals, cannot live in the present; he cannot lead a hand-to-mouth existence from moment to moment. This must finally bring him to ponder on topics where emotions blend with cold reason and where the answer is dictated by emotions though it is largely framed by reason.

What is the ultimate destiny of man and of mankind? What is the meaning of life and the relations between man and the universe? Whence have we come and whither are we bound, and what is the sense of all man's fears, sufferings, and disappointments? Metaphysics and religious speculation are as old as knowledge and as old as language itself. At the beginning they are extremely simple and crude. Animism and beliefs in magical force, fantasies about sorcery, ghosts, vampires, and totemism— that is, the belief in the spiritual affinity between man and nature—are the answers of primitive man to the fundamental riddles of life. Once we realize their real nature it is easy to perceive their great value. They are well adapted to the limited conditions in which primitives have to live, they contain the answer to the questions of whence and whither, and above all they supply man with ritual means of getting in touch with spiritual forces, of establishing communion with ancestral spirits, totemic beings, or divinities, and they allow man to secure his immortality and thus to give sense to his life.

Knowledge, magic, and religion are the highest, the most derived imperatives of human culture. Indirectly and through several relays they also are the outcome of man's organic needs. The craving for religion and for magical power, and scientific curiosity as well, are not instinctive. They are the outcome and the correlate of that intelligent adjustment of man to his environment which makes him the master thereof. Magic and to a much higher degree religion are the indispensable moral forces in every human culture. Grown out, as they are, of the necessity to remove internal conflict in the individual and to organize the community, they become the essential factors of spiritual and social integration. They deal with problems which affect all members of the community alike. They lead to actions on which depends the welfare of one and all. Religion and to a lesser extent magic thus become the very foundations of culture.

Summary and conclusions

By now, I trust, we all realize that there exist laws of cultural process, and that their discovery is the main task of scientific anthropology.

I have started with the affirmation that there is a science of culture. I hope that throughout the succeeding pictures of living cultures with their variety and diversity of forms, throughout the analysis of what these cultures have in common and how they differ, we have all realized that there is an underlying fundamental sameness; that it is possible to establish the common measure which is indispensable for the scientific treatment of any type of reality.

We have found everywhere that observation can be made fruitful, relevant, and convincing only if it is inspired by a theory of the nature of culture. Culture in the first place has to satisfy the organic needs of man. From the indirect, that is cultural, satisfaction of these, there arise further instrumental imperatives. Finally, in the spiritual realm, culture implies the integrative principles of knowledge, religion, ethics, and magical technique. Every human culture can be analyzed by the same universally valid concepts, derived from a theory which again consists of a system of general laws. At the same time, we have found that there is only one type of really scientific theory, and that is a theory which is dictated by observation and which can be tested by it.

The general concepts and laws I need not summarize for you. They result from the universal occurrence of such aspects of human culture as economics and education, law and political organization, magic, religion, art, and recreation. The cultural activities, again, in every society integrate into natural units, which we have called institutions. And here again it is possible to draw up a list or table of such institutions. The family, the extended kinship grouping, the clan, the village community, the tribe, and the nation are such universal institutions. If we add to them such more diversified types as occupational groups, economic teams, voluntary associations, we have a number of cultural entities each of which is amenable to laws and generalizations, and each of which must be studied by the same outfit of concepts.

In the vast system of institutional activities which corresponds to the fact of reproduction, we have listed such laws as the dominance of the initial situation; the principle of legitimacy, defining the legal aspect of parenthood; the further principle that marriage leads to the establishment of a domestic unit; the concept of the unilateral and bilateral kinship principles in reproduction, and the principle that the clan is not equivalent in influence to the family, but a derivate.

Whether we study economics as an aspect or whether we proceed to the definition of such specific economic institutions as agriculture, cattle-breeding, the organized activity of the hunting team, we can and must base our studies on a series of general laws or principles. We have to inquire into the economic process in its three phases: production, distribution and exchange, and consumption. We have to study these three phases as they permeate the whole of tribal life. We cannot understand the titles to property except through the role which they play in production and the influence which production exercises on property. Again, we find that unless we consider economics in conjunction with the organizing forces of religion and of magic, of law and politics, we shall always miss some of the most important realities of economics.

Had we more time, we should have been able to construct equally exhaustive theories of primitive law and primitive education, of the part played by recreation in primitive societies, and of the principles of artistic activities in their social and cultural aspect.[4]

In the course of our analysis we have had to emphasize the point that every cultural phenomenon presents to us three main facts: the material,

[4] The reader might perhaps compare my *Crime and Custom in Primitive Society*, 1926; the article, "Kinship," in *Man*, 1930, p. 19, where a bibliography of my publications on kinship will be found [see p. 153 of *Sex, Culture, and Myth*]; and the small book, *The Definition of Culture*, shortly to be published.

the social, and the spiritual. The first is best approached through the analysis of the material substratum of culture; the second by the study of institutions; the third through the linguistic approach. For, although I am not a behaviorist, I believe that it is best to study mental processes in their objective, outward manifestations.

Thus I maintain that the subject-matter of the comparative study of cultures does lend itself to sober, scientific treatment. I also maintain that this treatment is indispensable, especially from the point of view of actual research in the field.

I have tried to define the scope of anthropology, the pioneer among social sciences in the empirical approach to determinism. Determinism does exist in cultural process, and the scientific statement of this process must be deterministic, objective, fully documented, and unaffected by personal and impressionistic distortion. Scientific anthropology, as you have seen, must work on the foundations laid down by biology and physiology; it must work hand in hand with the psychologist; and it must learn as much as it can learn from the student of environment, the geographer.

Our plea for scientific anthropology, of course, is not tantamount to an indictment or exorcism of all the attractive and amusing speculations. Evolutionary *aperçus*, indeed, I regard as indispensable. Careful and sober diffusionist hypotheses seem to me quite profitable. To minimize or discard a really human interest in humanism would be a crime. To mix up or confuse the emotional or artistic approach with the scientific is a serious lack of judgment. The two approaches must be used simultaneously; they have to complement each other. But science must furnish the foundation.

The scientific theory of culture has also brought to light some really vital truths. Is the recognition of the universal stability and permanence of the family and marriage of no interest in these days when domestic institutions seem to be threatened on every side? The anthropologist might almost add: "As it was in the beginning, is now and ever shall be." That communism cannot be a panacea for all our cultural troubles may also be an interesting appreciation. We have seen that communism alone is never to be found in any culture, however primitive or complex. We have seen, also, why communism as an economic system cannot work except in conjunction with slavery. On the other hand, pure individualism does not exist anywhere either. So that some admixture of communism, that is, public control, has always worked and worked well. But it cannot work wonders, or cure all evils. We have defined the role of the supernatural as an integrating and organizing force in society. One of the implications of our analysis was that the abuse of law and political power must always lead to cultural disaster. Science and virtue, efficiency and endurance, courage and chastity can never be dictated by edicts, nor enflamed by oratory, nor yet forced into existence by a system of police spies and police brutalities. To replace religion and morality by the secret service of a totalitarian state is a disease of culture.

For we have fully acknowledged the existence of cultural maladjustment, and even of lethal ailments of civilization. The very concepts of adaptation and function imply degrees and qualifications, from excellence to decay.

Our present civilization is undoubtedly passing through a very severe, perhaps a critical stage of maladjustment. The abuse of legal and administrative power; the inability to create lasting conditions of peace; the recrudescence of aggressive militarism and magical trickery; the torpor of true religion and the assumption of a religious garb by doctrines of racial or national superiority, or the gospel of Marx—all this shows that, while we have become the masters of inanimate nature, we have connived at the complete enslavement of man by machine.

The greatest need of today is to establish a balance between the stupendous power of natural science and its applications, and the self-inflicted backwardness of social science and the consequent impotence of social engineering. To repeat a truism just mentioned, we have allowed the machine to overpower man. One of the reasons for this is that we have learned to understand, hence to respect and to handle, the mechanism. But we have failed to develop the really scientific spirit in humanism.

The following paragraph served as conclusion to the Harvard address:

Today the freedom to exercise purely scientific determinism is threatened in many countries. This freedom is even more essential for social than for natural science. It is, therefore, our duty on this occasion to insist on the necessity for this freedom. We are assembled here to celebrate the tercentenary of one of the greatest workshops of science and reason ever established by man. The founding of Harvard was an act of human behavior not outside reason and determinism. It was determined by wise foresight, and its existence and work have been enduring factors in developing reason and determining rational behavior. Harvard has always fostered that spirit of science which means freedom in the search for truth, for the laws of nature and of human behavior. Let this spirit preside over the development of the comparative science of man, and we may yet hope that the spirit of Harvard—that is, the spirit of science—will prevail in the conduct of human affairs.

8

MAN'S CULTURE AND MAN'S BEHAVIOR

The scientific basis of anthropology must be established, for anthropology as the theory of culture provides in many ways the scientific basis of all studies concerned with man, his behavior, and his achievements. Culture is clearly the fullest context of all human activities. It is the vast instrumentality through which man achieves his ends, both as an animal that must eat, rest, and reproduce; and as the spiritual being who desires to extend his mental horizons, produce works of art, and develop systems of faith. Thus, culture is at the same time the minimum mechanism for the satisfaction of the most elementary needs of man's animal nature, and also an ever-developing, ever-increasing system of new ends, new values, and new creative possibilities.

An understanding of what this reality is, how it works, how it is constituted and determined, is indispensable for all humanists alike. The archaeologist and the historian, who have to reconstruct the past cultural reality from partial data, monumental or documentary, must base their reconstruction on the laws determining the relations between a part and the whole, between economic and juridical phenomena, and between the structure of a society and its creative output. They must be in possession of a scientific theory of culture, or else indulge in more or less inspired, sound, but always intuitive guesswork. In economics and the science of law it is becoming increasingly recognized that the processes of production, exchange, and consumption do not happen in a vacuum, but within a cultural context; while legislation, the behavior of judges and juries, and the effective sanction of legal rules depend upon such factors as public opinion, economic necessities, the level of education, and the type of religion and ethics prevalent in a society. It seems hardly even necessary

This lecture was first presented before the Union College Symposium, "Science Views Man," March 1941, and published in American Scientist, *October 1941 (Vol. 29, No. 3 and 4), pp. 182–96; and January 1942 (Vol. 30, No. 1), pp. 66–78, and is reprinted by permission.*

to stress the fact that the student of contemporary social phenomena and also the psychologist must attack their problems within the real context in which these happen: the context of culture.

Science—to give an unpretentious yet clear definition or reminder—is the translation of experience into general laws which have predictive value. We have to inquire, then, whether it is possible to establish general rules and principles concerning cultural process and product. Such rules, to be scientific, must be inferred from observation and be subject to experimental test. They must be generalizations of universal validity. It is essential to have statements of principle which remain true whether applied to primitive or to highly developed culture, to an Arctic community or a tropical island tribe in the Pacific. We have to establish clearly determined relations between cultural variables embodied into formulae of general applicability.

From the slightly different point of view, it can be stated that science establishes order into its particular subject matter by isolating the relevant factors and forces. It will then be necessary to prove that such relevant factors of structure and forces controlling the process do exist in the domain of culture. Such systems of relevant concatenation would give us the clue for the observation of a new culture and the means of describing it adequately. They would also provide the common measure for the comparative, that is, theoretical treatment of all phenomena of organized behavior.

The legitimate subject matter of anthropology, as well as of other social sciences, is culture. The experimental approach to this subject matter must be based on direct observation of collective, organized behavior through field work. By field work I mean the study of living communities and their material culture, whether at a low level of development or within our own civilizations. Such study must be guided by the general theory of culture, whereas observation has to be stated in terms of general principle. As in all sciences, so also here, we shall have to inquire whether the final test of applicability through planned social engineering is possible in the case of social studies.

I am purposely omitting from my definition of the scientific approach the test of quantitative approach, the feasibility of mathematical or semi-mathematical formulation. It is clear that wherever phenomena amenable to counting and measuring are considered, the scientific approach would demand this type of operation. Also, in the rare cases where statistics yield sufficient data for curves or equations, these instrumentalities must be used. The general complexity of a subject matter makes it, as a rule, less amenable to quantitative treatment. In all such treatment, grave errors are introduced and increased in any algebraic manipulations whenever entities are counted or computed that are not really identical. The problem, therefore, of identity or of isolation of relevant factors and of their relations is one which must be solved first, and then only can we debate whether mathematical formulations are likely to introduce more clarity or more presumptuous error into our arguments. It goes without saying that in vital statistics, in certain economic transactions, and in the description of technical processes, especially at higher levels, the quantitative, as well as the mathematical, procedures have been already employed and cannot be left out of consideration.

As regards the primary character of science, that is, the cross-fertilization of observed fact and theoretical argument, the anthropologist has certain initial advantages and can claim certain achievements. Engaged as he is in the study of primitive cultures for which there are no historic records and very little archaeological documentation, the anthropologist, by the very nature of his material, was driven into the field. He had to become his own chronicler and to establish perhaps the first laboratory of social science in methodical ethnographic researches in the field. Since observation always implies theory, we find in modern anthropological studies that exchange of inspiration which comes from the simultaneous contact with facts and the striving to subsume them under general principles.

The wide range of cultural diversities was another motive that inspired the scientific bent in modern anthropology. Sound generalization must be derived from comparison and the use of the inductive method, and here again, unless there is some theoretical common measure of comparison, our induction fails.

As regards applications, anthropology has not as yet many achievements to its credit. Nevertheless, it may be said that social engineering presents certain facilities and a degree of viability when it comes to colonial affairs lacking under our own modern conditions. The colonial power has a control, legislative and administrative, over a primitive tribe, far greater than that admissible in a democratic commonwealth. Totalitarian experimentation, again, is not based in its sociological aspect on a scientific policy. In democratic countries, the typical politician is a disturbing link when it comes to the scientific guidance of public events. He is, as a rule, more keen to become a lawgiver than to be amenable to law in the scientific sense.

Obviously anthropology has no claims whatsoever to deal with the scientific problem of culture alone. It had certain initial advantages. To use them fully it must, first and foremost, disclaim some spurious pretenses. The savages are not the only representatives of man. We know full well that modern savagery is as illuminating as its primitive version. Thus, sociology, as soon as it becomes fully infected with the field-work habits of the anthropologist, will have at least quite as much to contribute to the scientific theory of culture as its humbler collaborator. Indeed, in the science of culture we would fail completely as anthropologists unless full cooperation is established between the study of the human mind, of modern societies and cultures, and of such well-established specialities as jurisprudence and economics.

The nature of cultural process

Considering culture as a whole, that is, at all levels and in any environment, recognition must first be given to its instrumental character. We might survey the organization of an Arctic community, a tribe living in the tropical jungle, a horde of lowest primitives, such as the Australian aborigines, and anywhere and everywhere we would find them wielding a body of implements, following rules of behavior, cherishing ideas and beliefs, engaging through all this in activities which integrate into a vast and complex instrumental apparatus. At higher levels of development, in the New World civilizations of Mexico or Peru, in ancient Egypt or in modern Europe, the apparatus and the activities are more highly developed, but the total effect is instrumental and so is every one of the differential phases. Man everywhere is maintained by his culture, allowed to reproduce, as well as instructed and assisted in this, supplied with techniques, knowledge, recreation, art, and religion.

Were one to look more closely at any particular culture, every activity would be found to be related to some organization or other. In each we would find a group cooperating, linked by common interests and a purpose. Members of such a group or institution own conjointly a portion of the environment, some implements or machines, and dispose of a quota of national wealth. They obey prescribed norms of conduct and are trained in particular skills. Through their activities thus normed and implemented, they achieve their purpose or intentions, known to everybody and socially recognized. They also produce an impression on the environment, social and physical; they achieve results which can be revealed through a sociological analysis.

We would find such groups in the homes of the people as family groups and domestic institutions, and that the food supply and the production of goods and implements is the result of such organized cooperative work. The temples and the courts of law are maintained and run by groups of people organized for a purpose, moved by definite motives or values, and having a special function in public life.

This surface impression, dictated by sound common sense, might lead the observer to the statement of a few generalizations. Culture as a whole is an extensive instrumental system of organized activities. It is exercised by a system of related institutions, that is, groups of people united by common interest, endowed with material equipment, following rules of their tradition or agreement, and contributing towards the work of the culture as a whole. The interests that supply the motive power and dictate the tasks of the group are at times physiological, as in food production, domestic life, and defense mechanisms. There are, however, other interests, values, and motives connected with science or with art which transcend any biological determinism. We are thus led to the fuller analysis as to what the drives or motives of human beings are, and also as to the principles and forces of human organization.

As regards the drives, man is obviously an animal; hence his organic needs will always give rise to a permanent biological determinism in all behavior. Men eat, sleep, reproduce, and protect their body from excessive temperature, as well as from physical destruction. There is a minimum of elementary conditions that has to be fulfilled so that the individual organism survives and the group retains its numbers. Even a slight, but progressive, deterioration of the healthy organic state would inevitably lead to cultural extinction.

It is equally important to realize that human beings live not by biological drives alone, but also by physiological drives molded and modified by culture. As regards nutrition, food and its intake are not a mere exchange between man and environment. In a primitive tribe or a civilized community, there is an organized system of production, distribution, storing, and preparing, which provides each member with his meals. Here again, consumption, that is, the intake of food, is fashioned by the taste, taboos, and hygienic rules, which partly limit and partly redirect the normal appetite. Propagation is determined, in its very impulse, by the ideals of beauty and desirability in which the sex impulse integrates with aesthetic, economic, and social considerations. The rules of specific taboo, such as incest and exogamy, as well as of preferential mating, dictate the type of courtship, whereas the production of children is universally defined by the law of marriage. Nor are the results of propagation merely biological. The extensive systems of kinship ties and grouping into clans, so prevalent in primitive communities, are the translation into sociological norms of the results of biological propagation. Bodily exercise is determined by economic labor and by systems of sports, recreational pursuits, or even artistic activities. Thus, man everywhere acts under culturally determined incentives; he submits to the norms prescribed by tradition; he cooperates and pools, or redistributes, the produce of his labor.

There are certain phases in human behavior even more removed from biological fact than those here described. In a primitive tribe there are objects of magical virtues or religious sanctity or economic value: the famous bull-roarers of central Australia, the totemic poles of the northwestern American tribes, or the millstones known from Micronesia. In order to understand the value attached to such objects and the activities that surround them, it would be necessary to enter a world of mythological antecedents or social and economic conventions. We would have to learn the meaning of the dogmatic principles and see how they are expressed in ritual, or economic transaction, or ethics. To understand why certain people indulge in head-hunting and others practice cannibalism, why in certain cultures valuable objects are produced only in order to be destroyed, would obviously require consideration of the formation of cultural value, of legal principle, as well as the native conceptions of wealth, social ranking, and the realities of magical or religious belief.

Accordingly, man is not merely impelled by hunger and thirst, by love, and the desire to sleep. There are other motives connected with ambition, rank, doctrine, and mythology which establish as powerful incentives for conduct as do those of an innate drive. Instrumentality obtains throughout. In other words, it is always found that a human being is impelled to a specific activity in order to attain a desired end. It is obvious, however, that culture solves not merely the simple organic problems, but creates new problems, inspires new desires, and establishes a new universe in which man moves, never completely free from his organic needs, but also following new ends and stimulated to new satisfactions.

All this does not imply that cultural determinism introduces a mere chaos of relativity in which we would have to resort to the arbitrary biddings of a *deus ex machina* of some specific tribal or cultural genius. We shall be able to give a clear definition and catalogue of the biological needs that are the prime movers of human behavior. We shall also clearly establish what we mean by derived needs or instrumental imperatives. Finally, it will be possible to show that the integrative values, such as ideas, belief, moral rule, are also determined and significant through their relation to culture as a whole. The needs of the organism and the raw materials supplied by the environment are the elements of the primary, or biological, determinism. The indirect cultural situation, however, in which the raw materials are obtained and elaborated and the human organism adjusted imposes new cultural, that is, instrumental and integrative imperatives, which are subject to determinism, hence also to scientific analysis.

The ability to establish and to maintain the cultural apparatus confers enormous advantages on mankind, advantages that consist, on the one hand, in a safer and fuller satisfaction of organic needs; and, on the other hand, in the gift of new impulses and new satisfactions. Culture thus satisfied first the minimum standard of living, that of organic survival. It also adds an increased artificial standard of enjoyment, in which man reaches what usually is described as intellectual, artistic, and ethical pleasures and satisfactions.

For all this there is a price to be paid in terms of obedience to tradition. Man must submit to a number of rules and determinants that do not come from his organism but from submission to his own artifact and machinery, to cooperation, and to the tyranny of words and other symbols. The oft-repeated opposition as between man and machine, in which man is often described as the slave of his self-produced mechanism, his Frankenstein monster, contains an essential truth. Even when man is not enslaved beyond the limits of real necessity, he becomes permanently dependent on his artifacts, once he has started to use them. Cooperation, the social give and take, implies a determined quota of contribution for which man receives, generally, a larger return, but has to remain bound to his social contract. As regards symbolic tradition, it does not always enslave, but it invariably redirects, limits, and determines human behavior.

The biological determinism of culture

We have seen that the biological determinants appear in every culture and that they are invariably refashioned and intertwined with other motives. The problem arises in what sense is it possible to isolate and define biological determinism? And further, in what way is it related to more complex cultural phenomena? The answer is contained in Figure 1, in

A. *Impulse* $\longrightarrow$	B. *Act* $\longrightarrow$	C. *Satisfaction*
drive to breathe; gasping for air	intake of oxygen	elimination of CO_2 in tissues
hunger	ingestion of food	satiation
thirst	absorption of liquid	quenching
sex appetite	conjugation	detumescence
fatigue	rest	restoration of muscular and nervous energy
restlessness	activity	satisfaction of fatigue
somnolence	sleep	awakening with restored energy
bladder pressure	micturition	removal of tension
colon pressure	defecation	abdominal relaxation
fright	escape from danger	relaxation
pain	avoidance by effective act	return to normal state

Fig. 1. Permanent vital sequences incorporated in all cultures

which the main types of biological determinism have been summed up severally and concretely. A set of vital sequences is there listed which, it is maintained, are always incorporated into every culture. The concept of vital sequence means that the central activity or biological act, listed in column B, must be performed regularly and permanently in every culture. This part of the performance is integrally incorporated into culture, with modifications, to be discussed later, as regards certain prerequisites and the conditions under which it is allowed to happen. The drive, listed in column A, invariably receives a profound modification, different from one culture to another. But although modified, the drive can be determined partly in its physiological character, partly in that it is always connected with the biological act. The items listed in column

C are again definable in terms of biological fact: satiation, detumescence, the freeing of the organism of waste matter, the restoration of muscular energy, and the using up of biochemical tensions through muscular exercise and breathing.

The three phases can be defined by the biochemist, the physicist, and the ecologist. The actual intake of air or food; the act of conjugation; sleep, rest, nutrition, or excretion, are clearly defined activities, in which several branches of natural science are interested. Thus, the concept of vital sequence is neither vague nor devoid of substance. It refers to happenings within the human organism as related to physical and cultural environment. However much the drive or satisfaction might be refashioned by culture, both drive and satisfaction must be of such a nature as to lead to the performance of each physiological act, adequate in terms of biology. We see here that the concept of form and function of human behavior is included, since each can be defined in terms of natural science.

The vital sequence is thus the projection of a complex cultural reality onto the physiological plane. We can now also define the concept of basic need over and above that of drive. In each culture there must be systems of standardized arrangements which allow of full, regular, and general satisfaction of all the individual drives. The basic need in its several varieties can, then, be defined as including all individual drives that have to be satisfied so as to keep the organisms of a community in a normal state of healthy metabolism. The non-satisfaction of any or every basic need would imply the gradual biological deterioration of the group, which, if cumulative, would lead to extinction. As regards procreation, the basic need here requires that a sufficient incidence of effective reproduction should occur to maintain the numerical strength of a community. In any culture where celibacy, chastity, vows, abstinences, or castration exceeded restricted numerical limits, we would have a process of gradual extinction. The concept of basic need differs from that of drive, in that it refers to the collective exercise of individual drives, integrated with reference to the community as a whole. The satisfaction of basic needs is predicated with reference to all the organisms, to environmental conditions, and to the cultural setting of the community. It need not be, perhaps, stressed that in the study of cultural realities, whether through field work or in theoretical analysis, we do not resort any more to our analysis in terms of individual drive, but have to rely on the concept of basic need. The drive → activity → satisfaction analysis contains an abstraction of great importance for the foundations of a sound theory of culture. In actual research, however, we do not meet this abstraction, but are faced always with culturally organized satisfactions of integral basic needs.

Figure 2 summarizes concretely and in a highly simplified manner the basic needs and the cultural responses to them. Its meaning will become

clearer in detail as our argument advances. For the present, it is clear
that it corresponds to a large extent to the list of drives. Several of them,
however, have been compressed into one entry in this figure as, for instance, the need of solid foods, liquids, and intake of oxygen. All these
are associated with the process of metabolism. Another important point
is that each entry is to be considered as integrally related with reference
to need and its linked responses. For, as we already know, in the human
species biological motive never occurs in a pure and isolated form. Human
beings breathe in closed rooms or caves; they have to combine breathing
with rules of politeness or taboo, since human breath is, in some cultures,
regarded as sacred and in others as dangerous. Nutrition, propagation, or

A. *Basic needs*	B. *Cultural re-sponses*	A. *Basic needs*	B. *Cultural re-sponses*
1. metabolism	commissariat	5. movement	activities
2. reproduction	kinship	6. growth	training
3. bodily com-forts	shelter	7. health	hygiene
4. safety	protection		

Fig. 2. Basic needs and cultural responses

bodily comforts occur as formed habits. Human beings eat according to
a definite daily sequence. They conjugate in accordance with rules of law
and morals, or else against them, and thus under cultural conflict. The
need for bodily comforts does not arise in an environmental vacuum and
then send off the organism in search of a satisfaction. Savages and more
sophisticated beings alike wear clothes, carry out a routine of cleanliness,
live in habitations, and warm themselves at some permanent sources of
warmth. Thus it is clear that the stream of necessities of motives arising
out of each need flows, as it were, parallel to the stream of culturally
obtainable satisfactions. In the daily round of life, as well as in the seasonal
cycle, the human being normally passes through a routine of instrumental
effort and of prepared satisfaction in which biological stimulus and organic
effort are not hooked up by *ad hoc,* short-circuited links of desire and
satisfaction, but are interwoven into two long chains: one of large-scale
organized work on culture and for culture; the other, a systematic drawing upon or consuming of already prepared cultural benefits and goods.

The instrumental phase of human behavior

To make the last argument more concrete and precise, let us again embody
it into a diagrammatic presentation:

Drive (1)—Instrumental performance—Culturally defined situation—
Drive (2)—Consummatory act—Satisfaction (meta-physiological)

Fig. 3. Instrumentally implemented vital sequence

This is obviously a much more accurate and less abstract representation than the vital sequence previously shown (Figure 2). Certain similarities between the two obtain. We are here still dealing with the vital sequence, one which includes a biological activity. There are in culture, as will be seen later, sequences that do not include such a link. In this figure there is a definite linkage in which all the phases are determined by the relationship between a biological drive and its satisfaction.

There are, however, differences. To be true to the reality of typical culture concatinations, it was necessary to split the drive into two parts. Drive (1) is the instrumental motive, the impulse to take the roundabout way that man follows when he produces or purchases his food, prepares it, and places it on his table. In this he acts to a certain extent like the learning animal in a maze, who has to discover and to use the devices which supply it with food. Sex leads the human animal not to conjugation directly, but to courtship and, in many cases, to marriage. In short, the entire training of the human organism teaches the individual to obtain biological ends through the recognition, appreciation, and the handling of the appropriate means.

Drive (2) represents the culturally determined appetite. Man very often does not eat by hunger, hardly ever by hunger alone. He eats at the right time, the right place, and in the right company. His tastes and values are highly shaped, and even when hungry, he will not touch food defined in his own culture as disgusting, unpalatable, or morally repugnant. "One man's meat is another man's poison": my cannibal friends in New Guinea developed a healthy appetite when confronted with missionary steak, but turned away in disgust from my tinned Camembert cheese, sauerkraut, or frankfurters, which latter they regarded as gigantic worms. Again, the impulse of sex which, in animal societies, occurs between any two healthy organisms, is culturally inhibited by such taboos as those of incest, of caste prejudice, and to a lesser extent, by appreciation of rank, class, and professional or racial discrimination. What is a comfortable means of sleeping to an African or a South Sea native would be torture to a pampered Parisian or New Yorker. Nor would our beds, bathtubs, and sanitary arrangements be convenient or even usable to a native from the jungle. Thus there is a two-fold redetermination of physiological drives. Cultural drive occurs in two forms, and each of them is determined by the tradition in which an organism is trained.

Satisfaction in this series has been modified by an adjective. It appears invariably as a cultural appetite rather than as the satisfaction of a pure physiological drive. Breathing, as carried on by certain European communities within the non-ventilated and heavily modified atmospheres of enclosed rooms, would not satisfy an Englishman accustomed to a superabundance of fresh air. The satisfaction of appetite by food discovered to be unclean ritually, magically, or in terms of what is repugnant in a culture does not lead to a normal state of satiety, but to a violent reaction, including often sickness. The satisfaction of the sex impulse in an illicit or socially dangerous manner produces detumescence, but also conflicts which may lead, in the long run, to functional disease.

Thus culture determines the situation, the place, and the time for the physiological act. It delimits it by general conditions as to what is licit or illicit, attractive or repulsive, decent or opprobrious. Although the act itself, as defined in terms of anatomy, physiology and interaction with the environment, is constant, its prerequisites as well as its consequences change profoundly.

The greatest modification, however, in this new diagram consists in the insertion of the two terms: Instrumental phase—culturally defined situation. The instrumental phase, as we shall see in a closer analysis, is always an integral part of a largely organized system of activities. The instrumentalities of food production would have to be connected with agriculture or hunting or fishing. The storing, preparing, and consuming of food happen in a home or a club or a restaurant. The instrumental phase is also the open door through which such elements of culture as artifacts, norms, and cooperative habits enter as essential constituents of human behavior.

Let us consider any instrumental phase. Primitive fire-making subserves the needs of cooking, warmth, and light. It implies the element of artifact, the knowledge and techniques of friction, and also the appreciation of the value of these objects and activities. In any food-producing instrumental phase we would discover the use of the digging-stick, the hoe, the plough; weapons, nets, or traps; and also the whole system of technique and knowledge, of cooperation and distribution with its legal and customary basis. In every instrumental phase of preparatory activities, the following factors are disclosed: (1) artifacts; (2) normed behavior; (3) organized cooperation; (4) symbolic communication by means of language or other signs. These four cardinal constituents of culture are present in each phase at any level of civilization.

One simple inference occurs immediately: the existence of culture depends upon the mechanisms and activities through which every one of these four constituents is produced and maintained, as well as generally distributed. First, therefore, there must exist in every culture forms or organization through which the material substratum of culture, that is, the body of artifacts, are produced, distributed, and consumed. The economic aspect of a culture is omnipresent.

The norms of behavior have to be known and they have to be enforced. Hence again we can postulate that some mechanisms for the statement, the interpretation, and the sanction of law and order must exist in every community. Accordingly at higher levels there exist everywhere legislative bodies, courts of law, and forces of police. In primitive communities such special institutions may be absent or rudimentary. Nevertheless, the equivalents of codifications, of adjudication, and enforcement are never absent. The essence of custom or norm is that it coordinates behavior; hence it has to be known by all those who cooperate. Many norms curb innate tendencies, define privileges and duties, limit ambition, and circumscribe the use of wealth. There is invariably a tendency to circumvent them. Together with the need of force implied in the imperative of social order, we have in authority a principle which implies the existence of force socially determined and physically implemented. We find everywhere, therefore, the political principle, that is, the socially or culturally determined distribution of force and the right to use it.

Finally, we found that communication, through language and other symbolic means, and the transmission of culture are essential parts of our extended instrumental sequence. Both can be subsumed under the concept of training, insofar as the skills, technical and social rules of conduct have to be implanted in the growing organism and maintained through precept and exhortation. Education, at all levels, can be differentiated into schooling and adult education. Thus the derived need of training or fashioning of the organism for its cultural tasks is one which can be listed as the fourth derived imperative of culture.

Figure 4 gives a condensed presentation of the instrumental needs of culture and of the organized responses to them. We have only to add

1. The cultural apparatus of implements and consumers' goods must be produced, used, maintained, and replaced by new production.
   Economics

2. Human behavior, as regards its technical, customary, legal, or moral prescription must be codified, regulated in action and sanctioned.
   Social control

3. The human material by which every institution is maintained must be renewed, formed, drilled, and provided with full knowledge of tribal tradition.
   Education

4. Authority within each institution must be defined, equipped with powers, and endowed with means of forceful execution of its orders.
   Political organization

Fig. 4. Table of instrumental imperatives

that the instrumental imperatives have the same degree of cogency as those derived directly from biological needs. We have shown that all vital sequences occur in culture through instrumental implementation. Hence no biological need, that is, no need of the community as a whole, can be normally and regularly satisfied without the full and adequate working of the instrumental responses. These latter constitute together the integral mechanism through which the whole set of basic need receives its regular flow of satisfaction in every culture. Since even the simplest culture raises the level of the quantitative and qualitative standard of living and thus alienates any human group from the direct hand-to-mouth satisfaction by contact with environment, the breakdown of the cultural machinery would imply at least gradual extinction.

Confirmation of this fact is evident when we look at the evidence of historical facts. A serious breakdown in the economic, political, or legal order which usually also implies deterioration in the systems of knowledge and ethics, leads human groups to disorganization and to the sinking of the cultural level. The breakdown of many simpler cultures under the impact of Western civilization and the extinction of many racial groups supply one sample. The ever-recurrent decay of once flourishing cultures, which are then replaced by others or else enter a period of Dark Ages, is another case in point. Even today we are faced with a serious threat to culture, that of total war, which is waged not merely in terms of destruction and physical aggression, but also as economic war against the systems of production and, above all, nutritive maintenance. As propaganda, it aims at the breaking down of moral and social resistance through the sapping of the constitutional principles of organization, both as regards defense and the normal working of institutions.

The emergence of culture

A clear definition of the symbolic process is still lacking. Its existence was implied throughout, especially in our statements concerning the codes of human behavior, the rules of conduct, the educational processes which largely consist in verbal instruction, and the inculcation of systems of value.

It will be helpful to turn once more to very simple cultural conditions that are on the borderline between the precultural behavior of man, the animal, and the emergence of truly cultural conduct. From the well-known facts of animal training, which have been now raised to a system of principles embodied in the psychology of stimulus and response, it is established that apes and lower animals can acquire habits and be taught to use artifacts. It is a fair assumption that precultural man, living under conditions of nature, was led frequently to the instrumental use of material objects. Whenever he was placed, with a fair degree of regularity, under conditions resembling those of an experimental maze in which the rat or the guinea pig is being trained, he probably developed individual habits. An individual habit implies at least the development of a skill, the appreciation of the instrumental value of an object and, finally, the retention of both skill and appreciation. This integral retention, diagrammatically embodied in our presentation of instrumentally implemented series, corresponds to the concept of reinforcement, so fruitfully used by Clark Hull and other contemporary psychologists, as the pivotal principle of animal learning. It is not difficult to see that reinforcement, which means the integral retention by an animal organism of a definite sequence in instrumental activities, contains two concepts of great importance to the student of culture, the concept of symbol and that of value.

Reinforcement, however, accounts only for the formation of habits, that is, of individual acquired types of behavior. As long as habit is not infectious or public, it is not a real unit of culture. Culture begins when the transition between habit and custom is made. Custom can be defined as a habit made public by communication from one individual to others and transferable, that is, capable of being ingrained by one generation on to the next.

We have to introduce two more factors as indispensable prerequisites for the transformation of habits into customs. First, the existence of a group in permanent contact and related on the genealogical principle must be assumed. We have further to assume the existence of means of communication which would make possible discourse and symbolic training. The means of communication, moreover, have to be linked and standardized into traditional statements that can be transmitted from the elder generation to the younger. Thus it is necessary to add two more factors to those previously listed.

And once more we come upon the same list of the cardinal constituents of culture: artifacts, skills, that is, norms of behavior; organized groups; and means of communications, that is, symbols and theoretical systems of precept and value.

The raw materials of both sociability and symbolism can also be assumed as pre-existent to the actual emergence of culture. The long infancy of the human species and the formation of families and of family groups was undoubtedly precultural. These are mere assumptions for which proof need not be given, but which are essentially plausible.

The same condition is evident with respect to the raw materials of symbolism. If precultural man was occasionally driven into developing habits, his behavior was determined by what the modern psychologist calls conditioned stimuli. Finding himself regularly within a context of situation and under the urge of a biological drive with no direct satisfaction, he would resort to instrumental behavior. In this the instrument, a piece of wood or stone, and the association of previous effective activity with this object would provide the cue or the conditioned stimulus to action. The fact that an environmental sign directs the organism to action is essentially symbolic.

Thus we can say that the artifact itself, the typical context of circumstance, the habitual technique, all these functioned symbolically, as well as instrumentally. It may also be assumed that the example of a performance was an act instilled with demonstrative symbolism. When this is added to such symbolic raw material as the bodily or facial expression of emotions, the deictic or otherwise significant gesture, and the natural sound symbols characteristic of many animal performances, it is apparent that symbolism, as significant direction of activity between one organism and another, may, indeed, must have been, precultural.

This allows us to define our idea of cultural emergence by relating a number of empirically substantial facts. The birth of culture probably occurred as a gradual, maybe age-long, process. It was not the miraculous occurrence of sudden speech or intelligence or invention or social organization. It consisted instead of the all-round systematic and effective integration of the partial increments of cultural behavior. As soon as the use of artifacts, the employment of skills gradually tended to become cooperative; in the measure as cooperation led to the development of significant signs and sounds, entering into concerted work as an integral system of links; and these systems of behavior became fixed into tradition; culture was born. The pervading principle of cultural behavior might perhaps be subsumed under the concept of value.

Value means a deep change in the whole organism, especially, no doubt, in the nervous system. It refers to all those attitudes which make for the retention of habits, the submission to traditional rules, the appreciation of and permanent grip upon material objects, and the adequate action and reaction in terms of an articulate sound or formally determined symbol. This latter aspect became, from the very outset, embodied in systems of theoretical knowledge, of belief, and of mythological or historical tradition.

The nature of symbolic interaction

Symbolism, as a type of human activity, as a means of communication, and as the basic substratum of tradition, needs some further consideration. It is necessary, first, to make clear the relation between the instrumental use of a device and its symbolic function. Insofar as an activity is performed as a means to an end—objects handled, devices constructed and used—it can be stated that the organism is engaged in the instrumental use of the apparatus. Even when a certain device is used in a cooperative manner, and there occurs an exchange of services in the concerted performance of the task, it can be stated that the cooperating organisms are instrumentally related. But the same artifacts, devices, and habits may act as signals or cues. One need only think of direct signaling at a distance or of one member of a hunting or fishing team following the lead of another when he sees him perform an activity or is made aware of it by a symbol. In this case the act, the object, or the sound play a symbolic role within the context of concerted action.

Even when we approach cooperative processes fully learned and well practiced, the distinction between the symbol and the instrumental function of any partial performance can be shown as relevant. It is only necessary to remember that no cooperative situation, no concerted human action is so fully a matter of routine that the need for reorientation or redirection would not enter. This need is always subserved by the occurrence of a symbolic gesture or a sound which thus is an essential element in all the improvised, reoriented, readjusted phases of human cooperation. The distinction between the symbolic and instrumental function is even clearer in the process of learning. The relevant cues or conditioned stimuli which lead the precultural animal or the learning human individual through the maze of a new situation stand out as the constant or unvarying signposts regularly encountered on the path to achievement. They are the symbolic elements which, together with the drive, the intrinsic instrumentality within the material setting, and the final reinforcement, lead to the acquisition of the habit.

The clear appreciation of the exact nature of symbolism in terms of learning, of cooperation, and of environmental factors will allow us rapidly to indicate the lines on which typical symbolic systems, of which language is the most important, gradually develop. Here, again, the misconception that a sound or a gesture "is made to stand for something else" must be restated into the correct assumption that the symbolic object or act is invariably a stimulus to action. The raw material for this can be found once more in the prearticulate sounds of infants. The cry of an infant is symbolic in that within the social context of domesticity, it summons another person, the mother, father, or nurse, and commands attention and help. Insofar as such sounds can be discriminated by those in charge as cries for food, for cleansing, or as symptoms of pain or anger, they are significant. Significance always depends on the context of situation, including the principal actors, on the requirements of one organism, and on the readiness of adequate response by others.

Exactly how articulate sounds developed from prearticulate grunts, exclamations, cries, or calls, can be left for the consideration of linguists, especially those who prefer to hunt for unverifiable hypotheses rather than to study the general determinism of language. The fact is that articulation has occurred and that it probably occurred very early in the development of human culture.

The assumption of the emergence of articulate words, however, does not imply the slightest divergence from our concept of symbolism. The articulate word, exactly as a material object, a gesture, or a prearticulate sound, is invariably the signal to action. On the prototype of infantile cries the development of significant names for members of a cooperative group can be assumed, and by names we simply mean here an unequivocal means of attracting, mobilizing, selecting a definite individual. Again, on the pattern of significant gestures, of the pointing out of an object, we can assume that articulate names for important factors of the environment gradually came into being. The distinction between stone and wood, between plants and earth, between food and non-edible objects, became incorporated into the human vocabulary. Such nominal elements in language function pragmatically in the concerted action of all primitives. Both for rapid instruction and effective cooperation they are indispensable. It can also be seen here how grammatical categories are determined, not by the logic of reflection, but by distinctions inherent in the pragmatism of concerted action on a sociological basis. The modification of nouns; that is, the various typical relations of ownership, dependence, physical position in space, were naturally implemented by the grammatical instrumentalities of accidence and of prepositional determination.

Certain qualifications of substances to be used, "cold" or "warm," "dry" or "wet," "hard" or "soft" had to be verbally implemented, since the definition of state or quality or utility as raw materials for an artifact must early have become part of instruction in training, in cooperation, and in planning.

Another type of influencing by signals must have been the imperative call to action, increasingly diversified and differentiated. Here also it is quite easy to see how articulate words became only more viable and effective substitutes for gesture and prearticulate sound. Verbs referring to forms of movement, the various modifications in the behavior of the human hand or leg, may have been first to appear. And here also the grammatical categories, in order to be effective in instruction, had to express temporal, as well as modal, modifications. The grammatical forms of conjugation must be related to commands and instruction concerning action in the pragmatic use of language as between elders and children and co-workers in concerted activity. The sociological basis of language obviously implies pronominal elements, inherent both in the modifications of verbs, insofar as the action is either that of *self* or of *thou* or of *the other*, and in the determination of nouns in possessive relations. Thus, vocabulary and grammar alike can be related to the categories of socially organized, traditionally defined, and coordinated systems of cultural activity.

The main source of scientific insight into the nature of language as an ingredient of all human activities is found in the study of linguistic learning by children and in the observation of how words are used pragmatically; that is, how they function in human work.

Language in proleptic instructions always refers to a future situation of activity, in that its understanding is always based on a past experience of words used within a similar context. The narrative, in its almost indefinite range of varieties, is comprehensible only through the fact that it refers to a past context, partially known but linguistically supplemented by certain variables also familiar from previous experiences. One type of narrative, the one couched in the most general terms, is neither more nor less than scientific theory. For scientific theory is, as we know, the most general statement of a type-situation empirically formulated with the proleptic intent of future guidance. Historical or traditional narratives very often refer to important events from the past, which have established a precedent in the legal, moral, or religious sense. The religious narrative or the sacred story or mythology of a tribe very often is an account of revelation; that is, of direct contact between man and the supernatural universe.

The integrative imperatives of human behavior: knowledge and belief

It has just been shown that the understanding of the symbolic function of language and other standardized signs leads directly to the existence of systems of knowledge and belief. Any system of signs, gestures, or sounds which, through instrumental behavior, supplies the means of defining an object, of reconstructing a process, of standardizing a technique, can be regarded as a primitive form of scientific theory. Indeed, such a symbolic system, in its very simplest form, had to be precise in the sense that it provided a correct formula for the permanent incorporation and transmission of the technical achievement to which it refers. The system was effective because the drive of the physiological need was transferred and permanently linked to the objects and habits which adequately, although indirectly, subserved the satisfaction of the drive.

Such systems could be neither prelogical nor mystical. Principles of human knowledge based on true experience and on logical reasoning and embodied partly in verbal statements, partly in the context of situation to which these refer, exist even among the lowest primitives. They must have existed from the very beginning of cultural tradition. Had this at any moment lapsed into mysticism or false interpretation of fact; or had it sinned against logic—that is, the principle of identity—human actions, techniques, and economic routine would have become false and useless, and the culture would have been destroyed in its very foundations. Knowledge, then, as the symbolic system organizing all the phases of reasonable human behavior—that is, behavior in which experience is logically integrated—is a permanent and essential imperative of human culture.

Knowledge, however, introduces certain new elements into the organic diathesis of man. Knowledge implies foresight, calculation, and systematic planning. In this it not only reveals to man how to achieve certain ends, but also lays bare the fundamental uncertainties and limitations of human planning, of his calculations, and, indeed, of his very existence. The very fact that man, however primitive, becomes accustomed to thinking clearly, to looking ahead, and also to remembering the past, makes him also aware of failures and potential dangers.

We have constantly emphasized that the birth and development of symbolism always occurs under the control of organic drives. Man becomes reasonable because his instrumental actions contain a strong dynamic, that is, emotional, tone. The principles of knowledge are always controlled by desire, by anticipation, and by hope. Their counterpart, the apprehension of failure, is equally strongly charged with emotions of fear, anxiety, or potential frustration. Man, even as his knowledge increases, becomes more and more aware of the fact that his desire is often thwarted, his expectations subject to chance, that there are always grave, incalculable potential dangers lurking ahead.

Man experiences ill health and physical disability in his own life. He sees kinsmen, friends, and neighbors removed by death or disabled by disease. He often finds that the best laid plans are crossed and disorganized by the unexpected intervention of chance and fate. Calamity or misfortune affect the individual and disorganize the group.

What new integrative imperative could be assumed to arise under such circumstances? The need arises from the conflict between hope—that is, positive expectation—and anxiety, or anticipation of possible failure. Any positive affirmations of success, stability, and continuity would satisfy this need. Here again we can indicate psychological foundations for the occurrence of such hopeful signs. A chance association, which might act as prognostic or be interpreted as good augury, could be described as the secondary symbolism of good omen. The normal reliance of the individual, especially the infant, on the protection of the group, might provide the prototype of the assumption of supernatural powers in those who are older, stronger, and more familiar with tradition. As regards death, the assumption of its being but an imaginary event, whereas reality consists in the survival of the soul, is brought near, not only by the natural strength of the general impulses of "self-preservation," but also by the collateral evidence of dreams, visions, and strong emotional memories.

Thus the dogmatic affirmations of religion and magic are brought near to us simply as standardized natural reactions of the human organism under conditions of conflict. The essence of much religious belief is the affirmation of man's dependence on Providence; that is, on some powerful, partly benevolent, partly dangerous principle pervading the universe. The other equally important source of religious attitudes is the affirmation of human immortality. Magic is, in its substance, the reinterpretation of the secondary causation in terms of good as against bad. It is thus the ritual production of favorable antecedents of luck and success.

Clearly, neither religion nor magic are mere dogmatic affirmations. Man believes in order to act with greater confidence. He also has to enact his belief. Accordingly to understand any magico-religious system, it is necessary to study ritual as the enactment of dogmatic reality, and ethics as the moral consequences of man's dependence upon supernatural powers.

This is not the place to enter into the details of the various religious systems from Totemism to Christianity, or to study minutely the varieties of magic, sorcery, and witchcraft.[1]

We are here interested primarily in the definition of knowledge, religion, and magic, as integrative systems in culturally regulated behavior. Let me briefly sum up the place of integrative imperatives within the theory of the hierarchy of needs here developed. The biological need was defined as the conditions imposed by the interaction of the human organism and environment upon behavior. These conditions determine the permanent incorporation of refashioned vital sequences into every particular culture. These needs are definable in terms of biology, and we have to put them on the map of anthropological studies insofar as they are all invariably incorporated, and also to the degree that they impose definite limits upon human conduct. The concept of instrumental need corresponds to the regular occurrence, and the permanent incorporation in every culture, of those types of activity which we have defined as economic, educational, legal, and political.

The concept of integrative need declares that in every culture coherent systems of a symbolic nature are found. There exist fixed and standardized texts, verbal or written. These texts are closely related with recurrent organized performances. These texts also appear in the processes of training the young and adolescent members; that is, the processes of their incorporation into organized groups or institutions. The continuity of culture, its transmission, and its maintenance depend upon the existence of those residues of action, crystallized into symbolic texts, diagrams, or inscriptions. The real functional identity of such symbolic systems is due to their having been developed as a by-product of experience and action. It may be the experience of training or the gradual adjustment of symbolic instrumental ability and activity in cooperation. Once formed, symbols can and have to be used, both in the context of the pragmatic situation and outside it.

It is thus evident that what is usually described as tradition closely corresponds to our concept of integrative imperatives. We have here linked up this concept with the other determinants of human behavior, and assigned it a definite place and function within the hierarchy of needs. The integrative imperatives are clearly as stringent as the instrumental ones. A lapse in knowledge and deterioration thereof would undermine the techniques of production, as well as the organization of all productive enterprise. The deterioration of belief and of ethics derived from it would mean the gradual disorganization of groups, as well as the occurrence of conflicts and disruptive forces. If knowledge, belief, and ethics were progressively lowered in any culture, then individual initiative and respon-

[1] The principles here developed will be found more fully documented in the little book entitled *The Foundations of Faith and Morals,* Oxford University Press, 1936. [See Chapt. 15 of *Sex, Culture, and Myth.*]

sibility, the social loyalties, and the organization of the institutions would perforce disappear, and thus leave the organism exposed to starvation, discomfort, and dangers. We see clearly that all three classes of imperative —basic, instrumental, and integrative—are linked, supplementary, and equally stringent.

It may be profitable to supplement the previous two diagrams of vital sequences, plain and instrumentally implemented, by diagrammatic representations of cultural sequence in which there is no physiological link, and the act itself is of a purely cultural nature. This obviously does not mean that such cultural sequences are not related to basic needs. Such a relationship invariably does exist. Yet, if we were to envisage a culture in which specialization has reached the point where a large number of people live exclusively by instrumental contributions, it would be seen that a great many sequences of activities start with a motive and move through an instrumental phase to a performance which has only a derived or instrumental value. The individual satisfaction as well as the drive, in such a case, are determined by the fact that achievements and contributions of this type receive an economic reward from their realization, by which the individual can satisfy all his basic necessities. If we think of the professional activities of a doctor or a lawyer or a clergyman, or of the type of work done in a factory by the business members, overseers, and workers, it would be found that it fits directly into our diagram of culturally instrumental sequence.

Motive (*economic interest*)—Cultural setting of instrumental institution —Act (*professional service or contribution of labor*)—Satisfaction (*economic and social reward*)

Fig. 5. Culturally instrumental sequence

In this series we obviously have simplified matters. The motive often includes elements of ambition, advancement, constructive interest. The satisfaction is invariably in terms of economic reward, since no man can work without maintenance. But it includes also the satisfaction of self-regard, the admiration enjoyed by a good worker, a constructive engineer, or creative scientist or artist. The middle links of our series mean that in order to satisfy the motive for employment, the workman, the professional, or the business man have to find some organized place of work. They can perform their act of professional or labor service only in a consulting room, business office, laboratory, workshop, or factory; in short, an institution. All such series of purely instrumental contributions obviously fit into our concept of vital, instrumentally implemented sequence. They are really part of the extremely complex instrumental phase, which, as already noted, becomes in highly differentiated cultures a long chain of linked instrumental cooperation.

We could have slightly modified our present diagram in order to apply it to certain acts, mostly found in religion and art, in which the act itself is not instrumental, but rather a direct satisfaction of spiritual needs corresponding to the integrative type of interest. When a believer repairs to a temple in order to participate in a sacramental act, a slight reinterpretation of the series is necessary. The sacrament of communion or of confession, like the enjoyment of a symphony or a theatrical performance, is to the believer or the artistically hungry man of culture an end in itself. To a certain extent, the concept of function breaks down in its instrumental character when some of the most highly derived spiritual needs of human beings are considered. The satisfaction felt by the mystic in complete union with Divinity, as also the satisfaction experienced by the composer or by the musical fanatic when he listens to the symphony, may be related in some ways to the general integration of culture. They have certain indirect influences on cohesion, solidarity, and unity of the group. The other aspect, however, their self-contained character of an end in itself, has to be put on record as well. This argument, as previously, can be set forth in a diagram.

Motive (*religious or artistic*)—Cultural setting—Act (*communion with the Supernatural; artistic experience*)—Satisfaction (*mystical ecstasy or artistic pleasure*)

Fig. 6. Cultural sequence of direct spiritual satisfaction

The organized systems of human behavior

In our analysis we certainly have not thrown overboard considerations of individual psychology or organic physiology. At the same time we were constantly faced by the fact of human organization. The cultural fact starts when an individual interest becomes transformed into public, common, and transferable systems of organized endeavor. It will be necessary to define the nature of such systems.

In the principle of prepared opportunities, previously discussed, it was evident that man never has to seek for the satisfaction of any of his needs, bodily, instrumental or spiritual; they are awaiting him, stored and prepared. We spoke of the two streams of requirement and satisfaction flowing parallel. Man finds his food, his shelter, the remedies for ill health, the redress of injuries, and spiritual comforts in definite places and within organized groups. Those are the home, the workshop, the hostelry, the school, the hospital, or the church. We shall describe such standardized systems of cooperation, as well as their material embodiment and the groups running them, by the term *institution*.

This reality was encountered in our analysis of the instrumental phase of a sequence. It was stated that such a phase was always the integral part of a larger unit of organization. Fire-making, as an instrumental phase, can happen at home and for the household, or during an organized enterprise, or else ritually, in a temple. Stone implements are produced to build a house or to pound the raw material of food or to engage in some organized agricultural work.

At a much higher level, we can see that no individual initiative is ever culturally relevant unless incorporated into an institution. The man who conceives a new scientific idea has to present it before an academy, publish it, teach it at a school, and compel its recognition by the organized profession before it becomes an accepted part of science. The inventor has to take out a patent, and thus obtain a charter. He has to organize the group of engineers and workmen, to finance them, and thus to implement the production of his practical device. He then has to find the market of consumers by creating new wants or redirecting old ones, and make the productive activity of his organization perform a function in satisfying a need.

In the analysis of the concrete structure of the instrumental phase of behavior, it was shown that it always consists in the concurrence of artifacts, organization of the personnel, norms of conduct, and a symbolic factor which functions in the establishment of that phase and in its co-ordination. From this we can proceed to a fuller definition of the concept of organized activities or institutions.

It is clear that the essence of organization implies *prima facie* three factors: a group of people engaged in the common performance of a task. These people must be equipped with instruments and have a definite environmental basis for their activity. We know also that in technique, law, and ethics, rules are the essence of human organization. As shown above, however, human groups do not organize for nothing. They have a purpose in common, they pursue an end, and thus they are bound together by a charter defining the purpose of their collaboration and its value. Right through our analysis it is evident that humanity, primitive and civilized alike, engages in work not only under the impulse of motives, but also towards the satisfaction of their real needs. This we have called function.

The function of an institution is the effect which it produces in the satisfaction of human needs. To the three concepts of personnel, norms, and material apparatus, we must add those of charter and function. Figure 7 summarizes this argument in associating the several co-effective

CHARTER

PERSONNEL   NORMS

MATERIAL APPARATUS

ACTIVITIES

FUNCTION

Fig. 7. Outline of an institution

factors of human organization. It can be read as follows: human beings organize under a charter that defines their common aims and that also determines the personnel and the norms of conduct of the group. Applying these norms and with the use of the material apparatus, the members engage in activities, through which they contribute towards the integral function of the institution.

Let us briefly define the concepts used in our institutional analysis. The charter is the system of values for the pursuit of which the group have organized. It may consist simply of a legal document, or, in the case of traditional institutions, it may be based on history, legend, or mythology. The personnel of an institution is the group organized on definite principles of authority and division of work and distribution of privilege and duty. The rules or norms consist, as we know, in all the acquired skills, habits, legal norms, and ethical commands. The distinction here made between norms and activities is justified. The norms represent the ideal standard of behavior, the activities their actual realizations. The distinction between charter and norms is based on the more fundamental character of the former. It defines the constitution of the group, its value and purpose for the members, as well as the command, permission, or acquiescence of the community at large.

The diagram would be as useful in ethnographic field work as in comparative studies where it supplies the common measure of comparison. It is related to our previous analysis in that the entries *personnel, norms, material apparatus* correspond to the instrumental phases of culture. The charter, as well as the verbal prescriptions referring to the norms, belong to the integrative class in our hierarchy of imperatives. The function is related to the theory of hierarchical needs in general.

The importance of the concept of institution as the legitimate concrete isolate of cultural analysis is seen also through the fact that we can draw up a list of the main types of institutions valid for all cultures. At first sight such a list does not look impressive, in that it appears entirely common sense. In reality it supplies the student with one of the most valuable proofs that universal laws of structure and process can be established in his field. The main types of institutional organization can be listed briefly under the following headings:

1. Family and derived kinship organizations
   (*Extended family; kindred groups; clan*)
2. Municipality
   (*Local group; horde; village; township; city*)
3. Tribe as the political organization based on territorial principle
   (*Primitive tribe; polis; state; state-nation; empire*)
4. Tribe as the culturally integrated unit
   (*Primitive homogeneous tribe; nation*)

8

5. Age-group
   (*Age-grades; age hierarchies; professional age distinctions*)
6. Voluntary associations
   (*Primitive: secret societies and clubs; advanced: benevolent, political, and ideological societies*)
7. Occupational groups
   (*Primitive: magical organizations; economic teams; artisan guilds; professional associations; religious congregations*)
8. Status groups based on the principle of rank, caste, and economic class

The analysis of this list would obviously require a textbook of cultural anthropology in full comment. Here I only want to point out that an institution like the family may change considerably from one culture to another. It is possible, nevertheless, to give a minimum definition that would serve in any comparative study as a common measure and for any type of ethnographic or sociological field work as a general guide. The family is the group consisting of husband and wife, parents and children. It is based on the charter of marriage contract, concluded on the foundation of the marriage law and religious sanctity of this bond as it is concretely formulated in each particular culture. This contract implies not only the definition of the relation between the consorts; it also determines the legitimacy and the status of the children.

The combination of the law of marriage and the law of kinship prevalent in any culture constitutes the minimum definition of the family. It is obvious that the family fulfils several functions: reproductive, educational, economic, legal, and often also religious and magical. Nevertheless, it is clear that the main function of the family is the culturally redefined production not merely of human infants, but the supply of young citizens of the tribe. The economic appurtenances, the legal prerogatives, the definition of authority and distribution of authority are all contingent on the main function. We can, therefore, define this briefly as the transformation of biological reproduction into culturally defined continuity of the group. We could supply analogous definitions in terms of charter and function of all the other entries in our table. This example must suffice. It shows that in each case we can define the integral function of an institution, while it would also be possible to show that the aggregate working of the community as a whole, that is, its culture, is carried along by the combined activity of all the institutions. These problems, however, refer already to the detailed and specialized province of social anthropology, and cannot be more fully developed here.

Conclusions

An attempt has been made in the present discussion to define cultural determinism; the influence of man's culture on man's behavior. We have seen that human beings act within the framework of institutional organization, and that the determinants of their activities can be defined in terms of what was described here as the hierarchy of needs. Our analysis of the various needs and, particularly, their relations proves that although cultural determinism supplies all the final motives of behavior, culture, in turn, is determined all along the line. We were not driven into the assumption of such concepts as cultural relativism, nor is it necessary to resort to research for specific tribal or racial geniuses or entities. It is evident that the driving forces of all behavior are biologically conditioned. The indirect instrumental satisfaction through culture engenders new needs of an instrumental and symbolic character. As shown, however, both the instrumentalities and the symbolic systems, again, submit to certain general principles which we were able to formulate.

Does this mean that we are denying here the diversity of cultural phenomena as encountered in various types of environment, at various levels of evolution, and even within nearly related cultures? By no means. The stress which was laid here on the uniformity is due primarily to the fact that we are here concerned with methods of approach, with common measures of comparison, and with instruments of research. These had to be built upon elements which are constant, recurrent, and which, therefore, lead to generalizations of universal validity.

The very concept of function, which was dominant throughout our analysis, however, opens the way for the introduction of variety and differentiation, as well as for the assertion that there is a common measure in this variety. In a fuller descriptive statement of what anthropology teaches about human nature, such differential characteristics would obviously have to be introduced. Some of them would undoubtedly lead us back to the differential influences of environment. We would find that the very basic needs have to be satisfied differentially in a desert, in an Arctic environment, in a tropical jungle, or a fertile plain, respectively. Other divergencies are accounted for by the level of development. Over and above such distinctions, we have to register fully and clearly that there occur in human cultures strange hypertrophies of custom, specific types of value, or else dominant interests in one or the other of the instrumental imperatives. In some cases they can be accounted for by a gradual integration of accidental events which gave to the development of a culture a specific twist. In such cases we could say that an historic explanation of such a hypertrophied economic institution as the Melanesian *kula* or the northwestern American *potlatch* can be given. In many cases the anthropologist, following the famous student of physics, has to admit simply and honestly his ignorance: *Ignoramus ignorabimus.*

As in all other studies, however, it is first necessary to establish the basis of research in formulating the universal principles of cultural analyses and thus providing a thoroughgoing classification of facts. On this basis it is then easier and more profitable to discuss the minor or partial problems of the subject matter: the deviations and the regional characteristics of cultures.

REFERENCES

Physiology and Psychology

Cannon, W. B., *Bodily Changes in Pain, Hunger, Fear and Rage,* D. Appleton & Co., 1929; *The Wisdom of the Body,* Morrow, 1932.

Ford, C. S., "Society, Culture, and the Human Organism," *Jour. Gen. Psych.,* 1939 (Vol. XX), pp. 135–79.

Hull, C. L., *Principles of Behavior,* in preparation [published in 1943].

McDougall, W., *An Introduction to Social Psychology,* 1st ed., 1908.

Murray, H. A., *Explorations in Personality,* New York, 1938.

Richter, C. P., "Animal Behavior and Internal Drives," *Quart. Rev. of Biol.,* 1927 (Vol. II), pp. 307–43.

Young, P. T., *Motivation of Behavior,* Wiley, 1936.

Anthropology and Sociology

Hertzler, J. O., *Social Institutions,* McGraw-Hill, 1929.

Linton, R., *The Study of Man,* Appleton-Century, 1936.

Lowie, R. H., *History of Ethnological Theory,* Farrar and Rinehart, 1937.

Malinowski, B., "Magic, Science and Religion," in *Science, Religion and Reality,* ed. by J. Needham, London, 1926.

Malinowski, B., "Anthropology," *Encyclopaedia Britannica,* 13th Edit., 1926; "Social Anthropology," *Encyclopædia Britannica,* 14th Edit., 1929; "Culture," *Encyclopaedia of the Social Sciences,* 1931 (Vol. IV); "Anthropology as Basis of Social Science," in *Human Affairs,* ed. by R. B. Cattell, 1937; *The Foundations of Faith and Morals,* Oxford Univ. Press, 1938 [see Chapt. 16]; "The Group and the Individual in Functional Analysis," *Amer. Jour. Sociol.,* 1939 (Vol. XLIV), pp. 938–964; "The Scientific Basis of Applied Anthropology," *Trans. VIII Volta Congress,* Roma, Reale Accademia d'Italia, 1940.

Miller, N. E., and Dollard, J., *Social Learning and Imitation,* Yale Univ. Press, New Haven, 1941.

Murdock, G. P., *Our Primitive Contemporaries,* Macmillan, 1934.

Panunzio, C., *Major Social Institutions,* Macmillan, 1939.

Sumner, W. G., *Folkways,* Ginn & Co., 1906.

Sumner, W. G., and Keller, A. G., *Science of Society,* Yale Univ. Press, 1927–28.

9

THE GROUP AND THE INDIVIDUAL

IN FUNCTIONAL ANALYSIS

Personality, organization, and culture

It might seem axiomatic that in any sociological approach the individual, the group, and their relations must remain the constant theme of all observations and argument. The group, after all, is but the assemblage of individuals and must be thus defined—unless we fall into the fallacy of "group mind," "collective sensorium," or the gigantic "Moral Being" which thinks out and improvises all collective events. Nor can such conceptions as individual, personality, self, or mind be described except in terms of membership in a group or groups—unless again we wish to hug the figment of the individual as a detached, self-contained entity. We can, therefore, lay down as an axiom—or better, as an empirical truth —that in field work and theory, in observation and analysis, the *leitmotiv* "individual, group, and their mutual dependence" will run through all the inquiries.

But the exact determination of what we mean by "individual," or how he is related to his "group," the final understanding of the terms "social organization" or "cultural determinism" presents a number of problems to be discussed. I would like to add that over and above individual mental processes and forms of social organization it is necessary to introduce another factor, which together with the previous ones makes up the totality of cultural processes and phenomena. I mean the material apparatus which is indispensable both for the understanding of how a culturally determined individual comes into being and, also, how he co-operates in group life with other individuals.

In what follows I shall discuss some of these questions from the

This article appeared in the American Journal of Sociology, *May 1939 (Vol. XLIV, No. 6), pp. 938–64.*

anthropological point of view. Most of my scientific experiences in culture are derived from work in the field. As an anthropologist I am interested in primitive as well as in developed cultures. The functional approach, moreover, considers the totality of cultural phenomena as the necessary background both of the analysis of man and that of society. Indeed, since in my opinion the relation between individual and group is a universal motive in all problems of sociology and comparative anthropology, a brief survey of the functional theory of culture, with a special emphasis on our specific problem, will be the best method of presentation.

Functionalism differs from other sociological theories more definitely, perhaps, in its conception and definition of the individual than in any other respect.[1] The functionalist includes in his analysis not merely the emotional as well as the intellectual side of mental processes, but also insists that man in his full biological reality has to be drawn into our analysis of culture. The bodily needs and environmental influences, and the cultural reactions to them, have thus to be studied side by side.

The field worker observes human beings acting within an environmental setting, natural and artificial; influenced by it, and in turn transforming it in co-operation with each other. He studies how men and women are motivated in their mutual relations by feelings of attraction and repulsion, by co-operative duties and privileges, by profits drawn and sacrifices made. The invisible network of social bonds, of which the organization of the group is made up, is defined by charters and codes—technological, legal, customary, and moral—to which every individual is differentially submitted, and which integrate the group into a whole. Since all rules and all tribal tradition are expressions in words—that is, symbols—the understanding of social organization implies an analysis of symbolism and language. Empirically speaking the field worker has to collect texts, statements, and opinions, side by side with the observation of behavior and the study of material culture.

In this brief preamble we have already insisted that the individual must be studied as a biological reality. We have indicated that the physical world must be part of our analysis, both as the natural milieu and as the

[1] When I speak of "functionalism" here I mean the brand which I have produced and am cultivating myself. My friend, Professor R. H. Lowie of Berkeley, has in his last book, *The History of Ethnological Theory* (1937), introduced the distinction between "pure" and "tempered" functionalism—my brand being the pure one. Usually Professor Radcliffe-Brown's name is linked with mine as a representative of the functional school. Here the distinction between "plain" and "hyphenated" functionalism might be introduced. Professor Lowie has, in my opinion, completely misunderstood the essence of "pure" functionalism. The substance of this article may serve as a corrective. Professor Radcliffe-Brown is, as far as I can see, still developing and deepening the views of the French sociological school. He thus has to neglect the individual and disregard biology. In this article functionalism "plain and pure" will be briefly outlined with special reference to the problem of the group and the individual.

body of tools and commodities produced by man. We have pointed out that individuals never cope with, or move within, their environment in isolation, but in organized groups, and that organization is expressed in traditional charters, which are symbolic in essence.

The individual organism under conditions of culture

Taking man as a biological entity it is clear that certain minima of conditions can be laid down which are indispensable to the personal welfare of the individual and to the continuation of the group. All human beings have to be nourished, they have to reproduce, and they require the maintenance of certain physical conditions: ventilation, temperature within a definite range, a sheltered and dry place to rest, and safety from the hostile forces of nature, of animals, and of man. The physiological working of each individual organism implies the intake of food and of oxygen, occasional movement, and relaxation in sleep and recreation. The process of growth in man necessitates protection and guidance in its early stages and, later on, specific training.

We have listed here some of the essential conditions to which cultural activity, whether individual or collective, has instrumentally to conform. It is well to recall that these are only minimum conditions—the very manner in which they are satisfied in culture imposes certain additional requirements. These constitute new needs, which in turn have to be satisfied. The primary—that is, the biological—wants of the human organism are not satisfied naturally by direct contact of the individual organism with the physical environment. Not only does the individual depend on the group in whatever he achieves and whatever he obtains, but the group and all its individual members depend on the development of a material outfit, which in its essence is an addition to the human anatomy, and which entails corresponding modifications of human physiology.

In order to present our argument in a synoptic manner, let us concisely list in Column A of the table on page 226 the basic needs of the individual. Thus "Nutrition (metabolism)" indicates not only the need for a supply of food and of oxygen, but also the conditions under which food can be prepared, eaten, digested, and the sanitary arrangements which this implies. "Reproduction" obviously means that the sexual urges of man and woman have to be satisfied, and the continuity of the group maintained. The entry "Bodily comforts" indicates that the human organism can be active and effective only within certain ranges of temperature; that it must be sheltered from dampness and drafts; that it must be given opportunities for rest and sleep. "Safety" again refers to all the dangers lurking in the natural environment, both for civilized and primitive: earthquakes and tidal waves, snowstorms and excessive insolation; it also indicates the need of protection from dangerous animals and human foes. "Relaxation" implies the need of the human organism for a rhythm of work by day and sleep at night, of intensive bodily exercise and rest, of seasons of recreation alternating with periods of practical activity. The entry "Movement" declares that human beings must have regular exercise of muscles and nervous system. "Growth" indicates the fact that the development of the human organism is culturally directed and redefined from infancy into ripe age.

SYNOPTIC SURVEY OF BIOLOGICAL AND DERIVED NEEDS
 AND THEIR SATISFACTION IN CULTURE

A	B	C	D	E	F
Basic needs (individual)	Direct responses (organized, i.e., collective)	Instrumental needs	Responses to instrumental needs	Symbolic and integrative needs	Systems of thought and faith
Nutrition (metabolism)	Commissariat	Renewal of cultural apparatus	Economics	Transmission of experience by means of precise, consistent principles	Knowledge
Reproduction	Marriage and family				
Bodily comforts	Domicile and dress	Charters of behavior and their sanctions	Social control		
Safety	Protection and defense			Means of intellectual, emotional, and pragmatic control of destiny and chance	Magic Religion
Relaxation	Systems of play and repose	Renewal of personnel	Education		
Movement	Set activities and systems of communication				
Growth	Training and apprenticeship	Organization of force and compulsion	Political organization	Communal rhythm of recreation, exercise, and rest	Art Sports Games Ceremonial

It is clear that the understanding of any one of these entries of Column A brings us down immediately to the analysis of the individual organism.

We see that any lack of satisfaction in any one of the basic needs must necessarily imply at least temporary maladjustment. In more pronounced forms, nonsatisfaction entails ill-health and decay through malnutrition, exposure to heat or cold, to sun or moisture; or destruction by natural forces, animals, or man. Psychologically the basic needs are expressed in drives, desires, or emotions, which move the organism to the satisfaction of each need through systems or linked reflexes.

The science of culture, however, is concerned not with the raw material of anatomical and physiological endowment in the individual, but with the manner in which this endowment is modified by social influences. When we inquire how the bodily needs are satisfied under conditions of culture, we find the systems of direct response to bodily needs which are listed in Column B. And here we can see at once the complete dependence of the individual upon the group: each of these cultural responses is dependent upon organized collective activities, which are carried on according to a traditional scheme, and in which human beings not merely co-operate with one another but continue the achievements, inventions, devices, and theories inherited from previous generations.

In matters of nutrition, the individual human being does not act in isolation; nor does he behave in terms of mere anatomy and unadulterated physiology; we have to deal, instead, with personality, culturally molded. Appetite or even hunger is determined by the social milieu. Nowhere and never will man, however primitive, feed on the fruits of his environment. He always selects and rejects, produces and prepares. He does not depend on the physiological rhythm of hunger and satiety alone; his digestive processes are timed and trained by the daily routine of his tribe, nation, or class. He eats at definite times, and he goes for his food to his table. The table is supplied from the kitchen, the kitchen from the larder, and this again is replenished from the market or from the tribal food-supply system.

The symbolic expressions here used—"table," "kitchen," etc.—refer to the various phases of the process which separates the requirements of the organism from the natural sources of food supply, and which is listed in Column B as "Commissariat." They indicate that at each stage man depends on the group—family, club, or fraternity. And here again we use these expressions in a sense embracing primitive as well as civilized institutions, concerned with the production, preparation, and consumption of nourishment. The raw material of individual physiology is found everywhere refashioned by cultural and social determinism. The group has molded the individual in matters of taste, of tribal taboos, of the nutritive and symbolic value of food, as well as in the manners and modes of commensalism. Above all, the group, through economic co-operation, provides the stream of food supply.

One general point which we will have to make throughout our analysis is that the relation is not of the individual to society or *the* group. Even in matters of commissariat a number of groups make their appearance. In the most primitive society we would have the organization of food-gatherers, some institutions through which the distribution and apportion-ment of food takes place, and the commensal group of consumers—as a rule, the family. And were we to analyze each of these groups from the point of view of nutrition, we would find that the place of the individual in each of them is determined by the differentiation as to skill, ability, interest, and appetite.

When we come to the cultural satisfaction of the individual impulses and emotions of sex and of the collective need for reproduction, we would see that human beings do not reproduce by nature alone. The full satis-faction of the impulse, as well as the socially legitimate effect of it, is subject to a whole set of rules defining courtship and marriage, prenuptial and extra-connubial intercourse, as well as the life within the family (Col. B, "Marriage and family"). The individual brings to this, obviously, his or her anatomical equipment, and the corresponding physiological impulses. He also contributes the capacity to develop tastes and interests, emotional attitudes and sentiments. Yet in all this the group not only imposes barriers and presents opportunities, suggests ideals and restric-tions, and dictates values, but the community as a whole, through its system of legal rules, ethical and religious principles, and such concepts as honor, virtue, and sin, affects even the physiological attitude of man to woman. Take the most elementary physical impulse, such as the attrac-tion of one sex by another. The very estimate of beauty and the apprecia-tion of the bodily shape is modified by traditional reshaping: lip plugs and nose sticks, scarification and tattooing, the deformation of feet, breasts, waist, and head, and even of the organs of reproduction. In courtship and in selection for marriage such factors as rank, wealth, and economic efficiency enter into the estimate of the integral desirability and value of one mate for the other. And again the fullest expression of the impulse in the desire for children is affected by the systems of legal principle, economic interest, and religious ideology, which profoundly modify the innate substratum of human physiology.

Enough has been said to point out that here once more any empirical study of the reproductive process in a given culture must consider both the individual, the group, and the material apparatus of culture. The indi-vidual, in this most personal and subjective concern of human life, is submitted to the influence of tradition which penetrates right down to the processes of internal secretion and physiological response. The selec-tive business of choice and of mating are constantly directed and influ-enced by the social setting. The most important stages (i.e., marriage and parenthood) have to receive a social hallmark in the contract of marriage. The legitimacy of the fruits of their bodily union depends upon whether they have conformed or not to the systems evolved in the community by traditional dictates.

Yet here once more we do not deal with the group and the individual, but we would have to consider a whole set of human agglomerations: the group of the two principal actors (i.e., marriage), the prospective family, the already developed families of each mate, the local community, and the tribe as the bearer of law, tradition, and their enforcement.

We must survey the other items of Column B more rapidly. The whole cultural system which corresponds to the necessity of keeping the human organism within certain limits of temperature, to the necessity of protecting it from the various inclemencies of wind and weather, obviously implies also the parallel consideration of individual and group. In constructing and maintaining even the simplest habitation, in the keeping of the fire alive, in the upkeep of roads and communications, the individual alone is not enough. He has to be trained for each task in technological and co-operative abilities, and he has to work in conjunction with others.

From the biological point of view the group acts as an indispensable medium for the realization of individual bodily needs. The organism within each culture is trained to accommodate and harden to certain conditions which might prove dangerous or even fatal without this training.

Here, therefore, we have again the two elements: the molding or conditioning of the human anatomy and physiology by collective influences and cultural apparatus, and the production of this apparatus through co-operative activities. Safety is achieved by organized defense, precautionary measures, and calculations based on tribal knowledge and foresight.

The development of the muscular system and the provision of movement are again provided for by the training of the individual organism and by the collective production of means of communication, of vehicles of transport, and of technical rules which define their use. The physical growth as guided by the influence of the group on the individual shows directly the dependence of the organism upon his social milieu. It is also a contribution of the individual to the community in that it supplies in each case an adequate member of one or several social units.

The instrumental imperatives of culture

In glancing at our chart and comparing Columns A and B, we recognize that the first represents the biological needs of the individual organism which must be satisfied in every culture. Column B describes briefly the cultural responses to each of these needs. Culture thus appears first and foremost as a vast instrumental reality—the body of implements and commodities, charters of social organization, ideas and customs, beliefs and values—all of which allow man to satisfy his biological requirements through co-operation and within an environment refashioned and read-justed. The human organism, however, itself becomes modified in the process and readjusted to the type of situation provided by culture. In this sense culture is also a vast conditioning apparatus, which through training, the imparting of skills, the teaching of morals, and the develop-ment of tastes amalgamates the raw material of human physiology and anatomy with external elements, and through this supplements the bodily equipment and conditions the physiological processes. Culture thus produces individuals whose behavior cannot be understood by the study of anatomy and physiology alone, but has to be studied through the analysis of cultural determinism—that is, the processes of conditioning and molding. At the same time we see that from the very outset the existence of groups—that is, of individuals organized for co-operation and cultural give and take—is made indispensable by culture.

But this first approach still remains chaotic and incomplete. On the one hand it is easy to see that certain fundamental types of human group-ing, such as family, village community, the politically organized tribe, or the modern state, appear almost everywhere in Column B. The family is not merely the reproductive group, it is also almost invariably a unit playing the more or less dominant part in the commissariat. It is as-sociated with the domicile and often with the production of clothing and other means of bodily protection (Col. B, "Domicile and dress"). The tribe or state which is primarily associated with protection and defense is also the group which takes cognizance of marriage law and family organization, which has its collective financial systems, and which at times organizes nutritive exploits on a large scale. Nor could we eliminate the role of the village community from any of the items listed in Column B, for this also functions at times as a food-producing group, or at least plays some part in the commissariat. It is an assemblage of households or tents providing the social setting for courtship and communal recrea-tions. Thus a further analysis of the integrated responses listed in Column B appears inevitable from the point of view of the organization into concrete units of collective activity—that is, institutions.

Our list is also incomplete in so far as certain institutions have not yet been listed. The church, for instance, to which in primitive communities there may correspond a totemic clan or a kinship group worshiping a common ancestor, is not yet on the map. Institutions corresponding to rank and hierarchy, to occupation, and to free association into groups, secret societies, and charitable insurance groups, have not yet been con-nected with any part of our argument.

Another element of confusion becomes apparent were we to cut short our analysis at this stage: for certain types of activities—economic, edu-cational, or normative—run right through every one of the cultural re-sponses of Column B.

Our further analysis thus branches off into a double line of argument. We can, on the one hand, consider the organization of human activities into certain concrete and, as we shall see, universal forms such as the family, the clan, the tribe, the age-grade, the association (club, secret society), the occupational group (professional or economic), or the church, and the status group or hierarchy in rank, wealth, or power. We have designated such organized groups, connected with definite purposeful activities and invariably united by special reference to environment and to the material apparatus which they wield, by the term "institution."

On the other hand, we can concentrate on the type and character of the activity and define more fully the several aspects of culture, such as economics, education, social control, knowledge, magic, and religion.

Let us start with a brief analysis of this second point. Man's anatomical endowment—which obviously includes not only his muscular system and his organs of digestion and reproduction, but also his brain—is an asset which will be developed under any system of culture when the individual is trained into a full tribesman or citizen of his community. The natural endowment of man presents also, we have seen, a system of needs which are, under culture, satisfied by organized and instrumentally adjusted responses. The empirical corollary to our analysis of basic needs has been that, under conditions of culture, the satisfaction of every organic need is achieved in an indirect, complicated, roundabout manner. It is this vast instrumentalism of human culture which has allowed man to master the environment in a manner incomparably more effective than any animal adaptation.

But every achievement and advantage demands its price to be paid. The complex cultural satisfaction of the primary biological needs imposes upon man new secondary or derived imperatives. In Column C of our table we have briefly listed these new imperatives. It is clear that the use of tools and implements, and the fact that man uses and destroys in the use—that is, consumes—such goods as food produced and prepared, clothing, building materials, and means of transportation, implies the necessity of a constant "renewal of the cultural apparatus."

Every cultural activity again is carried through co-operation. This means that man has to obey rules of conduct: life in common, which is essential to co-operation, means sacrifices and joint effort, the harnessing of individual contributions and work to a common end, and the distribution of the results according to traditional claims. Life in close co-operation—that is, propinquity—offers temptations as regards sex and property. Co-operation implies leadership, authority, and hierarchy, and these, primitive or civilized, introduce the strain of competitive vanity and rivalries in ambition. The rules of conduct which define duty and privilege, harness concupiscences and jealousies, and lay down the charter of family, municipality, tribe, and of every co-operative group, must therefore not only be known in every society, but they must be sanctioned—that is, provided with means of effective enforcement. Thus the need for code and for effective sanction is another derived imperative imposed on every organized group ("Charters of behavior and their sanctions," Col. C).

The members of such groups have to be renewed even as the material objects have to be replaced. Education in the widest sense—that is, the development of the infant into a fully fledged member of his group—is a type of activity which must exist in every culture and which must be carried out specifically with reference to every type of organization ("The renewal of personnel," Col. C). The need for "Organization of force and compulsion" (Col. C) is universal.

In Column D we find briefly listed the cultural systems to be found in every human group as a response to the instrumental needs imposed by the roundabout type of cultural satisfactions. Thus "Economics," that is, systems of production, of distribution, and of consumption; organized systems of "Social control"; "Education," that is, traditional means by which the individual is brought up from infancy to tribal or national status; and "Political organization" into municipality, tribe, or state are universal aspects of every human society (cf. Col. D).

Let us look at our argument and at our table from the point of view of anthropological field work or that of a sociological student in a modern community—that is, from the angle of empirical observation. Our table indicates that field research on primitive or developed communities will have to be directed upon such aspects of culture as economics, legal institutions, education, and the political organization of the unit. Our inquiries will have to include a specific study of the individual, as well as of the group within which he has to live and work.

It is clear that in economic matters the individual member of a culture must acquire the necessary skills, learn how to work and produce, appreciate the prevalent values, manage his wealth, and regulate his consumption according to the established standard of living. Among primitive peoples there will be in all this a considerable uniformity as regards all individuals. In highly civilized communities, the differentiation of labor and of functions defines the place and the productive value of the individual in society. On the other hand, the collective aspect—that is, the organization of economics—is obviously one of the main factors in defining the level of culture and in determining a great many factors of social structure, hierarchy, rank, and status.

As regards social control, anthropological field work in primitive communities has in my opinion missed two essential points. First of all, the absence of clearly crystallized legal institutions does not mean that mechanisms of enforcement, effective sanctions, and at times complicated systems by which obligations and rights are determined are absent. Codes, systems of litigation, and effective sanctions are invariably to be found as a by-product of the action and reaction between individuals within every organized group—that is, institution. The legal aspect is thus in primitive societies a by-product of the influence of organization upon individual psychology.

On the other hand, the study of the legal problem from the individual point of view reveals to us that the submission to tribal order is always a matter of long and effective training. In many primitive communities, the respect for the rule and the command is not inculcated very early in life—that is, parental authority is, as a rule, less rigidly and drastically forced upon children among so-called savages than among civilized peoples. At the same time there are certain tribal taboos, rules of personal decency, and of domestic morality that are impressed not so much by direct castigation as by the strong shock of ostracism and personal indignation which the child receives from parents, siblings, and contemporaries. In many communities we find that the child passes through a period of almost complete detachment from home, running around, playing about, and engaging in early activities with his playmates and contemporaries. In such activities strict teaching in tribal law is enforced more directly and poignantly than in the parental home. The fact remains that in every community the human being grows up into a law-abiding member; and he is acquainted with the tribal code; and that, through the variety of educational influences and considerations of self-interest, reasonable give and take, and balance of sacrifices and advantages, he follows the rulings of his traditional system of laws. Thus the study of how obedience to rules is inculcated in the individual during his life-history and the study of the mutualities of give and take within organized life in institutions constitute the full field for observation and analysis of the legal system in a primitive community. I would like to add that the science of modern jurisprudence could become inspired by anthropology in treating legal phenomena within the context of social life and in conjunction with other norms of conduct.

As regards education, we need only point out that this is the very process through which the total conditioning of the individual is accomplished, and that this always takes place within the organized groups into which the individual enters. He is born into the family, which almost invariably supplies his earliest and most important schooling in the earliest exercise of bodily functions, in the learning of language, and in the acquisition of the simplest manners of cleanliness, conduct, and polite behavior. He then may, through a system of initiation, enter into a group of adolescents, of young warriors, and then of mature tribesmen. In every one of his technical and economic activities he passes through an apprenticeship in which he acquires the skills as well as the legal code of privilege and obligation of his group.

The place of the individual in organized groups

So far we have been speaking of the instrumental aspects of culture. Their definition is essentially functional. Since in every community there is the need for the renewal of the material apparatus of tools and implements and the production of goods of consumption, there must exist organized economics at every level of development. All the influences which transform the naked infant into a cultural personality have to be studied and recorded as educational agencies and constitute the aspect which we label "education." Since law and order have to be maintained, there must be a code of rules, a means of their readjustment and re-establishment when broken or infringed. In every community there exists, therefore, a juridical system. This functional approach is based on the empirical summing-up of the theory of derived needs and their relation to individual biology and cultural co-operation alike.

What is the relation between these functional aspects of culture and the organized forms of activities which we have called "institutions"? The aspects define the type of activity; at the same time every one of them is carried out by definite groups. Co-operation implies spatial contiguity. Two human beings of different sex who are engaged in the business of reproduction, and who have to rear, train, and provide for their offspring cannot be separated by a great distance in space. The members of the family are subject to the requirement of physical contiguity in the narrow sense. They form a household, and, since the household needs food, implies shelter, and the whole apparatus of domestic supply, it must not only be a reproductive but also an economic as well as an educational group united by the physical framework of habitation, utensils, and joint wealth.

Thus we find that one of the universal institutions of mankind, the family, is not merely a group of people thrown together into a common nook and shelter of the environment, wielding conjointly the definite apparatus of domicile, of material equipment, and a portion of productive territory, but also bound by a charter of rules defining their mutual relations, their activities, their rights, and their privileges. The charter of the family, moreover, invariably defines the position of the offspring by reference to the marriage contract of the parents. All the rules of legitimacy, of descent, of inheritance, and succession are contained in it.

The territorial principle of integration produces yet another group: the village community, municipal unit, horde, or territorial section. People unite into villages or migratory hordes, roaming together over a joint territory—partly because there are many tasks for which the workers have to unite; partly because they are the natural groups for immediate defense against animals and marauders; partly also because daily contact and co-operation develop the secondary bonds of acquaintance and affection. And here also, apart from the territorial unity with its rules of land tenure, corporate or individual, apart from the joint ownership of certain instruments such as communal buildings, apart from the permanent personnel of which such a group consists, we have also mythological, legal, and legendary charters from which the sentiments that enter into the bonds of membership are largely derived.

Another institution determined by the spatial principle and united through it on a variety of functions is the widest territorial group, the tribe. This unit as a rule is organized on the joint wielding of collective defense and aggression. It presents, even in the most primitive forms, a differentiation and hierarchy in administrative matters, in ceremonial proceedings, and in military or legal leadership.

In many parts of the world political organization on the territorial basis and cultural identity have to be distinguished. We have in our modern world the minority problem; in primitive communities the symbiosis of two races or two culturally different communities under the same political regime. Thus, identity of language, of custom, and of material culture constitutes another principle of differentiation, integrating each component part, and distinguishing it from the other.

We see, thus, that the actual concrete organization of human activities does not follow slavishly or exclusively the functional principles of type activities. This refers more specifically to primitive groups. As civilization develops, we find that law, education, and economics tend more and more to become separated from such forms of organization as the family, the village, or the age-grade. They become institutionalized and bring into being specialized professions, spatially set off, with constructions such as factories, courts, and schools. But even in more primitive groups we find that certain occupations each tend to become incorporated into a definite organization. Such groups as magicians, shamans, potters, blacksmiths, or herdsman fall into natural teams, receiving, at least on certain occasions, a spatial unity—that is, specific rights to portions of the territory and to a material outfit that they have to wield under a differential charter of rules and traditional prerogatives. On occasions they work and act together and in separation from the rest of the community.

The analysis into aspects and the analysis into institutions must be carried out simultaneously, if we want to understand any culture completely. The study of such aspects as economics, education, or social control and political organization defines the type and level of the characteristic activities in a culture. From the point of view of the individual, the study of these aspects discloses to us the totality of motives, interests, and values. From the point of view of the group it gives us an insight into the whole process by which the individual is conditioned or culturally formed and of the group mechanism of this process.

The analysis into institutions, on the other hand, is indispensable because they give us the concrete picture of the social organization within the culture. In each institution the individual obviously has to become cognizant of its charter; he has to learn how to wield the technical apparatus or that part of it with which his activities associate him; he has to develop the social attitudes and personal sentiments in which the bonds of organization consist.

Thus, in either of these analyses the twofold approach through the study of the individual with his innate tendencies and their cultural transformation, and the study of the group as the relationship and co-ordination of individuals, with reference to space, environment, and material equipment, is necessary.

The cultural definition of symbolism

One more addition, however, we shall have to make to our analysis. Right through our arguments we have implied the transmission of rules, the development of general principles of conduct and of technique, and the existence of traditional systems of value and sentiment. This brings us to one more component of human culture, symbolism, of which language is the prototype. Symbolism must make its appearance with the earliest appearance of human culture. It is in essence that modification of the human organism which allows it to transform the physiological drive into a cultural value.

Were we to start from the most tangible aspect of culture and try to imagine the first discovery and use of an implement we would see that this already implies the birth of symbolism. Any attempt to reconstruct concretely and substantially the beginnings of culture must remain futile. But we can analyze some of the cultural achievements of early man and see what each of them implies in its essence.

Imagine the transition from subhuman to human management of any environmental factor: the discovery of fire, the use of such a simple un-fashioned implement as a stick or a stone. Obviously, the object thus used becomes an effective element in culture only when it is permanently incorporated into collective use, and the use is traditionally transmitted. Thus the recognition of the principle of its utility was necessary, and this principle had to be fixed so as to be communicable from one individual to another and handed on to the next generation. This alone means that culture could not originate without some element of social organization—that is, of permanent relations between individuals and a continuity of generations—for otherwise communication would not be possible. Co-operation was born in the actual carrying-out of any complex task, such as making fire and keeping it, and the use of fire for the preparation of food, but co-operation was even more necessary in the sharing and trans-mission even of the simplest principles of serviceability in production or use.

Incorporation and transmission implied one more element—the recognition of value. And it is here that we meet for the first time the mechanism of symbolization. The recognition of value means that a deferred and indirect mechanism for the satisfaction of an urge becomes the object of emotional response. Whether we imagine that the earliest human beings communicated by elementary sounds or by gesture and facial expression, embodied and connected with manual and bodily activity, symbolism was born with the first deferred and indirect satisfaction of any and every bodily need.

The urges of hunger and sex, the desire for personal comfort and security were refocused and transferred onto an object or a process which was the indirect means to the end of satisfying a bodily need. This transference of physiological urge on the secondary reality was in its essence symbolic. Any of the signs, gestures, or sounds which led to the definition of an object, to the reproduction of a process, to the fixation of technique, utility, and value were in essence as fully symbolic as a Chinese pictogram or a letter in our alphabet. For symbolism from its very inception had to be precise, in the sense that it provided a correct formula for the permanent incorporation and transmission of the cultural achievement. It had to be effective in that the drive of the physiological need was transferred and permanently hitched upon the object, which adequately though indirectly subserved the satisfaction of this drive. The sign, sound, or material presentation, the cultural reality to which it referred, and the bodily desire which was indirectly satisfied through it became thus integrated into a unity through the process of conditioned reflex and conditioned stimulus which has become the basis of our understanding of habit, custom, and language through the researches of Pavlov and Bechtyerev.

This analysis proves again that the most important and elementary process—the creation of cultural symbolism and values—cannot be understood without direct reference to individual psychology and physiology. The formation of habits, skills, values, and symbols consists essentially in the conditioning of the human organism to responses which are determined not by nature but by culture.

On the other hand, the social setting is indispensable, because it is the group which maintains and transmits the elements of symbolism, and it is the group which trains each individual and develops in him the knowledge of technique, the understanding of symbols, and the appreciation of values. We have seen also that organizations—that is, the personal bonds which relate the members of a group—are based on the psychology and physiology of the individual, because they consist in emotional responses, in the appreciation of mutual services, and in the apprenticeship to the performance of specific tasks by each man within the setting of his group.

The individual contributions and group activities
in knowledge and belief

The understanding of the symbolic process allows us to consider another class of necessities imposed upon man by culture. Obviously, the member of any group has to be able to communicate with his fellow-beings. But this communication is never, not even in the highly differentiated groups of today, a matter of detached, abstract transmission of thought. In primitive communities, language is used even more exclusively for pragmatic purposes. Early human beings used language and symbolism primarily as a means of co-ordinating action or of standardizing techniques and imparting prescriptions for industrial, social, and ritual behavior.

Let us look more closely at some of these systems. To every type of standardized technique there corresponds a system of knowledge embodied in principles, which can be imparted to those who learn, and which help to co-operate those who are already trained. Principles of human knowledge based on true experience and on logical reasoning, and embodied in verbal statements, exist even among the lowest primitives. The view that primitive man has no rudiments of science, that he lives in a world of mystical or magical ideas, is not correct. No culture, however simple, could survive unless its techniques and devices, its weapons and economic pursuits, were based on the sound appreciation of experience and on a logical formulation of its principles. The very first human beings who discovered and incorporated fire-making as a useful art had to appreciate and define the material to be used, its conditions, as well as the technique of friction and of fanning the spark in the tinder. The making of stone implements, and even the selection of useful stones, implied a body of descriptive rules which had to be communicated from one person to another, both in co-operation and in transmission from those who had the experience to those who had to acquire it. Thus we can list in Column E of our chart the necessity of general symbolic principles, which are embodied as a rule not merely in verbal statements but in verbal statements associated with the actual demonstration of technique and material, of physical context, and of utility and value (Col. E, "Transmission of experience by means of precise, consistent principles"). Thus knowledge, or a body of abstract symbols and verbal principles containing the capacity to appear as empirical fact and sound reasoning, is an implication of all cultural behavior even in its earliest beginnings.

In Column F we thus list knowledge as one of the systems of symbolic integration. By knowledge we mean the whole body of experience and of principle embodied in language and action, in techniques and organized pursuits—in food-gathering, with all it implies of natural history, in agriculture, hunting and fishing, sailing and trekking. Knowledge also implies, at every stage of development, the familiarity with the rules of co-operation and with all social obligations and privileges.

But once we realize that even the most primitive human beings developed systems of thought—that is, of foresight, of calculation, and of systematic planning—we are led to another psychological necessity connected with the cultural satisfaction of primary needs. The use of knowledge not only shows man how to achieve certain ends, it also reveals to him the fundamental uncertainties and limitations of his existence. The very fact that man, however primitive, has to think clearly, has to look ahead and also remember the successes and failures of his past experience makes him realize that not every problem can be solved, not every desire satisfied, by his own efforts.

From the point of view of individual psychology we see that reasonable processes and emotional reactions intertwine. The very calculations, and the fact that the principles of knowledge have to be built up into systems of thought, subject man to fear as well as to hope. He knows that his desire is often thwarted and that his expectations are subject to chance.

It is enough to remember that all human beings are affected by ill-health and have to face death ultimately, that misfortune and natural catastrophes, and elements disturbing the favorable run of food-providing activities, always loom on man's mental horizon. The occurrence of such acts of destiny engender not merely reflection, thought, and emotional responses; they force the human group to take action. Plans have to be reorganized whenever a natural catastrophe occurs. The group becomes disintegrated by the death of one of its members, especially if he is a leading individual. Calamity or misfortune thus affects the individual personally, even as it disorganizes the group.

Which is the new, highly derived, yet emotionally founded need or imperative which these considerations entail? We see that acting as he always does within an atmosphere of uncertainty, with his hopes raised and fears or anxieties aroused, man needs certain positive affirmations of stability, success, and continuity. The dogmatic affirmations of religion and magic satisfy these needs. Whether we take such early beliefs as totemism, magic, or ancestor worship; or these beliefs more fully developed into the concept of providence, a pantheon of gods, or one divinity; we see that man affirms his convictions that death is not real nor yet final, that man is endowed with a personality which persists even after death, and that there are forces in the environment which can be tuned up and propitiated to the trend of human hopes and desires.

We can thus realize the dogmatic essence of religion by the analysis of individual mental processes. But here also the group enters immediately and no purely physiological or psychological analysis of the human organism is sufficient. In the first place, the reaction of man to death and disaster cannot be understood merely in terms of his concern with himself. It is the care for those who depend on him, and the sorrow for those to whom he was attached and who disappear, that provide as much inspiration to religious belief as does the self-centered concern for his own welfare.

Religion, however, does not end or even begin with dogmatic affirmations. It is a system of organized activities, in ritual as well as in ethics. Belief at no stage, certainly not the primitive levels, is a mere metaphysical system. It is a mode of ritual activity which allows man, whether by constraint or persuasion, to manage the supernatural world brought into being by his desires, hopes, fears, and anticipations. All ritual behavior, whether at burial and mourning, at commemorative ceremony and sacrifice, or even in a magical performance, is social. It is social in the sense that often men and women pray, worship, and chant their magic formula in common. Even when a magical act is performed in solitude and secrecy, it invariably has social consequences. Ritual is also social in the sense that the end to be obtained, the integration of the group after death, the conjuring-up of rain and fertility, of a rich haul in fishing, and hunting, or of a successful sailing expedition, concerns the interests not of a single person but of a group.

Even sorcery and black magic conform with the stipulations of our argument. In the first place, sorcery, though carried out in secret, produces powerful though negative social results. Again, sorcery is, in correct functional interpretation, a primitive type of explaining and accounting for ill-health and death. The whole system of magical counteraction and cure, which is a regular counterpart of the belief in black magic, is the manner in which primitive man satisfies his individual cravings for some means of controlling a really uncontrollable evil. Sociologically it brings about the mobilization of the group consisting of the kinsmen, friends, and followers of the victim. Thus sorcery and the magical means of combating it again satisfy certain psychological needs and are accompanied by a sociological byplay of collective effort to deal with the disaster.

In all this we see once more that a parallel consideration of individual and organized group is indispensable in order to give us insight into the foundations, as well as the forms, of magic and religion. The structure of these cultural realities entails dogmatic thought—that is, positive affirmations about the existence of good and evil, of benevolent and hostile forces, residing in the environment and capable of influencing some of its responses. Such dogmatic affirmations contain recipes as to how the supernatural forces can be controlled through incantation and prayer, through ritual, sacrifice, and collective or individual sacrament.

Since religion consists by and large of collective efforts to achieve ends beneficent to one and all, we find that every religious system has also its ethical factors. Even in a magical ceremony, performed for a successful war or sailing expedition, for the counteracting of sorcery, or for the fertility of the fields, every participating individual and the leader of the performance is carrying out a task in which he subordinates his personal interest to the communal welfare. Such ceremonies carry with them also taboos and restrictions, duties and obligations. The ethics of a magical system consist in all these rules and restrictions to which the individual has to submit in the interests of the group.

The duties of mourning and burial, of communal sacrifice to ancestor ghosts or to totemic beings, also entail a number of rules, regulations, and principles of conduct which constitute the ethical aspect of such a ritual act. The structure of religion, therefore, consists in a dogmatic system of affirmations, in the technique of ritual, and in the rules and precepts of elementary ethics, which define the subordination of the individual to group welfare.

If we had time more fully to analyze the source of tribal rhythm, of emotional and bodily recreation, as well as their cultural satisfaction in artistic creation, in sports, games, and tribal ceremonial, we would find also that the need for any such cultural activity can only be understood by reference to individual psychology and to the needs of the individual organism. The type of satisfaction for each special need, however, implies immediately the elements of tradition, organization, and material equipment—that is, elements which cannot be discussed, still less understood, without the analysis of group life and group organization.

The gist of the foregoing argument has been condensed in our chart by the entry "Means of intellectual, emotional, and pragmatic control of destiny and chance" (Col. E), and in the corresponding entry of "Magic and religion" (Col. F). Again, the need for a "Communal rhythm of recreation, exercise, and rest" (Col. E) is satisfied by such cultural responses as "Art, sports, games, ceremonial" (Col. F).

Summary and conclusions

This brief outline of the functional approach to anthropological field work and comparative theory of culture shows that at every step we had to study, in a parallel and co-ordinated manner, the individual and the group, as well as their relations. The understanding of both these entities, however, must be supplemented by including the reality of environment and material culture. The problem of the relation between group and individual is so pervading and ubiquitous that it cannot be treated detached from any question of culture and of social or psychological process. A theory which does not present and include at every step the definitions of individual contributions and of their integration into collective action stands condemned. The fact that functionalism implies this problem constantly and consistently may be taken as a proof that, so far as it does, it does not neglect one of the most essential problems of all social science.

Indeed, functionalism is, in its essence, the theory of transformation of organic—that is, individual—needs into derived cultural necessities and imperatives. Society by the collective wielding of the conditioning apparatus molds the individual into a cultural personality. The individual, with his physiological needs and psychological processes, is the ultimate source and aim of all tradition, activities, and organized behavior.

The word "society" is used here in the sense of a co-ordinated set of differentiated groups. The juxtaposition and opposition of "the individual" and "the society," as an indifferentiated mass, is always fictitious and therefore fallacious.

From the structural approach we have found that social organization must always be analyzed into institutions—that is, definite groups of men united by a charter, following rules of conduct, operating together a shaped portion of the environment, and working for the satisfaction of definite needs. This latter defines the function of an institution.

Here, once more, we see that every institution contributes, on the one hand, toward the integral working of the community as a whole, but it also satisfies the derived and basic needs of the individual. Thus the family is indispensable to society in supplying its members, training them, and safeguarding their early stages. At the same time to consider the role of the family without reference to individuals in their sex drive, in their personal affections, as between husband and wife, parents and children, or to study the early stages of life-history of the individual outside the domestic circle would be absurd. The local group, as the organization for the joint use of an apportioned territory, as the means of collective defense, and as the medium for the primary division of labor, works as a part of society and as one of its indispensable organs. At the same time, every one of the benefits just listed is enjoyed by every individual member. His role and membership in that group have to be stated from the point of view of psychology, education, and also of the physiological benefits derived by each from the joint activities. The tribe and state carries out a collective policy in war and peace, in conquest and intertribal or international trade; but the very existence of tribe or state depends on the quality of citizenship, which is an individual fact and which consists in the contributions toward, and the benefits derived from, the participation of the individual in group life.

Were we to consider such institutionalized activities as those dependent on age, which are organized into primitive age-grades or the age hierarchies of our civil service, military organization, or professional work, we would find again that the problem must be stated in terms both of individual life-history and of age as a principle of social differentiation and integration.

In the genetic approach, the functionalist demands that, in field work and theory alike, the formation of such collective aptitudes and formed dispositions as taste, skill, principle, dogma, and value be stated in terms of both individual and group. No mental attitude or bodily skill can be understood without reference both to the innate individual and organic endowment and to the cultural influences by which it is shaped.

We have, in this article, followed the gradual transformation of biological needs into cultural imperatives and satisfactions. We have seen that, starting from the individual organism and its requirements, and studying the cultural satisfaction thereof, we come upon instrumental and integrative imperatives. In every culture there corresponds to these such types of organized activities as economics, education, political organization, and legal system; and again organized religion and magic, as well as artistic and recreational activities.

If space would allow we could show that, since every one of these integrative pursuits is carried on by a group, whether this be family, clan, or congregation; since dogma, mythology, and sacred history provide its charters; since every ritual implies a liturgical apparatus; and since the activities are integrated around a definite purpose or function, the communion with the supernatural—we would find that the integrative aspects of culture are again carried on in institutions, religious, magical, artistic, ceremonial, and recreational. The church, the congregation, the totemic clan, the magical or shamanistic corporations, as well as sporting teams and organizations of musicians, dancers, and actors, are examples of such institutions.

The individual, both in social theory and in the reality of cultural life, is the starting-point and the end. The very beginning of human civilization consists in acts of rudimentary mastery of implements, of production of goods, and of the incorporation of special achievements into a permanent tradition by means of symbolism. Society and its component groups are the carriers of verbal—that is, symbolic—tradition, the guardians of communal wealth, and the joint operators of the material and spiritual achievements of a culture. But in all this the ultimate modifying power, the creative inspiration, and all impulse and invention come from the individual.

Culture remains sound and capable of further development only in so far as a definite balance between individual interest and social control can be maintained. If this balance be upset or wrongly poised, we have at one end anarchy, and at the other brutal dictatorship. The present world is threatened in its various parts and through different agencies both with anarchy and with the brutal oppression in which the interests of the state, managed by small gangs with dictatorial powers, are made completely to overrule the elementary rights and interests of the individual. The theoretical discussion of the relation between the individual and the group has thus in our present world not merely an academic but also a deep philosophical and ethical significance. It cannot be too often repeated that any culture which kills individual initiative, and relegates the interests of most of its members to complete insignificance at the expense of a gang-managed totalitarian state, will not be able to develop or even to preserve its cultural patrimony.

10

MYTH AS A DRAMATIC DEVELOPMENT OF DOGMA

Walking through one of the suburbs of Innsbruck, the visitor might come upon a church not yet quite finished in one of the side streets; it stands in a backyard of a small suburban villa. Sometimes he might encounter people carrying bricks and other building material; if as an amateur ethnographer he were to stop and enquire, he would find that these are not professional masons and bricklayers but pilgrims—peasants and towns-people often coming from distant places who supply the material as well as the devotion and faith necessary for the construction of a new church. This is dedicated to St. Theresa and erected on a spot recently become renowned for its miraculous properties. The miracle started with a sensational event of no mean importance; its traditions, though recent, have already grown into the dimensions of a minor myth. A woman gave birth to twins: they came into the world practically still-born, the faith-ful say they were already dead on arrival. The mother, a pious woman, offered them to St. Theresa, prayed and made a vow that if they were restored to life she would worship the saint in a little wash-house in her backyard. The saint acceded to her vows and prayers, the twins lived, grew and prospered; minor miracles followed the principal one. The Church often indifferent and sometimes hostile to new-fangled miracles took cognizance of this.[1] The wash-house was transformed into a small

---

The typescript of this article is designated "Lecture I"; however, there is no indication in the records of when and where it might have been delivered. It appears to be a draft of an incompleted address.

[1] One has only to remember the case of Joan of Arc and the early hostility of the Church to the claims of Bernadette Soubirous at Lourdes. A few years ago the press reported throughout the world an interesting case from Hungary where three saints appeared to the faithful, drew large audiences and performed miracles. For some reasons of its own the Catholic Church refused to associate its authority with these miracles. The gendarmerie were summoned and finally the fire brigade were called and turned their hose on the faithful. The fire of enthusiasm of the faithful, deemed inapt by State and Church, was thus finally quenched.

chapel: its miraculous properties became known, the services were attended to overflowing, and finally a collection was made to build a large church.

This is a recent, well-attested and typical process by which among a religious people, a new minor cult, a new rallying point for belief and a new tradition spring up simultaneously. It is a close parallel to Lourdes, Loretto, to Santiago de Compostela and to the innumerable shrines, altars and places of miraculous power at which we Roman Catholics worship God through his saints: we believe that on the very spot in connection with a statue, a picture or a relic, miraculous grace can be attained.

Roman Catholicism does not stand alone. A visitor to Salt Lake City will naturally inspect the Tabernacle and the row of houses in which Brigham Young and his wives lived; he will admire the wonderful energy, social organisation and moral strength which created a flourishing community out of a desert. He would understand how a powerful religion can create a vigorous community and lead to great works. A scrutiny of the foundation of this faith sooner or later discloses the most interesting myth which tells of how God revealed to Joseph Smith the foundation of a new faith and a new social order. Again we have a new myth, a new ritual, a new morality growing as it were out of one event simultaneously and in close inter-relation. Whether we take Christian Science with its sensational birth in a miraculous cure and revelation or the Society of Friends with its almost complete denial of miracles, yet with its sacred tradition of the Founder and his supremely ethical personality, we would find everywhere that the works of religion and its beliefs must have sacred tradition as its groundwork, and that the miraculous element whether in a purely ethical or magical form must have precedence to be believed.

All this seems common-sense enough to escape being seriously questioned. It may, in fact, appear so simple as to be hardly worth consideration as an important scientific contribution to the comparative study of human religion. And yet the implication of the simple truth that myth must be studied in its social, ritual and ethical effects rather than as an imaginative and pseudo-scientific tale has been almost completely disregarded in the study of the subject. This I shall briefly show in the following pages.

For the present let me just indicate that the ethnographer, working among primitive people, will find everywhere similar conditions. Among the Palaeolithic inhabitants of Central Australia all the elaborate ritual of magic and religion is intimately bound up with the sacred body of tradition which might almost be called the totemic gospels of these people. Exactly as we carry out our ritual of baptism because of our doctrine of original sin, and believe in this dogma because of what we are told in the Book of Genesis, so they have to initiate their young in order to make them full human beings. And their belief is born from their primitive gospels where man was changed from an incomplete and uncircumcised creature into full bodily and spiritual man by the will of a benevolent totemic spirit. Among the Pueblo Indians, as we shall see, a rich mythology dictates the belief that fertility can be obtained by dramatic representation of ancestral doings, by a ritual appeal to those forces of nature which once upon a time were revealed in a personified form in great miraculous events of the past. In some parts of Melanesia magic performs miracles to-day because it is a repetition of spells and rites which once upon a time created the great miracles of the Golden Age.

A sociological definition of myth

What is then the fact of a myth? Briefly, that all the principal tenets of religious belief have a tendency to be spun out into concrete stories; in the second place, these stories are never mere accounts of what happened in the past. Every act of ritual, every artistic representation of religious subjects, in the worship of relics and sacred places in short, in all the visual signs of past sensational acts of grace every theme is revivified. The events of the mythological past play also a leading part in moral conduct and social organisation.

That myth is in a way a mere unfolding of dogma even a cursory glance at any religion will show. The belief in immortality, the dogma of individual survival, has given rise to the innumerable stories of how once man was made to live for ever on earth, how through a mistake of a supernatural messenger, or through his own sin, or through a mere technical error, man lost his eternal life.[2] The belief in Providence and in the great architect of the universe is embodied in numberless mythological cosmologies. On the shores of the Pacific and on its many islands, we are told how the world was fished out of the sea or moulded out of slime; or again, from other continents, we have stories relating how out of chaos the various parts of the universe have been shaped in succession, or how the earth was hurled from space, or out of darkness, by a divine maker. The wide range of beliefs which are usually labelled "nature worship" again have a rich mythology of totemic ancestors: of the early appearance and miraculous, though not always moral, behavior of nature gods, of the early contacts between man and his Guardian Spirit. In the analysis which follows of Australian totemic mythology, of the tales and sagas connected with Pueblo nature worship as well as the specimens of Melanesian mythology, I supply full documentation of this statement.

Wisdom, like charity, ought to begin at home. The principle here stated can be best appreciated by anyone, in relation to his own religious convictions. I suggest that if we were to take any of the living dogmas

[2] See Sir James George Frazer, *Folk-Lore in the Old Testament* [abr. ed., 1923], "The Fall of Man."

of our own religion, we would find that they are founded on our sacred traditions. The Roman Catholic may lay a greater stress on the teaching of the Church, the Protestant may go straight through the Bible, but in the long run it is the sacred tradition, oral or written, which supplies the foundation of all belief; the sacred tradition, of course, including the theological interpretation and additions.

I have already mentioned the dogma of original sin; the dogma of atonement is expressed in the whole of the New Testament and centred on the sacrifice on Mount Calvary; the dogma of real or symbolic presence in the sacrament has to be interpreted by reference to accounts of the Last Supper. The belief in the constitution of our Trinity, the three persons in their real relationship—a point on which a good deal of theological dispute and human blood has been spilt—finds its ultimate sources in the several events of the Bible. To indicate my own naive conviction from the time when I was a believing, practising Christian, I always thought at the Creation, God, the Father, acted in his private capacity, that later on, somehow, God, the Son, appeared on the stage, at first foreshadowed in the Old Testament, then as the full personality in the gospels. The Holy Ghost, to me always a somewhat shadowy, unsubstantial part of divinity, seemed to hover in the distance, present, no doubt, even when "darkness was on the face of the deep." In fact, I somehow felt that "when the spirit moved on the face of the waters" it might have done so most conveniently in a winged form—that of a dove. And aided, I think, by some pictures, I perceived the ship of God, the Father, floating above the dark waves of the primeval ocean. I am putting all this on record because I know from personal experience that no abstract dogma is sufficient substance for living belief. Belief, in its live form, turns to the real figures of sacred history as the act and word establishing salvation. Take, then, one living dogma after another. Whether we be Catholic or Protestant, Jew or Gentile, Buddhist or follower of Mrs. Eddy, Spiritist or Mormon, follow it up to its living roots and we will find that it leads back to some sacred events, or, at least, to some implication of a great picture emerging out of a story, of creation, of fall, of the tribulation of a chosen people, or of the fervent visions of the prophets.

It might not be so easy, perhaps, to do the reverse, to take an incident, even an important incident, in our holy writings, and to show how it has crystallised into a specific doctrine of faith, into a moral precept, or into a dogma of social behaviour. But of such an examination the results would be astonishing. The Flood, for instance, seems at first sight to be nothing but a dramatic tale. In reality—and here I speak again largely from personal experiences of living faith—the Flood is a mythological proof in vindication of God's moral vigilance. When humanity went completely astray, God was there to chastise men and women and to award one exception. The Flood was a miracle, and a miracle with a moral implication; it stands as testimony of God's interest in moral behaviour and to his supreme justice.

It is easier, perhaps, to treat Christianity in the anthropological spirit than to approach savage and primitive religions with a truly Christian mind. The un-Christian attitude displayed by many of us towards primitive beliefs, our conviction that they are just idle superstitions and gross forms of idolatry, has deeply affected the study of primitive religions by Europeans. Savage tales of a sacred character have often been taken as mere idle fiction. Had it been recognised that they are the counterparts of our own sacred writings, those who have collected them might perhaps have studied more fully the ethical, ritual and social influence of primitive mythology. Thus, ethnographic evidence has to be largely vitiated by a false theoretical approach to the subject. Again, in the study of some historical religions, of Egypt, Vedic India, Mesopotamia, of the ancient orient, we have a full documentation of their sacred writings, a much more limited account of their ritual, and hardly any data available of how their religions were actually lived in morals, social institutions and public life.

I am saying all this in order to draw the intelligent reader's attention to the fact that the best understanding of religion can be obtained by an objective view of what we believe in practice in our own society. The next best can be achieved by a really scientific study of exotic religions as they are practised to-day by non-Christian communities. The understanding of dead religions of which we have only scattered data and fragmentary documents and monuments is not the royal road for the comprehensive study of religion.

The point of view here developed has then as its main philosophic basis the principle that the most important thing about a religion is how it is lived. "Faith apart from works is barren." Since myth is an inevitable background of faith, its very backbone indeed, we have to study myth as it affects the life of people.

In anthropological jargon, this means that myth or sacred story has to be defined by its function. It is a story which is told in order to establish a belief, to serve as a precedent in ceremony or ritual, or to rank as a pattern of moral or religious conduct. Mythology, therefore, or the sacred tradition of a society, is a body of narratives woven into their culture, dictating their belief, defining their ritual, acting as the chart of their social order and the pattern of their moral behaviour. Every myth has naturally a literary content, since it is always a narrative, but this narrative is not merely a piece of entertaining fiction or explanatory statement to the believer. It is a true account of sensational events which have shaped the constitution of the world, the essence of moral conduct, and determines the ritual contact between man and his maker, or other powers that be.

It may be well at this point of the argument to pause for a moment and draw the attention of the reader, especially if he be a layman, to the fact that we are not elaborating a commonplace. It is maintained here that myth is an intrinsic part in the make-up of any religion, more precisely that it supplies the charter for ritual, belief, moral conduct and social organisation. This implies that myth is not a piece of primitive science, nor yet a primeval philosophic allegory of a semi-poetic, rhapsodic nature, nor yet a strangely garbled historic account. Hence the primary function of myth is neither to explain, nor to recount past historical events, nor to express the fantasies or crystallised day-dreams of a community. This view is not new or revolutionary; I have formulated it at an earlier period, more clearly, as it seemed to me then, too emphatically as was said by some of my colleagues, but the whole approach is an actual outcome of modern humanistic trends. The whole emphasis on the social aspect of religion, first recognised by Robertson Smith, later developed by Durkheim, by Hubert Morse and Radcliffe-Brown, brings near to us the question of the social aspect of mythology. The emphasis laid on behaviour and conduct in modern social sciences would also lead us to enquire whether mythology does or does not affect the ritual and moral behaviour of man. The psycho-analytic connection of myth with dreams and day-dreams, with fantasies and ideals, distorted though it might appear in many points to the unanalysed and uninitiated average citizen, does emphasise the dynamic aspect of myth, its connection with the constitution of the human family in its pragmatic aspect. But above all, the so-called functional approach, in the treatment of cultural phenomena, leads us directly to the study of myth through its cultural function. This approach insists on the fact that ideas, ritualised activities, moral rules, do not lead, in any culture, an isolated existence in water-tight compartments; that Man acts because he believes and he believes because the truth has been revealed to him in a miraculous presentation; that sacred tradition, moral standards, and ritual ways of approaching Providence are not isolated but that they work one on another, seems an almost self-evident assertion. That this is not the case a rapid survey of some theories of myth, current or recently advanced, will readily convince us.

Previous theories of folklore

Every one of these last-mentioned views has at one time or another dominated the scientific or pre-scientific conception of myth. Euhemerists, ancient and modern, hold that myth always centres round a kernel or core of historical truth, misrepresented by false symbolism and literary embellishments. Euhemerism still survives in all those approaches which used primitive tradition to establish historical fact. There is a great deal of truth in this view; the legends of Polynesia do contain undoubtedly a historical kernel. The reinterpretation of oriental mythology by Elliot Smith, Perry and [A. M.] Hocart has contributed to our knowledge of certain phases in the diffusion of culture. At the same time it is certain that the search for the historical kernel in the tribal tradition of the community touches but one aspect of the problem and probably not the most essential. It certainly does not define the actual sociological function of mythology. The main object of sacred tradition is not to serve as a chronicle of past events; it is to lay down the effective precedent of a glorified past for repetitive actions in the present. The historical assessment of myth, useful as it may be in many cases, has to be supplemented by the sociological theory of myth for two reasons. First of all, if the views here developed are correct, it is of the greatest importance that the field worker should not merely study the text of a sacred story or legend, but also, above all, its pragmatic effects on the social organisation, religious practices and moral conduct of the living society. In the second place, the theoretical explanation of miraculous, obscene, or extravagant elements in the myth cannot be achieved by treating such elements as distortions of historical facts. They, as well as many other motives of historical narratives, can only be understood by reference to ritual, ethical, and social influences of the story on present day conduct.

The theory that the nature of myth consists in an allegorical presentation of natural phenomena is associated in this country with the name of Max Müller. Here again, it would be wrong to reject his contribution en bloc. For there is no doubt that men's interest in certain phases of nature, above all in the growth of plants and in the reproduction of animals, has been expressed in religious rites, and these, as we know, are connected with mythology. But nature symbolism, especially as it is practised up to this very day by certain schools of thought in Germany, has short-circuited the problem by eliminating the intermediary link of ritual, prayer and religious belief. It has instead introduced two false concepts. One of them is the view that the real nature of myths is completely misconceived by those who now tell them and believe in them. In other words, that the allegoric or esoteric meaning of the combats, of the ordeals, of the crimes, triumphs and heroic deeds—which in reality are but cryptic accounts of the courses of the sun, of the phases of the moon, of the growth and decay of vegetation—corresponds to a primitive or a mythopoeic phase of humanity. This, our learned colleagues would tell us, can only be elucidated by a sound intuition, which allows us to guess at the inward meaning of the allegory. To the present writer, it is quite clear from his personal experience in the field, as well as from his perusal of literature, that this assumption of an entirely different mentality which created myths, and of another which practised them, is unsatisfactory. The events recounted in myths are so closely related to what human beings are doing now, albeit on a magnified, miraculous scale, that no esoteric explanation is satisfactory to account for the nature of myth. The other weakness in this type of explanation lies in their assumption not only that the whole substance of a mythological narrative is symbolic, but that all the symbolism refers to one or to another process of nature. Thus, according to some writers, all myths can be reduced to the course of the sun, and nothing else; or, according to others, to the phases of the moon; yet others see in them the processes of growth and development of plants or beasts only. But if the view here presented is right, and mythology follows belief, ritual and morality, then even these references to natural processes or astronomic events, which we find actually in myths, must differ from tribe to tribe and from region to region. Where climate and soil allow men to develop agriculture, the magic and religion of the people will centre round the life of plants, and myth will contain references to the growth and decay of crops, to the influences of sun, wind and rain. Hunter's moon, in any case, is important, because it regulates tribal life through its place in the calendar. Without underrating, therefore, the role of nature worship in religion and of references to natural processes in mythology, I would like to insist that both must be studied through the three-fold approach of religious dogma, ethics and ritual.

In combatting the allegorical interpretation of Max Müller, Andrew Lang developed the aetiological theory of primitive myth. In one way this was an advance because it assigned a more business-like role for myth in primitive culture. Yet it was vitiated by the way in which its sponsor formulated it. Let me quote his own words: "Savage men are like ourselves in curiosity and anxiety, causas cognoscere rerum, but with our curiosity they do not possess our powers of attention. They are as easily satisfied with an explanation of phenomena as they are eager to possess an explanation." "The savage stage of thought" which for civilised observers resembles a "temporary madness" (Müller) seeks an explanation of phenomena which presents itself "and that explanation he makes for himself or receives from tradition, in the shape of a myth. . . . Savage mythology, which is also savage science, has a reply to questions" (of the origin of the world, of man and of beasts).[3] Now the fact is that, on the whole, neither we, nor the savages, have a natural curiosity for the knowledge of causes. This curiosity in civilised man resides exclusively in the highly technical and differentiated scientific interest which is a product of a far-reaching division of labour. On the other hand, savages, like ourselves, must possess a sound, empirical, and practical knowledge which they need in all their technical processes, economic pursuits and collective activities on a large scale, such as war, sailing and trekking. To equate

[3] Article on "Mythology," by Andrew Lang, Encyclopædia Britannica, 12th Edit., 1922, pp. 131–32.

savage mythology with savage science is one of the greatest acts of violence perpetrated in the theoretical treatment of human culture. It has given rise to the later theories about the entirely different mentality of primitive man, about the prelogical mentality of savages and about the incapability of scientific or empirical thinking. The very fact that we have our own mythology quite as developed as a primitive for fulfilling the same function might have taught all the theorists of myth as an outcome of a different earlier mind, that their theories, to say the least, were insufficient. Yet all these views still influence modern scientific thought.[4] The somewhat eclectic and vague statement of the subject by Professor Ruth Benedict in the *Encyclopaedia of Social Science,* vide "Myth" and "Folklore," shows an advance from previous theories of myth. In this last-named article we find the following summing up: "Modern folklorist study is freeing itself from preconceptions and of far-fetched allegories and is founding itself upon the importance of folklore as a social phenomena, and as a means of expression by a social group of its own attitudes and cultural life. By regarding folklore as a cultural trait like technology, social organisation, or religion, any special consideration of communal authorship is made unnecessary, since myths are as much or as little due to communal creation as marriage or fertility rites. All cultural traits, including folk tales, are in the last analysis individual creations determined by cultural conditioning" (p. 291, 1931). And again, in article s.v. "Myth": "Myth is among some peoples the keystone of the religious complex, and religious practices are unintelligible, except by way of their mythology" (p. 180). But she considers that "The origin of religion is not to be sought in mythological concepts, nor the origin of myth in religion, but the two have constantly cross-fertilised each other, and the resulting complex is a product of both primary traits." The view taken that folklore *expresses* social attitudes or that mythology and religion cross-fertilised each other does not reach the clear recognition of

---

[4] Compare, for instance, the two last editions of *Notes and Queries in Anthropology.* In the last but one edition, we find the definition of myth as "stories which are intended to explain an abstract idea or vague and difficult conception," page 210. This is, of course, Andrew Lang with a vengeance. In the last edition, the substance of the theory here advanced was accepted completely; indeed, large chunks from a previous publication of mine are included (unfortunately without acknowledgements, without inverted commas, and without my permission). On page 329, lines 19 to 23 are the verbal repetition of a sentence on pages 119 to 120 of my *Myth in Primitive Psychology,* lines 24 to 33 are word for word with only slight abbreviations taken over from *Myth in Primitive Psychology,* page 124. Again the article on "Myth" in the 12th Edit. of the *Ency. Brit.* was written by Lang and contains a clear statement of the aetiological theory of myth. The 14th, the last one to contain a new article on myth, gives a brief summary of various theories and ends up with a statement of the functional and sociological interpretation of myth, and contains the quotation from *Myth in Primitive Psychology* by the present writer.

the specific social function of myth as a charter of ritual belief, ethics and social organisation. In fact, Professor Benedict explicitly criticises the views advanced by myself in her article on myth. She denies that the functional nature of myth as a charter of social organisation, religious belief, and ritual practices is universal.

We can therefore conclude that the view here advanced is making headway, but that it has not yet been universally accepted or clearly recognised. Yet it is by no means a new or original theory of the present writer. As in many other matters we owe the first flash of insight to that great Scot scholar Robertson Smith. Robertson Smith was perhaps the first clearly to recognise the sociological aspect in all human religions and also to emphasise, at times perhaps to over-emphasise, the importance of ritual as against dogma (*Religion of the Semites*, 3rd ed., 1927). Religion, according to him, is rather a fixed body of practices than a system of dogmas. There may perhaps be a slight exaggeration in his statement that "antique religions have, for the most part, no creed; they consisted entirely of institutions and practices" (*op. cit.*, p. 16). For in another place he is more correct in saying that "mythology takes the place of dogma. . . . The rite, in short, was connected, not with a dogma but with a myth" (p. 17). If we are correct in stating, not that each myth contains a dogma, but that most dogmas have their foundation in myth, we see that Robertson Smith has anticipated fully the point of view here, that "so far as the way of thinking expressed in a myth is not already expressed in the ritual itself, it had no properly religious sanction; the myth, apart from the ritual, affords only a doubtful and slippery kind of evidence." In this, Robertson Smith recognises clearly that any narrative has to be assessed by the function that it plays in organised religious behaviour. I would say that a myth that is not ex- pressed in ritual is not a myth but merely an old wives' or an old men's tale. In other words, any definition or classification of folklore that ignores its influence on ritual and also on social organisation must remain barren. This is implied already in Robertson Smith's view that "religion was the body of fixed religious practices . . . and practice preceded doctrinal theory" (p. 19). At present we do not worry so much over the prius-posterus, but we retain the principle that doctrinal theory and traditional practices are two aspects of the same thing; that they grow up together and that to study one without the other is a fundamental error of method.

Robertson Smith's view has influenced many subsequent writers; Dr. E. A. Gardner, writing on myth, in *Hastings' Encyclopaedia of Religion and Ethics*, [states] that "mythology, by its explanations and illustra- tions of the nature and character of the gods or other powers, would help man to keep his relations with them on the right basis." This might seem like a compromise between Andrew Lang and Robertson Smith, but as long as explanation is meant as a code and a charter for the correct carrying out of ritual practices, the essence of myth is correctly stated. The two volumes of Frazer's monumental work on the cults and myths of Adonis, Attis and Osiris contain a documentation of the point of view here developed, pervaded throughout as they are by the principles of Robertson Smith and the great insight of the author of *The Golden Bough* himself.

But where the inadequacy of the present state of anthropological knowledge makes itself most felt and the emphasis on the cultural function of myth is most necessary, is in the actual technique and methods of field work. A few first-rate writers, notably those whose work will be used in the subsequent pages, i.e., Spencer and Gillen, Fewkes, Cushing, A. R. Brown, Elsdon Best, as well as the younger field workers in the functional schools, Dr. Raymond Firth, Dr. I. A. Richards and Dr. H. Powdermaker, have supplied us with adequate data. But in many, even excellent, books, it would be difficult to find the co-relation between folklore and religion which would allow us to test and document the leading principles of Robertson Smith and his followers.

The final test of any theory in a branch of learning which claims to be scientific lies in its empirical value. Does the view here advanced open up new avenues of empirical research; does it force us to observe new facts and new relations between facts? Perhaps I can best bring home to you the significance of the present theory of myth by recounting briefly how I was forced to adopt this point of view in my field work. When I went out to New Guinea, I was already acquainted with the universally influential aetiological explanation of myth. This theory has, as we have seen, the fatal implication that we have to collect stories and regard them as self-contained documents of primitive science. I had to learn the lesson of functional co-relation between myth and ritual in the field.

11

SCIENCE AND RELIGION

I am speaking here about primitive religion and primitive science and about their relation to one another. I am speaking as an anthropologist, and anthropology, as you know, is the study of man in general and of primitive man or the savage, in particular.

The comparative study of religions and of the beginnings of science enters, therefore, within the scope of my speciality as one of its most important subject-matters. And in addressing you here, I feel it my duty not only to pronounce my personal views as to the relation of science to religion, but also to tell you what the science which specialises in the study of this relation has to give as its considered opinion. I shall try to lead you to the very sources of faith in the heart of primitive man. I shall also try to show you the earliest attempts of the human mind to deal with reality, that is the beginnings of science.

Has primitive man a religion? Or is he merely obsessed by savage superstitions, surrounded by the darkness of heathendom? This can be answered categorically: religious beliefs and practices, as well as religious morality, do exist among savages.

Has, then, primitive man also his science? Certainly. He employs his senses and his brains, he observes shrewdly and draws correct conclusions. He thus creates a body of knowledge and a tradition of knowledge—that is, genuine science.

The most important lesson from this talk will be that religion and science have existed from the very beginning, and that they have each occupied a different place in human activities. Each has its own task and its own province. It will be our business to define the respective tasks of religion and science.

What is, then, primitive religion? The reader of our classics, of Tylor

This was a talk over the network of the British Broadcasting Corporation, and appeared in The Listener, *October 29, 1930 (Vol. IV, No. 94), pp. 683–84, 716–17; it is reprinted by permission.*

and of Lord Avebury, of Andrew Lang, of Robertson Smith, or of Frazer will readily answer: Primitive religion consists in animism, totemism, nature worship, ancestor cult, and other similar things. All this sounds very well, and perhaps even very savage, but what is it all in reality?

Animism is the belief in the human soul; and in its survival after death. Hence, animism entails a cult of the dead. It also declares that Nature is animated by spiritual beings. Put in plain English, this savage belief is nothing else but faith in immortality and in a spiritual side to the world. There is, then, nothing so very strange or savage in it—in fact a great many of us are animists, all who believe in man's immortal soul, and in its survival after death.

How does primitive animism originate? The older anthropologists would tell you that the savage, pondering on dreams, visions, and cataleptic states, and trying to explain it all, arrives at a theory of the soul. But I should prefer to show you how animism works and what it does for man.

Follow me, then, for a few moments to a small island in the distant South Seas and a few years back in time. A native friend of mine, a Melanesian islander, is on his death-bed; he knows it and so do his nearest relatives and friends. Though mere savages, they are as deeply moved as any one of us would be. Those assembled at the death-bed are united by strong emotions. Fear and sorrow are unmistakable in the countenance of the dying man and of his friends.

Do they succumb to these emotions? Do they surrender to the horror of death? No! Moved they certainly are, but what controls them is an active purpose. They are carrying out certain traditionally prescribed acts by which they are able to save the dying man; that is, safely to conduct his spirit into the next world and to secure him a happy existence there.

They have covered the dying man with ornaments and flowers; they have put fruit and prepared dishes around him. Their most precious possessions are heaped on his body. All this—or rather its spiritual part—he will take on his journey to the other world. Messages are given him to transmit to those who have gone before. Some of those gathered round the death-bed seem to hear voices from the other world. The dying man is immersed in an atmosphere of affirmation. He is steeped in immortality, in the communion between the two worlds. Those whom he is about to leave take him by the hand, as it were, and lead him across the dividing line. As death approaches, the relatives and friends throng round the dying man, embrace him, rub his body with valuables and sacramental gifts and utter ritual words of comfort. I was forcibly reminded of the sacrament of Extreme Unction and of the Viaticum, as administered in the religion of my youth, in Roman Catholicism.

At last death occurs; the main actor has made his final exit. It is the most terrible and the most sacred moment of all religious experience. The helplessness of man and the hopelessness of the event are ruthlessly driven home to all who witness. Does religion merely express this fear and horror, this sorrow and despair? Is religion with its gods really made up of fear, as the famous Latin saying, and so many learned theories, would make us believe?

No. Here again religion orders man to act, and to act constructively. In an outburst of passionate grief, the survivors throw themselves on the corpse, fondle the dead remains, break out in loud wailing. They are seized, as it were, with a frenzy of ritualised sorrow. They tear out their hair; they gash their bodies; they rush round, destroying their material possessions.

But all this is ordered, foreseen, determined by tradition. More than that, it is all spiritually significant and morally effective. It helps the survivors, and it helps the spirit of the dead. Religion is never negative; it never allows man to surrender to fear, to doubt, and to despair. Religious ritual, and the belief which sustains it, transforms death from the most shattering experience into one solemn and serious, but never hopeless.

In the customs and manners of burial we find also the same principle: the horror of the corpse and the fear of the dead overcome, the relics sacralised, the terrible conflict of death solved. For there is a curious conflict between the desire to retain the corpse and the desire to get rid of it. In mummification, the body is preserved as far as is possible; in cremation, it is destroyed completely. In the infinite variety of mixed and intermediate modes, there is a conflict and a dilemma. You love the remains and you express your love ritually by clinging to the relics; you also loathe them and show this by cutting off all that has touched death from contact with life. Such is the ritual conflict as we find it in Central Australia and in South Europe, in Ancient Egypt or Babylon and in Melanesia.

This ritual conflict expresses something very deep and real. Death must inevitably remain mysterious and create a conflict in the human soul. It is the dreaded end of human life by all earthly measures. It is the transformation of a loved personality into something gruesome and decaying. It changes a benevolent being into a malignant and dangerous ghost. Death, then, either tears all significance out of human life, or else death has to be transformed and to be given an entirely new meaning.

Upon this conflict and chaos breaks the redeeming light of religious truth. It reveals to man that death is not an end, that the main principle of personality persists; that it is possible for the survivors to keep in touch with the departed spirit.

Animism, the belief in the immortality of the soul, is not a mere philosophic doctrine; it is the result of a deep emotional revelation. In animism, religion standardises the comforting, the saving belief, and thus it solves the dilemma of life and death, of survival and decomposition.

At the various ceremonies of death and after, in the ways of disposing of the dead and in the rites of burial, in ceremonies of commemoration and of communion with the dead, above all, perhaps, in ancestor worship, there is embodied a live faith in the immortality of the soul, the affirmation of the reality of spiritual existence.

The supreme crisis of life—Death—is thus sacralised or sacramentalised throughout humanity. Religion also puts its blessings on other vital crises and capital events of human existence. Birth, puberty, marriage, parenthood, are also made sacred by religious rites and ethical observances. Human existence is thus encased in that wonderful sacramental framework which is one of the main aspects and glories of religion. The main events of human life are surrounded with feelings of holiness; they are made public, morally momentous, and spiritually binding. In sacralising the crises of life, primitive religion does not trespass on the preserves of primitive science, any more than Christianity, for instance, in its sacraments of Baptism, Confirmation, Marriage, or Extreme Unction is guilty of usurping the task of the physicist, the chemist, or the historian.

But what about the really savage sides of primitive heathendom? Take magic, for instance, or fetishism. Surely here primitive man shows himself superstitious, as he also does in worshipping animals, plants, or totemic objects. And again, is it possible to have science side by side with all the magical *hocus pocus* and with the heathen worship of stick, stone, or beast?

To answer these questions let us inquire what is primitive man's real concern with his environment. He has to eat, first and foremost, and the surrounding nature is his living larder. He depends on the surrounding world for his raw material, for fair winds, for the open road, for sun, and for rain. At times, nature turns on him a friendly face; but then again it becomes unmanageable, dangerous, threatening him with wild animals, poisonous plants, with storms and accidents. And primitive man is much more at the mercy of the unexpected than are we.

Now here the most important thing to realise is that primitive man makes full use of his knowledge wherever he can. You must discard the notion that the savage is a child or a fool, a mystic or a nincompoop. I have seen the savage hunter at work: he knows his animals and their habits; he is familiar with the properties of his weapons, the strength of his spear and the flight of his boomerang. I have trusted myself to savage sailors on their frail craft over dangerous seas and under trying conditions. They understand wind and weather, stability and tides, in a truly reliable, that is, in a scientific, way. It is only because he is able to observe correctly and to think clearly, that, with his simple tools and limited co-operation, primitive man can master nature as well and as effectively as he actually does.

This, I trust, is convincing—but it is neither obvious nor generally accepted by modern science. Professor [Thomas H.] Huxley, in his first talk, gave us an admirable summary of the current anthropological views on our subject: yet he did not even mention primitive science. He and most contemporary thinkers would follow Sir James Frazer in identifying early magic with primitive science. Other learned anthropologists go even further and deny that logic, observation, or empirical thought are possible to the savage. He has been made, in fact, by some recent theories, into an incurably superstitious, mystical—to use the new-fangled technical term—into a "pre-logical" being. All this is good copy and pleasant reading—it makes us feel really civilised and superior—but it is not true to facts. Science, primitive as much as civilised, is the solid achievement of the human mind, embodied in the tradition of rational knowledge and put to practical purposes. As far as primitive man has really obtained the mastery of natural forces, and of the forces in his own nature, he relies on science and on science alone.

True, science advances, and modern science has grown out of all recognition from its humble origins. Science is conscious of its power and of its steady advances; proud of its ruthless conquests of fields hitherto left to mysticism and speculation, or to religious dogmatism. At times it becomes, therefore, arrogant and aggressive. Even more so because often it has had to be on the defensive. Religion and magic do not always give science its due, nor make way graciously and wisely. We had our fundamentalists from the time when Galileo was tortured, to the somewhat less dramatic but more dramatised performances of the late W. J. Bryan. Fundamentalism naturally exists in primitive savagery also, for their traditional routine, magically or religiously sanctioned, opposes all innovation and change. In *savagery*, fundamentalism is, on the whole, a beneficent force, though never a very amiable one.

The savage, I repeat, has got a firm grip on his science, even as his science keeps him well under its control. But his science fails him at times. Does our science, of which we are so proud and confident, never leave us in the lurch? It has not yet domesticated luck, chance, and accident. It cannot prevent earthquakes and famine, war, crime, or disease. So that even we, you and I, when too much at the mercy of hazard, become superstitious and repair to magic. You and I have our mascots and talismans, our signs and omens, our little ritual of salt and of mirrors, of new moons and of ladders. We smile at them but we practise them a great deal more seriously than our smiles might warrant. Nor can they be dismissed as insignificant survivals from primeval times. For they show as rank a growth on the most recent soil of human nature as on the most primitive.

We even see big systems of modern magic, of practical utilitarian belief, sprouting under our very eyes. Take Christian Science or the recently re-established astrology, faith-healing or theosophy, clairvoyance or the revelation of medium and table-rapping which calls itself spiritualism. One and all are new, strong, vital forms of modern civilised belief. They all contain a genuine response to a real need. But in my opinion they resemble primitive magic rather than religion, both in what they are and in what they do. With all that I regard them as highly respectable, for they seem to be indispensable.

And so within the context of primitive culture is also primitive magic, in which the savage tries to harness his luck and to bribe his chance, by spell, ritual, and taboo. Magic flourishes wherever man cannot control hazard by means of science. It flourishes in hunting and fishing, in times of war and at seasons of love, in the control of wind, rain, and sun, in regulating all dangerous enterprises, above all in disease and in the shadow of death.

We must guard against the mistake of assuming that magic represents primitive science. Magic never undertakes to do that which primitive man can easily achieve by knowledge, manual skill, and bodily effort. The savage never digs the soil by magic, nor does he throw his spears by ritual or sail his canoes by spell.

In Melanesia I studied an extensive and complicated system of garden magic. The soil was first blessed for fertility in general; then the plots were cleared by perfectly rational and practical procedures. A second magical ceremony followed to fumigate the cleared ground and thus prevent blights, pests, and insects. Then, again, came planting, done skilfully, practically, and scientifically. But when the plants sprouted and there was nothing better to do but to hope for good luck, magic again was enacted in ceremony after ceremony, designed to make the crops strong and good. And so, throughout the whole series, the rites alternated with the activities, each aspect, the rational and the magical, kept absolutely distinct from the other. The same is true of most Melanesian magic and of magic all the world over.

You can see, then, the relation of primitive magic to primitive science: they assist each other and co-operate, but never trespass on each other's preserves. You can see, also, the utility and the function of magic. Sociologically, it is an organising force; it brings order, rhythm, and control into the practical activities. The magician becomes the natural leader and often grows into the chief or the king. Individually, it gives man confidence and allows him to act firmly in the teeth of adversity and heavy odds.

Magic, then, has its own cultural task to perform. It has a value for primitive man and for primitive culture, and in all this its province and its function are different from those of primitive science.

It also differs from religion. For, apart from magic and from science, man also turns to nature in a religious spirit. Abundance of food and material welfare in general are, to primitive man, the primary needs of normal life. They are also the condition of any spiritual advance. But abundance of food and of goods is given to man independently of his efforts, often independently of his magic. Primitive man, even as civilised, feels an autonomous purpose in nature which at times rewards, at times punishes, and invariably follows its own mysterious way. Man naturally turns towards this purpose or providence; he personifies it and tries to propitiate it. This is the foundation of nature worship, which takes various forms, of which the most primitive, perhaps, is totemism. But all nature worship implies the deification of natural forces, the admission of a purpose, a providence, a personal guidance in the universe.

Our short, but, I trust, convincing glimpses into the drama of primitive life demonstrate one thing: the two main sources of religious inspiration are the desire for immortality and a craving for the communion with God. In affirming this I find myself in opposition to most current theories. Professor Huxley, who gave such a masterly summary of current views, specifically told us that God and immortality play no part in primitive religion. But I find that these are the twin needs which we all feel, which man has felt from the beginning, whenever he has been unable to face his destiny. In all this, religious belief is not a mere emotional effervescence, still less an intellectual interpretation. Religion promises immortality for man, and it reveals to him his God or his gods. It is this active or creative side of religion which seems to me to be the most important, and on which I have placed the greatest emphasis. Thus, the comparative science of religion compels us to recognise religion as the master-force of human culture. Religion makes man do the biggest things he is capable of, and it does for man what nothing else can do; it gives him peace and happiness, harmony and a sense of purpose; and it gives all this in an absolute form.

You can see that, throughout all this, I have spoken of religion in general, bringing the primitive and the civilised together, stressing the similarity between them. But I do not want you to forget all that is crude, cruel, and degraded in the religions of the savage, the ordeals and obscenities at initiation, the horrible rites of death, disgusting and murderous, the licence and degradation of the marriage ceremonial—all this and a great deal more could be adduced to make a heavy indictment of primitive heathendom. And yet, the cruelties and ordeals often function as tests of endurance. They assist the moral training in self-control which frequently goes with them. Licence at a wedding is often the final fling of pre-nuptial libertinage, a farewell to what is henceforth forbidden. The ritual at death serves to emphasise its solemnity and the solidarity of the dead with those who are killed to accompany them.

Black magic, again, which consists in the tampering with the health and life, as well as with the wealth and happiness of others, seems at first sight to be wholly evil; but it is often used for good, and it has its good and comforting sides. It makes disease and decay appear man-made and artificial, hence remediable. In fact, all savage sorcerers are able to cure as well as to kill. Black magic, also, though often used with malice for oppression or blackmail, is more frequently employed as an instrument of rough justice. It is used to redress wrongs and to buttress established power and privilege. It is a conservative force, and, as such, on the whole valuable in a primitive community. Black magic is like a sharp sword, two-edged, ready for justice and for crime, but, under primitive conditions, very useful. With all this, we do not want to indulge too freely in the apologetics of darkest primeval heathendom. Primitive religion has its shadows; so have our religions. The real point, however, which I want to make is that religion, even at its worst, is never completely useless or wholly evil. Even in its lowest forms it has a divine spark, and when I speak of "divine" I express simply the point of view of the believer and not my own. As an anthropologist I can speak of the "divine" only as it manifests itself to man and in man.

The comparative science of religions has no warrant to declare the absolute, transcendental truth of any one religion. Since religious revelation is an experience which, as a matter of principle, lies beyond the domain of science, either discipline is sovereign and independent, and neither can testify for or against the other. Speaking as an anthropologist, I have, therefore, to associate myself with the affirmation repeated by all my collaborators in this series—that religion and science need not be in open conflict, since their respective aims and provinces are distinct and independent.

You might like, however, to know my personal opinion as to the relation of science and religion. Let me, then, speak, not as a specialist, but simply as a thinking and feeling man.

Personally, I am an agnostic. I am not able, that is, to deny the existence of God: nor would I be inclined to do so, still less to maintain that such a belief is not necessary. I also fervently hope that there is a survival after death, and I deeply desire to obtain some certainty on this matter. But with all that I am unable to accept any positive religion—Christian or otherwise. I cannot positively believe in Providence in any sense of the word, and I have no conviction of personal immortality.

Thus, as you see, I profoundly differ from the confident rationalist or disbeliever of the past generation or two. We all know the story of La Place and the discussion which he had with Napoleon the First about his system of Celestial Mechanics. The Emperor asked him: "What place have you given to God in your system?" "Sire," was the answer, "this is an hypothesis of which I have never felt the need." It is the proud answer of a confident atheist, but it does not ring true to the humble agnostic. On the contrary, I should say that God is a reality and not a hypothesis, and a reality of which I am in the greatest need, though this need I cannot satisfy or fulfil. The typical rationalist says: "I don't know and I don't care." The tragic agnostic would rejoin: "I cannot know, but I feel a deep and passionate need of faith, of evidence, and of revelation." Personally, to me, and to those many who are like me, nothing really matters except the answer to the burning questions: "Am I going to live or shall I vanish like a bubble?" "What is the aim, and the sense, and the issue of all this strife and suffering?" The doubt of these two questions lives in us and affects all our thoughts and feelings. Modern agnosticism is a tragic and shattering frame of mind. To dismiss agnosticism as an easy and shallow escape from the moral obligations and discipline of religion—this is an unworthy and superficial way of dealing with it.

Is science responsible for my agnosticism and for that of others who think like me? I believe it is, and therefore I do not love science, though I have to remain its loyal servant. Science deals with truth and with evidence, and it develops a critical sense and a passion for full experience which spread beyond its own limited domain. Now, religious truth is vouched for by two sources of experience. We have in the first place the original revelation, handed on in religious teaching. This is the foundation of the great historical religions, notably of Christianity. And then there are the miracles and disclosures of the present day on which most of the new-fangled creeds are founded. Science has spoilt us for the unquestioning acceptance of truth at second-hand—the truth of tradition or of the Gospels. If there ever existed a real experience, if the truth of divine existence is there to be revealed, I rebel against the assumption that it has been shown in some dim past to my mythological forebears, and that it is not vouchsafed to me to-day and in a manner so convincing that there can be no doubt or cavil. The religious person would say, of course, that he does receive the revelation of divine truth. I can only reply that just here there seems to be an unbridgeable gulf between faith and agnosticism.

The comparative science of religions shows, moreover, that the same eternal cravings of the human soul have been satisfied by a variety of obvious fictions, which have worked as well as the nobler religious truths of our own culture. Thus, the realities of religious belief, however highly we may rate their value, appear almost as instruments created for a special need. The poison of pragmatism—truth measured by utility—is nowadays invading the comparative study of religions as well as all philosophy and science, and pragmatism is the death of religion as well as of metaphysics.

When I come, on the other hand, to the modern forms of revelation, to contemporary miracles, to faith-healing, to spiritualistic mediums, to palmistry, to the brass tablets of a Joseph Smith or the visions of a Mrs. [Mary Baker] Eddy, all my scientific morals of method and evidence are roused to protest. The evidential value of all this machine-made revelation, of this surreptitious communion with the beyond, I find worthless, and as an aesthetic or emotional experience, distinctly unattractive. Nor can I accept the inner revelation of Divinity as a system of ideals—such as Professor Haldane developed before us in a previous talk. His God is too abstract, too impersonal, to satisfy my craving for a real communion with the personal Guide of the Universe. A belief of that type contains no guarantee of personal survival after death. And without a personal God and the belief in immortality, I cannot conceive of a living religion. Moreover, is it true that the ideals of truth, and beauty, and goodness really unite all men or most men? Is the modern world, with its devastating wars, its racial, national, and class hatreds, with its mean rapacities and wholesale exploitations—is our world really governed by this inner and universal revelation of truth and harmony to all men alike? I see no trace of such control. I feel far nearer to the established, traditional creeds, which appeal to me aesthetically and morally—and for them I have a deep reverence.

Is there any hope of bridging this deepest gulf, that between tragic agnosticism and belief? I do not know. Is there any remedy? I cannot answer this either. What can help us, perhaps, is more and more honesty, more outspokenness and more sincerity.

It is in this spirit that I have described to you my personal position, because I felt it my duty to be sincere and outspoken. Those of you who are fortunate enough to believe, or equally fortunate positively to disbelieve, will not have detected any missionary accents in my confession of faith. All my scientific evidence tends to show that there are no reasons and no room for conflict between science and religion, but, in my personal experience I have found that science is dangerous, even, perhaps, when it does not destroy faith completely. Because, through it all and above all, though I am unable to worship any divinity, I have almost come to worship, certainly to revere religion.

In all its manifestations—animism and totemism, nature cults and ancestor worship, prayers to Providence and administrations of sacraments—religion, civilised or primitive, gives man what neither science nor magic can give.

Religion gives man hope of immortality and the ritual means of achieving it; it reveals the existence of God or Providence and tells how communion can be established: it affirms the meaning of the world and the purpose of life; and, through its sacraments, it allows men to obtain a greater fullness of life. Religion gives man the mastery of his fate, even as science gives him the control of natural forces, and magic the grip of chance, luck and accident.

A FUNDAMENTAL PROBLEM OF RELIGIOUS SOCIOLOGY

There are certain questions of principle in every branch of science which cannot be passed over in any comprehensive and thorough treatment of the subject, and upon the answer of which the further course of inquiry essentially depends.

Such questions are, as a rule, the most difficult to settle, because only an overwhelming amount of evidence gathered with the very problem in view allows of an unequivocal answer. In anthropology the mutual co-operation of the theorist and of the field-worker is essential in all such cases.

A question of this type presents itself at the outset in anthropological investigations of religion. Is there a sharp and deep cleavage between *religious* and *profane* matters among primitive peoples? Or, in other words: Is there a pronounced dualism in the social and mental life of the savage, or, on the contrary, do the religious and non-religious ideas and activities pass and shade into each other in a continuous manner?

This question is of utmost importance for the general theory of religion. Professor Durkheim postulates the existence of a perfectly sharp and deep cleavage between the two domains of the *sacré* and profane, and his entire theoretical construction stands and falls with this assumption.[1] Again, Dr. [Ronald R.] Marett is of opinion that, generally speaking, "the savage is very far from having any fairly definite system of ideas of a magico-religious kind, with a somewhat specialised department of conduct corresponding thereto." [2]

This view, although expressed in a somewhat different connection, undoubtedly implies the negation of Durkheim's dogmatic standpoint. Again, Mr. Crawley thinks that for the savage everything has got a religious dimension,[3] a view which also excludes the existence of any irreducible dualism of *magico-religious* on the one hand and *secular* on the other.

These examples show that the above question, fundamental as it is, is still unsettled and controversial. What answer does it receive from the ethnographic evidence? The great Australian ethnographers, Spencer and Gillen, whose researches have contributed to the advancement of our knowledge of primitive religion more than any other investigations, answer the question in the affirmative. The life of an aborigine of Central

---

This comment appeared in the Annual Report of the British Association for the Advancement of Science, 1914, *pp. 534–35, and is reprinted by permission.*

[1] *Les formes élémentaires de la vie réligieuse,* Paris, 1912.

[2] *Notes and Queries on Anthropology,* 4th ed., London, 1912. Article on religion.

[3] Article on religion in *Sociological Papers,* iii, London, 1910.

Australia is sharply divided into two periods: the one comprising his everyday life, and the other his magico-religious activities.[4] It is evident throughout Messrs. Spencer and Gillen's two volumes that the properly religious and magical practices and beliefs are strictly esoteric; that they are fenced off from everyday life by a wall of taboos, rules, and observances. Yet reading another standard work of modern anthropology, Dr. and Mrs. Seligman's monograph on the Veddas, one gets the impression that among these natives there does not exist anything like a radical bipartition of things and ideas into religious and profane.

Again, the views held by another recent investigator, Dr. Thurnwald, with regard to the magic of the natives of the Bismarck Archipelago and of the Solomon Islands, imply beyond doubt the absence of a clear-cut division between magico-religious and secular ideas,[5] the two classes merging into and blending with each other.

One conclusion seems to be inevitable: namely, that pending new evidence it would be rash to dogmatise on the subject under consideration. I venture to say more. The above-mentioned statements (which could easily be multiplied) point not merely to different personal equations, which, however, would be possible in such an enormously complex and general problem, but they point to real differences in the matter discussed. The consolidation of the religious life can be different amongst various peoples, depending as it does upon various social conditions. Thus religion seems to be best developed and possessing the highest relative social importance among the Central Australians, to a smaller degree among the Papuans studied by Thurnwald, still less among the Veddas. Where it is strongest the bipartition postulated by Durkheim seems to be most prominent. Wherever it is less pronounced the two domains shade into each other and begin to fuse.

Thus probably the division into *religious* and *profane* is not an essential and fundamental feature of religion, suitable to be considered as its very distinctive characteristic. It is an accidental feature, dependent chiefly upon the social part played by religion and connected possibly with some other factors, to determine the influence of which it is, however, necessary to have more ample evidence, gathered with the problem in view.

[4] *Northern Tribes of Central Australia*, p. 33.

[5] "Ethno-psychologische Studien an Südseevölkern," in *Beihefte zur Zeitschrift für angew. Psychologie*, Leipzig, 1913. Paragraph on magic.

12

ON SIR JAMES FRAZER

SCIENCE AND SUPERSTITION OF PRIMITIVE MANKIND

Sir James Frazer's *Golden Bough* is in many respects the greatest achievement of anthropology—a science the short life-history of which allows still of a rapid survey and a correct apportionment of values. The book, like no other work, expresses the spirit of modern humanism—the union of classical scholarship with folk-lore and anthropology. The marble forms of antique legend and myth are made to lend their beauty to the crude and queer customs of the savage and the uncouth usages of the peasant, while the Gods and Heroes of Olympus receive in exchange the vitalising breath of life and reality from their humbler yet more animate counterparts.

It is difficult to review a new version of the work in the ordinary manner. It would be as presumptuous to assess the value of a universally acknowledged masterpiece of literary art and a classic of scholarship as it would be unnecessary to indicate the scope of a work known to every cultured man, a work which has exercised paramount influence over several branches of learning and has created new lines of scientific research. But though it is superfluous to praise the book or to explain it, the appearance of the abridged edition seems an opportune occasion for us anthropologists to undertake a little examination of conscience with regard to this classic. We all admit that we owe an immense debt to the author of the *Golden Bough* and to his work, but have we acquitted ourselves well of an obligation, have we given him his due in return? By this I mean, have we taken all that has been offered to us and made the most of

This was a review of The Golden Bough: A Study in Magic and Religion *by Sir James George Frazer; it appeared in* Nature, May 19, 1923 *(Vol. III), pp. 658–62, and is reprinted by permission.*

it? Have we followed his lead to the end of the road, have we searched everywhere where the light of the *Golden Bough* has shone?

For this is the difference between the economic and the spiritual order of things: that in the former it is good to receive material benefits, and, speaking without cant, painful to give them; while in matters of the mind it is a joy to bestow but a burden to take, since this has to be done in an unselfish submission of the spirit, and requires obedience, discipline, and patience.

Surveying the immense influence exercised by this and Frazer's other works on contemporary humanistic literature, it might appear as if this quarry of inspiration and fact, however rich, must have by now become nearly exhausted. Literally half the subjects of modern anthropological argument and controversy have been submitted by Frazer for discussion: totemism, problems of the taboo, origins of kinship and chieftainship, primitive conceptions of the soul and spiritual life—the list could be drawn out indefinitely by going into more detail. In Great Britain, in France, in Germany and the United States, whole schools of anthropological science have flourished or grown rankly, respectively, on the ground broken and first cultivated by Frazer. It is enough to mention the names of Crawley, Marett, Durkheim, Hubert and Mauss, Van Gennep, [Wilhelm] Wundt, Freud and his school (in their anthropological studies), who in their work, some of it of the very first rank, are more or less dependent on Frazer and his initiative. Yet it would be easy to show that even this immense and most valuable Frazerian literature has left enormous areas within the enclosure of the *Golden Bough* ready for further cultivation.

It is not from the side of theory, however, that I wish to approach this great work, but, as a field worker, from the point of view of actual research among savage races. The test of a scientific achievement lies in its power of anticipation and of prophecy: a sound theory must be the forerunner of empirical discoveries, it must allow us to foreshadow new facts not yet ascertained by observation. It is not when a man talks to us about things we have seen already, but when, from his study, he can foretell unsuspected events, can direct us towards unforeseen treasures of fact, and guide our researches in unexplored countries, it is only then that the value of his theories is put beyond doubt or cavil. This is well known in natural science, where the value of a theory is always gauged by its lead in the laboratory or in the field. In humanistic and historical science the honour of a prophetic voice has been reserved to its youngest off-shoot, anthropology. For though "history never repeats itself" when we watch it over a relatively brief span, interested in its detailed course of accidental happenings, yet the evolution of culture, taken as a whole, is submitted to definite rules and regularities, and human nature, broadly viewed, as it

breaks through the media of various civilisations and stages of development, remains the same, and, being subject to laws, is thus capable of
prediction.

The *Golden Bough* has had a triumphant career in this respect. One
after the other the main supports of the lofty edifice, which at first might
have appeared entirely carved out of the author's creative imagination,
were traced to the solid bed-rock of fact by subsequent discoveries among
the backward races. The most fantastic feature in the ritual of Aricia,
the succession by murder, led the author to the theory of the killing of
divine kings, carried out by certain savages, in order to prevent their
end by disease or senile decay. This theory, when first emitted, had only
partial and meagre evidence in recorded fact. But the brilliant discoveries
of Dr. and Mrs. Seligman about the divine kings of the Shilluk, about their
violent end, regularly inflicted after a term of reigning, and about the
spiritual succession by the transmission of the soul, confirmed Sir James
Frazer's theoretical assumptions in every detail. Following this, field-work
has brought, and is still bringing, fresh evidence, enough to prove that
Frazer's researches have revealed an institution of the greatest importance
among backward races.

Sir James Frazer was the first to express the view that before humanity
had begun to worship spiritual beings there was a stage of belief and ritual,
essentially magical, in which man assumed a fixed order of Nature, subject to the power of specific incantations and rites. Modern research among
savages, in the measure as it penetrates more deeply into the comprehension
of native ideas, tends to establish the correctness, not only of the general
assumption of the magical stage in evolution, but also of Sir James's
detailed theories of the psychology of magic. The nature of primitive kingship and power; the paramount rôle played by the taboo and its psychology; the importance of harvest ritual and ceremonies among savages—
in all this it would be easy to show what copious results recent field-work
has produced by following the suggestions and inspirations of the *Golden
Bough*.

An irrefutable though somewhat external proof of this is to be found in
the ever-increasing bulk of the book as it passes through successive editions,
a score of new instances appearing to testify to the truth of some of
Frazer's fundamental propositions, where previous evidence was able only
to supply a few.

To mention only the other masterpiece of Sir James Frazer, *Totemism
and Exogamy*, we find again, after some thirty years, a small volume ex-
panded into four large ones by the rich harvest of facts which followed
the theoretical forecasts of the author. The ignorance of paternity, at first
observed by Spencer and Gillen among one tribe only, was at once recognised by Frazer as of extreme importance for the early forms of totemic
belief and organisation and kinship. Here again this forecast was confirmed,

not only by further researches of Sir Baldwin Spencer in the north of Australia, but also by the discoveries of Dr. Rivers in the New Hebrides, and by the findings of the present reviewer among a number of Papuo-Melanesian tribes of Eastern New Guinea. There this ignorance is of extreme importance in shaping the matrilineal ideas and institutions of the natives, and is also closely connected with their totemism.

There seems to be some need of emphasising this empirical fecundity of the book—that is, its essentially scientific value. The great admiration which this work has inspired as a literary masterpiece and as a classic of comparative history, folk-lore, and archaeology seems to have overshadowed the merits of the book as an organiser and director of field-work. These merits are due, not only to the learning and to the constructive craft of Sir James, but also mainly to his genius in understanding the fundamentals of human nature, especially of the nature of primitive man, such as we see him represented by the peasant and the savage. In no other work can we find the same intimate understanding of savage modes of thought and behaviour, the same unfailing capacity to interpret the savage's customs, ideas, and traditions from his own point of view, the same prophetic intuition of what is really important with the native and what is secondary. It is because of that that no other work of anthropological theory has received such brilliant confirmation from later researches in the field, nor is any one of them likely to stimulate future research to the same degree as the *Golden Bough*.

To substantiate this last forecast I should like to indicate, on one more point, this suggestive quality of Frazer's theories. I mean the very *leitmotiv* of the book, the importance of vegetable cults for primitive magic and religion, the enormous concern of primitive mankind for the soil's fertility and for its conditions, the sun, the rain, and the weather. Over and over again, in the course of the long and devious explanations of the ritual of Nemi, we meet with the magic of the skies and of the soil, with the worship of trees, with the belief in the influence of sex on vegetable fertility, with harvesting customs and superstitions, with gods and goddesses of the teeming forces of Nature.

The reader remains under the impression that the interest in the vegetable world has exercised an overwhelming influence over the formation of magical and religious belief and ritual; that these, like the luxuriant mantle of green which covers our earth, have grown out of the union of the skies with the earth's fertility.

This view, indeed, is not expressed by the author, who even, in the preface to this new, abridged edition, repudiates an extreme form in which this opinion had been imputed to him, the view, namely, that all religion starts from tree worship. "I am so far from regarding the reverence for trees as of supreme importance for the evolution of religion, that I consider it to have been altogether subordinate to other factors." This, of course, is quite true, but if, instead of tree worship, we take the wider complex of religious phenomena, the cult of vegetation, or rather of vegetable fertility and its conditions, I for one would fully endorse the view that here we have one of the very taproots of religious growth. I perceive, moreover, that this aspect of the Frazerian theories opens up new lines of empirical research of the greatest promise and importance.

The *Golden Bough*, in this regard, shows us primitive man as he really is, not an idle onlooker on the vast and varied spectacle of Nature, evolving by reflection a sort of speculative philosophy as to its meaining and origins, but an eager actor, playing his part for his own benefit, trying to use all the means in his power towards the attainment of his various needs and desires: supply of food, shelter, and covering; satisfaction of social ambitions and of sexual passions; satisfaction of some aesthetic impulses and of sportive and playful necessities. He is interested in all things which subserve these ends and are thus immediately useful. Round these he develops not only his material technique, his implements, weapons, and methods of economic pursuit, but also his myths, incantations, rites, and ceremonies, the whole apparatus of primitive science and superstition.

Among all forces of Nature useful to man, the earth's fertility occupies quite a privileged and special position in the mind of the savage. Vegetable life—in its perennial periodicity of active exuberance and relative rest in the tropics; of life and death in the cold and temperate zones; of barrenness and ' fertility in certain periodically irrigated deserts—exhibits a regularity and system, a dependence on causes and motives, which seem to be almost within the control of man, yet from time to time so baffling to all his endeavours as to keep his interests, hopes, and fears constantly alive. On this borderland, where man's self-sufficiency utterly fails him, yet where he perceives a clear order: on this ground, so vital to himself and so clearly subject to the play of some extraneous regularities or wills, here the ideas of magic and religion, always a cross-breed of reflection and emotion, flourish most abundantly. Especially where man begins actively to shape the forces of Nature in agriculture, magic ranges itself side by side with technical efforts and becomes a controlling factor of immense importance.

It would be natural to expect, therefore, that among savages there exists public magic of fertility, and that, on the sociological side, this leads to the early forms of chieftainship and kingship, while on the side of belief it leads to important developments of ritual and cult.

Here we touch on the sociological aspect of Frazer's theories of early magic. He clearly recognises the existence of a special class, who, by their magical knowledge, can acquire social importance: "the public magician occupies a position of great influence, from which, if he is a prudent and able man, he may advance step by step to the rank of a chief or king." The author further proceeds to show how very important these specialised magicians are, both in that they perform their services for the whole community, thus forming an integrating power, and also in that they are the first examples in the evolution of mankind of specialists freed from the ordinary burdens and occupations of their fellow-tribesmen, and able to devote themselves to one pursuit. The evidence which Sir James is able to adduce in support of his theory of public magic and of its sociological importance is great, but not quite adequate to substantiate all his theories. Thus, among the forms of public magic, Sir James can find examples only by referring to sunshine, rain, and weather. Even this material does not allow him to demonstrate in detail how political power and social influence arise from the exercise of the magical functions. We are led to inquire: If vegetable and fertility rites are so important, how is it that there are no departmental magicians of agriculture on record? Why does the public magician only control the conditions of fertility and not fertility itself? How can magical influence grow into political power? These questions seem at first sight to qualify and invalidate Frazer's theories of early kingship and magic. Yet here again, recent results of field-work among primitive people allow us to settle these doubts and cavils in a manner once more triumphant for the book, which shows itself to have been ahead of the material at the author's disposal.

In ethnographical researches done among some Papuo-Melanesian tribes of Eastern New Guinea, I found myself at once in the thick of a social and psychological situation such as is postulated by the *Golden Bough*. The office of the chief coincides there with that of the public magician. To the control of rain and sunshine the chief owes an enormous proportion of his executive power, which he uses to strengthen his position and to enforce his general will. A faithful disciple of the *Golden Bough*, I turned my attention to the institutions associated with agriculture. Then gradually I began to see that Frazer's theories of the sociologies of magic, of the rôle of the public magician, of the departmental control of natural forces, rested on much more solid foundations than he himself had been able to realise with the material in hand, and that this can be demonstrated on the book's own territory, that of vegetable cults. For not only do there exist in these tribes departmental magical rites of fertility, not only are they the most important ones, ranking even before the weather rites and always carried out by the chief, but also we can study there the sociological mechanism by which the garden magician obtains his political power.

In each community we find a garden magician, who performs his ritual for public benefit. These functions are always vested in the headman of the community. In villages which are capitals of a district and governed by a chief, he himself carries out the magic of vegetation. In this rôle, the headman or chief commands not only a high respect, as the man who has in his hands the forces of fertility and who knows how to tap them, but he also takes an actual lead in the practical pursuits accompanied by the magic. For the magical ritual is intimately bound up with the technical activities. It imposes a regularity in time, and compels people to work in order and in organised groups. This refers to several forms of public magic, such as canoe-building, fishing, and overseas expeditions, but most conspicuously to garden magic. In this, the magician controls the work of the whole community during the course of the year, gives the initiative to the various stages, has the right of reprimand and punishment, is regarded as the man responsible for success and failure, and receives tributes from his fellow-villagers.

Here again we see that, starting from one of those theories of the *Golden Bough* which go far ahead of the available evidence, field-work reaches interesting and important discoveries. In this case it leads to the study of primitive economics, a chapter very much neglected by the traveller and amateur ethnographer, and even by the specialist, which promises, however, to yield results of some importance. For I have no doubt that my confirmation of Sir James's theories from a limited ethnographical area will be followed by other more important discoveries all the world over.

Thus the *Golden Bough,* far from being a classic in the sense of having attained the fulness of its glory and deserving honourable rest, is a book which still has some hard service in the field before it, a book which should be in the kitbag of every ethnographic explorer. A modern ethnographer, in his researches among savages, must, while making his observations, remain still in contact with theoretical literature in order to receive from it constant inspiration and guidance, especially if he is bent on doing intensive field-work, if he is willing and able to remain for months and years among the same tribe and study it by means of their own language and by personally taking part in the tribal life. In such study I derived constant inspiration and benefit from the works of Westermarck, Karl Bücher, Ratzel, Marett, Hubert and Mauss, Crawley and Rivers, some of which I actually have re-read while in the field, others again in the intervals between my expeditions. Alas! at that time the twelve volumes of the *Golden Bough* were too heavy and costly a burden to carry across sago swamps, to paddle over lagoons in an out-rigger always ready to capsize, or to keep in a tent or thatched hut by no means rain and insect-proof. Now the more fortunate field-worker can easily take with him, handle, and constantly refer to the new, one-volume, abridged edition.

To the student in his library, this abridged edition will no doubt only serve as a handy guide, as a sort of explicit digest, or to the beginner as a preliminary introduction. The full version is indispensable to the student, and it is also the most fascinating and instructive reading to the layman. But no doubt many a one who was at first shy of tackling directly the *Golden Bough* will, in the short edition, find a bridge to the full work, which is not only the most important achievement of Sir James Frazer, but also the last word of modern anthropological scholarship.

THE DEEPER CRITICISM OF THE BIBLE

Though the *Golden Bough* will always rank as the greatest and most original achievement of Sir James Frazer, while again in *Totemism and Exogamy* he has given his most important contribution to scientific anthropology and sociology, the present book on folklore in the Old Testament, now abridged into one volume, makes an even greater appeal to the reader's general or philosophical interest than the other works, for it deals with the most important fact in human tradition and literature, and one associated with intimate personal experiences of all of us. In a field apparently made almost completely sterile by criticism, higher criticism, and uncritical speculations, Sir James contrives to revive dead questions and to reshape facts and situations familiar, yet always incomprehensible, until now they receive a new meaning in the light of comparative anthropology. In this work the learned author once more vindicates for anthropology its claim to be the ablest interpreter of all the documents of human tradition and culture.

In the opening chapters Sir James discusses the myth of myths—the biblical story of creation. This story has been lived through by every one of us. Every picture, every detail, has its deep, emotional associations, from earliest infancy, when they were taken as the paramount fairy tale, until the time when their literal sense had to be interpreted, perhaps even finally rejected. But at no time in a man's life of belief or doubt are the details of this myth mere incidents of a story or a fiction. The childish and naïve visions of paradise, the fears of punishment, the hopes of redemption, are all bound up with the great drama of Paradise Lost.

Yet, looking back to the youthful times when the fire of faith burned high, and when the deep, uncritical belief made the figures of paradise live and act in a world real and near to us, we can still perceive certain flickering shadows, certain blots on the picture. Besides the comprehensible and at times lovable figure of God, within the sunny garden where we felt quite at home with our first parents, there grows the strange tree with its dangerous fruits, there creeps the serpent around it, there happen such crude incidents as the moulding of Adam in clay, the transformation of a small bone into our first mother, and other events, showing a strange inconsistency of God and his unyielding vindictiveness, and creating hesitancy and lurking doubts.

Here Sir James takes us back once more to the vague apprehensions of

This article was a review of Folk-Lore in the Old Testament: Studies in Comparative Religion, Legend, and Law *by Sir James George Frazer; it appeared in* Nature, May 3, 1924 (Vol. 113, No. 2844), *pp. 633–34, and is reprinted by permission.*

our youth, revives our doubts, and formulates our questions anew. As we follow him, then, into the various parts of the world, where the Tree of Life grows on its native soil, where the first human beings spring naturally out of red clay, where the serpent beguiles the ancestors of man with good reason and to a sensible purpose, we begin to understand those incidents as they appear in a fragmentary and garbled form in our Bible. Above all, Divinity himself appears in a clearer light, in which he moves with more dignity, acts with greater consistency, and is led by a kinder purpose.

The mark of Cain, the covenant of Abraham, the tricks of Jacob and of Joseph; the vicissitudes of Moses, of the Judges and the Kings, the Witch of Endor, all their mysterious actions, their little lapses from morals and straightforward honesty, are analysed in the remaining chapters of the book. Sometimes Sir James shows us that the narrator of the biblical stories was aware of a certain sociological and customary context, which he took for granted with his readers, but which for us has to be reconstructed in each case by the hand of the skilful anthropologist. Sometimes a detail, obscure in itself, can be reinterpreted in anthropological terms, as when we realise that the mark of Cain might have been a disguise of immunity, or the kid-skins of Jacob may correspond to a rite of new birth.

The deeper biblical criticism of Sir James is not directed thus to the whitewashing of the biblical story. The blots on the Bible are not rubbed away, but painted into their full original forms, with the strong, variegated colours borrowed by Sir James Frazer from the peoples of all races, climates, and levels of civilisation.

There is no other work in which Sir James's admirable style, his quiet sense of humour, his true humanism are used to a more important purpose than in the present one. From his impartial and restrained attitude it is impossible to gauge whether he approaches the subject as a rationalist or as a mystic, or as a modern agnostic, who is neither entirely committed to reason nor absolutely absorbed by mysticism. The bigoted and dogmatic believer and the extreme rationalist may remain dissatisfied with the tone of the book. But both those who study the Bible for religious inspiration and those who regard it as a mere anthropological document will derive not only profit but also artistic pleasure from the present book. Both will be interested and grateful for the removal of absurdities, the imparting of a fuller and deeper meaning to the biblical account, for bringing God nearer to man, the creature to its Maker, whoever might be believed to be the one and who the other. Nowadays, when the modern believer seeks revelation in reality rather than reality in revelation, and when the modern agnostic has ceased to deny all reality to revelation, the two can meet on friendly terms in Sir James Frazer's anthropological workshop and discuss their differences amicably.

This makes one reflect on the distance between modern agnosticism and that of a generation ago. The longest chapter of this volume embodies the

Huxley memorial lecture, delivered by Frazer in 1916 before the Royal Anthropological Institute. It treats of the subject of the Great Flood, on which Huxley himself had written the famous essay. The great agnostic naturalist had still to combat the literal acceptance of the biblical story and show its absurdity in the light of geology and natural science. To-day, it is true, some people still believe in a flat earth and a universal deluge—but Huxley's writings have done their work, and he would scarcely write on the same lines now as he did in his time.

The modern agnostic does not take much trouble any more to establish the absurdity of biblical stories literally taken. He is not now disturbed by the absurdity of belief. Sometimes he even doubts whether his own disbelief is less absurd or more rational than the credulity of his opponent. He merely knows that he is entirely incapable of those acts of faith which give his luckier neighbour so much happiness, which seem to reconcile him to all the trials of life by apparently priceless promises of some future existence and spiritual compensation. The difference, he knows, cannot be mastered by reason or combated by rational argument. It lies deep in man's emotional constitution, and it sunders the black sheep from the white by an unbridgeable chasm.

It is the nature of the difference between the two which interests the modern disbeliever. He is fascinated by religious phenomena rather than shocked by them, and he contemplates and studies them with the same intensity of interest, almost with the same love and veneration, as the religious man. It is not the absurdity of the Great Flood which he wants to have proved; that he takes for granted. He wishes to find the foundations of this belief in the depths of human nature or in the vicissitudes of human history; and in this, Frazer's treatment of the Great Flood is more actual and modern than Huxley's, though not greater or more brilliant, for that is impossible! Each marks a milestone on the road of scientific and philosophic progress, each sums up an epoch in the relations between science and religion.

FRAZER ON TOTEMISM

Half a century ago, in 1887, there appeared in Edinburgh a small booklet entitled "Totemism." It was destined to exercise an influence on the science of man second only to that of another masterpiece by the same author —I mean of course Frazer's *Golden Bough*. Both works produced an immediate impression at home among scholars and abroad among workers in

This article was a review of Totemica: A Supplement to Totemism and Exogamy *by Sir James George Frazer; it appeared in* Nature, *March 19, 1938 (Vol. 141, No. 3568), pp. 489–91, and is reprinted by permission.*

the field. Both have since reappeared in a much fuller form; the first as *Totemism and Exogamy* (in four volumes, 1910); the second as a series of twelve volumes jointly named *The Golden Bough* (1911–15).

Each of the two great works has now received a valuable epilogue: *Aftermath*, a supplement to *The Golden Bough*, published last year; and now *Totemica*, giving the finishing touch to Frazer's work on totemism. To those of us who owe the main inspiration of our life-work to Frazer these recent events are both welcome and significant. The additional volumes bear witness not only to the vigour and creative power of the author but also to the value and vitality of the British school of anthropology.

Frazer, more than anyone else, has given the science of man wide currency among cultured people all over the world. It is largely due to the literary charm of his style and the profoundness of his insight that anthropological books are now extensively read, appreciated, and enjoyed. He also, above all others, has brought anthropology into line with classical scholarship. Nor is it an accident that the first systematic and planned scientific expedition was undertaken from Cambridge, Frazer's spiritual home and personal abode. The work of Spencer and Gillen in Central Australia, the researches of [John] Roscoe among the Baganda, the African classics of Smith and Dale, of Rattray, and of Junod, throughout bear witness to Frazer's genius and vision.

The direct imprint of Frazer's ideas on anthropological theory is not less remarkable. Take the range of its subject-matter: magic and kinship, social organization and the clan system, political power and problems of early science, of ritual and religion: in all these Frazer has given at least the initiative and in most cases the fullest and most adequate treatment of each subject. When the great Frenchman, Durkheim, was shaping his theory of primitive religion, he had in *The Golden Bough* an encyclopaedia of fact upon which to draw, and a compendium of theoretical points of view to inspire him. When Freud made his attempt to apply psychoanalysis to the "cave man" and his murderous and incestuous offspring, he turned to Frazer's *Totemism and Exogamy* and to *The Golden Bough*. Most modern schools of anthropology, whether "functionalism" or "structuralism," the search for "patterns of culture" or hunt for "tribal geniuses," largely depend for their inspiration on Frazer.

The present book is a review of evidence on totemism which has accumulated since 1910. It is arranged geographically, pride of place being naturally given to Australia: ". . . for it is to Australia, with its varied and very primitive forms of Totemism, that we must ultimately look, if we are ever to find a clue to the problem of the origin and meaning of the institution" (from the preface). From that continent some new and important facts have been brought to light in field-work organized from Sydney by Prof. A. R. Radcliffe-Brown and his successor Dr. A. P. Elkin. Some of the discoveries, such as those by R. Piddington and P. M. Kaberry,

W. E. H. Stanner and U. McConnel shed a new light on our theoretical conception of totemism.

Readers of Frazer, that is, all anthropologists, will note with interest that the new evidence establishes the widespread occurrence of two facts: the ignorance of physical paternity and the magical ceremonies for increasing totemic species. It is on these two ethnographic facts that Frazer founded his hypotheses of the origins of totemism.

Equally rich and interesting is the evidence from Oceania. It has been known since the times of Codrington that developed forms as well as the rudiments of totemism are to be found in Melanesia. Its occurrence among the Polynesians, foreshadowed by Rivers, has since been established through the recent researches of Drs. R. W. Firth and H. I. Hogbin. The data from Africa and India which Frazer is able to register in the present book, important as they are, do not add anything revolutionary to our knowledge. America, the continent in which totemism was discovered, has yielded only twelve pages.

Frazer himself keeps aloof in this book from controversy; nor does he work out his earlier theories any further. It is tempting, therefore, to inquire how far these have been strengthened or modified by recent discoveries and developments in anthropological doctrine. In his first theory, dating back to the original book of 1887, Frazer finds the origins of totemism in the widespread belief in the external soul, a belief in which primitive man associates his welfare and destiny with some symbolic object. Organized on a communal scale, that is, associating a whole clan with an animal or plant species, this belief becomes in substance totemism.

Frazer himself has discarded this view as a theory of the origins of totemism. We cannot, however, dismiss it as a contribution towards the understanding of the primitive tendency to symbolize, nor yet of the constitution of primitive society. An external symbol seems to be indispensable in the integration of primitive, and for that matter even of civilized, groups. Durkheim, developing Frazer's theories more fully, has rightly insisted on the functional value of the Australian *churinga* and of our modern flag, of the medieval scutcheon, and the crown and sceptre of contemporary monarchs. The appreciation of social symbolism, of the concept of the external soul in its wider setting, reveals to us some of the workings of the primitive, that is, essentially human mind, and of group integration at all levels of development. For the progress of civilization in a way consists in the imprint of things spiritual being given to matter, while shaped matter fashions spiritual processes in turn. The very essence of symbolism in thought, in speech and writing, in liturgy and in art is, after all, nothing else but the concept of "external soul" developed and refined beyond recognition and yet without any breach of continuity. Thus Frazer's first hypothesis can be regarded as the starting-point of some of the most important developments in the study of culture.

The second theory, formulated by Frazer after the sensational discoveries of Spencer and Gillen in Australia, links up totemism directly with magic. The Arunta and allied tribes perform magical ceremonies of totemic increase in which every clan acts as a co-operative unit in a vast enterprise of multiplying edible and otherwise useful animals and plants. The means to this practical end appear to us completely fictitious. This, however, does not detract from their social and even educational value. They bring home to the participants the importance of co-operation, the necessity of obeying rules and following tribal tradition—an aspect of ceremonial life brought out by Prof. Radcliffe-Brown in the second part of his *Andaman Islanders*.

The role of magic as an all-important organizing and integrating force can be seen even more clearly at a level higher than that of the Australian and Andaman islander. In the Trobriand Islands the garden magician, in virtue of his mystical power over Nature, becomes the leader and organizer of the enterprise: he acts as the agricultural expert and supervisor of work (cf. *Coral Gardens* by the reviewer). So also the man who magically controls wind and weather, the dangers of the open seas, and the vicissitudes of the commercial moods of his trading partners, acts as captain of the canoe and master of an overseas expedition (*Argonauts of the Western Pacific*). As regards Polynesia, the connexion between magic and practical activities has been well documented by Dr. R. W. Firth in his *Primitive Economics of the New Zealand Maori* (1929).

In his third and final theory of totemic origins Frazer reveals the significance of the primitive ignorance of physiological paternity. Here once more the Central Australians provide the cue. They believe that conception is due to the entry into a woman's womb of a totemic spirit-child. These are believed to reside in sacred spots, primarily deposits of bull-roarers (*churinga*), where mythical ancestors, half-human, half-totemic, had left their souls and their magical implements. This belief, argues Frazer, is sufficient to explain the reason why primitive man regarded himself as mystically bound up with an animal, plant, or inanimate object. It accounts also for the formation of clan bonds, and it explains why, through his totemic kinship with natural phenomena, primitive man claimed magical control over natural processes and objects.

At the time when Frazer was setting forth his theory, he was really generalizing boldly—some might even say, too boldly—from evidence confined to one insignificant tribelet in the deserts of Central Australia. Yet here once more Frazer's genius had anticipated the course of future discoveries. Animistic beliefs about conception have since been discovered in one tribe of Australia after another until their distribution map almost covers the continent. They have been signalled by Rivers from Melanesia, by the present reviewer from eastern New Guinea, and by Dr. Hogbin from Polynesia.

It is interesting to note that simultaneously with Frazer's *Totemica* there appears a monograph dealing with totemic paternity in aboriginal Australia. It is really a monument to Frazer's insight and vision, and to the value of his theories of totemism (M. F. Ashley-Montagu, *Coming into Being among the Australian Aborigines*, 1937). Dr. Ashley-Montagu concludes that, with very few and insignificant exceptions, "the orthodox doctrine of each tribe" in Australia is "that children are the result of the immigration into a woman of a spirit child which is of an origin going back into the far distant mythological past. . . . Thus it is that by means of this belief in the immigration of spirit children into women the proper totemic and moiety membership of the child is secured" (*op. cit.*, p. 199).

Taking any one of the three hypotheses in isolation, it might be contended that none of them alone is sufficient to account for the birth and nature of totemism. Taken in conjunction, they give a full and adequate explanation of the phenomenon. They all centre round the conception, almost the definition, of totemism which runs through Frazer's theoretical treatment and gives the perspective to his magnificent edifice of fact: totemism expresses ritually and mythologically man's selective interest in a number of animal or plant species; it discloses the primitive's profound conviction that he is in body and mind akin to the relevant factors of his environment. These he is able to control magically in virtue of the kinship; and towards them he has to observe a religious attitude of reverence and consideration.

In any theory of totemism, we have first and foremost to account for the linking of man with environmental forces and principles. In his third theory, Frazer makes the important suggestion that the primitive ignorance of reproductive physiology combined with beliefs of spirit-child incarnation is the natural basis of totemic kinship between man and Nature. This bond was to primitive man not merely an intellectual affirmation and a sentimental attitude; it became above all a means of action. Since his interest in his surroundings was pragmatic, that is, nutritive and utilitarian, and his earliest means of control magical, the main function of totemic belief consisted in the ritual of magical increase directed upon useful or practically important factors of the environment. Thus we are led inevitably to Frazer's second hypothesis, in placing the first within the context of primitive thought, feeling, and action.

Such terms and concepts, however, as "principles of fertility," "useful environmental factors" go beyond primitive man's intellectual horizon. He has to use concrete and tangible symbols, both ritually and psychologically. The principle of ritual symbolism, that is, the belief in the external soul, on which Frazer lays emphasis in his first theory, is the indispensable corollary to our understanding of the magical function of totemism and of its conceptual origins. The Australian *churinga*, for example, is the prototype of the external soul. In native belief it is also the main reservoir of spirit-children. In the increase ceremonies it becomes the main instrument of magical efficacy. This small object embodies as it were and epitomizes Frazer's hypotheses of totemic origin; and, let us remember, to the Central Australian the *churinga* is the most sacred and important object in the whole universe. It represents to him tradition, magical force, and the social unity of the clan, condensed but all-powerful. It stands for a long line of ancestors; it gives man the means of securing wealth and welfare; it is the source of human fertility. In "singing" to his *churinga*, in his mythologies and ritual actions, the Central Australian pragmatically bears witness to the intuition and insight of the great historian of totemism.

Frazer's theories explain not only the origins of totemism but also its functions. From the survival point of view, it is vital that man's interest in the practically indispensable species should never abate, that his belief in his capacity to control them should give him strength and endurance in his pursuits and stimulate his observation and knowledge of the habits and nature of animals and plants. Totemism, in the light of Frazer's theory, appears thus as a blessing bestowed by religion on primitive man's efforts in dealing with his useful surroundings, upon his "struggle for existence." At the same time it develops his reverence for animals and plants on which he depends, to which he feels in a way grateful, and yet the destruction of which is a necessity to him

Frazer's interpretation of totemism gives us still the best insight into the earliest phases of religion, of man's pious attitude of dependence, of his early seeking for permanent tangible values instinct with spiritual and moral substance. Within the framework of Frazer's interpretation we see how in totemism the beginnings of ethical attitudes are developed through the magical co-operation of clan members, and of the clans for the welfare of the whole community. Frazer has also shown that totemism, in its insistence on material symbolism, contains perhaps the earliest rudiments of sacred metaphor, that is, of abstraction, with all its possibilities of development into ritual, on one hand, and science on the other.

Frazer's contribution has been as essential to the progress in empirical field-work as to our theoretical understanding of primitive man. More than that, in his great works, *The Golden Bough, Totemism and Exogamy, The Fear of the Dead, The Belief in Immortality* and *Folk-Lore in the Old Testament,* Frazer has given us in outline a lasting philosophy of culture capable of indefinite development.

The extraordinary sympathy and insight with which the leader of the British school has treated primitive ways of thought and action, his fundamental humanism, his scientific acumen and artistic intuition have allowed him to reveal most of the problems with which modern anthropology is concerned. Frazer's vision has also led him to foresee the main currents of empirical discovery and to lay down the foundations of the comparative science of human cultures.

13

ELEMENTARY FORMS OF RELIGIOUS LIFE

It is superfluous to draw the attention of students to the importance of Prof. Durkheim's new work, for the appearance of a large volume from the pen of the leader of the French sociological school is a scientific event. The group of savants connected with *l'Année Sociologique* has achieved remarkable success in dealing with problems in primitive religion, and we have to thank it especially for the essays of MM. Hubert and Mauss on Sacrifice and Magic, and the articles of M. Durkheim on the Definition of Religious Phenomena, Classifications in Primitive Thought, and Totemism, and of M. Hertz on Funerary Rites.

To Prof. Durkheim the religious is the social *par excellence*. The distinctive characters of social and religious phenomena practically coincide. The social is defined, in *Règles de la méthode sociologique*, by its "exteriority to individual minds," by its "coercive action" upon individual minds; the religious, which is also "external" to individual minds, by its "obligatoriness." [1] It is obvious, therefore, that the present volume is of special importance, being the systematic and final expression of the best organized sociological school extant on a subject specially important to, and specially well mastered by, this school.

There is yet another reason why this book should particularly arouse the interest of the sociologist. It is Prof. Durkheim's first attempt to treat a "problem of origins" of such a fundamental and general social phenomenon as religion. In his methodological work, *Règles de la méthode sociologique*, he has strenuously insisted upon the treatment of social phenomena "as things," upon the necessity of excluding all forms of psychological explanations from sociology.[2] This postulate undoubtedly

---

This article was a review of Les Formes élémentaires de la vie religieuse: Le Système totémique en Australie *by Emile Durkheim, and appeared in* Folk-Lore, *December 1913 (Vol. XXIV, No. 4), pp. 525-31; it is reprinted by permission of The Folk-Lore Society.*

[1] See "Sur la Définition des phénomènes religieux," in *l'Année Sociologique*, Vol. II.

[2] *Op. cit.*, Table of Contents, cap. ii.

appears to many a rule rather artificial and barren in its practical applications—and especially to British anthropologists, who prefer psychological
explanations of origins; and this volume enables us to judge as to the
success of his method.

The book has several aspects and aims. It attempts to state the essential
and fundamental elements of religion, being thus a revision of the author's
former definition of *the religious;* it investigates the origins of religion;
it gives a theory of totemism; and it is designed as a substantial contribution to philosophy.

All these problems M. Durkheim seeks to solve by an analysis of the
beliefs of practically one single tribe, the Arunta. His keen eye detects
in the facts we owe to Messrs. Spencer and Gillen much that is not
patent to a less acute mind, and his researches through their two volumes,
completed by the records made by Mr. [Carl] Strehlow, yield him an
abundant crop of theoretical results. Nevertheless, to base most far-reaching conclusions upon practically a single instance seems open to very
serious objections. It is extremely dangerous to accept any people as
"the absolutely primitive type of mankind," or as "the best example of
elementary forms of social organization and creed," and to forego the
verification of conclusions by other available instances. For example,
when M. Durkheim, in trying to determine the fundamental aspect of
religion, finds it in an universal and absolute bipartition of men, things,
and ideas into "sacré et profane" (pp. 50 *et seq.*), he may refer to a
well-known passage by the Australian ethnographers,[3] and, in fact, a
sharp division of all things into religious and non-religious seems to be a
very marked feature of the social life of Central Australian natives. But
is it universal? I feel by no means persuaded. In reading the detailed
monograph by Dr. and Mrs. Seligman about the Veddas, no such division
is suggested as existing among that extremely primitive people. Again, it
would be difficult to maintain the existence of such a separation amongst
the Melanesian peoples of whom we have very copious records. This may
be due to a gap in our information, but, anyhow, it is not admissible to
base a system upon a mere assumption, instead of on certain knowledge.

One does not feel quite easy, also, about the assumption of totemism
being the elementary form of religion (liv. I, cap. iv), especially as here
again we find the investigation limited to the beliefs of the Central Australians.

Prof. Durkheim's theory of totemism is that the essence of totemism
lies in the totemic symbol and badge, and that the sacredness of the
totem is derived from the sacredness of the badge. A reconsideration,
from this new point of view, of the problem of totemism, grown slightly
wearisome owing to "totemic hyper-production" in recent times, cannot fail to be stimulating. M. Durkheim and his school accept, as is well

[3] *The Northern Tribes of Central Australia,* p. 33.

known, Dr. Marett's theory of preanimism. The totemic principle, the totemic force, is for Prof. Durkheim akin in nature to *mana*. This principle, inherent in the first place in the totemic badge and symbol, then in the species, and then in the clansmen, is thus explained: "Le dieu du clan, le principe totémique, ne peut donc être autre chose que le clan lui-même, mais hypostasie et représenté aux imaginations sous les éspeces sensibles du végétal ou de l'animal qui sert de totem" (p. 295). ["The god of the clan, the totemic principle, can therefore be only the clan itself, but hypostatized and manifested to the imagination in the physical form of the plant or animal that serves as the totem."] Undoubtedly this is a very interesting conception of religion, foreshadowed in our author's former works, in which so much stress is laid on the social nature of the religious—but here plainly expressed for the first time.

M. Durkheim proceeds to show how it comes about that society is the real substance, the *materia prima,* of the human conception of divinity. "Une société a tout ce qu'il faut pour éveiller dans les esprits, par la seule action qu'elle exerce sur eux, la sensation du divin; car elle est à ses membres ce qu'un dieu est à ses fidèles" (*ibid.*). ["A society, by its very power over the minds of people, has everything that is necessary to awaken in them the sensation of the divine; for society is to its members what a god is to his faithful."] Again, "Parce qu'elle a une nature qui lui est propre, différente de notre nature d'individu, elle poursuit des fins qui lui sont également spéciales; mais, comme elle ne peut les atteindre que par notre intermédiaire, elle réclame impérieusement notre concours" (*ibid.*). ["Because it has its own nature, different from ours as individuals, it pursues ends that are peculiar to it; but as it can attain them only through our intermediation, it imperiously demands our co-operation."] Let us note that here society is conceived to be the *logical subject* of the statement; an active being endowed with will, aims, and desires. If we are not to take it as a figure of speech (and M. Durkheim decidedly does not give it as such), we must label it an entirely metaphysical conception. Society conceived as a collective being, endowed with all properties of individual consciousness, will be rejected even by those sociologists who accept a "collective consciousness" in the sense of a sum of conscious states (as it is accepted, for example, by Messrs. McDougall, Ellwood, Davis, and, partly, by Simmel and Wundt). But, a few pages further, we read a statement which seems to allow of another interpretation. Speaking of "manières d'agir auxquelles la société est assez fortement attachée pour les imposer à ses membres," he says: "Les représentations qui les expriment en chacun de nous ont donc un intensité à laquelle des états de conscience purement privés ne sauraient atteindre; car elles sont fortes des innombrables représentations individuelles qui ont servi à former chacune d'elles. C'est la société qui parle par la bouche de ceux qui les affirment en notre présence" (p. 297). [Speaking of "modes of action to which a society is strongly enough attached to impose them on its members," he says: "The ideas that express them for each of us have therefore an intensity to which purely private states of consciousness could not attain, for they are strong in innumerable individual images which have served to form each of them. It is society that speaks through the mouths of those who affirm them in our presence."] Here we stand before a dilemma: either this phrase means that "social ideas" possess a specific character, because the individual who conceives them has the consciousness of being backed up by society in his opinion, in which case the statement is perfectly empirical; or the statement implies the conception of a non-empirical action of society upon the individual consciousness, in which case it conveys no scientific meaning.

The writer expresses himself again on the subject, from the genetic point of view: "En un mot, quand une chose est l'objet d'un état de l'opinion, la représentation qu'en a chaque individu tient de ses origines, des conditions dans lesquelles elle a pris naissance, une puissance d'action que sentent ceux-là mêmes qui ne s'y soumettent pas" (p. 297). ["In a word, when an opinion exists about a thing, the idea that each individual has of it comes from its origins, from the conditions giving birth to it, which are a force for action which even those who do not submit to it feel."] Here the author stands in front of the real problem. What are these specific social conditions in which arise "social consciousness," and consequently religious ideas? His answer is that these conditions are realized whenever society is actually gathered, in all big social gatherings: "Au sein d'une assemblée qu'échauffe une passion commune, nous devenons susceptibles de sentiments et d'actes dont nous sommes incapables quand nous sommes réduits à nos seules forces, et quand l'assemblée est dissoute, quand, nous retrouvant seul avec nous-mêmes, nous retombons à notre niveau ordinaire, nous pouvons mesurer alors toute la hauteur dont nous avions été soulevé au-dessus de nous-même" (p. 299). ["In the midst of an assembly inflamed by a common passion, we become capable of feelings and acts of which we are incapable when we are reduced to our own strength and when the meeting is over; when we are once more alone with ourselves and fall back to our ordinary level, we can then measure the height to which we had been raised above ourselves."]

This answer is somewhat disappointing. First of all, we feel a little suspicious of a theory which sees the origins of religion in crowd phenomena. Again, from the point of view of method, we are at a loss. Above we had been dealing (with some difficulties) with a transcendental collective subject, with a "society which was the creator of religious ideas": "Au reste, tant dans le présent que dans l'histoire, nous voyons sans cesse la société créer de toutes pièces des choses sacrées" (p. 304). ["Moreover, as much in the present as in history, we see society endlessly creating sacred things of all objects."] Then society was the divinity itself, i.e. it was not only creator, but the object of its creation, or at least reflected in this object. But here society is no more the logical and grammatical subject of the metaphysical assertions, but not even the object of these assertions. It only furnishes the external conditions, in which ideas about the divine may and must originate. Thus Prof. Durkheim's views present fundamental inconsistencies. Society is the source of religion, the origin of the divine; but is it "origin" in the sense that "the collective subject . . . thinks and creates the religious ideas"? This would be a metaphysical conception deprived of any empirical meaning; or is society itself the "god," as is implied in the statement that the "totemic principle is the clan," thought under the aspect of a totem? That reminds one somewhat of Hegel's Absolute, "thinking itself" under one aspect or another. Or, finally, is society, in its crowd-aspect, nothing more than the atmosphere in which *individuals* create religious ideas? The last is the only scientifically admissible interpretation of the obscure manner in which M. Durkheim expounds the essence of his theories.

Let us see how our author grapples with actual and concrete problems, and which of the three versions of "origins" just mentioned he applies to the actual facts of Australian totemism. He starts with the remark already quoted about the double form of the social life of the Central Australian tribesman. The natives go through two periodically changing phases of dispersion and agglomeration. The latter consist chiefly, indeed, almost exclusively, of religious festivities. This corresponds to the above-mentioned statement that crowd originates religion: "Or, le seul fait de l'agglomération agit comme un excitant exceptionellement puissant. Une fois les individus assemblés, il se dégage de leur rapprochement une sorte d'électricité qui les transporte vite à un degré extraordinaire d'exaltation. . . . On conçoit sans peine que, parvenu à cet état d'exaltation . . . l'homme ne se connaisse plus. Se sentant dominé, entraîné par une sorte de pouvoir extérieur qui le fait penser et agir autrement qu'en temps normal, il a naturellement l'impression de n'être plus lui-même. Il lui semble être devenu un être nouveau: les décorations dont il s'affuble, les sortes de masques dont il se recouvre le visage figurent matériellement cette transformation intérieure, plus encore qu'ils ne contribuent à la déterminer . . . tout se passe, comme s'il était réellement transporté dans un monde spécial, entièrement différent de celui où il vit d'ordinaire. . . . C'est donc dans ces milieux sociaux effervescents et de cette effervescence même que parait être née l'idée religieuse. Et ce qui tend à confirmer que telle en est bien l'origine, c'est que, en Australie, l'activité proprement religieuse est presque tout entière concentrée dans les moments ou se tiennent ces assemblées" (pp. 308, 312, 313). ["Now, the mere fact of gathering together acts as an exceptionally powerful stimulus. When the individuals are assembled a sort of electricity is released from their drawing together that quickly transports them to an extraordinary degree of exaltation. . . . It is easy to see that when he has reached this state of exaltation . . . man no longer knows himself. Feeling himself dominated, swept along by a kind of external power that makes him think and act differently than on normal occasions, he naturally has the impression of no longer being himself. He seems to have become a new being: the decorations with which he rigs himself out, the kind of masks with which he covers his face, materially represent this internal transformation, the more since they do not contribute to creating it . . . everything happens as if he were really transported into a special world entirely different from that in which he ordinarily lives. . . . It is therefore in these effervescent social spheres and from this effervescence itself that the religious idea appears to be born. And what tends to confirm the fact that this is indeed the origin is that in Australia religious activity itself is almost entirely concentrated in the moments when these assemblies are held."]

To sum up, theories concerning one of the most fundamental aspects of religion cannot be safely based on an analysis of a single tribe, as described in practically a single ethnographical work. It should be noted that the really empirical version of this theory of origins is by no means a realization of the "objective" method, in which M. Durkheim enjoins treating social facts as things and avoiding individual psychological interpretations. In his actual theory he uses throughout individual psychological explanations. It is the modification of the individual consciousness in big gatherings, the "mental effervescence," which is assumed to be the source of "the religious." The sacred and divine are the psychological categories governing ideas originated in religiously inspired crowds. These ideas are collective only in so far as they are general, i.e. common in all members of the crowd. None the less we arrive at understanding their nature by individual analysis, by psychological introspection, and not by treating those phenomena as "things." Finally, to trace back the origins of all religious phenomena to crowd manifestations seems to narrow down extremely both the forms of social influence upon religion, and the sources from which man can draw his religious inspiration. "Mental effervescence" in large gatherings can hardly be accepted as the only source of religion.

But, while one is bound to criticize certain points of principle in Prof. Durkheim's work, it must be added that the work contains in a relatively small bulk such thorough analyses of theories of religious facts—several of which, of first-rate importance, are original contributions by Prof. Durkheim or his school—as could only be given by one of the acutest and most brilliant living sociologists, and that these by themselves would make the book a contribution to science of the greatest importance.

14

THE LIFE OF MYTH

Myth, clothing the brutal and naked beauty of primeval thought with the dignity of tradition and the majesty of sacredness, exerts a singular attraction upon the human mind, civilized and sophisticated, as well as simple and untutored. The mixture of incompatible extremes, of the shameful and the holy, the graceful and the raw, the fleshly and the spiritual, the tragic and the clownish, surrounds myth with an atmosphere of mystery and gives it a meaning which has always inspired the artist and puzzled the student. From myth and folk tale have sprung the earliest as well as the ripest products of art: the savage enactment of myth at initiation and tribal feast as well as the tragedies of ancient Greece, the Elizabethan theatre, and the Wagnerian musical drama. In primitive, in pagan, and in Christian painting and sculpture, myth has supplied most of the subject matter and atmosphere.

The present volume, opening up one of the most wonderful and, for many reasons, least known regions of folk-lore, will be equally welcome to the scholar and the man of letters. It is a comprehensive survey of the mythological *Weltanschauung* of the Siberian and Finno-Ugric peoples, based on a polyglotic and extensive knowledge of the subject and, to a great extent also, on personal field work. It will be an important addition to the subject of general mythology, on which we have material enough, but not of the right sort.

The enormous variety of theories in comparative mythology and the wide range of opinions as to the true nature of a sacred tale is bewildering and disheartening. It shows how difficult to understand is the purely theoretical problem set by these tales, which come from a distant past and in which we seem to hear things both strange and familiar, almost incomprehensible messages which yet seem to convey a profound and

This article was a review of The Mythology of All Races, *Vol. IV,* Finno-Ugric, Siberian, *by Uno Holmberg, and appeared in* The Saturday Review of Literature, *April 7, 1928 (Vol. IV, No. 37), pp. 738–39.*

inevitable meaning. There are theories which make folk-lore into a muddled natural science, and the psychoanalytic interpretations which make myths into day-dreams charged with an incestuous desire; opinions which consider legends as but a slightly mangled tribal history, and others which make myth the outcome of unbridled imagination. At times myths are dismissed as the mystifications of priestly cunning, or again as a primitive *lapsus linguae*—the self-deception of the primitive mind by a self-made metaphor.

Most theories credit the savage with a too great propensity for arm-chair philosophizing and at the same time ascribe a too childish outlook to him. In fact he is not so silly as naïvely to personify natural objects, or to ignore the difference between men and beasts, animate and in-animate objects. Nor is he duped by his metaphors any more easily than is civilized man. On the other hand, he is neither idle nor speculative enough to spin out fantastic, semi-poetical explanations and rhapsodies; to standardize his day-dreams, or to record his tribal histories. His sense of historical accuracy and his interest in reconstructing the past is on the whole extraordinarily weak, as witness the almost complete absence of historical accounts from the immediate past, and the entire unreli-ability of such tales as can be checked from European chronicles. As to day-dreams in myth, the psychoanalytic theory stands and falls with the assumption of a "race memory" and a "race unconscious" which will be accepted by few anthropologists who do not belong to the inner ring of ardent Freudians.

The fact is that learned antiquarians, inspired psychologists, and vigorous protagonists of the "historical method" have all poured out their own opinions as to what the savage means by his story, why he tells it, and in what manner he relates his mythopoeic phantasies to reality. But they failed to ask the savage himself, or to look into the facts for an answer.

Myths in primitive culture are told with a purpose, and they are deeply rooted in the savage's interest and his social organization and culture. But the links which bind folk-lore to the rest of native life, the threads by which they are woven into the social fabric, have not only so far been ignored by the ethnographer, but have actually been severed by him. Stories have been taken down without any cultural context and projected out of native life into the ethnographer's note-book. Volumes of folk-lore have been published quite recently by first class ethnographers, in which the texts are given, as if from the begin-ning they had led a flat existence on paper (as for example, in Boas's *Tshimshian Mythology* or Rattray's *Ashanti Proverbs*).

And we find hardly any record of field work in which the cultural function of myth, legend, and folk tale are systematically studied; in which the ethnographer follows up all the connecting links between a sacred story and its influence on social organization, law, order, and ritual.

In order to explain a cultural product it is necessary to know it. And to know, in matters of thought and emotion, is to have experienced. The first necessity in the study of mythology, then, is to grasp how the natives *live* their myths. I maintain that the sacred tale is not told for amusement, as a simple entertainment. The "sacred" in early human societies is not an idle show or pretense imagined for the satisfaction of curiosity or even of emotional craving. The "sacred," both as a mental attitude and a form of behavior, is a dynamic principle of culture, governing some of the most important fields of human activity: magic, religion, morality, and social organization. In magic the "sacred," the power that resides in words and the efficacy that comes from appropriate gestures allows man to achieve supernaturally that which his practical means and abilities fail to accomplish: to inflict disease on an enemy and to restore the health of a friend; to enhance his own strength in battle, and to cow the adversary; to insure plenty in hunting, fishing, and in agriculture; to gain success in love and in social ambition. In religion, the "sacred" works as a life force which binds members of a group together and, by the establishment of moral values, integrates the mind of the individual in the crises of life—death, puberty, marriage, and birth. In conduct and organization, the "sacred" sanctions value, rule, and law.

Now what role does myth play in magic, religion, and morality? In all domains of the "sacred," man is required to act, often under considerable sacrifice to himself, in order to reach some ideal or goal. He has to undergo ordeals, to observe taboos, to forego comforts and endure privations, frequently for the benefit of others, always for advantages which are neither obvious nor immediate. To enforce the commandments of religion and magic a strong belief must exist that the promises or threats which sanction the commands are true. But man is more likely to believe in a future when he has some evidence of it from the past; he is more likely to act on a promise if there is a precedent to confirm it. There is no doubt, in fact, that the main cultural function of mythology is the establishment of precedent; the vindication of the truth of magic, of the binding forces of morals and law, of the real value of religious ritual, by a reference to events which have happened in a dim past, in the Golden Age of old, when there was more truth in the world, more divine influence, more virtue and happiness. Myth, coming from the true past, is the precedent which holds a promise of a

better future if only the evils of the present be overcome. It also usually indicates how the present can be vanquished with the help of ritual,
of religion, of moral precepts handed down from the past.

If with these principles in mind we look honestly at our own religion,
we can easily see how the story of Paradise, of the Fall, of the Expulsion,
of the Promise of a Redeemer, and finally, of the Redemption itself
gives the breath of life to Christian morality, to the Sacraments, and
even to such of the ritual as some of us follow. Nor are the savage
Australians, the Melanesians, or the African Negroes and Bantu different from us. Wherever we have a sufficiently full account of religion
and magic along with the narratives of folk-lore, it is possible to show
how deeply connected the two are, and how myth in its fundamental
function is neither explanatory, nor "wish-fulfilling," nor historical, but
essentially a precedent in support of religion and magical belief, or in
support of social and moral order.

To conclude then, we may say that no myth, no part of folk-lore
can ever be understood except as a living force in culture. The field
worker should not merely collect tales torn out of their context, but
observe the influence of myth on the social structure, the foundations
of man's power over nature as expressed in it, in short, he should study
the influence of mythological ideas on morality, on law, on magic, and
on the religious ceremonies side by side with the stories.

Dr. Holmberg's book makes a considerable advance toward the presentation of myth from this point of view. The volume gives remarkably
few stories, too few perhaps, and consists mainly in an account of the
various beliefs, practices, and institutions in which is embodied the
mythological world of the Siberian and Finno-Ugric races. The vivid,
convincing, and well documented picture of the material and spiritual
universe of the natives will rivet the attention of the casual readers
from start to finish, and prove invaluable as first-hand material to the
specialist. Scientifically the most important are those parts of the book
in which Dr. Holmberg shows the cultural life of sacred stories and
ideas and thus reveals the true nature and function of myth. Thus the
extraordinary cosmological concepts of some Siberians about the Pillar
of the World, which supports the sky and tethers the stars, are shown
to be connected with ancient forms of religious cult. Again in his account of Shamanism, Dr. Holmberg succeeds in giving a new, original,
and dramatic version. For he does not merely tell us about the Shaman,
nor is he satisfied to list the native beliefs on the subject; he shows us
the Shaman at work, predicting the future, curing sickness and causing
disease, surrounded by his familiar animals and guardian spirits, wielding
the instruments of his office: the hammer, the ring, and the drum—
and, withal, drawing a reasonable income from the supernatural trade

and enjoying considerable prestige. Dr. Holmberg also establishes a remarkable connection between Siberian Shamanism and totemism. He shows that both types of belief are rooted in the mythological idea that Shamanistic lineage on the one hand and magical powers on the other have been received from animals by human ancestors.

All these subjects will have an equal appeal to the student and to the layman, for Dr. Holmberg's style is vivid, his argument clear, and he knows the actors and the scenery from personal experience. The descriptions of the Arctic tundra, of the steppes, of the wide rivers of Eastern Europe and Siberia, are a fitting background to the contortions of the Shaman, to Spirits of Nature hovering among the stunted firs and birches, to the Living Stones—the Seide of Lapland—to the sacrifices of the Votiaks and Cheremiss made to their gods of nature among primeval groves on the plains of the Volga. All this Dr. Holmberg has seen with his own eyes and he conveys it to us well in his vivid description and in the excellent illustrations.

The insistence with which the real nature of myth and legend as the traditional precedent of belief, moral rule, and social organization is brought out in this volume is the natural outcome of a thorough knowledge of the material. And his method is the more convincing since the Finnish author does not seem to be aware of its theoretical importance. Indeed in the chapters on the Siberian Tree of Life and on the Mountain of the World with its manifold terraces, fascinated though we are by the narrative, we miss the fuller data which would allow us to judge whether these ideas are part of a larger system, or whether they influence ritual, cult, and conduct or whether they are mere literary fancies. Certain descriptions of nature-spirits, the Siberian beliefs on the stars and thunder, on fire and on wind, on the origin of the mosquito, as well as the Finno-Ugric account of ghosts are also incomplete in that the cultural context is not fully given. We would like to know how far the mythological belief in natural forces is connected with magical control of nature and how far this again is dependent upon economic pursuits.

The data on family gods, heroes, and household gods among Finno-Ugric peoples would gain by a fuller sociological account of tribal organization. But all such criticisms are merely the outcome of our appreciation of what Dr. Holmberg's work has already given us and a wish that, having gone so far on the right way he might have gone further. It might also be said that the author having shown the right way to approach myth, that is through the study of its cultural context, gives us perhaps too little of myth itself. No long narratives are told and even abridged stories are very sparsely adduced. They might almost be numbered on the fingers. It is certainly correct to start from the cultural approach to myth, but having reached it, it would be as well to indulge in a fuller treatment of it than is here given. Is myth inevitably condemned to fall between two stools, to be given only as an unintelligible story by one and to be practically omitted by the other?

In spite of this the volume is one of the best descriptions of primitive *Weltanschauung* and one of the most important additions to the science of myth that has recently been published. Great as is its intrinsic value, it becomes the more appreciable since the literature on Siberia and Eastern Europe is mostly written in Slavonic, Ugro-Finnish, or at best in Scandinavian languages, and is therefore inaccessible to the Western scholar. To read, moreover, an account of savage races written by a highly civilized member of one of them—even though that race has reached perhaps the highest level of culture—provides a rare anthropological thrill. And again, the peoples in the heart of Asia and Eastern Europe have, in many ways, influenced human history and human culture to a greater extent than any other race, partly because in their constant invasions of their richer, sedentary neighbors—the Chinese, the Europeans, the Semites, and the Hindus—they provided the dynamic factor of human history and progress, partly because they provide, most likely, the real link between the Old and the New World.

15

THE FOUNDATIONS OF FAITH AND MORALS

Preface

Anthropology is the comparative science of human cultures. It is often conceived as the study of man's savagery and of his exotic extravagances. Modern developments in the world's history, however, have made us uncertain whether we can trace a sharp line of distinction between *culture* and *savagery*. The student of human institutions and customs is, as a matter of method, also feeling less and less inclined to confine himself to the so-called primitive or simple cultures. He draws on the savageries of contemporary civilization as well as on the virtues and wisdom to be found among the humbler peoples of the world. By this very fact the Science of Man has a lesson to teach.

But the specifically scientific task of anthropology is to reveal the fundamental nature of human institutions through their comparative study. An inductive survey establishing the intrinsic similarity which underlies fortuitous variations discloses the nature of law and religion, of property and co-operation, of credit and moral confidence; it also yields the correct definition of such institutions as human marriage, family, Church, and State. What is common to all of them, *quod semper, quod ubique, quod ab initio*, constitutes obviously their essential character. In all this the Science of Man is gradually falling into line with other sciences, above all with the exact and natural disciplines.

To many a thinking man and woman one of the most important questions of the day is the place of religion in our modern culture. Is its influence on the wane? Has it failed us, say, in the last war and in the framing of the ensuing peace? Is it gradually receding from the

The following articles comprised the Riddell Memorial Lectures delivered before the University of Durham at Armstrong College, Newcastle-upon-Tyne, February 1935, and were published as a booklet by the Oxford University Press, London, in 1936.

dominant place which it ought to occupy in our public life and private concerns? The attacks on religion nowadays are many, the dangers and snags innumerable and obvious. Yet, here again, the comparative study of civilization teaches that the core of all sound communal life has always been a strong, living faith. What about our own civilization? Is there not a slight shifting of the function and substance of religious belief? Do we not observe the infiltration of extraneous dogmas, political and economic, into the place of the spiritual truths on which Christianity is based? Is it true that some modern political movements, Communism or Fascism, the belief in the saving power of the totalitarian state and of new Messiahs, brown-, red-, or black-shirted, are becoming, in form and function, the effective religion of the modern world?

From the scientific point of view we must first arrive at a clear conception of what religion is. And this can be best achieved by a comparative study of religious phenomena, carried out in the anthropological spirit. Such a survey will show that, as regards religion, form, function, and substance are not arbitrary. From the study of past religions, primitive and developed, we shall gain the conviction that religion has its specific part to play in every human culture; that this is fundamentally connected with faith in Providence, in immortality, and in the moral sense of the world; and that this faith in turn demands a technique for its expression, a technique which offers possibilities of communion and prayer, of revelation and miracle; finally, that every religion implies some reward of virtue and the punishment of sin.

The argument which will be presented in these lectures will carry to the thoughtful reader the lesson that substance and expression are deeply interwoven in all religious manifestations. It is a tragic error, therefore, to apply religious technique to ends which are extraneous to true faith, to ends which are partisan, political, or economic. A sound social life must be based upon a truly religious system of values, that is, one which reflects the revelation to us of the existence of spiritual and moral order. This does not mean that all the members of the society controlled by religious belief and ethics should be bigoted sectarians, or even practising believers. To plead for the application of ethical principles and the recognition of spiritual values in public life and national policy is not tantamount to the declaration of one's own adherence to any metaphysical or dogmatic system.

I, personally, am unable to accept any revealed religion, Christian or not. But even an agnostic has to live by faith—in the case of us, pre-war rationalists and liberals, by the faith in humanity and its powers of improvement. This faith allowed us to work in freedom of thought and independence of initiative for the progress of science and for the establishment of a commonwealth of free human beings. It allowed us to exercise our intellectual and artistic faculties, safeguarded as we were by democratic institutions, looking forward, as we were able, to the welfare of generations to come. This faith has been as rudely shaken by the War and its consequences as that of the Christian. Science has suffered. It has become enslaved and subordinated to political and partisan ends. Science, too, like Christianity, has failed us as a foundation for ethics and for constructive action. So that as a rationalist and a believer in the development of human personality and of a liberal commonwealth of free men, I find myself in the same predicament as that of a believing Christian. It is high time that the old, now essentially unreal, feud between science and religion should be ended, and that both should join hands against the common enemy. The common enemy, in my opinion, is the planned misuse of force on a large scale, and the national organization for an aimless and destructive struggle between the members of what is really one commonwealth, united by economic, cultural, and ethical interests.

For some time past I was working on the foundations for a full and reasoned statement of my belief in the value of religion. Keeping to my anthropological last, I was engaged in the collection of material for a book or a memoir, in which I proposed primarily to analyse the technique of religious expression in myth and dogma, in ritual and ceremonies, in ethics and the social influence of faith.[1] When I was invited to give the Riddell Memorial Lectures for the Session 1934–5, I felt that the scope of my inquiries fitted well into the terms of the Charter: "The subject-matter of the Lectures is to be the relation between Religion and contemporary development of Thought . . . with particular emphasis on and reference to the bearing of such development on the Ethics and Tenets of Christianity." I decided to submit a preliminary statement of my results, and thus to demonstrate the integrative function of Christianity in our own culture. The text of the lectures here presented must be regarded as a preliminary statement of my conclusions, documented by the most relevant and most telling facts. I have to thank the Committee of the Riddell Memorial Lectures for the permission granted me to republish, at a later date and in a fuller form, the material and conclusions here outlined. Since, however, the more extensive publication will be of a strictly technical character, and will be addressed primarily to the specialist in anthropology and comparative History of Religion, the lectures as they stand will in no way be superseded.

Department of Anthropology   B. M.
University of London

[1] In the collecting of the extensive material, only part of which is incorporated in this pamphlet, I was greatly helped by Miss Iris Harris and Miss N. Cohen, whose assistance was made possible by the generosity of the Rockefeller Foundation.

I

THE THREE ASPECTS OF RELIGION

Religion is a difficult and refractory subject of study. It seems futile to question that which contains the answers to all problems. It is not easy to dissect with the cold knife of logic what can only be accepted with a complete surrender of heart. It seems impossible to comprehend with reason that which encompasses mankind with love and supreme wisdom.

Nor is it easier for an atheist to study religion than for a deeply convinced believer. The rationalist denies the reality of religious experience. To him, the very fact of religion is a mystery over which he may smile, or by which he may be puzzled, but which, by his very admission, he is not qualified to fathom; it is difficult seriously to study facts which appear merely a snare, a delusion, or a trickery. Yet how can even a rationalist lightly dismiss those realities which have formed the very essence of truth and happiness to millions and hundreds of millions over thousands of years?

In another way the believer, too, is debarred from impartial study. For him one religion, his own, presents no problems. It is the Truth, the whole Truth, and nothing but the Truth. Especially if he be a fundamentalist, that is, unable to understand the foundations of human faith, he will simply disregard most religious phenomena as "superstitions" and will uphold his own views as Absolute Truth. And yet every one, the bigoted fundamentalist always excepted, might well pause and reflect on the way of his Providence which has vouchsafed the Truth to a small part of humanity, and has kept the rest of mankind in a state of perpetual darkness and error and thus condemned them to eternal perdition. Yet there may perhaps be room for a humble approach to all facts of human belief, in which the student investigates them with a sympathy which makes him almost a believer, but with an impartiality which does not allow him to dismiss all religions as erroneous whilst one remains true.

It is in this spirit that the anthropologist must approach the problems of primitive religion if he is to be of use in the understanding of the religious crises of our modern world. We must always keep in sight the relation of faith to human life, to the desires, difficulties, and hopes of human beings. Beliefs, which we so often dismiss as "superstition," as a symptom of savage crudeness or "prelogical mentality," must be understood; that is, their culturally valuable core must be brought to light. But belief is not the alpha and omega of religion: it is important to realize that man translates his confidence in spiritual powers into action; that in prayer and ceremonial, in rite and sacrament, he always attempts to keep in touch with that supernatural reality, the existence of which he affirms in his dogma. Again, we shall see that every religion, however humble, carries also instructions for a good life; it invariably provides its followers with an ethical system.

Every religion, primitive or developed, presents then three main aspects, dogmatic, ritual, and ethical. But the mere division or differentiation into three aspects is not sufficient. It is equally important to grasp the essential interrelation of these three aspects, to recognize that they are really only three facets of the same essential fact. In his dogmatic system, man affirms that Providence or spirits or supernatural powers exist. In his religious ritual he worships those entities and enters into relation with them, for revelation implies that such a relation is possible and necessary. Spirits, ancestral ghosts, or gods refuse to be ignored by man, and he in turn is in need of their assistance. The dependence on higher powers implies further the mutual dependence of man on his neighbour. You cannot worship in common without a common bond of mutual trust and assistance, that is, of charity and love. If God has created man in His own image, one image of God may not debase, defile, or destroy the other.

In discussing dogmatics, especially in primitive religions, we shall be met by what might be described as the mystery of myth. In all religions, Christianity and Judaism not excepted, we find that every tenet of belief, every dogmatic affirmation, has a tendency to be spun out into a long narrative. In other words, the abstract system of dogmatic principles is invariably bound up with a sacred history.

Minor characteristics, extravagances, and peculiarities of mythology have mostly attracted the interest of the student in the past and aroused his passion to explain them. The stories are at times crude, in some cases even obscene. This, within the general scope of our analysis, we shall not find difficult to understand: religious beliefs enter deeply into the essential facts of life, of which fertility and procreation are an essential part. Another peculiarity of myth is the frequent reference to natural phenomena, to features of the landscape, to quaint habits of animals and plants. This has often been accounted for in learned theories by the assumption that mythology is primitive science, and that its main function is to explain natural phenomena and the mysteries of the universe. Such theories we shall to a large extent have to dismiss or at least to correct. Primitive man has his science as well as his religion; a myth does not serve to explain phenomena but rather to regulate human actions.

The main problem of myth is in my opinion its relation to dogma; the fact that myth is an elaboration of an act of faith into an account of a definite concrete miracle. Why is this necessary? In the course of our analysis I hope to show that this is due to the very nature of life and faith. Faith is always based on primeval revelation, and revelation is a concrete event. In revelation God, or ancestral spirits, or culture heroes create and mould the universe, manifest their will and power to man. All this is a temporal process, a concrete sequence of activities, a set of dramatic performances. Man in turn reacts to this manifestation of supernatural power, he rebels and sins, gains knowledge, loses grace and regains it once more. Small wonder, then, that most of the dogmatic systems of mankind occur as a body of sacred tradition, as a set of stories stating the beginning of things and thus vouching for their reality. Again, since in myth we have an account of how Providence created man and revealed its reality to him, we usually find that myth contains also the prescription of how man has to worship Providence in order to remain in contact with it.

Thus the discussion of myth leads us directly to the riddle of ritual. Here, again, we shall not tarry over the sensational peculiarities of detail. We shall proceed at once to the central and fundamental problem: "Why ritual?" We may start here with the extreme Puritan's scorn and rejection of all ritualism, for this represents the voice of reason against the sensuous, almost physiological attitude of naïve faith. Incense, pictures, processions, fireworks are as incomprehensible, hence repugnant, to the highly refined and reflective type of religious consciousness as they are to the anti-religious rationalist. Ritualism is to reason, pure, or sublimated in religious feeling, always a form of idolatry, a return to magic. To the dispassionate student of all religions, who is not prepared to discount Roman Catholicism because he feels a deep admiration for the religion of Friends, nor yet to dismiss totemism because he appreciates its distance from the religion of Israel, ritual still remains a problem. Why has man to express such simple affirmations as the belief in the immortality of the soul, in the reality of a spiritual world, by antics, dramatized performances, by dancing, music, incense, by an elaboration, richness, and an extensiveness of collective action which often consumes an enormous amount of tribal or national energy and substance?

Here, again, our argument will not be a mere tilting at windmills. The usual scientific treatment of ritual, primitive and civilized, does not seem to me to be quite satisfactory. The conception, for instance, of primitive magic as "a false scientific technique" does not do justice to its cultural value. Yet one of the greatest contemporary anthropologists, Sir James Frazer, has to a certain extent given countenance to this conception. Freud's theory that magic is man's primitive belief in the "omnipotence of thought" would also dismiss primitive ritual as a colossal piece of pragmatic self-deception. The views here advanced will be that every ritual performance, from a piece of primitive Australian magic to a Corpus Christi procession, from an initiation ceremony to the Holy Mass, is a traditionally enacted miracle. In such a miracle the course of human life or of natural events is remodelled by the action of supernatural forces, which are released in a sacred, traditionally standardized act of the congregation or of the religious leader. The fact that every religious rite must contain an element of the miraculous will not appear to us an outgrowth of human childishness, of primeval stupidity (*Urdummheit*), nor yet a blind alley of primitive pseudo-science. To us it represents the very essence of religious faith. Man needs miracles not because he is benighted through primitive stupidity, through the trickery of a priesthood, or through being drugged with "the opiate for the masses," but because he realizes at every stage of his development that the powers of his body and of his mind are limited. It is rather the recognition of his practical and intellectual limitations, and not the illusion of the "omnipotence of thought," which leads man into ritualism; which makes him re-enact miracles, the feasibility of which he has accepted from his mythology.

The enigma of ethics, the question why every religion carries its own morals, is simpler. Why, in order to be decent and righteous, must man believe in the Devil as well as in God, in demons as well as in spirits, in the malice of his ancestral ghosts as well as in their benevolence? Here, once more, we have a host of theoretical conceptions, or misconceptions, dictated by hostility to religion or by the partisanship of sectarians. In order to safeguard ourselves against the superficial view that a sadistic priesthood has invented hell-fire so as to cow believers into doing what it wishes, we shall have to make an attempt at a real understanding of the phenomena. For, with all our sympathy for the religious attitude, we shall also have to reject the theological view that morality must be associated with dogma, because both have been vouchsafed to mankind by the One True Revelation. The correct answer to our problem lies in the social character of religion. That every organized belief implies a congregation, must have been felt by many thinkers instructed by scholarship and common sense. Yet, here again, science was slow to incorporate the dictates of simple and sound reason. Tylor and Bastian, Max Müller and Mannhardt treat religious systems as if they were philosophical or literary productions. The initiative in putting the sociological aspect of religion on the scientific map came from the Scottish divine and scholar, Robertson Smith. It was elaborated with precision, but also with exaggeration, by the French philosopher and sociologist, Durkheim.

The essentially sound methodological principle is that worship always happens in common because it touches common concerns of the community. And here, as our analysis will show, enters the ethical element intrinsically inherent in all religious activities. They always require efforts, discipline, and submission on the part of the individual for the good of the community. Taboos, vigils, religious exercises are essentially moral, not merely because they express submission of man to spiritual powers, but also because they are a sacrifice of man's personal comfort for the common weal. But there is another ethical aspect which, as we shall see, makes all religions moral in their very essence. Every cult is associated with a definite congregation: ancestor-worship is primarily based on the family; at times even on a wider group, the clan; at times it becomes tribal, when the ancestor spirit is that of a chief. The members of such a group of worshippers have natural duties towards each other. The sense of common responsibility, of reciprocal charity and goodwill, flows from the same fundamental idea and sentiment which moves clansmen, brothers, or tribesmen to common worship. I am my tribesman's brother, or my clansman's totemic kinsman, because we are all descended from the same being whom we worship in our ceremonies, to whom we sacrifice, and to whom we pray. We have only to change the word *descended* into *created* in order to pass to those religions which maintain as a fundamental principle the brotherhood of man, because he owes his existence to a Creator whom he addresses as "Our Father which art in Heaven." The conception of the Church as a big family is rooted in the very nature of religion.

These conclusions may seem simple, once they are stated directly. Fundamental scientific truths in physics and biology, as in the science of man, are never sophisticated. Yet, as I shall show later, even now anthropologist and missionary alike deny ethics to the heathen.

I hope that the perusal of the following lectures will supply the reader with what might be called a sound theoretical framework for the appraisal of other religious phenomena, primitive and civilized, ancient and modern, healthy and pathological.

II

A SOCIOLOGICAL DEFINITION OF MYTH

The central problem of myth has already been raised, and its answer foreshadowed. The problem is why dogma has a tendency to develop into a story; the answer suggested was that, since all dogmas are revealed, the story of the revelation has to be told so that the truth of the dogmas be founded in real historical fact. Turn to a collection of material such as Frazer's *Golden Bough* or his *Folk-Lore in the Old Testament* and you will find our contention fully documented. The belief in Providence and in the Great Architect of the universe is embodied in numberless mythological cosmologies. On the shores of the Pacific and on its many islands we are told how the world was fished out of the sea or moulded out of slime; or again, from other continents, we have stories relating how out of chaos the various parts or elements of the universe have been shaped in succession, or how the earth was hurled from space, or out of darkness, by a divine maker. The wide range of beliefs which are usually labelled "nature-worship" again have a rich mythology of totemic ancestors, of the early appearance and miraculous, though not always moral, behaviour of nature gods.

There is no doubt that all the stories of creation, of the first appearance of man, of the loss of worldly immortality and the translation to another world after death account to a certain extent for the existence of the world, of man, of after-life. But they are not scientific explanations. They are not taken as items of ordinary knowledge. They are regarded by the people as sacred; they are enacted by them in religious mysteries, sacrifices, and ceremonies; and they form the foundation, not only of faith, but also of religious law. To tell how God created the world is to affirm that God is not only the cause but also the end of all existence, the giver of all that is good and the source of all the laws of life. To tell how man lost eternal life on earth, and then was given an after-life, is to impart the dogma of the immortality of the soul, and through this to give the foundation of ancestor-worship, as well as the ritual of burial and mourning. To describe how man at one time descended from the animals gives a charter of totemic relationship for the members of a clan, who are still regarded as related to the animal species and can therefore control that species through ritual and magic.

Right through we can see, even at a cursory glance, how myth is a living reality, is active in ritual and in ethics, and is dramatically convincing as the foundation of dogma. The best way, perhaps, to bring home the significance of myth as a charter of belief, ritual, and ethics, is by analysing one example fully. It will provide us with what I understand is called, in the technical language of the moving pictures, a "close-up." I shall briefly show how I was forced to adopt this theory in the course of my experiences in field-work in Melanesia.

When I first went there I knew that every good ethnographer must collect "folk-lore." By the time I was able to use the vernacular, I was eagerly writing down any story which was told to me by a native. I collected tales about ogres and flying canoes, about malicious stepmothers and daring sailors, about the beginnings of magic and the queer pranks of an avaricious harlot. Gradually, however, it dawned on me that the natives themselves were aware of points in the performance which I was constantly missing; for I was collecting texts but disregarding contexts. In the course of time, I realized that the manner of telling a story and the way in which it was received, the circumstances under which the story was told and its immediate and also indirect influence, were quite as important as the text itself.

I missed not only the context of situation but very often the context of further elaborations and commentaries on the part of the natives.[2] After telling me some important or sacred story, the narrator would often

* The reader acquainted with the present writer's *Coral Gardens and their Magic,* 1935, and especially with the linguistic arguments of Vol. II, will understand what is meant by the term "context of situation" and the theoretical importance of this in the ethnographic treatment of human speech and folk-lore.

continue into what seemed to me entirely irrelevant verbosities. I still can remember the first time I was told the myth about the brother and sister incest.[3] After the tragic account was finished, my friend, who belonged to the community which "owns" this myth, began to boast: he told me how they and they alone have the power to enact properly the love-magic which is associated with the myth; how they have the right to levy toll on neighbouring communities; how certain spots in the territory are important for the correct carrying out of the magic. Feeling that the narrator was "rambling," I cut him short and told him that if the narrative was not finished he ought to continue it, but that if he had nothing more to tell of the story, I was not interested in his bragging. It was only later that I realized that in this very bragging lay what was perhaps the most important aspect of myth. My informant, in a characteristically boastful manner, was simply stating how the myth acts as a warrant for the correct performance of the magic; how it gives a right of ownership and control to the natives of the community where the magic originated, and from whence it draws its miraculous powers. He was, in short, giving me the sociological function of myth, in his naïve, concrete, and strongly personal manner. In the course of my work I discovered that such epilogues or appendixes to a narrative very often contain new and unexpected sidelights on ritual, on the rank or privileges of the communities, clans, and individuals, and on the way in which the very validity of magic was established in native belief.

In fact, with a better knowledge of the vernacular, I was forced to discriminate between several categories of folk-lore, and I had to base my discrimination not so much on differences in text, but rather in cultural setting.[4] I found that there is a class of stories which might be called fairy-tales or folk-tales. The natives call them *kukwanebu*. These are told during the rainy season when people are largely confined to the villages and, especially in the evenings, have nothing to do. They are told entirely for entertainment. Their subject-matter consists of grotesque, miraculous, and often bawdy events which appear in the same light to the natives as to the European listener. These stories definitely form what may be called tribal fiction—tales told for mere entertainment—and they do not convey any important truths, moral precepts, or ritual directions.

A second class, called *libogwo*, consists of historical legends, believed to be true, and usually told to enhance or define the status of a community, clan, or family. These stories as a rule contain little or nothing that is actually miraculous or extravagant, although they are not always free from exaggerations in the heroic line.

There is a third class of story, told for a very serious purpose, and

[3] Compare the last chapter of *Sexual Life of Savages,* and Part 2, Chapt. IV, of *Sex and Repression.*

[4] Compare *Myth in Primitive Psychology,* pp. 24–36.

connected with religious belief, social order, or moral issues, and last but not least with ritual. These stories, like the fairy-tales, have a strong tinge of the supernatural. But here the supernatural is not a mere trick of fancy, not an idle satisfaction of day-dreaming, but a miracle which is firmly believed in, a miracle, moreover, which, as likely as not, will be re-enacted in a partial and modified form through the ritual of native magic and religion.

Thus there exists a special class of story regarded as sacred, embodied in ritual, morals, and social organization, and constituting an integral and effective part of religion and magic. These stories do not live by idle interest; they are not narrated as historical accounts of ordinary facts. They are to the natives a statement of a higher and a more important truth, of a primeval reality, which is still regarded as the pattern and foundation of present-day life. The knowledge of the mythological past supplies man with the incentive, as well as with the justification, for ritual and moral action; it furnishes him with a body of indications and directions for the correct performance of the sacred acts.

If I wanted to convince you briefly of the correctness of my conclusions, and if I had the opportunity of transporting you to the Trobriand Islands for a short visit, I would first make you participate in a typical social gathering at which fairy-tales are recounted. You would find yourself among a hilarious gathering of people, invariably at dusk or at night, sitting round the fire, at times engaged in some manual work and listening to stories which they all know almost by heart, but to which they always respond with interruptions, repartees, and laughter. Many a man or woman "owns" a number of fairy-tales, that is, tales which he or she has appropriated by custom and practice. Such tales are often punctuated by ditties in which the other natives join in chorus. The jokes are often ribald and the audience responds or caps them with additional remarks.

It would have been an entirely different setting in which you would hear a native legend told naturally and spontaneously in the course of tribal life. We would have to visit some distant community, and there, perhaps at an historic spot, or in reference to the rights of ownership of another village, or in order to flatter the pride of a subclan, we would be told a tale which has all the hall-marks of an historical account. Stories of that nature would also be related at times of overseas sailing, or, in olden days, during a war between two groups of villages. We would then hear about famous exploits, shipwrecks and rescues, victories and fierce battles.[5]

But it is when tribal festivities or magical ceremonies are to be performed that the time for telling the most sacred tales is at hand. Thus,

[5] Some such stories the reader will find in my *Argonauts of the Western Pacific,* in Professor Seligman's *Melanesians of British New Guinea,* and in Dr. Fortune's *Sorcerers of Dobu.*

during the sacred season of harvest rejoicing, the younger generation are reminded by their elders that the spirits of their ancestors are about to return from the underworld and visit the ancestral village. The dogmatic substance of Trobriand belief about the fate of the soul after death, the nature of the underworld, and the various forms of communion between the living and the dead, are stated at that season more frequently than at any other time. The reality of the spirit world would also be present both in the mind and in the conversation of the natives on the occasion of death or when a big ceremonial distribution of wealth occurs to commemorate a recently deceased person.[6]

Thus during harvest and after, at the season of Milamala, when the spirits come for a few weeks and settle again in the villages, perched upon the trees or sneaking about the houses, sitting on high platforms specially erected for them, watching the dancing and partaking of the spiritual substance of the food and wealth displayed for them, the knowledge of the whole dogmatic system concerning spirits is necessary, and it is then imparted by the elder to the younger. Every one as yet uninformed is told that after death the spirit has to go to Tuma, the nether world associated with the small island of that name. He has to pass through a narrow cleft in the rocks which is the entrance to the nether world. On the way he encounters Topileta, the guardian of the spirit world, who must be offered gifts, the spiritual substance of the valuables with which the body is covered at death. After he has passed the entrance and satisfied the guardian of the dead, the spirit is received by friends and relatives to whom he tells news of the world of the living. And then he settles down to a second life, built very much on the pattern of the previous existence.

In order to keep in touch with the supernatural realities and happenings of the Milamala, it is necessary for every one to be instructed in the ways of spirits and on their behaviour: how they manifest their existence and how they can be reached by the living; how they show their anger and their pleasure. On the whole, adherence to custom and tradition pleases the ancestral ghosts, while neglect angers them. The rules of conduct of man towards spirits and their reactions to them are given, not in the form of abstract principles and precepts, but by telling the story of an occurrence. This is at times a recent event, at times very ancient, but it always points a moral and establishes a precedent. These stories have very often only a local currency. In one village I was told that three years ago the spirits spoiled a whole feasting and dancing season by inducing bad weather, destroying the crops, and sending sickness on the people, because the community had not obeyed its chief who wanted them to

<hr />

[6] A fuller documentation of the native belief in the spirit world will be found in an article entitled "Baloma, Spirits of the Dead in the Trobriand Islands," in the *Journal of the Royal Anthropological Institute*, 1916.

carry out their fishing magic according to old custom. Elsewhere, it was the unsatisfactory performance of a big mortuary feast, due to the meanness of the headman, which had irritated the spirits and made them show their displeasure by sending a set of calamities.

III

THE SPIRIT WORLD IN MYTH AND OBSERVANCE

But over and above such local minor myths there exist one or two stories referring to very ancient times and defining several of the fundamental tenets of native belief. The very existence of the other world and its place beneath the surface of the earth, in a different dimension, so to speak, is established by the story which might be called the Trobriand "myth of myths" about the first arrival of human beings on earth. Humanity, once upon a time, led an existence similar to that which the spirits now lead underground, in a shadowy world different from the present one. From thence they ascended to earth by crawling out through places of emergence, "holes" or "houses" as they are called.

The fact of broken existence, that is, the fact of death and continuance afterwards, is embodied in a tale of original immortality, of its loss, and of its partial retention in the survival after death. Originally every one was able to rejuvenate by the process now observed in snakes and other reptiles, by sloughing the skin. This might have continued up to the present, but for an original error or lapse of an innocent girl. It happened in the village of Bwadela. An old woman who dwelt there with her daughter and granddaughter went out one day for her regular rejuvenation trick. She took off her skin and threw it on the waters of a tidal creek, which, however, did not carry it away, as it was caught on a bush and stuck there. Rejuvenated, she came back as a young girl and joined her granddaughter, who was sitting at a distance. But the girl, instead of welcoming her grandmother, failed to recognize her, was frightened, and drove her away—a very serious insult among Trobrianders. The old woman, hurt and angry, went to the creek, picked up her old skin, donned it again, and came back in her wrinkled and decrepit form. From that moment, and in the fulfilment of the curse which the old woman put on her daughter and granddaughter, the rejuvenation process was lost once and for ever. It is characteristic here that we have, in a matrilineal society, one of the most important and dramatic occurrences in human history taking place between women of three generations. It is also characteristic that a small localized event has cast its blight upon the whole of humanity, even as an event happening in a small garden somewhere in Mesopotamia has blighted the life of that vast branch of humanity who

believe in the Old Testament. This story obviously receives its full significance only when we place it within the context of belief about death,
immortality, and the communion between the living and the dead.

On this last point the story is supplemented by another myth. For,
though human beings lost immortality and eventually died, yet the ghosts
remained in the villages and took part in ordinary life, even as these spirits
now do on their annual return after harvest. It was only when one of
the poor invisible ghosts, sneaking in at meal-time and snatching the
crumbs of the living, was scalded with hot broth, that a new crisis arrived.
After the spirit had expostulated, she, for it again was a woman, was told
by her daughter, "Oh, I thought you were away, I thought you were
only returning after harvest." The old woman, with insult and mortifica-
tion added to injury, retorted, "Good, I shall go to Tuma and live in the
underworld." From that time on, the spirits have dwelt in their own
realm and returned only once a year.

There is another set of beliefs, essential to our understanding of the
Trobrianders' attitude towards life and death and survival. These natives
might be said hardly to recognize death as an inevitable event, inextricably
bound up with the process of life and setting a natural term to it. Although they will admit that some people might die of old age or of an
accident, yet in the course of my inquiries I never came across a single
concrete case of "natural death." Every form of disease was conceived as
the result of witchcraft. An old man may be more susceptible to witchcraft, but the real cause of his death is always a specific act of sorcery,
to which also are attributed all the fatal accidents. Here, once more, we
have a rich mythology. A number of stories are told of how witchcraft
was brought upon mankind. These, perhaps, are less primeval in their
nature, for the Trobriander believes that witchcraft always existed outside his district, and he feels only the necessity of relating how it came to
the Trobriand archipelago. One story tells how a crab flew through the
air from a southern island nearer the mainland of New Guinea, and came
down on a spot on the north of the main island of the Trobriands, in a
district which now enjoys the reputation for most efficient sorcery. This
crab taught the members of the local clan how to bewitch others and kill
them, and this knowledge is still retained by the clansmen of to-day. On
the south of the island, again, we are told how a bad and malicious being
travelled in the hollow of a bamboo, and was stranded on the southern tip
of the main island. In another story we hear about a big tree, in which
malignant demons resided. When it was felled its tip touched the southern-
most point of the Trobriands, which became immediately peopled with
carriers of sorcery.

The mythology of witchcraft accounts for the fact that Black Art
flourishes in its most efficient form in the two districts, the one where
the crab fell and the other where the evil beings were conveyed from the

south. But the story does not contain merely an explanation. It is a sociological charter for the local inhabitants, who derive part of their income and most of their prestige from the fact that they are the accredited sorcerers of the district. They also teach sorcery to others for a substantial payment.

I have briefly summed up the main stories which refer to the phenomena of death and its causes, to survival and immortality, and to the communion between living and dead. Take one of these stories alone, and at first sight it might appear as if it were just a tale told in "explanation" of the loss of immortality, of the removal of spirits to another world, of the occurrence of witchcraft, of sickness and of death. This to a certain extent is true, for, if our theory is right, the essential nature of myth is that it serves as a precedent, and every precedent contains an element of explanation, for it is a prototype for subsequent cases.

But a precedent is not an explanation in the scientific sense; it does not account for subsequent events through the relation of cause and effect, or even of motive and consequence. In a way, it is the very opposite of scientific explanation, for it relates a complete change in the order of the universe to a singular dramatic event. It shows how the outburst of passion in the heart of an insulted and injured woman makes her throw away the benefits of immortality, undergo the ordeal of decrepitude and death, and all this in order to be able to curse posterity with the loss of eternal life. In short, myth is not a pseudo-science of nature; it is a history of the supernatural. It invariably refers to a unique break in the history of the world and mankind.

It is only by the ambiguous use of the word "explanation" that we could defend the aetiological theory of myth. Once this ambiguity is recognized there is no harm in fully illuminating how far and to what extent myth really satisfies the craving for explaining or accounting. The answer is that myth explains in so far as a precedent establishes new procedure; or as a creative act brings forth a new reality; or as a miracle accounts for something which is unaccountable on the basis of scientific knowledge. Mythology, then, is definitely the complement of what might be called the ordinary knowledge or science of primitive man, but not its substitute. It is true that the appearance of the Holy Virgin to Bernadette Soubirous explains the miracles of Lourdes, but we must distinguish this explanation from the axioms of biology, the generalizations of bacteriology, and the empirical rules of medical knowledge. Those who mistake primitive mythology for an equivalent of science should reflect on the relation of our own myth to our own academic disciplines. Perhaps the greatest shortcoming of the aetiological theory of myth is its denial of primitive knowledge. The so-called primitives do distinguish between natural and supernatural. They explain, not by telling a fairy-tale, but by reference to experience, logic, and common sense, even as we do. Since they have their own science, mythology cannot be their system of explanation in the scientific sense of the word. If in turn we try to define more clearly the exact manner in which myth *accounts for* the order of the universe and the life of man, we see immediately that the function of myth is specific: it serves as a foundation for belief, and establishes a precedent for the miracles of ritual and magic.

We can draw another conclusion from our analysis. It is incorrect to take one incident from a narrative or even one narrative in isolation from the others. It is only when we treat the whole cycle of stories connected with the fact of death and survival, and when we place this cycle within the context of native ritual behaviour and their moral attitudes, that we do justice to the cultural character and role of myth. The theory of myth, then, here propounded, implies a different treatment of empirical reality; it assigns to myth a different function from that of either explanation or allegory; it shows that the whole complex of cultural practices, beliefs, and myths expresses man's pragmatic reaction towards life and its vicissitudes; it refers to his emotions, forebodings, and to the ritualized behaviour in which these mental attitudes are expressed.

Let me further substantiate this by a brief summary of other types of Trobriand mythology. If I am correct in my theoretical handling of the facts, we ought to find sacred stories whenever there is an important dogma, a vital ritual, or some fundamental ethical process at stake. Apart from health, disease, and self-preservation, man is perhaps most concerned about two things: the satisfaction of his hunger and of his erotic impulses. As regards the first, the complex and elaborate system of food-providing processes intervenes between nature and man's square meal. The Trobrianders procure their food in several ways, of which two are primarily important. First, the fruits of the jungle are collected and the tubers of the gardens cultivated; second, the fish of sea and lagoon are caught. Now, as regards vegetable food, agriculture is highly developed and supplies them with their staple sustenance. Agriculture, therefore, constitutes for them the primary interest in life, since success in gardening means plenty and wealth, while failure means misery and starvation. There is a twofold set of activities connected with the raising of crops, the rational and the magical. In connexion with magic, there exists a mythology telling how a culture hero, Tudava, originally apportioned different measures of fertility, together with spells and rites, for the raising of crops. Those districts where he received a warm welcome were given good gardens, those who received him with hostility were penalized by arid soil and meagre gardens. This mythology serves to buttress the natives' confidence in their magic. Side by side with the main myth about the culture hero there exist also minor local myths, sometimes extremely brief and succinct but very important, myths in which the members of a community relate how their own local system came into being and why it is so very effective. But I need not enter into this aspect of magic and myth, for I have elaborated it elsewhere.[7]

Fishing, again, has an elaborate system of magic, and, connected with it, myths telling how the fishing of red mullet was instituted, again by Tudava, the culture hero; also how shark-fishing and its magic came into being in one of the villages of the north shore. In the matter of fishing, an interesting correlation can be established in the Trobriands. Wherever the pursuit is dangerous and its issues uncertain, there we have a highly developed magic and, connected with it, a mythology. Where, as in fishing by poison, there is no question about success and no tax on human skill, endurance, or courage, we find no magic and no mythology. And when it comes to minor economic pursuits, such as arts and crafts, hunting, the collection of roots, and the gathering of fruit, again neither magic nor mythology is to be found.

Returning once more to the main source of sustenance, that is, the soil and its products, one condition of fertility is essential, the right incidence of rain and sunshine. Since in this part of the world there is never danger of too much rain, while droughts occasionally occur, it is the timely arrival of rain which is the main source of anxiety. If rain fails for more than a year, the whole district suffers drought and famine sets in. Historical accounts of terrible years of starvation are told by the natives; and drought with its incident famine is always assigned to magic. The magic of rain and sunshine is vested in one person and one person only, that of the Paramount Chief of the district. It makes him the general benefactor of the whole tribe when things go well, even as he is the dispenser of punishment when his subjects have given him grounds for displeasure. The complex and elaborate system of rain and drought magic is again based upon a myth. This tells us how rain was born of a woman; how it had to be stored in one or two sacred spots, ever since important in magical ritual; and how the privilege of using this magic became finally vested in the family of the Tabalu, the paramount rulers of the district. In many ways this magic is the ultimate source of the chief's political power and of his personal prestige.

The most ambitious seafaring enterprise of the natives, the circular trade of valuables called *kula*, also has a system of magical practice and a number of myths associated with it.[8]

Love, like hunger and the fear of death, is always fraught with strong emotions, and anxieties, and forebodings. Nor does the course of love ever run smoothly. We are not surprised, therefore, to find a mythology and a magic associated with love. Here, the story of how an incestuous love-adventure between brother and sister was caused by the accidental misuse

[7] *Coral Gardens and their Magic,* 1935.

[8] Compare *Argonauts of the Western Pacific,* where a full description of the *kula* and its magic has been given.

of magic supplies not the explanation of the existence of love, nor yet of the use of magic. It establishes a powerful precedent and gives a certain community the charter for its performance.

The "close-up" of Trobriand mythology has allowed us to appreciate the cultural nature of myth on one example. Mythology, the system of sacred stories, constitutes the charter of social organization and the precedent of religious ritual. In this, mythology supplies the foundations of all belief, especially the belief about life after death and about the miraculous powers of magic and ceremonial. The sacred stories of the Trobrianders reveal how humanity has experienced the greatness of ancestors and culture heroes; how through dramatic events a new order became established or new principles introduced into human life; how the power of magic was given to men, how it was used or misused. Our analysis has proved to us also that, in Melanesia at least, myth must be studied within the context of social life. Since myth does not live by myth alone, but in so far as it influences art and dancing, social organization and economic activities, directly or indirectly through the ritual connected with them, the life of myth is not in its telling, but in the way it is fully enacted in tribal custom and ceremonial.

IV

THE SACRED STORY AND ITS CONTEXT OF CULTURE

Let us for the moment look up and away from the narrow technicalities of ethnography, and see what our conclusions mean as regards the nature of religion in general. First of all, our facts teach us one truth regarding the structure of Trobriand religion. Myth, ritual, and ethics are definitely but three facets of the same essential fact: a deep conviction about the existence of a spiritual reality which man attempts to control, and by which in turn man is controlled. Dogma, ritual, and ethics are therefore inseparable. Take the facts presented above about the mythological cycle of death, immortality, and the spirit world. We started from stories, but we were immediately led into a discussion of action directed towards the subject-matter of these stories, that is, a discussion of ritual. At Milamala we see how the ritual of give and take, the sacrifices to the spirits and their response, are the expression of the truth contained in mythology. And here ethics come in immediately, because the spirits and their reaction are determined by moral principles. You give offerings to the spirits of your own kindred, and they show their pleasure or displeasure by supernatural symptoms. But the spirits expect not only material gifts but also good behaviour. The spirits are in general conceived of as guardians of tradition. They will be satisfied when people follow custom, scrupulously carry out magic and observe taboos, conform to rules of family life, kinship, and of tribal organization. The two stock answers always given to the question why custom is observed and tradition followed are: "It has been ordained as of old," or else, "The spirits would be angry if we did not follow custom." If you press further as to who it is that has "ordained of old," reference will be made immediately to a specific myth; or you will perhaps be told, "Our ancestors in olden days always did that. They live now as spirits in the other world. They like us to behave as they did. They become angry and make things bad if we do not obey custom." In other words, the general principle of the observance of custom has its spiritual backing. It is directly connected with the whole body of tradition, and with the ritual enactment of this tradition. Take away from the natives the belief in the reality of their sacred lore, destroy their sense of the spirit world as it exists and acts upon them, and you will undermine their whole moral outlook.

The consideration of the norms and practices connected with death, burial, and mourning shows the close correlation between moral behaviour towards living and dead, ritual practice, and dogmatic belief. At the death of an individual a whole system of mortuary duties devolves on his immediate relatives.[9] The essence of these duties, from the sociological point of view, is that they reaffirm the bonds of marriage and the duties of children towards parents. In short, in its moral aspect, mortuary ritual is the religious extension of the ethical rules of conduct as between the members of the family, of the wider kindred group, and of the clan. Later on, when the spirits enter into a permanent or periodic and seasonal communion with the living, the family bonds and other social relations contracted in life become extended to the spirits beyond.

Such a communion between the living and the dead, based upon the pattern of earthly existence, is to be found wherever there is a belief in spirits, or any form of ancestor-worship or Manism. In Christian Europe on All Souls' Day, when people according to sect and nation commemorate at graves or carry out memorial services in the church, there exists this spiritual interaction between a man and the dead ones of his own family. The dead depend upon the prayers, masses, or, at least, on the loving memory of the survivors. The living turn to the dead for intercession in Heaven. The African, again, lives in a world determined for good and evil by ancestor spirits, the dispensers of good fortune and adversity alike. Health and disease, affluence and famine, victory and defeat are generally attributed to the goodwill of ancestral ghosts or to their displeasure respectively.

The relation between living and dead is realized in three ways. In every form of ancestor-worship, the belief is founded on that specific mythology which consists in family tradition, the knowledge of ancestral names, the personalities and exploits of the forebears in direct

[9] *Sexual Life of Savages*, Chapt. VI; *Crime and Custom*, pp. 33–34.

line, especially in the miraculous aspect. The ritual of sacrifices and devotion to ancestors is essential. Ritual, in turn, is necessarily permeated with ethics: the ancestors in spirit form, as the living parents, punish for bad behaviour and disrespect, and reward for good conduct and dutiful services. In all this we have gone beyond the Trobriands: our conclusions hold good for the Communion of Saints in Christianity, or for ancestor-worship in China or ancient Rome, in Bantu Africa or among the Pueblo Indians, in Australia or the Egypt of the pharaohs.

And here we can see how the substance of religious belief is not arbitrary. It grows out of the necessities of life. What is the root of all the beliefs connected with the human soul, with survival after death, with the spiritual elements in the universe? I think that all the phenomena generally described by such terms as animism, ancestor-worship, or belief in spirits and ghosts, have their root in man's integral attitude towards death. It is not mere philosophical reflection on the phenomena of death, nor yet mere curiosity, nor observations on dreams, apparitions, or trances, which really matter. Death as the extinction of one's own personality, or the disappearance of those who are near, who are loved, who have been friends and partners in life, is a fact which will always baffle human understanding and fundamentally upset the emotional constitution of man. It is a fact about which science and rational philosophy can tell nothing. It cuts across all human calculations. It thwarts all practical and rational efforts of man.

And here religious revelation steps in and affirms life after death, the immortality of the spirit, the possibilities of communion between living and dead. This revelation gives sense to life, and solves the contradictions and conflicts connected with the transience of human existence on earth. Religion, moreover, does not merely affirm an abstract truth as an idle comfort for thought and emotion. Through the revealed truth, and on its foundations, religion tells man how to behave, how to enter into relationship with the dead, how to better their existence and to gain their favour and assistance in turn. Mortuary ritual is the enactment of the truth of immortality. And, since the relations between living and dead are based on the moral principle of give and take; since they carry over the affection and mutual assistance from this world across the dividing line, they supply the supernatural sanction for family ethics. The affection of parents for their children, founded as it is in the physiology of reproduction, receives an additional dimension. Parents value their children and have to look after them with an additional concern, because, after death, they will be dependent on their services. The children grow up in a system under which parents and forebears are not only the dispensers of the good things of this world, but even after death will be able to assist or to harm with a supernatural might.

I have enlarged upon the one aspect of religion, illustrated by perhaps the most important myth of the Trobrianders and their most elaborate ritual, because I am convinced that the concern in the immortality of the soul is one of the two principal sources of religious inspiration. This belief is not in its essence a philosophical doctrine. It does not encroach upon the domain of knowledge. It is the outcome of the deepest human cravings, the result of that desire for continuity in human life and the traditional relationship between the generations, which is the very essence of human culture. Ceremonies and rites which immediately follow the death of an individual, services at burial, the commemoration of and the communion with the dead, are universal and are perhaps the most conspicuous phenomena of human religions. They are all the expression of this one main source of human faith, the desire for immortality.

What about the other myths and ceremonies which we have met in our brief survey of Trobriand religion? They consist mostly of mythology connected with magic—magic of love and of gardens, of war and of ceremonial exchange, of hunting, fishing, and sailing. Here we have an entirely different dogmatic element. The affirmation contained in this type of myth refers to a primeval power which man wielded over the unconquered and unconquerable forces of nature. Thus in one myth we are told that, since rain was born of a woman, she and her kindred, being of the nature of rain, were able to control it completely. The birth of rain was a miracle, and through this miracle man in a certain lineage was given the power of re-enacting minor miracles. In the same way, some people brought the magic of love with them. The myth tells us how the force of its magic was once revealed in breaking through the strongest prohibition, that of incest between brother and sister. That miracle, dreadful and wonderful at the same time, is the pattern on which at present the minor miracles of love-magic are believed to be possible. In pursuits where there is well-founded knowledge and where practice and hard work achieve part of the results, magic is resorted to in order to overcome those forces and elements which are governed only by chance. Thus in agriculture, in hunting and fishing, in war and in dangerous sailing, magic effects in a spiritual manner that which man cannot attain by his own efforts. Here the relation of mythologically founded dogma and ritual is as close as in the case of the communion between living and dead. It is only because man is in need of magic wherever his forces fail him that he must believe in his magical power, which is vouched for by myth. On the other hand, the primeval myth of the magical miracle is confirmed and repeated in every act of subsequent magic.

What is the common measure of all these beliefs in man's magical power, primeval and present? They are of the same substance as our belief in Providence. In almost every myth which has a charter of magical efficacy we have the affirmation of a fundamental bond of union

11

between man and the forces of nature and destiny. The mythology, which assigns common parentage to a particular lineage of man with rain or the fertility of plants, an animal species or wind, establishes a common measure between man and the relevant aspects of his environment. It submits those forces of rain, weather, fertility, vegetation, and fauna, which man needs, yet cannot practically master, to a superadded, supernatural control. Whether we call this type of belief totemism or zoolatry, or the religion of Mana, or preanimism, they achieve one main end. They humanize the outer world; they put man in harmony with his environment and destiny; they give him an inkling of a working Providence in the surrounding universe.

Here again it is very important to realize that the whole substance of Trobriand magic—and this is also true of Central Australian totemism, or of the fertility ritual of the Pueblo Indians, or of the rain ceremonial of the divine kings of Africa—remains completely outside the legitimate domain of science. It is an indispensable complement or counterpart of man's practical activities, but it never confuses or stultifies them.

V

TOTEMIC MIRACLES OF THE DESERT

We must, however, turn to some other ethnographic area and look at the facts more in detail once again. Unfortunately, few cultures have been studied with the all-round interest so indispensable to all functional analyses, that is, analyses of the mutual influence of religion and ordinary life, of magic and economics. We know a great deal, however, about the beliefs and practices of a small group of people in Central Australia, thanks mainly to the pioneering work of Spencer and Gillen.

Their ordinary existence, common to men and women, and concerned with the obtaining of food, with amusements, and the daily round of camp life, is based upon a different type of tradition. There is a body of rules, handed from one generation to another, which refers to the manner in which people live in their little shelters, make their fire by friction, collect their food and cook it, make love to each other, and quarrel. This secular tradition consists partly of customary or legal rules, determining the manner in which social life is conducted. But it also embodies rules of technique and behaviour in regard to environment. It is this aspect of secular tradition which corresponds to knowledge or science. The rules which we find here are completely independent of magic, of supernatural sanctions, and they are never accompanied by any ceremonial or ritual elements. When the native has to produce an implement, he does not refer to magic. He is strictly empirical, that is, scientific, in the choice of his material, in the manner in which he strikes, cuts, and polishes the blade. He relies completely on his skill, on his reason, and his endurance. There is no exaggeration in saying that in all matters where knowledge is sufficient the native relies on it exclusively. If you want to appreciate the amount of such knowledge, as well as the practical skill necessary for the production of the technological apparatus of the Central Australians, study chapters xxvi and xxvii in volume II of *The Arunta*, by Spencer and Gillen. The authors refer to the judicious choice of material suitable for a ground axe, or again for a chipped one. They tell us that in one case the "shape and finish is simply a question of material available," or again, we find that the hafting, in technique and material, depends on the purpose for which it is made. That this secular tradition is plastic, selective, and intelligent, and also well founded, can be seen from the fact that the native always adopts any new and suitable material. "Even amongst tribes that have had very little intercourse with white men, iron is beginning to replace stone." We might add that bottle-glass is rapidly ousting quartz or obsidian, woven materials are used instead of animal skins or bark-cloth, and kerosene-tins in Australia, as elsewhere, have become the most widely used water-vessels.

In his organized hunting the native also obeys an entirely secular tradition. He displays a great deal of skill, but also a considerable amount of knowledge, in stalking the kangaroo or wallaby, in following the emu and the euro. He knows the habits of the game, their watering-spots, the characteristics of the terrain. His capacities for finding his way where the European would get lost, in discovering hidden water or food-supplies inaccessible to the white man, are well known from the history of early exploration in Australia.

In short, the Central Australian possesses genuine science or knowledge, that is, tradition completely controlled by experience and reason, and completely unaffected by any mystical elements. I am emphasizing this because, in order to understand the supernatural, we have to see how the natural is defined in a given culture. The distinction, I believe, is universal. It is a mistake to assume that, at an early stage of development, man lived in a confused world, where the real and the unreal formed a medley, where mysticism and reason were as interchangeable as forged and real coin in a disorganized country. To us the most essential point about magic and religious ritual is that it steps in only where knowledge fails. Supernaturally founded ceremonial grows out of life, but it never stultifies the practical efforts of man. In his ritual of magic or religion, man attempts to enact miracles, not because he ignores the limitations of his mental powers, but, on the contrary, because he is fully cognizant of them. To go one step farther, the recognition of this seems to me indispensable if we want once and for ever to

establish the truth that religion has its own subject-matter, its own
legitimate field of development; that this must never encroach on the
domain where science, reason, and experience ought to remain supreme.
To-day this truth is important, not so much perhaps in the clash between science and religion, but rather in the encroachment of political,
economic, and pseudo-cultural doctrines of the Fascist and Communist
types upon the preserves of legitimate religion.

The Stone Age primitives whom we are considering, the Central Australians, do not make such a mistake. Their sacred tradition is concerned only with those things where experience and reason are of no
avail. The Central Australian may be guided by his own excellent knowledge in hunting and collecting, in finding water and in preparing his
implements, but one thing he cannot control, and that is the general
fertility of his environment, which depends upon the rainfall. If this be
adequate, then "as if by magic, the once arid land becomes covered
with luxuriant herbage"; plants, insects, marsupials, and birds abound,
and the native's prosperity sets in. If, on the other hand, the rainfall
fails, the species do not multiply, and he is faced with starvation and
misery.

Now in order to appreciate the essential difference between the technique of magical and ceremonial life on the one hand, and that of
ordinary economic activities on the other, let me once more describe
one totemic ceremony in detail. Were we to arrive at the proper time
of the year, before the beginning of the rains, somewhere near Alice
Springs in Central Australia, we could witness a typical ceremony, that
of the witchetty grub totem, and observe the behaviour of the men,
which is not that of ordinary everyday routine. Those who are about
to take part in the ceremony have to leave the camp quietly; they slink
out to a meeting-place which is not far off, but which is not supposed
to be known to any one who does not belong to the totem group. Only
a few of the older men of this group will remain in the camp, to keep
an eye on what is happening there. The performers are thus a group
united by the bonds of totemic identity; they are all reincarnations of
mythological ancestors, who once roamed the country and used to perform ceremonies identical in substance with the ones which their descendants are performing now. The group is organized: there is a leader;
there are distinctions according to age, degree of initiation, and of traditional knowledge.

The men adopt a behaviour, costume, and a mental attitude entirely
different from that of ordinary life. No one is allowed to carry weapons
or decorations; they must go quite unarmed, naked, discarding even the
hair-girdle, which is the one constant article of clothing worn by men.
Only the very old men are allowed to eat; the others, we are told, must
on no account partake of any food until the whole ceremony is over.

Even if some game is caught, this must be handed over to the old men. It is not only the season which is determined, but also the time of day. They start at dusk, so that they can spend the first night at a special camp. Place, like time, is strictly defined by tradition, which in this, as in everything else, follows mythological precedent.

In fact, since the whole country has been created with close reference to the concern and interests of man, above all to his ceremonial pre-occupations, there exists what might be described as a totemic geography or, at least, topography of specially sacred spots, which have been defined as the result of ceremonial activities of the past.[10]

> Every prominent, and many an insignificant, natural feature through-out this strip of country—the most picturesque part of the great central area of the continent—has some history attached to it. For example, a gaunt old gum tree, with a large projecting bole about the middle of the trunk, indicates the exact spot where an Alchera man, who was very full of eggs, arose when he was transformed out of a witchetty grub (*The Arunta*, p. 327).

It is in this scenery, impregnated with traditional memories of ancestral acts, that the ceremonies take place.

Each ancestral act was a creative miracle producing either a permanent feature of the landscape, or a sacred implement, or else directly producing animals or plants. For the time of the totemic ancestors was largely taken up with the enactment of totemic miracles, ceremonies through which individuals belonging to plant or animal species were created. And the rites of to-day are nothing else but repetitions, as exact as possible, of the ancient miracles, the tradition of which is preserved from generation to generation, not merely in memory, but also by the very fact that year after year they are performed, and their dramatic substance thus perpetuated in the behaviour of man.

The aim of the ceremonies is the same as it was; the technique is identical, and so is the social organization on which they are based. For, as already mentioned, even the members of the present-day group are the incarnations of individuals who lived in the Golden Age. Only the ceremonies have abated as regards miraculous intensity. To-day the totemic people cannot create mountains or canyons, cannot produce

[10] Cf. *The Arunta*, Vol. I, Chapt. V, where the formation of the landscape by the creative acts of the original world-makers is described. On pp. 88–91 a minute description with plans and diagrams is given of the spot at which the present ceremony takes place. This should be collated with the account of the ceremony in Vol. I, pp. 148–53. The mythological story of how both landscape and ceremony originated will be found on pp. 326–34. I am giving this information, since the writers do not cross-reference. The fact that they are apparently not aware how important is the parallelism between myth, ceremony, and the spiritual essence of the landscape increases the documentary value of their material.

fresh animal species or individuals, cannot change the shape of man or nature. The only thing which they can achieve is to contribute towards the fertility of their own totemic species.

Let us once more join our witchetty grub local clan and follow their ceremonial behaviour on the morning when they start their beneficent ritual. First of all they have to provide themselves with the liturgical implements; the men have to pluck twigs from the eucalyptus, while the leader carries a small wooden trough. This latter represents the *meimba*, the sacred vessel in which the culture hero, called Intwailiuka, carried his store of spirits and sacred bull-roarers. Here again the mythological implement, the original *meimba*, was miraculous in the extreme; its counter-part to-day still carries, as we shall see, some of its magical power. Provided with their liturgical implements, the natives now follow, with their leader in front, the path traversed by Intwailiuka, the totemic ancestor, who first created the ceremony and also the landscape. They reach the Great Cavity, high up on the western wall of the ravine. In spite of its name, it is only a shallow cave with a large block of quartzite surrounded by smaller stones. The culture hero was of course also responsible for producing these stones miraculously, and they represent the large body of the witchetty grub, which is the totemic animal of the group, whilst the small stones are the eggs. The head man of the group begins to sing, tapping the stone with his wooden trough, while the other men tap it with their twigs, and also chant songs. We are not given the text of these, but the authors tell us that the burden of them is an invitation to the animal to lay eggs. Complicated manipulations follow: the ceremonial stones are tapped with twig and trough; the leader takes up one of the smaller stones and strikes each man in the stomach, telling him, "You have eaten much food." The tapping of the stone produces grubs; the magical songs invite the animal to lay eggs; the anatomical ritual refers to the satiety which follows the plentiful supply of grubs, which again is the theme of the magic.

We cannot follow in detail all the acts. We should have to chant further with the natives at a place where the totemic ancestor used to cook, pulverize, and eat the grub. He was a great producer and also apparently a Gargantuan consumer of his totem. Then we should have to repair to the drawings (*op. cit.*, Fig. 44, facing p. 141), which were placed on the rocks, not by Intwailiuka, the totemic ancestor, but by Numbakulla, the First Creator. These drawings, as a matter of fact, also refer to subsequent events by one of those proleptic or prophetic acts of creation by which the First Creator anticipated the future. The totemic ancestor Intwailiuka used to stand here, throwing up the face of the rock numbers of sacred bull-roarers, and this is imitated now by the leader of the performing group. Although we are not told so explicitly, this also obviously contributes towards the fertility of the grub. A number of other ceremonial spots are visited; once more they chant, carrying on ritual activities in imitation of ancestral acts; over and over again the leader repeats the words, "You have eaten much food," thus magically anticipating plenty. There seem to be some ten of such spots, and at each of them the ceremony is carried out again. The totemic group of performers then move back towards the main camp, and not far from it they are met by the rest of the local population, men and women alike, who henceforth play a small and collateral part in the rest of the proceedings.

One element of these latter must be mentioned. While the totemic performers had been away, a long, narrow hut had been built, which is intended to represent the chrysalis case from which the fully developed insect emerges. When the party return, the people of the other moieties and the women assemble behind this hut-chrysalis. They range themselves, men of the other moiety in one group, the women of the same moiety in another, the women of the other moiety in a third. The totemic and class differentiations come always very much to the fore in such ceremonies. Now, in and around this hut-chrysalis, an important stage of the ceremony is performed, the men wriggling in and out, chanting songs about the animals in their various stages and about the sacred stones with magical import, created in ancestral, mythological times.

The most characteristic feature of the subsequent phase of the ceremony, where others participate, is the kind of ceremonial or magical give and take. This can only be understood by referring it to the social organization of these natives and to certain economic principles of their ceremonialism. The rites for the multiplication of the totemic species can be performed only by the members of the clan. It is not only their privilege, but also their duty towards the community as a whole, to carry out such rites. The natives believe deeply that the fertility of animals and plants depends on the magical co-operation of the totemic clans. Most totems are edible animals and plants, and apparently there is no important food-supply but is represented on the totemic list. There can therefore be no doubt that, in the aborigines' economic conception of the world, totemic co-operation is indispensable to human existence. The essence of this as a system among the Arunta consists, therefore, in each clan carrying out the ceremonial for the benefit of the rest. Although a man is not absolutely forbidden to eat of his totem, he eats sparingly, usually not at all, and he is debarred from eating the best part of his totem animal, when this is large and succulent, as the emu, the kangaroo, or the wallaby.[11] The clan as a whole, therefore, derives little if any benefit from its ceremony.

The ceremonial by-play which now takes place must be considered against the background of this totemic co-operation. The performing

[11] Cf. *The Arunta*, pp. 80–87.

party are expected by the others; they are welcomed by them, and at certain stages they receive food, which has been cooked for them, while they in return distribute some of their ornaments to the other people. The leader says: "Our increase ceremony is finished, the *Mulyanuka* (men of the other moiety) must have these things, or else our increase ceremony will not be successful, and so harm will come to us." Then the men of the other moiety approach, and the objects are divided among them.[12]

The dependence of present-day religious ceremonial on the supernatural reality of the Golden Age manifests itself in every detail of the above account. As regards the nature of the acts, that is, the magical rites, we can see at once that they have nothing to do with any practical work. To describe that sort of magic as pseudo-science, or the primitive counterpart of science, is not correct. There is in many details of the ceremonial an element of imitation, but the imitation is not of the animal, nor is it based on natural history. It is the imitation of ancestral behaviour, and it is based on the sacred tradition of myths. The native identifies himself with his totemic animal, but here again the identification is not between man as he is to-day and the kangaroo, emu, or grub as it now exists. In his ceremonial life, man becomes Alchera, that is, totemic ancestor, and he acts as an Alchera. The witchetty grub man goes back to the Golden Age, in which men and women of this clan were supposed "to have been full of eggs which are now represented by rounded water-worn stones," many of which, as we have seen, are actually manipulated in the sacred ceremony. Every act of this, and of any other, totemic ceremony in Central Australia is not an imitation of the animal species, but an imitation of the primeval, supernatural, half-animals half-men of which mythology teaches, and which were the ancestors of the present-day clan.

The Alchera were creative in a supernatural sense; the powers and influence of magic are again creative and supernatural in the very same sense, but with enormously reduced intensity. The supernatural, to the Arunta, is that power which the totemic ancestors fully possessed, since they were able to create the world, transform the landscape, make men, animals, and plants, and institute social order, customs, and ceremonies. Of this power man participates only in those activities which are ceremonial, and which have been handed down from the Alchera. In all other things man can only achieve what he produces by hard labour, by skill, and on the basis of his empirical knowledge.

In the analysis of the Central Australian tribes we have again found

[12] The full account of this ceremony will be found in *Native Tribes,* pp. 170 *sqq.,* and in *The Arunta,* Vol. I, pp. 148 *sqq.* Comparing the latter, which is also the later book, the student will be interested to note that the amplifications emphasize even more strongly the dependence of ritual on tradition.

a confirmation of our theory of myth and sacred tradition. We were able to arrive at conclusions which emphasized the profound difference between acts achieved by magic and religion, on the one hand, and those based on knowledge, on the other. This distinction is necessary for our theory of myth; it also implies this theory. Sacred tradition, we perceive more and more clearly, does not explain things; it tells us how they were created. This is not a scientific explanation, but a religious truth.

Let us go one step farther. What is the place of ceremonial or magic or ritual or religion, or whatever you like to call it, within the scheme of culture? What does the whole totemic ritual contribute to the tribal life of a Central Australian? From one point of view, we have to class it as a delusion or superstition, following in this the footsteps of Tylor. But there are elements in it which must be appraised in an entirely different manner. Taking native mythology and ritual together, we see that they contain two elements. From the dogmatic point of view, the creation of the world, the natural affinity between men and animals and plants, the reinterpretation of the landscape and all the natural features in terms of human interest, one and all establish a deep bond between man and his environment. Here, once more, we find a belief closely akin to our idea of a beneficent Providence, even as we have found another counterpart in the Trobriands. The Central Australian, living as he does in an arid, inhospitable, hostile country, has developed a system of beliefs which humanize the environment. Above all, the mythology and its dogmatic contents establish a close affinity between the socially organized groups of the natives and the vast range of animal and plant species, including most, probably all, of those which are useful to man. The limited knowledge of the Central Australian allows him to collect plants, grubs, and small marsupials, and to hunt the bigger animals. It allows him to produce the implements which he needs for this purpose, and the clothing and ornaments necessary in that climate. Where his knowledge fails him, where his scientifically logical and empirically orientated mind tells him that no effort of his body or mind will bring any results, there sacred tradition steps in.

Pragmatically speaking, this tradition helps him in the effective carrying out of his practical work. At the time when rains are due to come, and favourable weather may either fulfil his great expectations or adverse drought blight all his hopes, the native, instead of merely waiting in idle and demoralizing anxiety, marks time in carrying out his totemic ceremonies. Mythology teaches him that these ceremonies will contribute towards the fulfilment of his hopes. Far from being a harmful delusion which diverts his energies from useful pursuits, totemism brings about an integration of the individual mind, and an organization of collective activities, both directed towards the desired end. Magic is a system of collective suggestion, which at that critical season tells the Central Australian that all will be well, on condition that man obeys the behests of tradition and enters into communion with the supernatural essence of his world.

We have seen above that the totemic increase ceremonies are based on the ethical principle of co-operative services rendered by each totemic group to the whole community. That the benefits are, from the rational point of view, illusory does not diminish the ethical elements contained in this work done unselfishly for the benefit of others. It would be possible to go even farther and to show that the totemic ritual of the Central Australians exercises an important influence on the development of purely economic virtues. The ceremonies foster foresight, regularity, and organization of effort; they involve, perhaps, the greatest quantity of collective labour carried out by these natives. The fact that purely religious ceremonial creates labour-gangs, trained to work systematically, to obey the leadership of one man, to work for the benefit of the community as a whole, with direct reference to practical ends, is of no mean importance for economic evolution.[13]

I am enlarging on this, because the real importance of the so-called functional method in modern anthropology consists in the parallel study of mutually dependent phenomena or aspects of tribal life. The functional principle teaches that if you want to understand magic, you must go outside magic, and study economic ritual within the context of those practical activities in which it is really embedded. This principle, the theoretical importance of which I first conceived from the excellent material of Spencer and Gillen, I have later applied in field-work.

In the appreciation of Melanesian magic there is perhaps no more important truth to be recognized than its influence upon practical activities and the way in which it is determined by them. Those who glance over the pages of one or two of my books (*Argonauts*, but especially *Coral Gardens*) will find that magic is essentially an integrating and organizing force. It provides that spiritual strengthening of the individual mind and that discipline and preparation of the group which are necessary whenever the natives are confronted with a task difficult and not altogether controllable by knowledge and skill. Take their sailing, for instance. In the construction of their canoes, the organization of their crew, their choice of season, route, and sailing technique, they depend on a rational tradition. But the vicissitudes of sailing—wind and weather, reefs and calms—are beyond the control of Trobriander and European alike. So also, to a certain extent, is the reliability of the material from which a canoe is built, and the human element which the Trobriander will meet

[13] This was the thesis of my earliest essay, written in English and published under the title "The Economic Aspect of the Intichiuma Ceremonies," in *Festskrift tillagnad Edvard Westermarck*, Helsingfors, 1912.

at the other end of his expedition. For these unaccountable, uncontrollable elements, there exists magic: of mist and of wind, of shipwreck and of malevolence, of success in trading, and of benevolence of potential enemies. Individually, this magic means for every man confidence, optimism, preparedness. Socially, this magic emphasizes the prestige of its master. It gives him additional power and adds an element of strength to the social organization of the crew and of the whole body of the sailing expedition.

In agriculture, as I have shown with an almost tedious elaboration of detail, the same also obtains. Magic never encroaches on rational and practical work. The domain of intelligent effort and enlightened persistence on the one hand, of good luck on the other, are mutually exclusive. But magic adds to the zest and beauty of work: it introduces rhythm, punctuality, discipline, and order into the collective activities of the gardening team; it provides this team with a leader.

While the Australian evidence shows that economic virtues may be developed by magic in anticipation of their subsequent utility in organized production, the conditions in the Trobriand Islands present us with the economic function of magic fully established. An intermediate stage in this development we might perhaps find in the fertility ceremonies of the Pueblo Indians, with which we shall deal very briefly, only showing that the functional nature of myth and ritual in that area falls within the scope of our analysis.

VI

THE EVIDENCE OF OTHER ETHNOGRAPHIC AREAS

In a brief and simple statement of anthropological theory it is always best to demonstrate the principles by giving one or two examples, taken from well-known and fully documented areas. I have based my conclusions on Central Australia because our material is exceptionally good, and on the Trobriand Islands because I know this region from personal experience. What about the wider validity of the present theory?

I have been attempting to demonstrate that the substance of religion, that is, its subject-matter, is not arbitrary. The twin beliefs in immortality and in Providence grow out of the necessities of human life. They step in as all-powerful, beneficent cultural forces, integrating the individual mind and organizing social grouping. The two beliefs, moreover, as we have seen, would not be alive if they were mere abstract formulae. They are believed because they are human experiences present and past. All religion is founded on revealed truth because man had to experience the reality of the supernatural in order to accept it. This revelation may be contemporary: miracles must occur, and do occur, in every live religion. As a rule, however, the great miracles of religion come from the past. They are handed down through an age-long, venerable tradition. Conformity, whole-hearted submission to traditional biddings, is perhaps the most important moral force in any healthy society, primitive or civilized. The existence of such ethical influence we have fully established both in Central Australia and in the Trobriand belief in spirit life and magical power. The other active and pragmatic manifestation of every religious belief is the enactment of limited miracles of magic and ritual.

In one way, perhaps, it is the concept of miracle which forms the core of my theoretical approach. The word "miracle" is, in theology, restricted to more spectacular events, above all to the tangible, concrete, sensuously appreciable workings of supernatural force, which fall outside the established course of nature. Thus the theologian would class the production of wine at Cana, the multiplication of bread and fishes, the resurrection of Lazarus, as miracles, but he would refuse the title of miracle to the supernatural processes which take place in the Sacrament.[14] For the theologian regards these events as falling under the law of nature of the supernatural.

I submit, however, that the anthropologist, or any scientific student of the history of religions, must redefine the crude, popular language which, in this case, the theologian seems inclined to accept. To the scientific mind any event in which supernatural forces manifest themselves, whether to the bodily eyes or to the vision of faith, must belong to the same category. The transformation of the earthly substance of bread and wine into the real body and blood of Jesus Christ, for instance, is a miracle in so far as the Real Presence is assumed. Again, the complete change of the substance of the human soul in the sacrament of the remission of sins is as genuine a miracle as a complete change in bodily metabolism produced, let us say, by the water of Lourdes. In one way, the scientific approach is here more religious and reverent than that of the theologian. The anthropologist dissociates himself resolutely from doubting Thomas and the theologian alike; he places the spiritual reality assumed by religious faith on the same level as the material reality accessible to the senses. Actually, what the scientist follows in his classification is the whole cultural setting and attitude of the faithful. He draws the line of distinction, not by the naïve, crude criteria of sight, sound, touch, or smell, as opposed to mystical experience. The line of demarcation must be scientifically drawn between phenomena where nothing but physical events occur, and those where supernatural forces enter as cause or effect.

Let me exemplify my point by the miracle of Bolsena. Here we have a

[14] Cf. the articles s.v. "Miracles" in *Hastings' Encyclopaedia* and the *Roman Catholic Encyclopaedia*.

genuine myth, not only attested by Catholic writers, but embodied in one of the most magnificent churches of Christendom, and in some of the most famous paintings, notably the *Stanza* of Rafael. Those who have seen the latter, especially the detail of the bleeding Host, those who have visited the Cathedral of Orvieto, where the miracle is confirmed by the sacred relic and represented in fresco and enamel work, will realize how myth becomes monumentally translated into works of art. The story itself tells how a Bohemian priest, sceptical as to the doctrine of transubstantiation, became convinced by a miracle which occurred between his own fingers while he was celebrating the Holy Mass in the town of Bolsena. In the very act of consecration, and between the words, he had an access of doubt, and then the miracle happened. Blood overflowed in the chalice; the Host became covered with drops of blood; the whole congregation saw this. Indeed, the whole of Christendom was so impressed by this visible manifestation of the Real Presence that the Pope not only ordered the building of the Cathedral of Orvieto, but also instituted the festival of Corpus Christi. We have here in one event the ritual consequence of the myth.

But what is really important here is the relation between the ordinary miracle of consecration and its spectacular manifestation at Bolsena. From the religious point of view it would be worse than heresy to affirm that the true miracle of our religion, the Real Presence of the body and blood of Jesus Christ, was any more genuine, or real, or factual on that one occasion than on any other.[15] The miracle did not change anything in the true substance of the mystical reality. It was merely a sign; but even this sign to the truly faithful is unnecessary, since the sacrament itself is the sign. Where does the miracle then reside? Its reality lies in the invisible grace which makes the sacrament of transubstantiation the very epitome of everything that the Catholic believes: the incarnation of the Second Person of the Trinity, His sacrifice on Calvary, and the institution of the sacrament by which He perpetually reappears on earth and unites Himself with every believer in the Sacrament of the Communion.

From this one example we can see that the only scientifically correct definition of miracle is as an event in which supernatural realities are created by ritual acts. The miracle of magic, the utterances of words, and the performance of gesture are supernatural forces which, through a supernatural mechanism, bring about natural events. In the miracles of sacrifice or sacrament we have again words and gestures which bring about events as real and true, but supersensuous because spiritual in nature. The reality of both has to be vouched for by experience: we know that the Sacrament of Communion is true because it was instituted

[15] I am writing this, of course, as a good anthropologist, from the strictly Roman Catholic point of view, in which, moreover, I was brought up.

by Jesus Christ during the Last Supper, and also because at every Communion the believer mystically experiences the divine grace which comes from the union with God. We know that the miracles at Lourdes are true, because there is a running tradition of miraculous healing, but above all, because the Virgin Mary appeared to the poor shepherdess.

And here we come immediately upon the very essence of myth: it is above all, as has been so often emphasized, the affirmation of primeval miracles. I think it would be interesting to survey from this point of view other examples of belief and ritual. There is no doubt that in some religions the element of the miraculous is almost negligible. Let us take an area known to me from a four weeks' visit, in which I was, however, conducted by an expert anthropologist who had remained there two years, Dr. I. A. Richards, to whom I am entirely indebted for the following information, given me both in the field and in London. The religious life of these people, the Bemba of Northern Rhodesia, is almost completely devoid of anything which would fall into the category of the directly miraculous. They very seldom even ask for a specific result of prayer, sacrifice, or rite. The ancestral spirits are asked for blessings in general, for peace, health, and prosperity of the land. "May we go in peace, give us life, give us children." The spirits are begged in general to promote the welfare of the group, heal sickness, or bring rain.

Consequently, since there is no definite request or attempt to bring about a specific effect, there is very little need for an empirical testimony of clear-cut results. The mythology of the Bemba is accordingly extremely poor. But even they have a legendary cycle connected with the first man who, from the north-west, entered the territory at present occupied by the tribe. This man, Lucelenganga, received the knowledge of medicine and of magic from the High God. Before that, "All the magical trees and herbs were in the country, but we did not know how to use them." The tradition was carried on because Lucelenganga selected the most intelligent men living and taught them the magic of healing medicine. This legendary background is not a mere story, but lives in ritual. The witch-doctor, *shinganga,* to-day calls upon Leza the High God when digging his herbs and roots, and addresses Lucelenganga by name when mixing his medicines or divining. A witch-doctor utters these words: "You, Lucelenganga, who left your footsteps on the rock and the footsteps of your dog, give strength to my medicine." Or else he repeats the same initial words and says ". . . make the words of my divination true." A witch-doctor has also to add the names of the actual ancestors or predecessors from whom he has bought or learnt the use of the medicine. The footsteps mentioned in the incantation refer to a natural feature in the landscape which the natives still show, and which they attribute to the heavy tread of Lucelenganga as he first passed through the country.

We have here, therefore, not a complete absence of mythology, but rather mythology reduced to a bare outline. In its sober and limited way, we have the same appeal to the continuity of tradition, the same reference to the divine sources of supernatural power. The mentioning of names of predecessors and of ancestors is, incidentally, a very prominent feature of the Melanesian language of magic.[16]

From my very rapid and rather superficial survey of East African tribes, I have come to the conclusion that mythology is not completely absent, though it plays a far more limited part than in Melanesia or in Central Australia. But here only very careful analysis of the character of ritual and its supernatural context, with direct reference to what might be called the historical records of the effects of ritual, can give a satisfactory answer. For mythology flourishes not only in the dim, distant past: there is also the living, current mythology of contemporary miracle or supernatural manifestation of divine power. In Lourdes such mythology is recorded in the scientifically attested chronicle of miraculous healings. Manifestations of the supernatural power of saints are recorded again in the chronicles of Roman Catholic hagiology. Such records have to be kept, because the canonization of saints is contingent on the occurrence of at least two well-attested miracles. Christian Science, spiritism, faith healing, palmistry attract and retain their faithful, or their customers, by alleged empirical proof or claim of miracles achieved.

Once we define myth as a sacred tradition which exists in order to attest the reality of any specific vehicle, channel, or mechanism by which the supernatural can be tapped or moved, it becomes quite clear that, on the one hand, it is idle to argue whether there are myths unconnected with religion. On the other hand, it is equally barren to study any religious ritual or ethics without seeking to discover how far the dogmas involved have that empirical and historical background of attested occurrences which we define as the only legitimate sphere of mythology or sacred tradition.

The point of view, therefore, here adopted with regard to myth really turns on the question whether we define myth in a purely mechanical and formal way, or functionally, that is, by the role it performs in culture. As long as the purely formal approach dominates, we shall have in ethnography collections of "folk-lore" and descriptions of "ritual" and "ceremonialism" entirely unrelated to each other, and it will be difficult to prove the point of the present theory, or to appreciate the living reality of religion in such artificially dissected material. The formal point of view of which I am complaining still does predominate. Even a competent American anthropologist tells us that it is quite impossible "to generalise

---

[16] Cf. the present writer's *Coral Gardens and their Magic*, Vol. II, part vi, "An Ethnographic Theory of the Magical Word," and part vii, "Magical Formulae."

as to the degree to which myth is dynamic in religion." [17] This misconception is based simply on a formal and, to me, barren definition of the term "myth." This writer, incidentally, affirms that the "dairy ritual of the Todas seems unsupported in myth, and the gods mentioned in the prayers are on the level of mere abracadabra" (*loc. cit.*). Yet the student who turns to the source, the book by W. H. R. Rivers on the Todas, can see from pp. 182 *sqq.*, and also p. 246, that a knowledge of their mythology is indispensable in order to understand the ceremonies and the prayers connected with the dairy or with the village. The prayers contain "references to various incidents in the lives of the gods, and many of the clauses would be unintelligible without a knowledge of these lives." The Toda god is distinctly anthropomorphic, lives the same life as the present-day Toda, and tends his dairies and buffaloes. So close is the relation between present-day life and the mythological background that the Todas regard their sacred dairies as the property of the gods, while the dairymen are looked upon as priests. Indeed, Rivers tells us that there was "a period when gods and men inhabited the hills together. The gods ruled the men, ordained how they should live and originated the various customs of the people"; and again, "According to tradition, the most sacred dairies . . . date back to the time when the gods were active on earth and were themselves dairymen."

This is, I think, sufficient to show how badly my critic has selected her negative example to prove the inadequacy of my theories. Were we engaged in a specialized anthropological discussion, it would be possible and also advisable to scrutinize the material presented by Rivers about the Todas more in detail. It would confirm our theory of myth and its relation to ritual, and the essential correlation between ethics and religion. We might discuss some of the interesting material collected by Professor Radcliffe-Brown on the mythology and religious ritual of the Andaman Islanders, and their influence one on the other. I should have liked to join issue with this author in his theoretical interpretation of myth. For he regards myth as a form of primitive philosophy by which early man establishes his system of social values. These latter, however, Radcliffe-Brown does not attempt to correlate with practical activities.

Polynesian mythology and its place in religion would lend itself especially well to a functional analysis of the ethical and cultural influence of tradition.

The area, however, to which I should like to refer the specialist, and about which I should like to say a few words to the general reader, is that known in ethnography as the Pueblos. To the popular imagination they have been made attractive by the writings of D. H. Lawrence and Aldous Huxley, by the glamour of their archaeological past still surviving in

[17] Dr. Ruth Benedict in the article on "Myth" in the *Encyclopaedia of Social Sciences,* New York, 1933.

mighty ruins, and by the legendary stories which have hung round them ever since the early Spanish explorations. We have also some really good anthropological material on these people, and, what is useful to the layman, one or two excellent summaries of their main cultural and social characteristics.[18]

The religion of these Indians is dominated completely by their dependency on rain and sunshine, by their interest in their fields, and also by their desire for the fertility of women. The religion is carried out partly in the form of public ceremonies, partly by private prayers and offerings. These are directed to superhuman beings associated with such natural phenomena as the sun, the earth, fire, and water. It is about these beings that a very rich mythology flourishes.

There is, however, another class of supernatural beings, the Kachinas, who are regarded as ancestors, and of which the visible representation appears during the ceremonial season in the form of masked dancers. Most of the ceremonial is, from the social point of view, connected with the organization of the Pueblos into religious fraternities or priesthoods. These are often named after animals and objects of worship, and they claim mystical affinities with snake and with fire, with antelope and with lightning, affinities again recorded in the stories of native mythology.

A brief outline of the nature of Hopi religion will best be given in the words of Dr. Murdoch, who, without any theoretical preconceptions in favour of our thesis, yet summarizes the state of affairs almost in the terms adopted in the present essay.

> An agricultural people inhabiting a cool and arid region needs, above all things, warmth and rain for the growth of its crops. It is understandable, consequently, that Hopi should worship a Sky God who brings rain, an Earth Goddess who nourishes the seed, and a Sun God who matures the crops, as well as a special Corn Mother and a God of Growth or Germination. Moreover, the essential summer rains fall only in sudden torrential thunderstorms at irregular and unpredictable inter-

[18] A good, brief, and comprehensive account of one of the groups of the Pueblos is given by G. P. Murdoch in *Our Primitive Contemporaries*, New York, 1934. The chapter on the "Pueblos of New Mexico" in *Patterns of Culture*, London, 1935, by Dr. Ruth Benedict, gives a very vivid picture, based partly on her own observations. My own brief survey was enriched by information generously given me by Mrs. Robert Aitken (Miss Barbara Freire-Marecco), who has intensively studied the Tewa on the First Mesa. During a short visit there and among other settlements of the Pueblo, I was able to gain a concrete impression, and had the good luck to be present at one of the Kachina dances at Oraibi. The writings of Fewkes, of Voth, and of Curtis, valuable though they are, suffer from the "false anatomy," the complete severing of mythology from ritual and the treatment of the latter as if it were performed by marionettes. A good compensation for that is to be found in the short but excellent monograph by Dr. H. K. Haeberlin, *The Idea of Fertility among the Pueblo Indians*, 1916, which is one of the pioneering works in functional anthropology.

vals; sometimes they fail entirely, or an unseasonable frost or severe windstorm blights the crops. Thus man's very existence depends upon an element of chance which manifests itself in ways so violent and seemingly arbitrary that they suggest the agency of supernatural powers as capricious as they are mighty. It is but natural, therefore, that the Hopi should bend every effort to control these unseen powers through propitiation and coercion.[19]

It remains only to add that all the efforts to control the Unseen Powers are carried out according to prescriptions mostly derived from the mythological past.

The function of Hopi religion, therefore, is identical with that which we established on the basis of the Trobriand material and which we also discovered in Central Australia. For these natives too have conceived of a vast supernatural world, superimposed on their empirical reality. To propitiate this supernatural world by ritual, to establish concord between man and the Universe by the observance of ethical rules, occupies half of the Pueblos' existence. For the ethical element is prominent in Pueblo religion. ". . . the Pueblos show a great advance over many primitive tribes in that their legends and their priests reiterate constantly that 'prayer is not effective except the heart be good' ".[20]

In scanning the detailed descriptions of Pueblo ritual contained in the many volumes of Curtis, Fewkes, or [Henry R.] Voth, we can see that this inner purity of heart is actually obtained by following a whole system of lustrations, of abstinences, and by keeping a strict control of passions. "One of the obligations that rest upon every priest and official during the time when he is actively participating in religious observances is that of feeling no anger." [21] Virtue and morality in ordinary conduct of life are also enjoined under supernatural sanctions. The failure of crops

[19] *Op. cit.*, p. 348.

[20] M. R. Coolidge, *The Rainmakers (Indians of Arizona and New Mexico)*, 1929, p. 204. The same writer speaks also about the goodness, unselfishness, truth-telling, respect for property, family and filial duty of the natives, and affirms that these virtues are "closely connected with religious belief and conduct, but not their principal object." With this latter part I would agree, but it is the connexion of ethics with religious belief and ritual which is too often overlooked in ethnographic theories and observations.

[21] R. Benedict, *op. cit.*, p. 61. This author adds that "anger is not tabu in order to facilitate communication with a righteous god who can only be approached by those with a clean heart. It is rather a sign of concentration upon supernatural affairs, a state of mind that constrains the supernaturals and makes it impossible for them to withhold their share of the bargain. It has magical efficacy." I cannot follow this argument. The very fact that a complete concentration of mind is necessary and that all passions must be excluded when we approach God is essentially a moral rule. The fact that, in order to attain magical efficacy, we must pay undivided attention to our spiritual communion, demands what every theologian as well as the anthropologist or the man in the street would call "a clean heart."

is attributed to adultery quite as much as to insufficiency in ceremonial. And here it is interesting to note that such moral precepts are based on mythological foundations. For one of the main culture heroes of the people, Alosaka, is described in one of the myths as being so thoroughly disgusted when his wife was seduced and the people ravished women and attacked the old, that he departed from this earth together with the miraculous bounty he had brought, and returned to his mother, the Earth Woman. The ethical *motif* can be found throughout Pueblo mythology. Politeness, goodwill, offerings on the part of the culture heroes towards gods are rewarded; evil deeds are punished.

I cannot enter, however, into the details of myth and ritual, and must remain satisfied with the brief indication that, in Pueblo culture, not only are myth and ritual closely connected with each other and with ethics, but the whole religion is a by-product of man's adaptation to his environment.

VII

CONCLUSIONS ON THE ANATOMY AND PATHOLOGY OF RELIGION

From our brief ethnographic survey we can conclude that the scientific analysis of religion is possible, for there are common elements in all religious systems as regards substance, form, and function. Every organized faith, we have seen, must carry its specific apparatus, by which it expresses its substance. There must be a dogmatic system backed by mythology or sacred tradition; a developed ritual in which man acts on his belief and communes with the powers of the unseen world; there must also be an ethical code of rules which binds the faithful and determines their behaviour towards each other and towards the things they worship. This structure or form of religion can be traced in totemism and animism, in ancestor-worship as well as in the most developed monotheistic systems.

We find, moreover, that there exists an intrinsically appropriate subject-matter in every religious system, a subject-matter which finds its natural expression in the religious technique of ritual and ethics, and its validation in sacred history. This subject-matter can be summed up as the twin beliefs in Providence and in Immortality. By belief in Providence we understand the mystical conviction that there exist in the universe forces or persons who guide man, who are in sympathy with man's destinies, and who can be propitiated by man. This concept completely covers the Christian's faith in God, One and Indivisible though present in Three Persons, who has created the world and guides it to-day. It embraces also the many forms of polytheistic paganism: the belief in ancestor ghosts and guardian spirits. Even the so-called totemic religions, based on the conviction that man's social and cultural order is duplicated in a spiritual dimension, through which he can control the natural forces of fertility and of the environment, are but a rude version of the belief in Providence. For they allow man to get in touch with the spiritual essence of animal or plant species, to honour them and fulfil duties towards them, in return for their yielding to his needs. The belief in Immortality in our higher religions is akin to that of primitive creeds, some of which only affirm a limited continuance after death, while others assume an immortality consisting in repeated acts of reincarnation.

The substance of all religion is thus deeply rooted in human life; it grows out of the necessities of life. In other words, religion fulfils a definite cultural function in every human society. This is not a platitude. It contains a scientific refutation of the repeated attacks on religion by the less enlightened rationalists. If religion is indispensable to the integration of the community, just because it satisfies spiritual needs by giving man certain truths and teaching him how to use these truths, then it is impossible to regard religion as a trickery, as an "opiate for the masses," as an invention of priests, capitalists, or any other servants of vested interests.

The scientific treatment of religion implies above all a clear analysis of how it grows out of the necessities of human life. One line of approach consists in the study of sacraments, that is, those religious acts which consecrate the crises of human life, at birth, at puberty, at marriage, and above all at death. In these religion gives a sense and a direction to the course of life and to the value of personality. It binds the individual to the other members of his family, his clan or tribe, and it keeps him in constant relation with the spiritual world.

Another empirical approach shows how magical and religious phenomena are directly dictated to man by the stresses and strains of life, and the necessity of facing heavy odds; how faith and ritual must follow the darker, more dangerous, and more tragic aspects of man's practical labours. Here the material foundations of man's life ought to be scrutinized. Agriculture, with its principal condition of rainfall and sunshine, leads to the magic of fertility, to an elaborate ritual of sowing, flowering, harvest, and first-fruits, and to the institution of divine kings and chiefs. Primitive food-gathering produces ceremonies of the Intichiuma type. Hazardous pursuits, such as hunting and fishing, sailing and distant trading, yield their own type of ritual, belief, and ethical rules. The vicissitudes of war and love are also rich in magical concomitants. Religion, no doubt, combines all these elements in a great variety of designs or mosaics. It is the object of science to discover the common elements in them, though it may be the task of the artist or of the mystic to depict or to cherish the individual phenomenon. But I venture to affirm that in not a single one of its manifestations can religion be found without its firm roots in human emotion, which again always grows out of desires and vicissitudes connected with life.

Two affirmations, therefore, preside over every ritual act, every rule of conduct, and every belief. There is the affirmation of the existence of powers sympathetic to man, ready to help him on condition that he conforms to the traditional lore which teaches how to serve them, conjure them, and propitiate them. This is the belief in Providence, and this belief assists man in so far as it enhances his capacity to act and his readiness to organize for action, under conditions where he must face and fight not only the ordinary forces of nature, but also chance, ill luck, and the mysterious, ever incalculable designs of destiny.

The second belief is that beyond the brief span of natural life there is compensation in another existence. Through this belief man can act and calculate far beyond his own forces and limitations, looking forward to his work being continued by his successors in the conviction that, from the next world, he will still be able to watch and assist them. The sufferings and efforts, the injustices and inequalities, of this life are thus made up for. Here again we find that the spiritual force of this belief not only integrates man's own personality, but is indispensable for the cohesion of the social fabric. Especially in the form which this belief assumes in ancestor-worship and the communion with the dead do we perceive its moral and social influence.

In their deepest foundations, as well as in their final consequences, the two beliefs in Providence and Immortality are not independent of one another. In the higher religions man lives in order to be united to God. In the simpler forms, the ancestors worshipped are often mystically identified with environmental forces, as in totemism. At times they are both ancestors and carriers of fertility, as the Kachina of the Pueblos. Or again the ancestor is worshipped as the divinity, or at least as a culture hero.

The unity of religion in substance, form, and function is to be found everywhere. Religious development consists probably in the growing predominance of the ethical principle and in the increasing fusion of the two main factors of all belief, the sense of Providence and the faith in immortality.

The conclusions to be drawn with regard to contemporary events I shall leave to the reader's own reflection. Is religion, in the sense in which we have just defined it—the affirmation of an ethical Providence, of immortality, of the transcendental value and sense of human life—is such religion dead? Is it going to make way for other creeds, perhaps less exacting, perhaps more immediately repaying and grossly satisfactory, but creeds which, nevertheless, fail to satisfy man's craving for the Absolute; fail to answer the riddle of human existence, and to convey the ethical message which can only be received from a being or beings regarded as beyond human passions, strife, and frailties? Is religion going to surrender its own equipment of faith, ritual, and ethics to cross-breeds between superstition and science, between economics and credulity, between politics and national megalomania? The dogmatic affirmations of these new mysticisms are banal, shallow, and they pander directly to the lowest instincts of the multitude. This is true of the belief in the absolute supremacy of one race and its right to bully all others; the belief in the sanctity of egoism in one's own nationality; the conviction of the value of war and collective brutality; the belief that only manual labour gives the full right to live and that the whole culture and public life of a community must be warped in the interests of the industrial workers.

Those of us who believe in culture and believe in the value of religion, though perhaps not in its specific tenets, must hope that the present-day misuse of the religious apparatus for partisan and doctrinaire purposes is not a healthy development of religion, but one of the many phenomena in the pathology of culture which seem to threaten the immediate development of our post-war Western society. If this be so, these new pseudo-religions are doomed to die. Let us hope that our whole society will not be dragged with them to destruction. Let us work for the maintenance of the eternal truths which have guided mankind out of barbarism to culture, and the loss of which seems to threaten us with barbarism again. The rationalist and agnostic must admit that even if he himself cannot accept these truths, he must at least recognize them as indispensable pragmatic figments without which civilization cannot exist.

INDEX

164; family as source of, 133; formation of ties, 70–71; Frazer and, 270; Functional approach to, 75; group, 55, 56, 136; hypertrophy of primitive bonds, 135; in human culture, 132; individual and collective, 136–137; Initial Situation of, 59–60, 69–70, 76, 81, 83, 138, 141, 157, 158, 163, 193; laws of, 183; matrilineal, 117; modes of counting descent, 134; primitive, 47–58; terms, 29; theories of, 150–153; ties, 200; twofold nature of, 78; unilateral counting of, 77

Kipling, Rudyard, 173
Kiwai Papuans, 8
Köhler, Wolfgang, 34, 46, 157, 164
Koita, 15
Konde, 7
Koppers, 34, 57n, 94, 124
Koryaks, 5, 10, 15, 29
Kotas, 8
Kovalesky, Maxime, 34, 93
Kroeber, Alfred L., 34, 57n, 123, 151, 152n
Kubary, Jan Stanislaw, 93
Kubu, 4
Kukis, 7, 27
Kulaman, 10
Kulngo, 5
Kumbi, 5
Kutchin, 27
Kwakiutl, 13

La Place, P. S., 263–264
Land tenure, 186
Lang, Andrew, 34, 55, 93, 94, 123, 136, 157, 252, 253n, 255, 257
Lango, 30
Language, 211–213, 224. See also Homonyms
Lawrence, D. H., 330
Legitimacy, 6–7, 19; principle of, 62–63, 64, 68, 69, 106, 128, 139–140, 158, 163, 193
Lenape Indians, 29
Lengua Indians, 7
Levirate, 15, 16, 21, 52, 54
Lévy-Bruhl, Lucien, 94, 125
Leza, 328
Lindsey, Judge Ben B., 43, 110, 112
Line Islanders, 27
Lippert, Julius, 13, 34

Lisu, 6
Lobola. See Bride-price
Lotuko, 15
Lowie, R. H., 34, 45n, 123, 134, 136, 151, 152n, 154, 224n
Lucelenganga, 328

Madi, 7, 15
Magic, 188–192, 259; and chance, 265; and sacrifice, 283; as man's primitive belief, 300; dogmatic affirmations of, 214–215, 239–241; identified with primitive science, 260; linked to totemism, 280; objects of, 200; Polynesian garden, 261; primitive, 261; psychology of, 270; public, 272–274; sociological, 272–273. See also Black magic
Magico-religious-secular theory, 266–267
Mailu, 7, 153n
Maine, Sir Henry, 52, 92, 133
Makololo, 30
Malinowski, Bronislaw: and kinship theory, 136, 152; and marriage theory, 34; bibliography, 153n; books cited, 68, 127, 128, 152n, 164n, 193n, 215n, 280, 324; personal belief of, 263, 296–297
Man and machine, 201–202
Mandan, 5
Mandingo, 5
Manism, 313, 316
Mannhardt, 301
Maori, 7, 8, 10, 15, 26, 27
Marett, Ronald R., 266, 269, 274, 285
Marquesans, 10, 27
Marriage, 3–35; "Adam and Eve" theory of, 92, 93; among primitive mankind, 117–122; and Functional anthropology, 97; and kinship, 76; and love, 4; and sexual conduct, 39, 67–68; and the State, 39, 41; as a legal contract, 16–17; as license for parenthood, 39, 65; bibliography, 35; Boas on, 99; by capture, 19, 20; by purchase, 14–16, 19, 20, 38; ceremonies, 26; "companionate," 110; conflicting anthropological theories, 52–53, 93; contemporary, 90–91; cross-cousin, 21, 52, 54; determined by social and financial considerations in Europe, 21; dissolution